Arguing, Reasoning, and Thinking Well

Arguing, Reasoning, and Thinking Well offers an engaging and accessible introduction to argumentation and critical thinking. With a pro-social focus, the volume encourages readers to value civility when engaged in arguing and reasoning. Authors Gass and Seiter, renowned for their friendly writing style, include real-world examples, hypothetical dialogues, and editorial cartoons to invite readers in. The text includes a full chapter devoted to the ethics of argument, as well as content on refutation and formal logic. It is designed for students in argumentation and critical thinking courses in communication, philosophy, and psychology departments, and is suitable for students and general education courses across the curriculum.

Robert H. Gass is a Professor Emeritus of Communication Studies at California State University Fullerton.

John S. Seiter is a Distinguished Professor of Communication Studies in the Department of Languages, Philosophy, and Communication Studies at Utah State University.

D0162534

Arguing, Reasoning, and Thinking Well

Robert H. Gass and John S. Seiter

Routledge
Taylor & Francis Group

NEW YORK AND LONDON

First published 2019
by Routledge
52 Vanderbilt Avenue, New York, NY 10017

and by Routledge
2 Park Square, Milton Park, Abingdon, Oxon, OX14 4RN

Routledge is an imprint of the Taylor & Francis Group, an informa business

Library of Congress Cataloging-in-Publication Data
Names: Gass, Robert H., author. | Seiter, John S., author.
Title: Arguing, reasoning, & thinking well / Robert H. Gass, John S. Seiter.
Description: First edition. | New York, NY : Routledge, 2019. |
    Includes bibliographical references.
Identifiers: LCCN 2018060732| ISBN 9780815374329 (hardback) |
    ISBN 9780815374336 (paperback) | ISBN 9781351242493 (ebk)
Subjects: LCSH: Persuasion (Rhetoric) | Reasoning.
Classification: LCC P301.5.P47 G38 2019 | DDC 808—dc23
LC record available at https://lccn.loc.gov/2018060732

ISBN: 978-0-815-37432-9 (hbk)
ISBN: 978-0-815-37433-6 (pbk)
ISBN: 978-1-351-24249-3 (ebk)

Typeset in Bembo
by Swales & Willis Ltd, Exeter, Devon, UK

Visit the eResource: www.routledge.com/9780815374336

To my parents, Delores and Richard, who loved me beyond reason.

John S. Seiter

To my dear old mom, Lorena P. Gass, who encouraged my education every step of the way. I hope I've made you proud.

Robert H. Gass

Contents

Preface

If 18th-century Europe represented the Age of Reason, then 21st-century America may be aptly titled the age of unreasonableness. Indeed, we live in what has been dubbed the "post-truth" era (Oxford Dictionaries, 2016) and a "post-fact society" (Manjoo, 2008). Where facts were once considered stubborn and persistent, they must now compete with "alternative facts." Where truth once reigned over falsehoods, it has been subverted by assertions that "truth is not truth" (see Giuliani, 2018).

In addition, we live in an era where people all too commonly have strong opinions on issues, yet possess little knowledge or understanding of those issues (Somin, 2016). By way of illustration, at a town hall meeting hosted by representative Bob Inglas, a Republican from South Carolina, an attendee reportedly told the congressman, "keep your government hands off my Medicare" (cited by Ceska, 2009). But Medicare is, after all, a government program. As another example, many Americans support the U.S. Constitution wholeheartedly, yet 37 percent of those polled in a recent survey could not identify a specific right guaranteed by the First Amendment (Annenberg Public Policy Center, 2017). The same survey revealed that 33 percent of Americans could not name any of the three branches of government (Annenberg Public Policy Center, 2017).

True, we are living in the information age, technology age, or digital age depending on the terminology one prefers. Information, however, exists alongside misinformation campaigns. Technology, especially social media, is often used as a platform to promote hate, instill fear, and sow discord. Facebook, Instagram, Twitter, and other social media platforms rely on algorithms to curate and filter news, a practice that tends to isolate users into bubbles of like-minded others. Despite all the information and technology available, we seem to be less informed, more opinionated, more intellectually lazy, and more verbally aggressive than ever.

A major contributor to these problems is that we often lack the ability, knowledge, or motivation to think, reason, and argue well. What's more, while readily pointing fingers at others' opinions and behaviors, we don't always question our own. For instance, when flitting from link to link online, we may lose the capacity for sustained, in-depth thinking. When witnessing multiple TV pundits talking over one another, we may assume that pontificating is what wins the day. When watching reality TV ("talk to the hand"), we may come to accept that rudeness trumps reasoning.

The ability to think, reason, and argue—not just make assertions—is in high demand and short supply. Aristotle called humans the "rational animal." But he never lived to watch an episode of *Big Brother* or *Real Housewives*. A survey by Hart Research Associates asked 400 employers what skills they valued most in new hires (2013). The results showed that nearly all those surveyed (93 percent) agreed that, "a candidate's demonstrated capacity to think critically, communicate clearly, and solve complex problems is more important than their undergraduate major" (Hart Research Associates, 2013, p. 1). Clearly, then, the ability to argue, think, and reason well is a desideratum.

In writing this text, our goal is to improve your arguing, thinking, and reasoning skills. At the same time, we hope to instill a desire to grapple with arguments, not avoid them or escalate them. We strive to improve your ability to advance a cogent, well-reasoned case, while avoiding verbal aggression. We also seek to improve your reasoning skills in a variety of ways, such as evaluating the credibility of sources, applying tests of evidence, exposing fallacies in reasoning, and refuting opposing arguments.

We realize this is a tall order. Our approach relies on a readable, accessible writing style. Along the way, we also present theories and concepts, offer social scientific evidence, and provide numerous examples and illustrations of reasoning, both good and bad, to show how the material applies to ordinary, everyday arguments. We rely on excerpts from arguments in the public sphere, along with hypothetical dialogues, and a dose of humor here and there to (hopefully) hold your attention. This approach has served us well in our other text, *Persuasion, Social Influence, and Compliance Gaining*, which is now in its 6th edition.

As you read this text, we hope that you learn a good deal about the nature of argument, improve your arguing skills, and have fun in the process.

References

Annenberg Public Policy Center (2017, September 12). *Americans are poorly informed about basic constitutional provisions*. Retrieved on August 29, 2018 from: www.annenbergpublicpolicycenter.org/americans-are-poorly-informed-about-basic-constitutional-provisions?utm_source=news-release&utm_medium=email&utm_campaign=2017_civics_survey&utm_term=survey&utm_source=Media&utm_campaign=e5f213892a-Civics_survey_2017_2017_09_12&utm_medium=email&utm_term=0_9e3d9bcd8a-e5f213892a-425997897.

Ceska, B. (2009, September 5). Keep your goddamn government hands off my Medicare. *Huffington Post*. Retrieved on August 29, 2018 from: www.huffingtonpost.com/bob-cesca/get-your-goddamn-governme_b_252326.html.

Giuliani, R. (2018, August 19). Interview with Chuck Todd on *Meet the Press*. New York: NBC.

Hart Research Associates (2013). *It takes more than a major: Employer priorities for college learning and student success*. Washington, DC: American Association of Colleges & Universities and Hart Research Associates.

Manjoo, F. (2008). *True enough: Learning to live in a post-fact society*. Hoboken, NJ: John Wiley.

Oxford Dictionaries (2016). *Word of the year 2016 is post-truth*. Retrieved on August 29, 2018 from: https://en.oxforddictionaries.com/word-of-the-year/word-of-the-year-2016.

Somin, I. (2016). *Democracy and political ignorance: Why smaller government is smarter*. Stanford, CA: Stanford University Press.

Acknowledgments

We are extremely grateful to the folks at Routledge/Taylor & Francis for their assistance with this project. In particular, we appreciate Laura Briskman for sharing our early vision for the book. We also thank Nicole Salazar for her legendary patience, and Brian Eschrich, Judith Harvey, and Sonnie Wills, who helped us with editing and other essentials down the home stretch.

John Seiter is grateful to Matthew Volk, Dave Aadland, Adam Milroy, Sidi Becar Meyera, and Charlie Huenemann for helping with materials, feedback, and ideas. In addition, he'll never forget how kind his friends and colleagues at Utah State University are. Thanks, especially, to Jennifer Peeples and Bradford Hall for tolerating him throughout all of these years. John is also forever grateful to his first argumentation teacher and forensics coach Pat Ganer, who gave him a "D" on his first debate assignment, yet managed to light a spark all the same. Most importantly, for all her love and support, John Seiter thanks Debora—his kindred spirit, devil's advocate, and guardian angel all rolled into one amazing wife.

Robert Gass expresses endless thanks to Susan, his high school sweetheart, for matching wits with him, making him laugh, and sharing the journey with him. He is also grateful to the marvelous instructors and debate coaches who taught him about argumentation over the years; Daniel Miller at Cal. Poly Pomona, Lucy Keele at Cal. State Fullerton, Donn Parson at the University of Kansas, Pat Ganer at Cypress College, and all his fellow Jayhawk debate assistants. He also gained a wealth of knowledge from his colleagues, John Reinard, Jeanine Congalton, Jon Bruschke, and Erika Thomas with whom he coached debate and taught argumentation classes at Cal. State Fullerton.

Chapter 1

Why Study Argument?

"Kiddie" Arguments

One of the authors was enjoying a cheeseburger at a local fast food chain when two toddlers, accompanied by their parents, took a seat in a nearby booth. It wasn't long before an argument broke out:

"Yes, you did."

"No, I didn't."

"Did too."

"Did not."

"Did too."

And so it went.

Listening to little tykes argue is both fascinating and frustrating. Their arguing skills are underdeveloped, yet they understand that arguing is supposed to be a back and forth process. They try to emulate the give and take format they see adults using. Although they may imitate the form of adult arguments, children's arguments are typically lacking in substance. They know they are supposed to refute their opponent's arguments, but they don't quite know how. They may add snappy comebacks to their argumentative repertoire, such as "I know you are but what am I?" but their arguments remain superficial. Unfortunately, not all people outgrow this. Indeed, in the fast food restaurant, it wasn't the toddlers who were arguing. *It was their parents.* The two children, along with the author, sat quietly soaking it all in.

Arguing as a Developmental Process

Child prodigies are fascinating. Pablo Picasso learned to draw before he learned to speak. He was admitted to Barcelona's School of Fine Arts when he was 13. Garry Kasparov, considered by many to be the greatest chess player of all time, began playing at the age of five and was the USSR chess champion at 13. And then there's Wolfgang Amadeus Mozart, who wrote his first symphony when he was only eight.

Feeling old? If so, you can take solace in the fact that, when it comes to arguing, there are no childhood geniuses.[1] You won't, for instance, find any eight-year-old "whizz kids" presenting cases before the Supreme Court. This is because *the ability to think, reason, and argue well is a developmental process.* As Mercier and Sperber observed, "there is no evidence that [reasoning] occurs in preverbal children" (2011, p. 57). As their cognitive functioning and language abilities improve, children improve their argumentation skills (Amsterlaw, 2006; Jasna, 1992; Kuhn & Udell, 2003; Ricco, 2015). Young-uns soon learn to make more substantive arguments. For example, most kids quickly learn to invoke the "fairness principle" as an effective strategy. If a parent says, "Lulu, it's your bedtime," the child might respond, "That's not fair! Henry gets to stay up late."

Children also learn social norms that govern arguing, such as not engaging in name-calling, taunting, or hazing (okay, *some* kids learn these norms), and they develop what has been called a *theory of mind* (Wellman, 1992). That is, they begin to see things from another person's point of view, a crucial skill that helps them tailor their arguments to a particular audience. As a result, after asking her mom, "Can I stay up an hour later to watch this show?" Lulu might add, "It's educational!" Lulu's argument demonstrates perspective-taking.

Argumentation skills continue to develop during the teen years. One study (Weinstock, Neuman & Glassner, 2006) found that students' ability to identify informal fallacies improved with grade level. Another study demonstrated that adolescents (7th and 8th graders) were proficient in advancing arguments for their own side, but were not as adept as young college students (freshman and sophomores) at refuting the arguments of the opposing side (Felton & Kuhn, 2001).

The Importance of Context and Culture

While the ability to argue is learned, it is important to keep in mind that this ability is learned somewhat differently across cultures and over time. Arguing is contextual and is situated in a particular culture, time, and place. By way of example, what might have been perceived as a cogent argument for the use of torture in the 1500s, during the Spanish Inquisition, would not be perceived as a reasonable argument today. Moreover, while arguments for a number of questionable medical practices—e.g., bloodletting or lobotomies—might have held water at one time or another, they'd certainly be considered unreasonable today.

What's more, culture and context not only influence perceptions about the content of arguments, but also perceptions about whether, when, and how to disagree. Likewise, orientations toward arguing, such as whether to be direct and assertive or avoid confrontation, vary between Asian and Western cultures (Xie, Hample & Wang, 2015). We address these differences in more detail in Chapter 4.

Adult Arguers

Research suggests that arguing ability continues to develop into adulthood (Grossman, Na, Varnum, Park, Kitayama & Nisbett, 2010; Kuhn & Udell, 2003; Moshman, 1998). By the time most people finish high school or enter college they have acquired basic argumentation skills. You may be asking yourself, then, "If I've got the basics down, why do I need this book?" The answer is that it is one thing to develop basic argumentation skills, and another thing altogether to become a skillful arguer. Parents, for instance, frequently resort to a fallacy called *appealing to the crowd* when they utter remarks such as "I don't care if your friends ride their skateboards in the street. If they jumped off a cliff would you do it too?" Other examples

Figure 1.1 Sometimes people act first, and think second.
© Peter Mueller/*The New Yorker* Collection/www.cartoonbank.com.

of adult arguers making rather childish arguments are just a couple of clicks away on your remote control. The *Judge Judy* show, for example, relies on plaintiffs' and defendants' feeble arguments as a form of entertainment. Other low-brow TV fare also appeals to people's baser argumentative urges. Hey, we love to watch these shows too, but we don't expect to hear exemplary reasoning when doing so.

Faux Reasoning

Unfortunately, in everyday life the situation isn't much better. Consider the sham conversation below.

Naomi: "Why?"
Bernie: "Because."
Naomi: "Because why?"
Bernie: "Just because."

Figure 1.2 "Punny reason giving."

J.C. Duffy, Fusco Brothers, 10/23/2008 Cartoonist Group, image 27509. © J.C. Duffy/Fusco Brothers/cartoonistgroup.com.

Although Bernie offers the semblance of an argument, it is not an actual argument. Perhaps he can't come up with a good reason or maybe he is being cognitively lazy. The slang phrase "I want this because of reasons," which was also a popular meme, embodies this same empty reasoning. The phrase, which is sometimes shortened to "because of reasons," is used ironically to acknowledge that a person *should have* reasons, but cannot be bothered to come up with any.

Another faux argument involves making a questionable claim, and then adding "I'm just sayin'" as a means of shirking any obligation to provide proof. Imagine, for example, two office gossips discussing their boss's attire:

Ralph: "Is Lester on the prowl? He's sporting a new wardrobe."
Amos: "I don't think so. He and his wife just celebrated their 20th anniversary."
Ralph: "Still . . . that's an awfully nice suit he has on. I'm just sayin'."

Think about Ralph's claim for a moment. By adding "I'm just sayin'," he isn't strengthening his argument. The phrase is tacked on to avoid offering additional reasons or proof.

The proverbial response, "What*ever* . . ." (accent on the *ever*) also entails a pretext of reasoning. "What*ever* . . ." is a way of conveying annoyance or disdain without conceding or refuting the point. If you've ever used this response, you should know that people find it irritating. In fact, in one series of polls, "whatever" was voted the "most annoying" word for seven years in a row (*Marist Poll*, 2015)! Other tired tropes, such as "It is what it is," can be aggravating as well. Although offered as an excuse for doing nothing, it relies on circular reasoning, a topic we will cover later in this book.

Angry Argument

Worse still, some adult arguers don't simply offer empty arguments, they get mad too. They resort to *verbal aggression*, such as threats or name calling. Participants on reality shows, such as *Big Brother* or *Real Housewives*, often rely on such tactics. The dialogue below illustrates a hypothetical encounter characterized by aggressiveness.

Vic:	"Oh yeah?"
Rex:	"Yeah!"
Vic:	"Sez who?"
Rex:	"Sez me. Wanna make somethin' of it?"
Vic:	"I'd like to see you try."
Rex:	"Keep yappin' and I'll slap the ugly right off your face."
Vic:	"Bring it on, fool."
Rex:	"So you're admittin' you're ugly?"
Vic:	"Not as ugly as you're gonna be."

The form of the above argument involves point–counterpoint, but there is little or no substance to the "arguments." Blustering and threats have replaced reasoning and rationality. Argumentation scholars (Infante, 1987; Infante & Rancer, 1982; Infante & Wigley, 1986) view verbal aggression as a *skill deficiency*. When arguers lack appropriate argumentation skills, they resort to name calling and put downs. We will have more to say about verbal aggression in the following chapter.

Aims and Goals of This Book

Improving Your Knowledge and Skills in Argumentation

The good news is that it is quite possible to improve your arguing, reasoning, and thinking skills. Hence this book. One of our primary reasons for writing this text is to help increase your knowledge and understanding of basic principles and processes of argumentation which, in turn, will improve your argumentation skills. Whatever your current level or ability, you can improve. In this respect, arguing is analogous to dancing. You might already have a decent "Moonwalk" or "Tango," but there is always room for improvement. First, you'll need a better understanding of how argumentation works. Then you'll need practice. And lots of it. Just as one can't learn to scuba dive solely by reading about it, you can't become a more competent arguer without practicing your skills. As van Gelder (2005) emphasized, "for students to improve they must engage in critical thinking itself. It is not enough to learn about critical thinking" (p. 43). At best then, we can point you in the right direction. But, ultimately, you'll need to complete the journey yourself. We promise it'll be worth your while!

Improving Your Thinking and Reasoning Ability

Our second goal is to improve your critical thinking ability. Critical thinking and argumentation go hand in hand. Before you can develop a cogent argument, you need to understand the issues surrounding a controversy. That requires researching the issues and analyzing them in depth and detail. Unfortunately, not everyone understands this. Indeed, according to a survey of 400 companies, fewer than 1 in 3 employers rated college graduates as excellent in critical thinking skills (Schoeff, 2007). Another survey revealed that 93 percent of employers agreed that "a candidate's demonstrated capacity to think critically, communicate clearly, and solve complex problems is more important than their major" (Hart Research Associates, 2013, p. 1).

What's more, some people are convinced that they are "right" and that conviction alone is enough to prevail in any argument.[2] Not so. When pondering an important issue, it is worth taking differing perspectives into account. Strong convictions aren't sufficient for winning an argument. In fact, they may even blind people from recognizing weaknesses in their own positions.

Improving Your Ability to Argue Appropriately

Arguing well isn't just about winning either. Our third goal in writing this book is to help you improve your ability to argue in socially appropriate ways. Arguing well isn't about winning at all costs. To be a *competent* arguer you must argue effectively *and* appropriately, which means that in addition to advancing a well-reasoned case, you should make arguments that are suitable for your audience, the context, and existing social norms. People who are rude, boorish, or verbally aggressive may win the battle but lose the war. They may prevail in a particular argument, but damage their relationships, identities, or reputations in the long run. A competent arguer, then, demonstrates respect for others, without resorting to name calling, threats, or ultimatums. All three of the above goals—improving your argumentation skills, cultivating your critical thinking skills, and learning to argue in appropriate ways—are major themes of this text. More about the positive side of arguing is explained in Box 1.1.

Box 1.1   Arguing Is a Prosocial Endeavor

The Common Sense View of Argument

Arguing is not a dirty word, although many people seem to think so. In everyday life the word "argument" often carries a negative connotation. Some people equate having an argument with having a fight. Rather than using the word "argument" to refer to an interaction, people often opt for euphemisms such as, "We were merely having a *discussion*." Words such as "discussion," "quarrel," "tiff," or "spat" sound less pejorative. In everyday parlance, being labeled "argumentative" also has a negative connotation. "Floyd is an argumentative person" someone might say, meaning that Floyd is hard to get along with.

Emotional Excess

These negative connotations are understandable. Sometimes arguing is associated with an *excess of emotion*. When some people argue, they become angry, scornful, and vehement. These are the parents you see, for example, hurling expletives at the referee during their eight year old's soccer match. However, such behavior is actually the result of a *lack* of argumentation skills. Screamers lack argumentative competence. Their hostility is a sign of a skill deficiency.

Emotionlessness

Sometimes arguing is associated with an *absence of emotion*. When some people argue, they become cold and calculating. They lack compassion. Imagine an inflexible professor who says to a student, "Your paper is five minutes late. That'll cost you a letter grade." When the student begins to explain, the professor states matter-of-factly, "It's in the syllabus. I suggest you read it." Other examples include a lawyer who enjoys humiliating witnesses, a boss who turns every minor request by an employee into a performance review, or a parent who translates every mistake a child makes into an "I told you so" lecture.

Being cold and calculating, however, is not an intrinsic feature of arguing. An absence of emotion also may reflect a skill deficiency. To argue *appropriately*, we must demonstrate respect for the other person and tolerance for his or her point of view. Arguing competently and appropriately requires using our heads and our hearts.

An Enlightened View of Argument

Our view is that arguing is actually a *prosocial* form of human interaction. First and foremost, arguing is a peaceful means of managing conflicts. Arguing is democratic; all the participants get to have their say. That doesn't guarantee that they will leave with a warm, fuzzy feeling. Still, arguing is one of the best ways of handling disagreements. People can disagree, but in constructive ways.

Arguing also clears the air. When we argue with other people, we get issues out into the open. As Makau and Marty (2001) emphasized, "Whether within families, organizations, or nation-states, efforts to suppress or otherwise avoid addressing disagreements almost inevitably lead to even greater conflict" (p. 8). Arguing lets people know where they stand in the relationship. This doesn't mean that every argument produces a happy ending. People may disagree so fundamentally over an issue that it ends their relationship. But that is better than perpetuating a relationship that is fundamentally flawed for the sake of avoiding conflict.

Arguing also signifies respect and tolerance. When one person has all the power in a relationship, there is no need to argue. The person who holds all the cards can simply order the other person to do his or her bidding. In a relationship characterized by equality, each party wants to *convince* the other person, not compel him or her (Ehninger, 1970).

Arguing with another person is a sign of respect for her or his intelligence. Arguing requires rational actors. To argue with another person is to acknowledge that she or he is capable of understanding good reasons when they are put forth. The boss who yells, "I'm not paying you to think. I'm paying you to do what you're told" is not displaying respect. Giving orders is efficient, arguing is not. Saying "Because I'm the boss," implies that the recipient of the message doesn't deserve an explanation.

The enlightened view of argument offered here does not suggest that arguing is always enjoyable, although it often can be. Arguing can be unpleasant, even when all the parties to an argument are arguing effectively and appropriately. We can all recall arguments that we dreaded having. We can all recall arguments that ended badly, with one or both parties feeling wounded. We become emotionally involved in arguments. Our egos are at stake, not just our arguments.

Why Learn About Argumentation?

The Advocacy Function: Stating Your Case

There are multiple benefits to improving your arguing, reasoning, and thinking skills. The first is what we call an *advocacy function*. By learning how to present a well-reasoned argument you'll become a more effective advocate for your own ideas. Sometimes, it isn't enough to have a good idea; you have to convince others it is a good idea too. In almost every career path, especially the "people professions" such as advertising, law, ministry, politics, public relations, sales, social work, and teaching, to name just a few, you must be able to make a convincing case.

The Defensive Function: Jiu Jitsu for Your Brain

The second benefit is what we call the *defensive function*, which means that by learning about arguing, reasoning, and critical thinking you'll be better prepared to fend off bad arguments made by others. Whether it is marketers trying to convince you to buy something, politicians vying for your vote, or Nigerian princes trying to give you $10 million, you need to be able to spot weak arguments when you encounter them. For example, most "work at home" offers are pure scams (Leamy, 2008; Von Bergen, 2010). Despite their claims, most people *cannot* earn $100,000 or more per year sitting at home in their pajamas.

An important aspect of the defensive function is recognizing common fallacies in reasoning. As just one illustration, testimonials for "miracle diets" are often based on a *hasty generalization* fallacy. The persons featured in such ads are hand-picked and the fine print accompanying such ads often states "results not typical" or "results may vary." A working knowledge of such fallacies will help you maintain your guard against unscrupulous advocates. Several chapters of this text are devoted to helping you spot such fallacies.

The Decision-Making Function: Getting It Right

The third benefit to improving your arguing, thinking, and reasoning skills is the *decision-making and problem-solving function*. People don't always make good decisions. As an example, more than one in five Americans believe that winning the lottery is the most practical way for them to accumulate a retirement nest egg (Coombs, 2006). Sadly, it is poorer, less educated people who spend a disproportionate amount of their income on lottery tickets, rather than saving or investing (*Investopedia*, 2018). Yet, saving even a small amount each week or month over a period of many years is a much surer way to accumulate wealth. People make important decisions throughout their lives. When buying a car, voting in an election, or deciding whether to ask your doctor if an advertised prescription medicine is right for you, you need to be able to separate the wheat from the chaff to make a good decision.

The Knowledge Function: How Do You Know What You Know?

A fourth function, the *knowledge function*, is based on the realization that arguing is *epistemic*, which means that arguing is a "way of knowing" (see Scott, 1967). Epistemology is the study of how we know what we know (or what we *think* we know). For instance, we know some things through instinct (pain hurts, avoid pain) and others through experience (in real estate, it's location, location, location). We learn some things through reading and study (the Rosetta Stone was discovered by a French soldier, Pierre-François Bouchard, in 1799), and others through tradition and culture (avoid making eye contact on the subway). Sometimes, however, we don't actually know what we believe until we argue about it. We don't always have pre-formed opinions on issues. We discover what we believe in and through the process of having an argument.

The Dialectical Approach: Back and Forth

One way this happens is through something known as the *dialectical method*. This approach involves testing competing arguments in the marketplace of ideas, and seeing which ones survive careful scrutiny. Also called the *Socratic method*, this approach involves a back and forth process of asking and answering questions and, ultimately, getting at the heart of a matter. Question asking and answering is at once collaborative and adversarial. The discussants adopt opposing positions with a view toward discovering the best answer to a question, the best solution to a problem, or the best decision that can be made. Through dialogue, people may discover things about themselves, about other people, or society in general that they didn't already know.

Going Out On a Limb

As a way of knowing, *arguing inherently risks the self* (Brockriede, 1975; Ehninger, 1970). In other words, when we choose to argue with someone we run the risk of changing our own ideas. When we lay our arguments on the line, we put our egos on the line too. By choosing to argue, we risk our belief system, our view of the world, and ourselves. Although the process is sometimes painful, it is healthy in the long run to question one's assumptions.

The Social Competence Function: Don't Be a Jerk

A fifth benefit of studying argumentation is the *social competence function*, which suggests that, by improving your argumentation skills, you will become more adept at managing disagreements. Some people don't know how to deal with conflicts so they avoid them. That doesn't make conflicts go away, however. In fact, it may cause an issue to fester. It can also lead to passive-aggressive behavior (e.g., getting back at another person in a roundabout way). Other people deal with conflicts by escalating them. As we noted above, such people get in someone's face, engage in trash-talking, or resort to threats and ultimatums. As an alternative, arguing effectively and appropriately is one way of keeping conflicts from getting out of hand.

The Citizen Participation Function: All In

A sixth benefit of learning to argue, reason, and think well is the *citizen participation function*, which is based on the idea that democracy depends on an informed public. That may sound hackneyed, but the sad fact is that many people are woefully uninformed. Consider this: A poll conducted by Zogby International (2006) revealed that 77 percent of Americans could name at least two of Snow White's seven dwarfs, yet only 24 percent could name two or more Supreme Court Justices. What's more, 73 percent of those polled identified all Three Stooges correctly, but only 42 percent could identify all three branches of government. Sixty percent knew Homer was Bart Simpson's father, but only 21 percent knew that another Homer wrote the epic Greek poems the *Iliad* and the *Odyssey* (Doh!). This doesn't necessarily mean that people are stupid. It does suggest, however, that many people pay more attention to popular culture than current events, government, history, or literature.

In the absence of an informed citizenry, abuses of power are more likely to occur and fundamental rights are more likely to be eroded. As historian Barbara Tuchman observed, "wooden-headedness, the source of self-deception, is a factor that plays a remarkably large role in government" (p. 7). To prevent such wooden-headed thinking, people need to be engaged. Unfortunately, too few citizens participate in the decision-making process. By way of illustration, more people voted in the finale of *American Idol* in 2008 and 2012 than in the presidential elections in those same years (De Moraes, 2012; Elsworth, 2006; Liptak, 2012; Sweney, 2006). Yes, we're aware that *American Idol* viewers don't have to be 18 or registered to vote. *Idol* viewers can vote more than once and can vote by phone or online. But consider this: a survey conducted by Pursuant, Inc., a polling firm, found that "35 percent of *American Idol* voters said their votes for favorite singers were *just as important* as their votes for president of the United States" (italics added, cited in Belcher, 2006, p. 8). That's scary. If an *Idol* winner is a bust, the worst case scenario is weak song or CD sales. If a president is a disaster, the results can be catastrophic.

Besides that, you never know when you may be confronted with an issue that affects you personally. One of our colleagues, for instance, found herself involved with a group of fellow citizens who learned that some organization or agency was dumping chemical and toxic waste in their neighborhoods. They wanted to speak out, but lacked the skills to do so. We believe people should be capable of making their voice heard at a city council meeting or other public forum by offering a well-reasoned argument. All people should be able to write, phone, or email an elected official and express their position on a controversial issue. They should be capable of writing a letter to the editor of a newspaper and make a convincing case. To participate in public policy decisions that affect your life requires effective argumentation skills.

The Sensitivity Function: I Can Appreciate That!

Want to challenge yourself? Try this: find something you care about and then try building a case *against* it. Better yet, find someone with an opposing point of view and have a debate in which you argue for the *other* person's side. You might be surprised at what you learn. In our experience, students who attempt this exercise often walk away with a newfound appreciation, cultivating not only an open-minded approach to different perspectives, but also an enriched sensitivity to other people, including those from different backgrounds and cultures. That's because arguing invites us to consider different people and viewpoints. While it's true that clinging to our own way of thinking is probably more comfortable, opening ourselves to alternative ways of seeing the world can be richly rewarding. Don't mistake us. We're not suggesting that you abandon your perspectives. We do believe, however, that your time will be well spent exploring the bases of your values, opinions, beliefs, and viewpoints.

Arguing as an Intellectual Challenge: The Fun Function

People often enjoy matching wits with one another. An eighth and final benefit to arguing, then, is that it is a form of intellectual stimulation, or what we call the *fun function*! This may not be everyone's cup of tea, but some people enjoy verbal jousting and witty banter. Such arguments serve as a form of language play. Suppose, for example, that Mario and Luigi have the following conversation.

Mario: "Spiderman versus Batman? No contest. Spiderman has *super powers*. The Caped Crusader is just a buff, rich dude with a bunch of gadgets."

Luigi: "*Mais non!* Batman would own Peter Parker. Spidey has no formal martial arts training. Batman mastered the Keysi Fighting Method."

Mario: "Spiderman wouldn't get close enough for hand-to-hand fighting. He'd wrap Batman up in webbing from a distance."

Luigi: "Yo. Ever heard of a Batarang? Batman would just cut the webs and sweep the leg."

Mario: "You're forgetting that Spiderman has spider-senses, and he'd sense Batman's every move."

Luigi: "You're forgetting that Batman's tool-belt includes stun grenades, which would disrupt Spiderman's senses."

Of course, Batman, who is a DC Comics character, and Spiderman, who is a Marvel Comics character, live in different imaginary worlds. And their abilities vary depending on whether one is relying on the comic book characters or their film versions. Since neither Spiderman nor Batman actually exists, the outcome of such a duel is pure conjecture. Nevertheless, such mental sparring can be fun.

One of the author's fondest memories of growing up includes listening to his father and uncle arguing at the kitchen table. It was one of their favorite pastimes. The author's father was fairly conservative, the uncle fairly liberal. They argued about politics, religion, science, art, and all manner of other topics. At times their disagreements became heated, but they respected one another's views. Their arguments were also infused with humor. For example, one such dispute had to do with whether dogs or cats were better pets. The author's father claimed dogs were superior to cats and offered to sell the uncle the family dog for $10,000. The uncle quickly countered, "Suppose I trade you our two $5,000 cats?" The point is that if participants display respect for one another, arguing can be intellectually stimulating, enjoyable, and even playful. Now that you have a clearer understanding of the importance of arguing well, let's dive right in. Next we examine the beginning stages of engaging in an argument.

Argumentative Overtures

We don't advise you to pick arguments with random strangers. Next time you use Uber, resist the urge to challenge the driver to an argument; "Gun control: Pro or con?" Plenty of opportunities for arguing will arise in the course of your everyday life without having to force the issue. Suppose, however, that you and another person happen to disagree about something. How should you initiate an argument when you perceive that you are at odds? The first step, we suggest, is to attempt to establish rapport with the other person. To do this, you'll need to focus less on "winning" and more on reaching agreement.

Finding Common Ground

A good place to begin an argument is by finding common ground. Look for shared goals and common values that you and the other party have in common. Highlight the points on which you agree. This helps reduce defensiveness.

"We" Statements

One technique is to use "we" rather than "you" statements. A "we" or "us" approach is less adversarial than a "you" versus "me" mentality. Imagine that the parents of second-graders are arguing about whether their children should be trading items in their school lunches. One parent cautions that trading foods could trigger allergic reactions. Another worries that healthy foods, like apples or bananas, will be swapped for sugary snacks and sodas. To diffuse the tension, one parent might highlight their mutual interests.

- "We have the same goal. We all want our children to have healthy, nutritious lunches."
- "None of us want kids to trade for foods that would cause an allergic reaction or, worse, result in anaphylactic shock."
- "Let's highlight what we agree on. Can we agree that trading one healthy food for another, say, an apple for a banana or vice versa, would be okay?"

By emphasizing similarities rather than differences and using "we" rather than "you" statements, a cooperative relationship among the parents is more likely to take hold.

Identification and Empathy

Another helpful technique is to establish a connection with the other person and demonstrate empathy on a personal level. Showing that you understand how the other person feels will help avoid antagonism. Some examples of this technique are provided below.

- "I wish more parents cared as much as you do."
- "I hear you. We should all take an active interest in our kids' nutrition."
- "I share your concerns. I worry about what my kids are eating too."

Taking the time to establish rapport, instead of rushing headlong into an argument, will reduce the chance of getting off on the wrong foot. You and the other person may disagree, but there is merit in trying to identify points on which you also agree.

Respect and Tolerance

Another way to develop rapport is to acknowledge the other person's opinion in a constructive way. You might say, for example:

- "You raise an important issue."
- "You make a good point."
- "That's an excellent question."

Such statements demonstrate that you are listening, not just hatching objections, and that you see the merits of the other side. Of course, none of these approaches are guaranteed, but using one or more of them can go a long way in earning the other person's trust and respect.

Transitioning into Argument

Suppose you've done your best to be friendly and obliging. You've emphasized shared goals and displayed empathy, but it is clear that you and someone else hold incompatible views on a subject. What should you do next?

Partial Agreement

One method of transitioning into argument is to partially agree with the other person's position. If you naysay everything the other person says you'll come across as petty or badgering. Some examples of partial agreement include:

- "I agree with most of what you said."
- "You are right about . . . where I differ with you is . . . ."
- "Point taken. I'm still uncomfortable with one thing . . . ."
- "I'm with you, right up to the point where you say . . . ."

If you can do this without using the dreaded word "but," all the better. When you express partial agreement, the other person may be anticipating that you'll say "but . . . you are completely wrong," or some other variant of total rejection. "But" tends to put people on the defensive. Try using "that said . . .," "nonetheless . . .," or "even so . . ." as alternatives. Avoiding the trigger word "but" will allow you to segue into disagreement while the other party is "waiting for the other shoe to drop."

Respectfully Disagree

As you transition into argument you can disagree without seeming disagreeable. We suggest that you be assertive, but polite. It will be more difficult for the other person to take offense if you are courteous when disagreeing. Some examples of this approach are found below.

- "I don't entirely agree with what you said."
- "I respect your opinion. Can I share mine too?"
- "I may be mistaken. My understanding is that . . . ."
- "With all due respect . . . ."

Phrase Your Initial Objection as a Question

Another way of transitioning into argument is to pose your initial objection as a question rather than a declarative statement. This demonstrates that you are listening to what the other party has to say.

- "If you don't mind my asking, how do you know that?"
- "And what makes you think that . . .?"

- "Are you sure that's a good idea?"
- "I'm unclear about something. Can you explain why . . .?"

Use Perception-Checking

Ask for clarification to make sure you understand the other person's position on the issue. An advantage of this approach is that it prompts the other person to commit to a position. Once the person clarifies his or her position, it will be harder for him or her to vacilate later.

- "Correct me if I misunderstood . . . Are you saying . . .?"
- "Tell me if I'm hearing you correctly . . . ."
- "Can you clarify what you mean by . . .?"
- "Just so I'm clear, are you saying . . . or are you saying . . .?"

Use Paraphrasing

This strategy is similar to perception-checking, but involves making statements rather than asking questions. To do this, try to summarize the other person's position clearly but briefly. Capture the essence of what the person is saying in a single sentence without parroting exactly what the other person just said. By doing this, you show that you are listening in a fair-minded way.

- "So it's your position that . . . ."
- "Let me make sure I understand. Your objection is . . . ."
- "Tell me if I've got it right. Your point is that . . . ."
- "What I'm hearing you say is that . . . ."

As with perception-checking, this strategy helps you. Once another person agrees that you have summarized her or his position fairly, the person will find it harder to "waffle."

Finding common ground is an important step before engaging in argument. In addition to cultivating a respectful communication climate, doing so could even resolve the issue from the get go. Indeed, we can't count how many times we ourselves have been arguing with other people, only to discover that we actually agreed with them from the very start. We just assumed we were at odds, not taking time to find out whether we shared common goals. As such, before spending an hour arguing with someone, take a few minutes to see if you really disagree in the first place.

Chapter Summary

By way of summary, then, children are fairly naïve or unsophisticated arguers. Skill at arguing evolves over time. The ability to argue well requires cognitive development and a mastery of language skills. Arguing effectively also depends on socialization processes, such as learning social norms for arguing. By the time people reach early adulthood they have acquired a basic repertoire of arguing skills. That said, you cannot simply "grow up" to become a better arguer, thinker, and reasoner. These skills are not like getting taller; they don't just happen. They must be developed. People who default to verbal aggression have a skill deficiency in argumentation.

The goals of this text are to improve your argumentation skills by increasing your knowledge and understanding of argument, to improve your critical thinking and reasoning ability, and to help you argue in appropriate ways. Eight functions or benefits of improving your argumentation skills were identified as well. Before charging forth into an argument, look for areas on which you and the other person(s) may agree. A variety of techniques were identified for reducing defensiveness in the early stages of an argument.

Notes

1 A few "Wunderkinds," as the Germans call them, have left their mark in literature and philosophy. Jeremy Bentham, for example, studied Latin at age three and entered Queens College, at Oxford, at age 12. However, all of his well-known accomplishments, such as his writings on utilitarianism, came later in life. H.P. Lovecraft, the science fiction writer, began writing poetry at the age of six, but didn't publish his first work, the *Tomb and the Dragon*, until age 27. Occasionally one hears of child evangelists, such as Marjoe Gortner, who was ordained as a minister at age four. He was, according to some accounts, coached relentlessly by his parents to memorize all his lines and inflections (Conway & Siegelman, 1978). For the most part, such childhood "verbal geniuses" are simply working from a script; parroting a series of phrases they have committed to memory. Their communication is strictly unilateral. If they were interrupted and their statements were challenged, they couldn't defend their positions fluently or cogently. In its 60-year history, a pre-teen or adolescent has never won the National Debate Tournament, even though many child prodigies begin college at age 12 or so. Freshman, aged 18–19, have won the tournament or been selected as top speaker, but no one younger.
2 One could have "truth" on one's side if the argument were over a factual issue, such as the number of U.S. presidents who were assassinated while in office. In disputes over value and policy issues there isn't *a* correct answer and even some factual disputes hinge on the definitions one employs.

References

Amsterlaw, J. (2006). Children's beliefs about everyday reasoning. *Child Development*, 77(2), 443–464, doi: 10.1111/j.1467-8624.2006.00881.x.

Belcher, W. (2006, May 3). Devoted voters for *American Idol* do their duty on a presidential scale. *The Tampa Tribune*, p. 8.

Brockriede, W. (1972). Arguers as lovers. *Philosophy and Rhetoric*, 5(1), 1–11. Retrieved February 22, 2019 from: www.jstor.org/stable/40237210.

Brockriede, W. (1975). Where is argument? *Journal of the American Forensic Association*, 11(4), 179–182, doi. org/10.1080/00028533.1975.11951059.

Conway, F. & Siegelman, J. (1978). *Snapping: America's epidemic of sudden personality change* (2nd Ed.). New York: Stillpoint Press.

Coombs, A. (2006, January 13). Lottery is seen by some as best chance to accumulate wealth; many underestimate the value of consistent saving over time. *The Buffalo News*, p. D-9.

De Moraes, L. (2012, May 24). CBS triumphs in 2011–2012 network ratings war. *The Washington Post*, p. C6.

Ehninger, D. (1970). Argument as method. *Speech Monographs*, 37, 101–110, doi.org/10.1080/036377 57009375654.

Elsworth, C. (2006, May 26). U.S. pop show victor attracts more votes than any president. *The Daily Telegraph* (London), p. 18.

Felton, M. & Kuhn, D. (2001). The development of argumentative discourse skill. *Discourse Processes*, 32(2–3), 135–153, doi: 10.1177/0741088315590788.

Grossman, I., Na, J., Varnum, M.E.W., Park, D.C., Kitayama, S. & Nisbett, R.E. (2010). Reasoning about social conflicts improves into old age. *Proceedings of the National Academy of Sciences*, 107(16), 7246–7250, doi.org/10.1073/pnas.1001715107.

Hart Research Associates (2013). *It takes more than a major: Priorities for college learning and student success*. Washington DC: American Association of Colleges & Universities and Hart Research Associates. Retrieved on August 1, 2018 from: www.aacu.org/publications-research/periodicals/it-takes-more-major-employer-priorities-college-learning-and.

Infante, D.A. (1987). Aggressiveness. In J.C. McCroskey & J.A. Daly (Eds), *Personality and interpersonal communication* (pp. 157–192). Newbury Park, CA: Sage.

Infante, D.A. & Rancer, A.S. (1982). A conceptualization and measure of argumentativeness. *Journal of Personality Assessment, 45*(1), 72–80, doi.org/10.1207/s15327752jpa4601_13.

Infante, D.A. & Wigley, C.J. (1986). Verbal aggressiveness: An interpersonal model and measure. *Communication Monographs, 53*(1), 61–69, doi.org/10.1080/03637758609376126.

Investopedia (2018, January 8). The lottery: Is it ever worth playing? *Investopedia*. Retrieved on January 12, 2018 from: www.investopedia.com/managing-wealth/worth-playing-lottery.

Jasna, M. (1992). The collaborative development of children's arguments. *Argumentation & Advocacy, 29*(2), 77–89, doi.org/10.1080/00028533.1992.11951557.

Kuhn, D. & Udell, W. (2003). The development of argument skills. *Child Development, 74*(5), 1245–1260, doi: 10.1111/1467-8624.00605.

Leamy, E. (2008, February 11). Creative consumer: Avoid work at home scams. *ABC News*. Retrieved May 21, 2010 from: http://abcnews.go.com/Business/SmallBiz/story?id=4263388&page=1.

Liptak, K. (2012, November 8). Report shows turnout lower than in 2008 and 2004. *CNN Politics*. Retrieved January 4, 2013, from: http://politicalticker.blogs.cnn.com/2012/11/08/report-shows-turnout-lower-than-2008-and-2004.

Makau, J.M. & Marty, D.L. (2001). *Cooperative argumentation: A model for deliberative community*. Prospect Heights, IL. Waveland Press.

Marist Poll (2015, December 21). "Whatever" most annoying word for seventh year. *Marist Poll*. Retrieved February 22, 2019 from: http://maristpoll.marist.edu/1221-whatever-most-annoying-word-for-seventh-year.

Mercier, H. & Sperber, D. (2011). Why do humans reason? Arguments for an argumentative theory. *Behavioral and Brain Sciences, 34*(2), 57–111, foiz: 10.1017/S0140525X10000968.

Moshman, D. (1998). Cognitive development beyond childhood: Constraints on cognitive development and learning. In W. Damon (Series Ed.), D. Kuhn & R. Siegler (Vol. Eds), *Handbook of child psychology: Vol. 2. Cognition, language, and perception* (5th Ed., pp. 947–978). New York: Wiley.

Ricco, R. (2015). The development of reasoning. In R.M. Lerner (Ed.-in-Chief), L.S. Liben & U.M. Müller (Vol. Eds), *Handbook of child psychology and developmental science, Vol. 2: Cognitive processes* (7th Ed., pp. 519–570). Hoboken, NJ: John Wiley.

Schoeff, M. Jr. (2007). Skill levels of U.S. grads leave employers cold. *Workforce Management, 86*(7), 14. Retrieved August 13, 2010 from ABI/Inform Global.

Scott, R.L. (1967). On viewing rhetoric as epistemic. *Central States Speech Journal, 18*(1), 9–16, doi.org/10.1080/10510976709362856.

Sweney, M. (2006, May 26). *American Idol* outvotes the president. *The Guardian*. Retrieved July 16, 2004 from: www.guardian.co.uk/international/story/0,,1783339,00.html.

Tuchman, B.W. (1984). *The march of folly: From Troy to Vietnam*. New York: Random House.

van Gelder, T. (2005). Teaching critical thinking: Some lessons from cognitive science. *College Teaching, 53*(1), 41–46, doi.org/10.3200/CTCH.53.1.41-48.

Von Bergen, J.M. (2010, February 18). Federal crackdown on work-at-home scams. *Philadelphia Inquirer*, p. C-1.

Weinstock, M.P., Neuman, Y. & Glassner, A. (2006). Identification of informal reasoning fallacies as a function of epistemological level, grade level, and cognitive ability. *Journal of Educational Psychology, 89*(2), 327–341, doi.org/10.1037/0022-0663.89.2.327.

Wellman, H.M. (1992). *The child's theory of mind.* Cambridge, MA: MIT Press.

Xie, Y., Hample, D. & Wang, X. (2015). A cross-cultural analysis of argument predispositions in China: Argumentativeness, verbal aggressiveness, argument frames, and personalization of conflict. *Argumentation, 29*(3), 265–284, doi.org/10.1007/s10503-015-9352-8.

Zogby International (2006, August 15). *New national poll finds: More Americans know Snow White's dwarfs than Supreme Court judges, Homer Simpson than Homer's Odyssey, and Harry Potter than Tony Blair.* Zogby Analytics, Soundbites. Retrieved September 17, 2006 from: www.zogby.com/Soundbites/ReadClips. dbm?ID=13498.

Chapter 2

Arguing Ethically

The Meltdown

When one of the authors was a college student, he got clobbered by a professor he barely knew. The professor seemed amicable enough, but you know what they say about judging a book by its cover. While usually an easygoing fellow, once this professor stepped on a basketball court, an unsettling Jekyll-n-Hyde transformation took place. His "win-at-all costs" attitude turned what was intended to be a friendly Saturday morning game into an ugly spectacle. Your author, the unfortunate target of the professor's ire, got knocked for a loop when attempting an easy shot. As the author watched little birdies circling his head, the professor yelled "offensive foul" and a dispute ensued. When other players—even some from the professor's team—took the author's side, the professor hurled profanities, then insults, then threats, and finally the basketball itself at the author's face. Fortunately he missed, but the author was stunned nonetheless. Sure, he'd experienced hostility before, but this case seemed too trivial to provoke such an extreme reaction. You might expect such a lack of decorum from professional wrestlers or bridezillas, the author figured, but why would a professor stoop so low? Of course, the author was being naïve. Professors are not above behaving badly and, unfortunately, they are not alone.

To be sure, there is a lot of anger out there. As Amy Alkin observes in her book, *I See Rude People*, "Rudeness isn't just contagious; it's epidemic" (2010, pp. 18–19). Try Googling "little league fights," for example, and you'll find a wide selection of videos featuring players, coaches, and parents "getting in each other's grill." And, if that's not enough, you can almost always find television reality or talk shows (e.g., *Mob Wives, Real Housewives, Hell's Kitchen*) that have managed to market tantrums as entertainment. Politicians, of course, are not above the fray, and who hasn't heard of internet trolling, flaming, and cyberbullying? We could go on, but you get the point—incivility is not in short supply.

With that in mind, this chapter is devoted to examining how to argue ethically, with civility and decorum. In addition to discussing the different goals you should consider when engaging in an argument, we examine a number of perspectives on cooperative and constructive argumentation. First, however, we turn to a discussion of some principles related to the topic at hand.

Argument Is Not a Dirty Word

One of the authors once had a conversation with a couple that went like this:

Husband:	(proudly) "We've been married for two years and never had a fight."
Author:	"What do you mean by fight?"
Wife:	"An argument."
Author:	"You're telling me that in two years you've *never once* argued?"
Husband and wife:	(in unison) "Nope!"

Upon hearing this, the author's first thought was "Uh Oh." An absence of argument in a relationship isn't necessarily something to be proud of. In fact, compared with couples that argue effectively, those that avoid arguments are 10 times more likely to have unhappy relationships (see Hill, 2018). An absence of argument might, for instance, signal relational inequality. One partner might be more emotionally or financially dependent on the other and dare not disagree. When our relationships are rooted in equality, we feel free to argue because we are confident enough in the relationship to do so. Don't get us wrong. We're not endorsing constant bickering and endless sniping. We are recommending that couples argue about important issues, those that affect their relationships. Regrettably, the "happy" couple in this story divorced within a few years.

When it comes to connotations associated with the word "argument," the couple in this story is not alone. Unfortunately, the word "argument" often carries with it a pejorative connotation. In one study by Benoit (1982, cited in Hample, 2003), for example, undergraduate students were asked to recall and describe an argument in which they had recently been involved. Results indicated that the students' view of an argument was largely negative, involving "overt disagreement, loud and negative voices, irrational emotional displays, closed-mindedness by both parties, and negative relational consequences" (Hample, 2003, p. 447).

Viewing Argument Positively

Do you also view argument negatively? After reading this chapter, we hope not. If you do, however, you may be selling yourself short. Indeed, according to argumentation scholar Dale Hample (2003), the ability to understand and reframe arguing as a positive process is essential to becoming a skillful arguer. We couldn't agree more. In fact, one of our main objectives in this book is to dispel negative attitudes about what argument is and does. We encourage you to think of argument in a positive light. Arguing about things that matter is an asset, not a liability, to a relationship.

That said, a willingness to argue, while necessary, is not sufficient to make you a competent arguer. You also need to argue ethically. How you argue has the potential to affect your relationships, the way in which you perceive yourself and others, and the effectiveness of what you say. Accordingly, in this chapter we offer some basic principles and practical skills that should help you argue more appropriately. Beforehand, however, we'd like to add a disclaimer. While we encourage you to consider our guidelines, we do not believe we have a corner on the ethics market. Although we try to practice what we preach, we've committed our fair share of blunders during arguments. Our views, and those of others that we examine, are not sacrosanct. Moreover, some of our guidelines do not apply in every situation. That said, we hope our guidelines are helpful as you begin to think through the bases for your own ethical standards and come to terms with what you consider to be good and bad behavior when arguing. With this in mind, we begin by examining some traits and behaviors related to competent argumentation.

Arguing (In)Competently: Traits and Behaviors of Effective and Ineffective Arguers

Human beings are natural categorizers. We like to group and label things, including the movies we watch (e.g., comedy, drama, . . .), the music we listen to (e.g., rap, rock, polka, . . .), and even the people with whom we argue. By way of example, communication scholars have identified a wide array of traits that affect the manner in which people approach, participate in, and react to arguing. Although we do not have space to cover them all, we discuss several that have the potential to either facilitate or short circuit constructive argumentation.

Argumentativeness and Verbal Aggressiveness: You Say Tomato, I Throw Tomatoes

Remember the old saying, sticks and stones may break my bones, but words will never hurt me? If you've ever been called a "fatso," "wimp," or "nerd," you know that saying isn't always true. Some insults cross a legal line and are classified as hate speech. There is little doubt that aggressive communication can hurt, but is all aggressive communication bad? According to Dominic Infante (1987), comments directed at another can be either constructive or destructive, depending on whether they are a manifestation of assertiveness or hostility, respectively. Here, we discuss two distinct styles of communication; *argumentativeness*, which is good, and *verbal aggressiveness*, which is a skill deficiency (Infante & Wigley, 1986) (see Table 2.1).

Verbal Aggression: If You Can't Say Anything Nice, Go Ahead and Say It

Rather than attacking the substance of what you are saying, people who are verbally aggressive attack your self-concept by saying things like, "You're either a liar or an idiot. I can't tell which." Verbally aggressive people are prone to using threats, profanity, and ultimatums. Their approach to winning arguments is to insult people's character, competence, background, appearance, and so forth. As such, verbal aggressiveness wreaks havoc on relationships. As you might have guessed, abusive relationships are characterized by higher verbal aggressiveness than are non-abusive ones (Infante, Chandler & Rudd, 1989). To argue appropriately, you should strive to be *low in verbal aggressiveness* (for a possible exception, see Box 2.1).

Argumentativeness: Don't Shoot the Messenger

In contrast to verbal aggressiveness, argumentativeness is a form of assertiveness and is a constructive trait (Infante & Rancer, 1982). Compared with high verbal aggressives, who abuse others, individuals who are high in argumentativeness tend to focus on the substance of an argument. Moreover, compared with low argumentatives, who tend to avoid and withdraw from arguments,

Table 2.1 Constructive and destructive communication styles.

Hostility	Assertiveness
Subtype: verbal aggression	Subtype: argumentativeness
Consequences: destructive to relationships	Consequences: constructive for relationships

Box 2.1   Enough Said? A Case for Incivility

Is civility overrated? It is, according to Craig Shirley (2015), a political biographer who recently argued, "The last thing we need in American politics is more civility. What we need is more focused anger. Anger begets debate and debate begets change" (para. 5). According to Shirley, elites endorse civility in politics as a way to control the citizenry, when, instead, anger would serve us better. Along similar lines, Thornton (2015) suggested that:

> A dislike of political rancor is at heart a dislike of democracy . . . If the citizenry comprises multiple factions free to seek their interests and express their passions, one would expect political speech to be spirited, angry, and brutal, for passionately held beliefs in fundamental principles, which seldom can be reconciled with conflicting beliefs and principles, frequently form the substance of political speech. (paras 4 and 13)

An alternative perspective, advanced by Susan Herbst (2010) in her book *Rude Democracy*, is that both civility and incivility are best understood as political tools that are used strategically to achieve specific goals. The lines between them, she suggests, are often fuzzy. As such, rather than bemoan the prevalence of incivility in today's society, we'd be better served by cultivating a thicker skin, learning to tolerate disagreement, developing better listening skills, and embracing a culture of argument.

Finally, although, so far, we have suggested that competent arguers tend to focus their attention on positions rather than people, we admit that there may be exceptions. For example, we have argued elsewhere (Seiter & Gass, 2010) that the primary purpose of political disputes, particularly campaigns, is to provide information that an audience can use to make decisions. With that in mind, attacks on a candidate's personal attributes may be fair so long as such attacks are characterized by veracity, relevancy, and decorum (Seiter & Gass, 2010). In other words, fabricating stories about an opponent's illegal activities is clearly a no-no. Moreover, some attacks seem more relevant than others. For example, in 1972, some people questioned whether George McGovern's presidential running mate, Thomas Eagleton, who had undergone shock treatment and been hospitalized repeatedly for depression, was able to withstand the stress of the office were he to take over as president. This, to us, is obviously more relevant than the jeers we saw in 2016, when, for example, presidential candidate Marco Rubio insulted Donald Trump for having small hands and a spray tan, and Trump insulted Rubio for being short and sweaty. Finally, decorum requires that people adapt appropriately to the contexts and circumstances in which they find themselves. Thus, while providing voters with truthful and relevant information should take priority over politeness, it's one thing to say your opponent "lacks experience" and quite another to label one's opponent as a "moron" or "idiot."

high argumentatives tend to have a positive view of arguments and, therefore, do not avoid them. Previous research indicates that high argumentatives are perceived as being more credible than low argumentatives (Infante, 1981). Furthermore, high argumentatives tend to be more difficult to provoke (Infante, Trebing, Shepherd & Seeds, 1984), that is, it is harder to "push their buttons." They are also more successful in college and relationships (Infante, 1982; Rancer & Avtgis, 2006). To argue appropriately, you should strive to be *high in argumentativeness* (see Table 2.2).

Table 2.2 Argumentativeness and verbal aggressiveness: finding the sweet spot.

	High Argumentativeness	Low Argumentativeness
High Verbal Aggressiveness	Eager to argue, but hostile when doing so.	**The worst balance**: Prone to engaging in name calling, insults, put-downs.
Low Verbal Aggressiveness	**The best balance**: Willing to engage in argument, but focuses on issues, not personalities.	Avoids or withdraws from arguments.

Based on this research and more (see Avtgis & Rancer, 2010; Rancer & Avtgis, 2006), it is clear that arguing appropriately and ethically involves avoiding personal attacks and, instead, focusing on the issue at hand (for more on this topic see Box 2.2). We are not suggesting that people should start instigating arguments whenever and wherever possible. Obviously, lack of argumentative discretion can lead to problems. For example, one of the authors and his wife hosted a dinner party several years ago. During the main course, one of the guests started a debate, pointing out what he claimed were serious flaws in a certain religion. The problem? Two of the other guests were members of that religion. Clearly, silence or small talk would have been preferable to the heated exchange that ensued, not to mention the chilly silence that followed. Argumentative acumen requires knowing when it is appropriate to disagree and when to bite your tongue. Neither avoiding arguments completely nor rushing headlong into every argumentative fray is desirable (see Table 2.2).

Box 2.2   Timing Is Everything: On Procrastination and Sandbagging

Although we have told you that appropriate arguers focus on attacking positions rather than on attacking people, the simple act of focusing on positions will not make you an appropriate arguer. There are other things to consider. For instance, the saying, "Timing is everything," applies to arguments as well. It may not matter, for example, how position-oriented your argument is if you present it when another person is in a bad mood or exhausted. Sometimes waiting for a better time is the best approach. That being said, procrastinating can also be a problem. Indeed, another key principle that is related to arguing positively is to argue about issues in the "here and now." If something is bugging you, bring it up as soon as it is appropriate to do so. Raise the issue while it is still relevant. When you get an issue out in the open, the other person knows where she or he stands. If you wait too long, the other person may feel ambushed. "Why didn't you say something before?" the person may ask. Moreover, avoiding an argument won't make the problem go away. It will allow the conflict to fester. The result may be passive-aggressive behavior or a huge verbal donnybrook later on. Conflicts that simmer have a tendency to boil over. It is much better to address an issue, head on, by arguing about it.

Related to the above, you should avoid what is known as *sandbagging*, whereby you save up a number of issues and drop them on another person all at once. Suppose Osbaldo naïvely asks his neighbor for a favor.

Osbaldo:	"Hey Edna, would you mind dropping me off at the train station tomorrow morning? My car is in the shop."
Edna:	"No, I wouldn't mind, as long as you return my blender—the one you borrowed for your party last month."
Osbaldo:	"Oh. Sorry. I forgot I even had it."
Edna:	"And stop hammering and sawing in your garage late at night."
Osbaldo:	"Sure, I . . . I had no idea."
Edna:	"And pick up after your dog when he poops on my lawn. He does it all the time."
Osbaldo:	"Uh, er . . .."
Edna:	"Then I wouldn't mind dropping you off at all."

Osbaldo will probably feel like he's been sandbagged. In response to what he believes to be a simple request, he gets coldcocked by a litany of complaints. If Edna wants to remain on good terms, she would be better advised to raise issues one at a time, when they are much more manageable.

Tolerance for Disagreement: Yours Is Not to Reason Why?

According to the Center for Relationship Abuse Awareness (2017), one of the signs or "red flags" for identifying a potentially abusive person is to ask yourself whether you are afraid to disagree with that person. Unfortunately, some people are not to be trifled with. Of course, not all people react violently in the face of disagreement. Some, as we saw earlier, withdraw from or avoid disagreements altogether. The point is that some people tolerate disagreement better than others. Communication scholars define *tolerance for disagreement* (TFD) as "the amount of disagreement an individual can tolerate before he or she perceives the existence of conflict in a relationship" (Richmond & McCroskey, 1992, p. 125). Unlike people with a high TFD, those with a low TFD tend to see disagreements as more than mere differences of opinion; instead, they equate disagreements with conflict, involving competition, suspicion, distrust, and hostility (McCroskey & Wheeless, 1976; Teven, McCroskey & Richmond, 1998). We also suspect that people with a low TFD have a negative view of argument. Not surprisingly, one study found that supervisors with a low TFD had less satisfied employees than supervisors with a high TFD (Richmond & McCroskey, 1979).

Unfortunately, the negative consequences of a low tolerance for disagreement reach further than employee dissatisfaction. As Martinson (2005) argued:

> one of the more troubling aspects of contemporary American culture is the considerable number of persons who feel no obligation to support freedom of speech and/or freedom of the press . . . Those who disagree are perceived as dangerous. There are right answers and wrong answers, and to suggest that one might learn something from those who espouse ideas other than one's own quickly leads to a charge that one is "selling out" . . . That is perhaps the reason the contemporary American political scene has been characterized by what has been called the "politics of demonization." (pp. 118, 119)

Such demonization and intolerance for disagreement can have other negative consequences as well. It might, for instance, contribute to a phenomenon Janis (1972) called *groupthink*, which occurs when members in a group are so concerned with maintaining consensus and getting along with each other that they refrain from arguing. Poor decisions are often the result. In fact, a number of blunders—e.g., Roosevelt's complacency before Pearl Harbor, Kennedy's Bay of Pigs fiasco, Nixon's Watergate break-in, the space shuttle *Challenger* disaster, and the invasion of Iraq—have been attributed to groupthink (see Badie, 2010; Griffin, 1997; Janis, 1972).

With this in mind, cultivating a tolerance for disagreement is clearly important to arguing appropriately. It is not always easy, but two steps in the right direction include building *respect for dissent* (see Wallace, 1955) and being *open-minded*. In recommending this, we are not implying that all ideas are equally good. We are suggesting that people should stand up for what they believe in, while, at the same time, paying attention to the considered opinions of others (see Martinson, 2005).

Acknowledge Good Arguments: When You're Right, You're Right

Of course, being open-minded and building respect for dissent are only the first steps to arguing appropriately. Such attitudes should also be communicated. For example, if the person with whom you are arguing makes a good argument, you should acknowledge it. There's no harm in admitting, "I agree with you on that point," or "you're right about that," or "you know, I hadn't thought of it that way." You needn't concede the entire debate. By acknowledging the other person's good arguments, you'll be modeling fair-mindedness, thereby encouraging the other person to do the same.

Use Active Listening: Good Arguers Are Good Listeners

Similarly, building and communicating respect and open-mindedness requires active listening skills. Some arguers begin to mentally rehearse their counter-arguments as soon as another person opens his or her mouth. Some even prepare a "canned rant" the night before such an encounter. Listen instead. Make sure you clearly grasp the other person's arguments. After all, you can't refute someone's position unless you understand what his or her position is.

Paraphrasing: What I Hear You Saying

A skill we mentioned in Chapter 1 bears repeating here: to demonstrate that you are listening, use *paraphrasing*, which involves summarizing the other person's argument in your own words. An arguer might say, "If I understand you correctly, your main objection to the death penalty is that it is discriminatory." Or the arguer might say, "What I hear you saying is that legalizing physician-assisted suicide is a matter of states' rights."

Perception-Checking: Am I Hearing You Correctly?

Another skill identified in Chapter 1 is *perception-checking*. You can use perception-checking by asking if you've understood the other person's point correctly. You might ask, "Are you saying that . . .?" or "Are you upset because . . .?" or "Am I correct in inferring that . . .?" Not only will the use of paraphrasing and perception-checking demonstrate that you are paying attention to what the other person is saying during an argument, but doing so will also help you to pin down the other person's position. Clarifying the other person's position discourages later waffling.

Taking Conflict Personally: How Thin Is Your Skin?

Taking conflict personally (TCP), a trait identified by Hample and Dallinger (1995), is associated with having negative emotional reactions to disagreements. Although the trait is typically discussed in literature on interpersonal conflict, it is easy to see how it relates to arguing competently as well. Like people who are low in argumentativeness (see above), those who are high TCPs do not like to argue. They not only avoid arguments, they believe that disagreements hurt relationships and create stress. Moreover, as the name of the trait implies, high TCPs take disagreements personally, often feeling persecuted, stressed, and less satisfied in their relationships with other people (Hample & Richards, 2015). Considering this, it's hard to imagine high TCPs engaging in productive argumentation. They are too concerned about their own feelings. Keeping that in mind, approaching arguments non-defensively is an important skill. Similarly, being able to distinguish verbally aggressive communication from argumentative communication is essential. If someone is making arguments that counter *positions* you adhere to, having a hissy fit is not a constructive approach.

If someone is attacking you personally, however, that's another matter altogether. An effective approach to deal with such behavior is to disrupt the attack cycle. Try to redirect the person's focus to positions not personalities. For instance, a person might say, "We were arguing about where to spend Thanksgiving, not about whether I'm selfish or inconsiderate" or "Let's deal with that issue in a minute. I want to get back to what we were just talking about." In the argument below, Eunice defuses Ernie's anger toward the issue.

Ernie: "What's it like, being stupid 24/7?"
Eunice: "Rather than focusing on my shortcomings, let's concentrate on getting this project finished."
Ernie: "Your teeth are brighter than you are."
Eunice: "Ernie, insulting me isn't going to help solve this problem."
Ernie: "I'll be nicer, when you get smarter."
Eunice: "I'll try my best. Now, shall we tackle this project?"

Eunice refuses to be baited by Ernie into a name-calling contest. She deflects Ernie's insults and focuses on the task instead.

Of course, if verbally aggressive people persist in attacking, it's also fine to ask them to stop or to leave the conversation. You might say, "If you insist on name-calling, I'm going to leave." If you know a person tends to be hot-tempered, have the argument in a public place. As an alternative, you can also invite a third party to observe the interaction. Hopefully, this will cause the hot-head to engage in more self-monitoring. Nobody deserves to be verbally abused.

Goals: Winning Isn't the Only Thing

Sometimes people become so obsessed with winning that they lose track of everything else. Think modern politics is nasty? It is, but in the presidential election of 1828, John Quincy Adams was described by political foes as a tyrant and pimp, while Andrew Jackson was accused of murdering his own soldiers and being the son of a prostitute (Swint, 2008). How about sports? In 1997 heavyweight boxer Mike Tyson bit off a piece of his opponent's ear, while in 2006 French soccer great Zinedine Zidane infamously head-butted a defender during the World

Cup final. And don't forget the entertainment industry, which saw rapper Kanye West storm the stage and grab the microphone from Taylor Swift, who had just won an award that Kanye believed Beyoncé deserved.

If that's not bad enough, the desire to win arguments seems just as ingrained. Consider, for example, the following book titles on Amazon.com:

The Art of Always Being Right: The 38 Subtle Ways to Win an Argument (Arthur Schopenhauer and A.C. Grayling)

How to Win an Argument: Surefire Strategies for Getting Your Point Across (Michael A. Gilbert)

Win an Argument: 40 Stratagems & Drills to Verbally Crush Any Opponent (Roma Solodoff)

How to Argue and Win Every Time: At Home, At Work, In Court, Everywhere, Everyday (Gerry Spence)

The menu of books with a similar theme is longer, but you get the idea. Winning is extolled as a virtue. Hence such common sayings as "Winning isn't everything, it's the only thing" and "Everybody loves a winner." Unfortunately, some people believe it, often losing sight of other goals that are important, like maintaining healthy relationships. The key point we want to stress here is that being a skillful arguer is enormously dependent on your goals. So important, in fact, that Dale Hample (2003) argued:

In trying to understand why some people are better at arguing than others, and what may be done to help those who are less skilled, I think that the most fundamental question to answer is, *What do people think they are doing when they are arguing?* . . . When people argue badly, and especially when incompetence constitutes social inappropriateness, the problem is likely to be that they have misframed what they are doing. (p. 443)

Given that, in this section we examine some of the "*other* things"—specifically, some other goals besides "winning"—that are essential to being an appropriate and ethical arguer.

Goals to Pursue While Arguing: That's a Lot to Juggle!

Competent arguers are not only successful at convincing others, they do so without violating normative standards for civil dialogue. Winning at all costs won't do you much good if the costs include your family, friends, co-workers, and other relationships. According to Hample (2003), two important goals for *argumentation competence* are *effectiveness* and *appropriateness* (also see Spitzberg & Cupach, 1984). We agree. Arguers who continually fail to convince anyone lack competence and need to improve their argumentation skills. Arguers who continually engage in inappropriate behaviors, such as name calling, threats, and ultimatums, lack appropriateness and also need improvement. A competent arguer makes both effective and appropriate arguments.

Goals–Plans–Action: A Goal Without a Plan Is a Wish

In pursuit of these more general goals (i.e., effectiveness and appropriateness), however, our framework for arguing competently suggests that it is also useful to examine more specific goals that might arise in argumentative encounters. To do so, we rely on research conducted in the field of persuasion that we extend for our purposes here. Specifically, in his *goals–plans–action model*, James Dillard (2004, 2008) argued that people may pursue different types of goals when they are trying to influence someone. That is, in addition to being persuasive, people may or may not be concerned with goals such as saving face and creating good impressions ("conversation management goals"), maintaining and improving relationships with others ("relational resource goals"), maintaining ethical and moral standards for behavior ("identity goals"), enhancing health and resources ("personal resource goals"), and maintaining desirable emotions ("affect management goals").

Dillard's discussion of these goals is, of course, *descriptive* in nature; it is based on empirical research (Dillard, Segrin & Harden, 1989) and *describes* the types of goals that people say they might consider when they are creating persuasive messages. In our framework for arguing appropriately, we not only suggest that these goals play a role in argumentative encounters but we also address these goals in a *prescriptive* way. That is, we suggest that, as general guidelines, keeping these and similar goals in mind before or while engaging in an argument will make you a more appropriate arguer. In other words, you *should* not simply consider these goals, you should implement them as well.

Goal 1. Managing Favorable Images of Yourself and Others: About Face

Our faces are part of who we are. Our physical faces, however, are only one of the "faces" that we wear. Indeed, according to *face theory* (Goffman, 1955), "the word *face* is a metaphorical allusion to one's desired social identity or image(s)" (Shimanoff, 2009, p. 374). When people interact in everyday life, they engage in *facework* or *impression management* in order to project a desired public image. Of course, this public image, or face, can be lost or threatened. If, for instance, you've ever done something embarrassing in public—e.g., wet your pants, burped accidentally, claimed Arizona was a country—you may have felt that you "lost face," damaging the image you were trying to project.

As you may have imagined, the way you communicate does not simply affect your own public image, it can support or threaten others' face as well. To illustrate how, *politeness theory* (Brown & Levinson, 1987) posits that all people are motivated to maintain two kinds of face: positive and negative. *Positive face* refers to the desire to be liked, respected, and approved of, while *negative face* refers to the desire to be free of impositions, constraints, or encroachments imposed by others. During an argument, for example, accusing other people of being moronic, dishonest, or as interesting as cottage cheese might threaten their positive face, while constantly interrupting them or not giving them a chance to speak might threaten their negative face.

It turns out that if you decide to engage in such face-threatening behaviors, you might, at the same time, hamper your goal of creating a favorable image of yourself. Several experiments conducted by one of the authors and his colleagues support this assertion (Seiter, 1999; Seiter, Abraham & Nakagama, 1998; Seiter & Weger, 2005; Seiter, Weger, Jensen & Kinzer, 2010). In these studies, when debaters disparaged their opponents by using negative nonverbal cues (e.g., rolling their eyes, grimacing) they were perceived as less credible, less likable, and inappropriate.

Given what we've said so far, what advice can be offered to arguers who wish to present a desirable image? One tip is to acknowledge the face needs of others. Be compassionate toward those with whom you disagree, rather than mocking or humiliating them. Encourage others to share their ideas and opinions, rather than constantly interrupting or stifling them. Treat people as if they were equals rather than inferiors. As Sellers (2004) said:

> Rules of civility encourage taking the well-being of every member of the community equally into account in public discourse and treating every participant in the conversation as a fellow citizen whose interests deserve respect and whose views merit careful consideration. This requires listening to the arguments made by others in the public discussion, trying to understand them, and responding as if they were made in good faith by making reasoned responses even to incoherent or transparently self-interested views. (p. 18)

Goal 2. Maintaining Ethical and Moral Standards: Speak No Evil

The way we conduct ourselves while arguing does not simply affect the way others see us, it affects the way we see ourselves. Our self-image, in turn, affects the way we behave while arguing. As such, if you see yourself as kindhearted, you're likely to avoid telling people that they smell like the bilge water on an abalone trawler. Likewise, if you catch yourself insulting someone, you might feel guilty. That is because most people have beliefs about what is right and wrong and are motivated to behave consistently with those beliefs (see Festinger, 1957). With that in mind, one measure of appropriateness is the degree to which arguers' behavior makes them feel good about themselves when all is said and done.

Of course, not all people have the same ethical standards. In addition to being accountable to our own consciences, we should be accountable to other people as well. Considering what others use as ethical standards for judging behavior is time well spent. Sure, you could let another person drag you into the gutter based on their arguing style. You could also help that person onto the sidewalk by modeling constructive arguing behaviors instead.

HONESTY: GIVE IT TO ME STRAIGHT

One ethical principle that is commonly discussed by philosophers and communication ethicists is honesty. David Nyberg (1993), for instance, argues that deception is ethically neutral. Others, such as Sissela Bok (1999), disagree, arguing that because deception devastates trust, the foundation of relationships, acceptable lies are few and far between. We can come up with a long list of lies that we consider justified and/or harmless (e.g., bluffing in poker when all players agree it is part of the game, planning a surprise party, pretending nothing happened when grandma passes wind).

When it comes to arguing, however, we presume that a person's mode of communication should follow the old adage that "honesty is the best policy." Can you picture, for example, what might happen in argumentative contexts if deception were the *modus operandi*? Imagine watching a political debate in which the candidates lied about everything (admittedly, little imagination is required). It would be like playing chess with no rules. All the argumentative moves would be meaningless. Any conclusion reached would be useless. In short, effective argumentation depends on honesty.

GRICE'S MAXIMS

This notion resonates in the writings of Grice (1989). Specifically, his *cooperative principle* describes four maxims that participants in an interaction are expected to follow and that enable effective communication. Although Grice did not present these maxims as ethical guidelines, we suggest that, in the pursuit of being honest, arguers should attempt to satisfy the requirements of each of the following maxims.

First, the maxim of *quality* says that communicators are expected to provide information that is not false or that does not lack adequate evidence (Grice, 1989). Unfortunately, violations of this maxim are all too common. Consider the spate of fake news that plagued the 2016 presidential election. Counterfeit news sites, including trolls and bots, within and outside the U.S., swelled. In the months leading up to the election, fake news stories were read and shared more than legitimate news stories (Lee, 2016). Examples of such stories included false headlines claiming that "Pope Francis Shocks World, Endorses Donald Trump for President" and "FBI Agent Suspected in Hilary Email Leaks Found Dead of Apparent Murder-Suicide" (Lee, 2016).

Likewise, recent years have seen the rise of "post-truth politics," and "alternative facts," featuring politicians who cling to their talking points even after those points have been identified as false. Considering this, it's not surprising that the *Oxford Dictionary*'s word of the year for 2016 was "post-truth," a concept we revisit in Chapter 5.

The second maxim, *quantity*, suggests that communicators are expected to provide neither more nor less information than is required (Grice, 1989). If we transform this into an ethical principle, it is that arguers should provide information that is needed to satisfy the purposes of the interaction. This, of course, does not always happen. For example, when former President Bill Clinton claimed, "I did not have sexual relations with that woman, Miss Lewinsky," he left out the part about oral sex, which, he claimed, did not fit the definition of "sexual relations." While to some, his statement seems a clear violation of the quality maxim, there is little doubt that he could have been more forthcoming about the nature of his relationship with Monica Lewinsky.

The third maxim, *relation*, says that communicators are expected to make their messages relevant to the topic. Some time ago, a student of one of the authors violated this maxim while making arguments about a research paper she submitted. She claimed she deserved a higher grade because another student in class, one she mentioned by name, received an "A" on his paper even though he partied and got drunk a lot. Although such smear tactics are clearly irrelevant, they are quite common, particularly in politics.

Finally, the maxim of *manner* says that communicators should not be obscure and ambiguous (Grice, 1989). Thus, this maxim is violated when certain words or phrases make the meaning of an argument or message unclear. To illustrate, consider these two statements, created by Robert Thornton (2003), for recommending someone with questionable qualifications:

- If the person is chronically absent: "A man like him is hard to find." (p. 19)
- If the person is lazy: "In my opinion, you will be very fortunate to get this person to work for you." (p. 5)

These examples, of course, are just for fun, but when arguers use such statements to intentionally mislead someone, they are ethically suspect.

Although we have focused almost entirely on deception and ambiguity in this section, maintaining ethical and moral standards involves much more than being honest. In fact, it involves many of the concepts we discuss in other sections of this chapter. One of these includes the manner in which we handle relationships while arguing. We examine that topic next.

Goal 3. Creating and Maintaining Healthy Relationships: There's No "I" in Argument

Trust is a prerequisite for cooperation. If you want to work together with people, you must first earn their trust. Viewing arguments as collaborative encounters, rather than adversarial ones, is one way of doing so. Earlier in this chapter we explained that competent arguers tend to frame arguing as a positive, constructive process rather than as something negative and destructive. In addition to discussing this manner of framing arguments, Hample (2003) suggested that there are two other ways that people might frame them. The first is to view arguments purely instrumentally, as a means of getting a raise, establishing dominance, winning an election, and so forth. To us, a person who frames arguments solely for his or her self-benefit is suspect. Argument, to such a person, is about getting what he or she wants without considering others.

In contrast, a second way to frame arguments is to consider whether people try to coordinate their goals with those of another arguer. Skillful arguers, according to Hample, tend to "integrate their own goals with the other's cooperatively, not competitively" (2003, p. 470). This, to us, underlines the relational nature of argument. When people in an argument—for example, a married couple deciding whether or not to adopt a child—treat each other with respect and dignity, attempting to fasten their goals together, arguments will be more competent, satisfying, and constructive. With this as a backdrop, we turn to a discussion of what others have written about the importance of relationships and cooperation in argumentation.

"I'm not yelling <u>at</u> you, I'm yelling <u>with</u> you."

Figure 2.1 *The New Yorker*, 2/19/2001.

RELATIONAL METAPHORS FOR ARGUING: I'M A LOVER NOT A FIGHTER

In a widely acclaimed essay, one of our favorite former professors, Wayne Brockriede (1972), used a relational metaphor to discuss the different ways that people show regard for others while arguing. Specifically, he suggested that arguers could be classified as rapists, seducers, and lovers. The first group, *rapists*, view others as inferior and attempt to dominate, control, and bully them. They use coercive argument strategies such as threats and force. They are verbally aggressive, resorting to personal attacks to assert power and superiority. The second group, *seducers*, also has little regard for others in an argument. Unlike the rapists, however, seducers try to charm or trick their victims into agreeing with them. Deceit, insincere flattery, and beguilement are tactics they might use to pursue their own interests at the expense of others.

In contrast to rapists and seducers, *lovers* treat those with whom they are arguing as equals. They address others as persons, not objects. They respect both themselves and others, attempting to reaffirm the other person's sense of self-worth. They try to empower others to contribute their ideas in an argument. Rather than coerce or seduce, they promote free choice and honesty in interactions. Because they emphasize cooperation over competition, relationships are more important than outcomes of an argument.

To this list of "lover" attributes, we might add another, as well as an additional category. Earlier, for example, we discussed low argumentatives, people who behave like "celibates," avoiding arguments because they view them as negative interactions. Using this same metaphor, high verbal aggressives are like "sex addicts"—they argue constantly and have no boundaries when doing so. In contrast, lovers embrace arguments, understanding that arguing, if done properly, is a means of strengthening relationships.

COOPERATIVE APPROACHES TO ARGUMENTATION: IF YOU'RE NOT WITH ME, YOU'RE NOT AGAINST ME EITHER!

Although we do not have the space to detail them all here, a number of other communication frameworks are consistent with Brockriede's metaphor of arguers as lovers. These approaches support a cooperative and relational approach to arguing. In this section we list several of these approaches and briefly note some of their highlights.

Cooperative Argument   First, Makau and Marty (2001) provide a framework of *cooperative argumentation* that promotes collaboration over competition and deliberation over persuasion. To them, people's fundamental interdependence provides one of the main reasons why we must take others' perspectives seriously and engage in cooperative dialogue, which they define as "a process of communicating **with** (rather than at, to, or for) others and the sharing of a mutual commitment to hear and be heard" (p. 46). Such dialogue emphasizes equality. It leads to a deeper understanding of our own and other's perspectives, and, as such, helps us grow, make better decisions, and build relationships with each other. It involves empathy, open-mindedness, self-awareness, and listening skills. Finally, it requires us to view others as "resources rather than as rivals" (p. 88).

Dialogues, Not Diatribes   Similarly, previous scholars have pointed to the desirability of viewing communication, and, by extension, argumentation, as a dialogue rather than as a monologue.

While monologue is associated with treating humans impersonally, dialogue does not. More specifically, Johannesen, Valde, and Whedbee (2008) summarized the principal ethical components of the *dialogical perspectives* of communication. These include authenticity (being direct, honest, and straightforward), inclusion (attempting to see another's viewpoint without sacrificing our own), confirmation (expressing warmth for others and valuing them as unique and worthy human beings), presentness (bringing our total and authentic beings into an encounter while avoiding distraction and risking attachment), a spirit of mutual equality (avoiding the exercise of power or superiority), and supportiveness (non-judgmentally encouraging the other to participate).

An Invitational Approach to Argument   Many of these values are championed by feminist scholars as well. Some, for example, have argued that the traditional, male, patriarchal view of communication focuses on winning and conquest at the expense of relationships. Sally Miller Gearhart (1979, cited in Johannesen et al., 2008), for example, equated the intent to persuade with violence. Similarly, Foss and Griffin (1995) wrote that the traditional, adversarial approach to communication "devalues the lives and perspectives of others" (p. 3). As an alternative, they propose an *invitational rhetoric*, which focuses on being open, nonjudgmental, and protecting others' integrity through equality and respect. The goal of invitational rhetoric is not to change people, although change might occur. It is to share perspectives, to strive for understanding, and to create an environment where people feel safe and free to choose.

Although we agree that cooperative, dialogic encounters are an ideal to which all arguers should aspire, we are not as critical as some scholars in the way we view traditional argumentation. Specifically, we believe that argument is a complex activity that can fulfill many functions. In some cases, it is cooperative and deliberative. In others it can be a means of inquiry and decision making. Sometimes, however, there are situations that are inherently competitive, where rolling up your sleeves and engaging in hard bargaining is necessary. Relationships are not always a top priority in such cases. In an academic debate or a trial, for example, where winners and losers are declared, the traditional model still fits. That being said, just because an event is competitive in nature and relationships are not emphasized, it does not mean that respect, decorum, and integrity should be thrown out the window. Instead, some standards apply to almost any argumentative encounter.

Goal 4. Handling Your Emotions: Don't Get Bent Out of Shape

"Chill out," "Simmer down," and "Count to ten," are all expressions about controlling your emotions. Although we know some people who might suggest that there is no room for emotion in arguments, that's not what we'll tell you. To ignore the emotional aspects of arguing would seem to dehumanize it. If you, or the person with whom you are arguing, are passionate about an issue, you're bound to experience emotions during an argument. In fact, not getting riled up about certain topics (e.g., child molestation, human trafficking) would be callous. That said, there are some practical guidelines you can follow when expressing feelings. Adhering to these guidelines will increase your appropriateness when expressing emotion and responding to others' expressions of emotion.

First, present your arguments in the "here and now." If someone says or does something that bugs you, speak up in the moment. Don't stew for a week. That can lead to passive-aggressive behavior. And when you finally do confront the other person, she or he may feel ambushed. "If you resented me borrowing your pickup truck, why didn't you say so? I would have rented one."

Second, you should "own" your emotions. Don't blame the other person for your feelings. Saying, "You are making me so upset!" or "You make me so mad," implies that the other person is responsible for your feelings. Instead, say, "I'm so upset with you" or I'm really angry at you right now."

Third, you should respond appropriately to another person's disclosure of emotion. When another person expresses his or her feelings, try not to judge the person. For instance, telling someone "Stop feeling sorry for yourself" or "You have no right to be angry at me," implies that the person is not entitled to his or her own feelings. A better approach is to acknowledge how the person feels. Respond by saying, "I can see how upset you are," or "I know how stressful this must be for you." That way you aren't judging or denying the other person's feelings. Neither are you accepting blame for how the other person feels. You are simply acknowledging her or his feelings. You may be surprised at how well this approach works in defusing tension. If someone you are arguing with starts to cry or hyperventilate, there is little point in continuing the argument. Stop arguing and deal with the emotional and relational issues first.

"And just what the hell is that supposed to mean?"

Figure 2.2 Emotions creep in.

© Danny Shanahan/*The New Yorker* Collection/www.cartoonbank.com.

Fourth, in some cases you or the other person may be so worked up that it is better to postpone the argument to another time—but a time certain. That is better than letting anger boil over. In other cases, you may want to avoid a public spectacle by "airing your dirty laundry" in front of everyone. Note, you should still let the person know you take issue with something and arrange a time to talk. Suppose you are at a dinner party and your spouse says something you perceive as insulting. Rather than starting a row at the dinner table, you could lean over to your spouse and say, "I feel humiliated by the remark you just made. I want to talk about it when we get home." And, as we suggested above, if the other person is prone to temper tantrums in private, suggest having the argument in a public place or having a third party present.

Fifth, don't try to provoke someone with whom you are arguing. If you enjoy pushing other people's buttons or relish watching them lose their cool, it's probably time to re-examine your motives for arguing. Moreover, if you catch yourself trying to hurt and or make people angry as a way of punishing them for disagreeing with you, or as a means of establishing dominance, it is time to stop.

Final Thoughts: You've Got the Power

If you are familiar with the superhero Spiderman, perhaps you know the mantra that drives him: *With great power comes great responsibility*. This, we believe, is true for superheroes and arguers alike. Indeed, many of the concepts presented in this book teach you to think more critically and to argue more effectively. In that respect, you have more power than you did before you read these chapters. With that in mind, we believe you have a responsibility. As with most things (e.g., a gun, a hammer, knowledge), the ability to argue persuasively can be used for good or evil. After reading this chapter, we hope you'll choose to use your arguing skills wisely.

Summary

This chapter examined important features of competent and ethical argument. First, it discussed several traits, some fostering competent argumentation (i.e., argumentativeness, tolerance for disagreement) and some not (i.e., verbal aggressiveness, taking conflict personally). Next, it examined several goals that communicators should keep in mind when arguing. First, arguers should attempt to create favorable images of themselves and others by respecting the positive and negative face of others. Second, arguers should consider their own and others' moral and ethical principles, which should include creating messages that are truthful, unambiguous, and relevant. Third, arguers should attempt to create and maintain favorable relationships while arguing by valuing others and treating them with compassion, dignity, and equality. Finally, arguers should manage their emotions while being mindful of the emotions of others.

References

Alkin, A. (2010). *I see rude people: One woman's battle to beat some manners into impolite society*. New York: McGraw Hill.

Avtgis, T.A. & Rancer, A.S. (2010). *Arguments, aggression, and conflict: New directions in theory and research*. New York: Routledge.

Badie, D. (2010). Groupthink, Iraq, and the war on terror: Explaining US policy shift toward Iraq. *Foreign Policy Analysis*, *6*(4), 277–296, doi: 10.1111/j.1743-8594.2010.00113.x.

Benoit, P.J. (1982, November). The naïve social actor's concept of argument. Paper Presented at the annual meeting of the Speech Communication Association, Louisville, KY.

Bok, S. (1999). *Lying: Moral choice in public and private life*. New York: Vintage Books.

Brockriede, W. (1972). Arguers as lovers. *Philosophy and Rhetoric*, *5*(1), 1–11.

Brown, P. & Levinson, S. (1987). *Politeness: Some universals in language usage*. Cambridge: Cambridge University Press.

Center for Relationship Abuse Awareness (2017). *What is relationship abuse?* Palo Alto, CA: Center for Relationship Abuse Awareness. Retrieved August 28, 2017 from: http://stoprelationshipabuse.org/educated/warning-signs-of-abuse.

Dillard, J.P. (2004). The goals-plans-action model of interpersonal influence. In J.S. Seiter & R.H. Gass (Eds), *Readings in persuasion, social influence, and compliance gaining* (pp. 185–206). Boston, MA: Allyn & Bacon.

Dillard, J.P. (2008). Goals-plans-action theory of message production: Making influence messages. In L.A. Baxter & D.O. Braithwaite (Eds), *Engaging theories in interpersonal communication: Multiple perspectives* (pp. 65–76). Los Angeles, CA: Sage.

Dillard, J.P., Segrin, C. & Harden, J.M. (1989). Primary and secondary goals in the production of interpersonal influence messages. *Communication Monographs*, *56*(1), 19–38.

Festinger, L. (1957). *A theory of cognitive dissonance*. Stanford, CA: Stanford University Press.

Foss, S.K. & Griffin, C.L. (1995). Beyond persuasion: A proposal for an invitational rhetoric. *Communication Monographs*, *62*(1), 2–18, doi.org/10.1080/03637759509376345.

Goffman, E. (1955). On face-work: An analysis of ritual elements of social interaction. *Psychiatry: Journal for the Study of Interpersonal Processes*, *18*(3), 213–231, doi.org/10.1080/00332747.1955.11023008.

Grice, P. (1989). *Studies in the way of words*. Cambridge, MA: Harvard University Press.

Griffin, E. (1997). *A first look at communication theory* (3rd Ed.). New York: McGraw-Hill.

Hample, D. (2003). Arguing skill. In J.O. Greene & B.R. Burleson (Eds), *Handbook of communication and social skills* (pp. 439–477). Mahwah, NJ: Erlbaum.

Hample, D. & Dallinger, J.M. (1995). A Lewinian perspective on taking conflict personally: Revision, refinement, and validation of the instrument. *Communication Quarterly*, *43*(3), 297–319, doi.org/10.1080/01463379509369978.

Hample, D. & Richards, A.S. (2015). Attachment style, serial argument, and taking conflict personally. *Journal of Argument in Context*, *4*(1), 63–86, doi: 10.1075/jaic.4.1.04ham.

Herbst, S. (2010). *Rude democracy: Civility and incivility in American politics*. Philadelphia, PA: Temple University Press.

Hill, A. (2018, February 13). Couples who argue together, stay together, research finds. *The Guardian*. Retrieved February 22, 2019 from: www.theguardian.com/lifeandstyle/2018/feb/13/couples-who-argue-together-stay-together-research-finds?CMP=twt_gu.

Infante, D. (1981). Trait argumentativeness as a predictor of communicative behavior in situations requiring argument. *Central States Speech Journal*, *32*(4), 265–272, doi: 10.1080/10510978109368105.

Infante, D. (1982). The argumentative student in the speech communication classroom: An investigation and implications. *Communication Education*, *31*(2), 141–148, doi.org/10.1080/03634528209384671.

Infante, D. (1987). Aggressiveness. In J.C. McCroskey and J.A. Daly (Eds), *Personality and interpersonal communication* (pp. 157–192). Newbury Park, CA: Sage.

Infante, D., Chandler, T.A. & Rudd, J.E. (1989). Test of an argumentative skill deficiency model of interspousal violence. *Communication Monographs*, *56*(2), 163–177, doi.org/10.1080/03637758909390257.

Infante, D. & Rancer, A.S. (1982). A conceptualization and measure of argumentativeness. *Journal of Personality Assessment*, *46*(1), 72–80, doi.org/10.1207/s15327752jpa4601_13.

Infante, D., Trebing, J.D., Shepherd, P.E. & Seeds, D.E. (1984). The relationship of argumentativeness to verbal aggression. *Southern Speech Communication Journal*, *50*(1), 67–77, doi.org/10.1080/10417948409372622.

Infante, D. & Wigley, C.J. (1986). Verbal aggressiveness. An interpersonal model and measures. *Communication Monographs, 53*(1), 61–69, doi.org/10.1080/03637758609376126.

Janis, I. (1972). *Victims of groupthink.* Boston, MA: Houghton Mifflin.

Johannesen, R.L., Valde, K.S. & Whedbee, K.E. (2008). *Ethics in human communication* (6th Ed.). Long Grove, IL: Waveland Press.

Lee, T. (2016, November). The top 20 fake news stories outperformed real news at the end of the 2016 campaign. *Vox.* Retrieved on December 5, 2016 from: www.vox.com/new-money/2016/11/16/13659840/facebook-fake-news-chart.

Makau, J.M. & Marty, D.L. (2001). *Cooperative argumentation: A model for deliberative community.* Long Grove, IL: Waveland Press.

Martinson, D.L. (2005, January/February). Building a tolerance for disagreement. *Clearing House, 78*(3), 118–122, doi.org/10.3200/TCHS.78.3.118-122.

McCroskey, J.C. & Wheeless, L. (1976). *An introduction to human communication.* Boston, MA: Allyn & Bacon.

Nyberg, D. (1993). *The varnished truth: Truth telling and deceiving in ordinary life.* Chicago, IL: University of Chicago Press.

Rancer, A.S. & Avtgis, T.A. (2006). *Argumentative and aggressive communication: Theory, research, and application.* Thousand Oaks, CA: Sage.

Richmond, V.P. & McCroskey, J.C. (1979). Management communication style, tolerance for disagreement, and innovativeness as predictors of employee satisfaction: A comparison of single-factor, two-factor, and multiple factor approaches. In D. Nimmo (Ed.), *Communication yearbook 3* (pp. 359–373). New Brunswick, NJ: Transactional Books.

Richmond, V.P. & McCroskey, J.C. (1992). *Organizational communication for survival.* Engelwood Cliffs, NJ: Prentice Hall.

Seiter, J.S. (1999). Does communicating nonverbal disagreement during an opponent's speech affect the credibility of the debater in the background? *Psychological Reports, 84*(3), 855–861, doi.org/10.2466/pr0.1999.84.3.855.

Seiter, J.S., Abraham, J.A. & Nakagama, B.T. (1998). Split-screen versus single-screen formats in televised debates: Does access to an opponent's nonverbal behaviors affect viewers' perceptions of a speaker's credibility? *Perceptual and Motor Skills, 86*(2), 491–497, doi.org/10.2466/pms.1998.86.2.491.

Seiter, J.S. & Gass, R.H. (2010). Aggressive communication in political contexts. In T.A. Avtgis & A.S. Rancer (Eds), *Arguments, aggression, and conflict: New directions in theory and research* (pp. 217–240). New York: Routledge.

Seiter, J.S. & Weger, H. (2005). Audience perceptions of candidates' appropriateness as a function of nonverbal behaviors displayed during televised political debates. *The Journal of Social Psychology, 145*(2), 225–235, doi: 10.3200/SOCP.145.2.225-236.

Seiter, J.S., Weger, H., Jensen, A.S. & Kinzer, H.J. (2010). The role of background behavior in televised debates: Does displaying nonverbal agreement and/or disagreement benefit either debater? *The Journal of Social Psychology, 150*(3), 278–300, doi: 10.1080/00224540903510811.

Sellers, M. (2004). The ideals of public discourse. In C.R. Sistare (Ed.), *Civility and its discontents: Essays on civic virtue, toleration, and cultural fragmentation* (pp. 15–24). Lawrence, KA: University Press of Kansas.

Shimanoff, S.B. (2009). Facework theories. In S.W. Littlejohn & K.A. Foss (Eds), *Encyclopedia of communication theory* (Vol. 1, pp. 374–377). Los Angeles, CA: Sage.

Shirley, C. (2015, July 30). In defense of incivility: Beware the press and politicians who bemoan the 'tone" in politics. *PoliZette.* Retrieved on December 26, 2017 from: www.lifezette.com/polizette/in-defense-of-incivility.

Spitzberg, B.H. & Cupach, W.R. (1984). *Interpersonal communication competence.* Beverly Hills, CA: Sage.

Swint, K. (2008). *Mudslingers: The twenty-five dirtiest political campaigns of all time.* New York: Union Square Press.

Teven, J.J., McCroskey, J.C. & Richmond, V.P. (1998). Measurement of tolerance for disagreement. *Communication Research Reports*, *15*(2), 209–217, doi.org/10.1080/08824099809362115.

Thornton, B. (2015, September 22). Three cheers for political incivility. *Defining Ideas*. Retrieved on December 26, 2017 from: www.hoover.org/research/three-cheers-political-incivility.

Thornton, R.J. (2003). *Lexicon of inconspicuously ambiguous recommendations*. Naperville, IL: Sourcebooks.

Wallace, K.R. (1955). An ethical basis of communication. *The Speech Teacher*, *4*(1), 1–9, doi.org/10.1080/03634525509376710.

Chapter 3

Argument Theories, Models, and Definitions

Conceptualizing Argument: What Is an Argument Anyway?

How do you know when you are having an argument? If two friends refuse to talk to each other, are they having an argument? How about a father and son who haven't spoken in 10 years? What if a person made a "bald-faced" assertion that "the sun revolves around the earth," with no accompanying reasons or evidence?[1] If two people are screaming at each other, does that count as an argument or something else? Is it possible to argue with yourself, for example, as in Hamlet's soliloquy?

When presented with these questions, some of our students have no firm opinion, while others have strong convictions about what counts as an argument. Given the range of views on the subject, let's examine the ways in which argument has been defined and conceptualized by the people who study it most. Along the way, we'll also consider some of the better known theories and models of argument. By the end of the chapter, we hope that you will have a clearer understanding about what is and isn't an argument.

Argument as Reason-Giving: "Give Me One Good Reason . . ."

One of our favorite holiday television shows features Linus, of *Peanuts* fame, demanding that his sister Lucy gives him one good reason to do something that he doesn't want to do. "I'll give you five good reasons," Lucy replies, counting each of her five fingers while forming a fist. "Those are good reasons," Linus replies. Lucy, of course, has not offered real reasons, only the threat of a knuckle sandwich.

Although definitions of the term argument are many and varied, most share a common assumption that the core of argument involves reasoning and rationality (Johnson, 2000; Rowland & Barge, 1991). At its most basic, *argumentation is a form of communication that emphasizes reason-giving*. An argument may include emotional appeals, such as pity, guilt, or fear, but the defining feature of argument is that a person is advancing an idea or position through reasoning. The arguer may rely exclusively on reasoning, or the arguer may offer other forms of proof, such as statistics, quotations, or physical evidence to accompany the reasoning. The reasoning need not be particularly good. One can reason, even if one is reasoning badly, just as one can sing, but sing badly. However, when one is arguing, one is normally *trying* to reason well.

*"Say what's on your mind, Harris—the language
of dance has always eluded me."*

Figure 3.1 Robert Mankoff cartoon, published in *The New Yorker* 1/14/1991.
© Robert Mankoff/CartoonCollections.com.

Argument₁ and Argument₂: Of Nouns and Verbs

To further clarify, the term "argument" can be used in two different senses (Legge & DiSanza, 1993; O'Keefe, 1977, 1982). In the same way that the word "dance" can refer both to a thing (I went to the dance) or an activity (let's dance), so too can the word "argument." Specifically, "argument" can be used as a *noun*, e.g., "Roscoe made a good argument," or as a *verb*, e.g., "Arguing with Lola is futile. She won't listen to reason." O'Keefe labels the first type, a message unit, as *argument₁*. He labels the second type, the act of arguing, as *argument₂*.

To illustrate, suppose a young couple is discussing whether to have a baby right away or postpone having children until they have established their careers. The wife says, "My biological clock is ticking. The older I get, the greater the risks associated with pregnancy." The husband says, "I know, but if we both have good jobs we'll be better able to afford a child."

The *specific points* each partner is making are arguments$_1$. The *type of discussion* they are having is an argument$_2$. In answer to the question posed at the beginning of this chapter, then, if two friends refused to talk to each other they would be having an argument$_2$, but not making specific arguments$_1$. In answer to another of the questions, a person who made a bald-faced assertion *without reasoning or evidence*, would be advancing a claim, but not making an argument$_1$. And if two people were screaming at one another they would be having an argument$_2$, and being jerks about it. With this distinction in mind, let's examine some well-known theories and models of argument$_1$ and argument$_2$.

Theories and Models of Argument

Although we do not have sufficient space to examine all models of argument, we highlight some of the major approaches in the sections that follow. First, no examination of argumentation theories would be complete without a discussion of Aristotle's contributions. Next, we examine more modern perspectives on argumentation, which can be classified as *monological, dialogical,* or *rhetorical* in their approach (Bentahar, Moulin & Bélanger, 2010).

The Aristotelian Approach: The Roots of Modern Argumentation

Among Aristotle's many works, *The Rhetoric,* written in the 4th century BC, reveals how argumentation and persuasion evolved in the world's first democratic society. "Aristotle's writings," write Rapp and Wagner (2013), "provide a fundamental point of reference not only for historical approaches to argumentation theory, but also for some important modern theories of argumentation" (p. 8).

Aristotle defined rhetoric as "the faculty of observing in any given case the available means of persuasion" (sec. 1365). He further classified the means of persuasion into three types: *logos* or the use of logic and reasoning, *ethos* or source credibility, and *pathos* or appeals to emotion. As he stated,

> There are, then, these three means of effecting persuasion. The man who is to be in command of them must, it is clear, be able (1) to reason logically, (2) to understand human character and goodness in their various forms, and (3) to understand the emotions – that is, to name them and describe them, to know their causes and the way in which they are excited. (sec. 1365a)

Aristotle also identified a variety of fallacious arguments (*Sophistical Refutations,* 165b30–168a17, see also Walton, 1995). Some, such as *equivocation* (using the same term with multiple meanings) and *amphiboly* (being intentionally ambiguous or vague), were based on language. Others, such as *begging the question* (basing an argument on an unproven assumption) and *faulty cause* (making an erroneous cause–effect inference), were not based on language. We'll examine these and other fallacies in Chapters 8 and 9, which address the topic of fallacious reasoning.

Aristotle's most enduring contribution to argumentation was his endorsement of the *enthymeme,* which he viewed as the primary means of persuasion. What's an enthymeme? To understand, it helps to know what a syllogism is. In its most basic form, a *syllogism* is a deductive argument comprised of two premises and a conclusion. For example, the argument "All cows have four stomachs. Bessie is a cow. Therefore, Bessie has four stomachs," is a syllogism.

Syllogistic reasoning is based on formal logic, such that *if* the premises are true, the conclusion necessarily follows. That is, *if* all cows have four stomachs (actually one stomach with four compartments), and *if* Bessie is a cow, then it logically follows that Bessie has four stomachs too. We'll return to this topic in Chapter 11, which is devoted to understanding rules about when a syllogism is valid or invalid. For now, though, it is enough for you to know that a syllogism is a three-part argument, in which there are two premises that establish a conclusion.

In contrast, the enthymeme is often described as an abridged syllogism. That's because an enthymeme omits one of the premises, or sometimes the conclusion, allowing for a shorter argument. For example, the argument "This car's engine is warm, so it must have been driven recently," includes only one premise, followed by the conclusion. The omitted premise is that "driving a car makes the engine warm."

There are two important differences between a syllogism and an enthymeme. First, in a syllogism, each premise is stated explicitly. All the assumptions are spelled out for the listeners. With an enthymeme, because one premise or step is unstated, listeners have to fill in the missing premise on their own. Second, in a valid syllogism, the conclusion of an argument is certain. It necessarily follows from the premises. With enthymematic reasoning, however, the conclusion is probabilistic. That is, the conclusion is a matter of probability, not certainty. In the argument above, for example, while it's *probably* true that the car has just been driven, there's no way to be certain. Indeed, perhaps it's a hot day without shade, or maybe the car was simply idling.

Because the listener, reader, or viewer must mentally complete an enthymeme, this form of reasoning is participatory in nature. Bitzer (1959) highlighted this important feature, noting that "the enthymeme succeeds as an instrument of rational persuasion because its premises are always drawn from the audience" (p. 408).

There are times, of course, when listeners are unable to fill in the missing premise on their own. They may not possess the same knowledge as the source, may not share the same beliefs or assumptions as the source, or may not perceive the inference as the source intended. In the latter case, the audience would see the argument as a *non-sequitur*, that is, an inference that doesn't seem to follow. To illustrate, if Marjorie said, "It's going to snow soon, we should get a toboggan," most people would understand that tobogganing is a winter recreational activity. However, if Marjorie said, "It's going to snow soon, we should get a pony," most people would not be able to figure out the missing premise. "Why a pony?" someone might ask, "Is it going to pull a sled?" "Will we eat the pony if it is a harsh winter?" another one might wonder.

The beauty of enthymematic reasoning is that listeners draw on their own beliefs, attitudes, and values to make sense of arguments. Moreover, arguments are shorter and more efficient because premises already held by listeners can be taken for granted. At the same time, the conclusions of enthymemes are only probable at best.

Monological Models: Part and Parcel

Just as a good chef must know the ingredients that go into making a particular dish, an effective arguer needs a solid grasp of the "ingredients" that make up an argument. *Monological models* are useful because they help identify such ingredients, and, in turn, help evaluate the argument. Specifically, monological models focus on the structure of the argument itself (Bentahar, Moulin & Bélanger, 2010), similar to the argument₁ perspective discussed earlier. We begin by examining the work of Stephen Toulmin, a British philosopher and educator, who presented one of the most well-known and important monological models of argument. Toulmin was frustrated with the ability of formal logic to explain ordinary argument. As such, his model emerged out of his notion that ordinary reasoning, which characterizes arguments that we hear and make in our daily lives, is more practical than formal logic, a topic we cover in a later chapter. What's more, Toulmin believed that we could better appreciate the quality of everyday arguments by understanding their structure.

The Toulmin Model of Argument

Toulmin's (1958, 1984, 2003) model separates an argument into distinct elements, which can be grouped into two "triads." The first of these triads is comprised of the most basic ingredients of an argument. Specifically, it consists of a *claim, grounds,* and *warrant*. The second triad, which extends the model, adds the elements of *qualifier, backing,* and *rebuttal*. Let's take a closer look at these elements and how they are related.

The First Triad: Claims, Grounds, and Warrants

CLAIMS: GETTING TO THE POINT

Suppose a friend, Stan, told you that "Facebook has diluted the concept of friendship." Stan has just made a claim. The *claim* is the point Stan is trying to make. It is the proposition he is advancing. Claims often follow *clue words* such as "hence," "therefore," and "thus." There are various types of claims, which we examine in Chapter 5. For now, it is enough to know that different types of claims require different forms of support.

GROUNDS: PROVIDING PROOF

Speaking of support, imagine that after hearing Stan's "Facebook claim," you asked him to back it up. *Grounds*, the second element of Toulmin's model, are used to do just that. Specifically, *grounds* are synonymous with proof and may consist of reasoning, statistics, reports, quotations, physical evidence, or other support for a claim. For instance, Stan might support his Facebook claim by adding, "For example, although some people on Facebook have 5,000 friends, Robin Dunbar (2010), an anthropologist, maintains that the number of people with whom we can have meaningful friendships is limited to 150."

Here is a useful tip: Grounds often follow such *clue words* and phrases as "because," "since," "given that," or "for example." Grounds also include premises accepted by your target audience. Some arguments are accompanied by multiple grounds, that is, several different forms of proof. For example, a father might advise his son, "Don't be a coal miner, Dale. The pay is lousy, the work is dangerous, and there are no benefits." The claim "don't be a coal miner" is supported by three different grounds. For each argument below, see if you can distinguish between the claim and the grounds.

"Charlotte is an Australian citizen because she was born in Sydney."

"It looks like rain. You'd better take an umbrella."

"I think Nigel got in a fight. He is sporting a black eye."

WARRANTS: CONNECTING THE DOTS

The third element in the Toulmin model, the *warrant*, establishes the connection between the claim and grounds. The warrant in an argument authorizes the *inferential leap* that connects the grounds with the claim. That is, the warrant ties the claim and grounds together. For example, if one detective told another, "there are three cigarette butts on the ground outside the victim's window, which suggests the killer watched the victim for some time," the detective would be making an inferential leap (sign reasoning, in this case) that cigarette butts are a telltale sign that someone was watching and waiting. Although the detective didn't state the warrant explicitly, it might go something like this (warrant in italics): "There are three cigarette butts on the ground. *It takes a long time to smoke three cigarettes*, which suggests that the killer watched the victim for some time." Similarly, if the other detective declared, "The window was broken from the outside, not the inside. You can tell because the broken glass fell inside the room," the detective would be making another inferential leap (this time, a cause–effect inference). If the detective had stated the warrant explicitly, it would go something like this: *striking a window from the outside (cause) would result in the broken glass falling inward (effect)*.

To help visualize the role of the warrant, imagine an argument as if it were a stone arch (see Figure 3.2). The interlocking stones work together to support the arch. The claim and grounds are analogous to the *voissoirs*, the wedge-shaped stones that form the curved portions of the arch. The warrant is analogous to the keystone. Just as the keystone locks the *voissoirs* into place, the warrant holds the claim and grounds together. Without the keystone, the arch would collapse. Without a warrant, an argument collapses. Absent a warrant, a claim and grounds constitute a *non-sequitur*, or simply, two unrelated statements.

MORE ABOUT WARRANTS

In the example above, the detectives did not state their warrants explicitly, a common practice in real-life argumentation. Indeed, warrants are usually *implicit* (Brockriede & Ehninger, 1960; Voss,

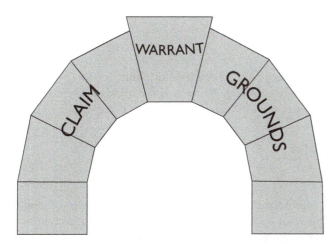

Figure 3.2 The warrant is the keystone that holds the grounds and claim together.

2005), meaning that when people make arguments, they usually don't say what the warrant is. Instead, warrants function as *unexpressed premises*,[2] requiring the recipient to figure out the connection between the grounds and the claim. If you're thinking that this reflects our discussion of enthymemes above, you are right! Since the recipient must complete the warrant or "connect the dots," ordinary arguments, like enthymemes, are necessarily *interactive* or *participatory* in nature. The arguer usually supplies the claim and grounds; the listener makes sense of the two by filling in the warrant.

Moreover, in the same way that some arguments are multi-grounded, arguments can be multi-warranted as well, meaning that more than one inferential leap can be made by recipients. A warrant might be based on source expertise, for example, yet also rely on the use of an analogy.

The implicit nature of warrants often leads to confusion in everyday arguments. If you can't grasp the warrant, you might be left saying, "I don't get it." Imagine, for example, how you'd react if someone told you, "Don't trust Edna, because she plays a saxophone." You would probably be at a loss trying to make sense of the seemingly unrelated statements. On the other hand, imagine the person said, "Don't trust Edna, because she is a con artist." In this case, you would have no trouble making the connection; con artists are not to be trusted.

THE FIRST TRIAD COMBINED

Now that you understand the basic elements of Toulmin's model, let's consider a more serious argument to see how all these elements fit together. Consider the argument "The legal drinking age in the U.S. should be lowered to 18, because the current age of 21 encourages binge drinking by under-age drinkers." Before continuing, read the argument again and see if you can identify the three elements. If you've got a good grasp of the three elements, you came up with the following (see Figure 3.3):

- The *claim* is that the legal drinking age should be lowered to 18.
- The *grounds* are based on the current law's effect on under-age drinkers; it encourages binge drinking.
- The *warrant* or inferential leap is based on a *cause–effect inference*; the current age limit is the cause of the problem.

Of course, the argument could be flawed. Lowering the legal drinking age to 18 might cause 15–17 year olds to engage in more binge drinking. As long as the arguer's inferential leap is understood, however, the connection between the claim and grounds is established.

Extending the Model: The Second Triad

QUALIFIER

Imagine you are going to make an argument, but you anticipate objections. If so, you might try to pre-empt challenges by including what is called a *qualifier*. A qualifier consists of any words or phrases that limit the strength or scope of a claim, such as "probably," "possibly," "most likely," or "perhaps" (Brockriede & Ehninger, 1960; Freeman, 2005). If, for example, Spencer

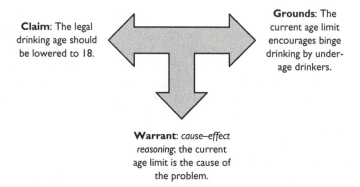

Figure 3.3 The basic Toulmin model.

Note: It doesn't matter particularly if the claim is placed on the left or right. An arguer might state the claim first, followed by the grounds. Conversely, an arguer might state the grounds first, followed by the claim.

said, "Nabila is a Muslim. She wears a hijab," he would be making a *universal* or *unqualified claim*, whereas if Spencer said "Nabila is *probably* a Muslim, because she wears a hijab," he would be making a *qualified claim*. Adding a qualifier to his argument acknowledges the probabilistic nature of his reasoning. In some cases, a qualifier may be used to strengthen a claim (Jonsen & Toulmin, 1988, p. 10). Words such as "certainly," "undoubtedly," or "absolutely" might be used increase the force of a claim. If Spencer said, "Nabila is *undeniably* a Muslim," he would be using a qualifier to strengthen the claim.

BACKING

Another element of the extended Toulmin model is *backing*. Because backing reinforces the warrant, arguers who suspect that their warrants might be challenged can offer additional backing. To illustrate how, let's say that two buddies, Arlo and Gus, are playing a round of golf. Arlo shanks a drive that careens off the fairway and rolls onto the golf cart track. They have the following argument:

Arlo: "I'm allowed to move my ball, because it's on the track" (Arlo's unstated warrant is that the rules permit moving the ball in this situation).
Gus: "No way. You gotta' play the ball where it lies."
Arlo: "Nice try, but rule 24-2b states that 'a golfer is entitled to free relief from a cart path if the ball comes to rest upon the path.' Wanna see the rule book?"
Gus: "Naw, I'll take your word for it. I'm going to beat you anyway, you Shankasaurus."

In this case, Arlo reinforces the original warrant by citing the rule book. In many arguments, however, backing isn't necessary because the warrant alone is sufficient to legitimize the inferential leap.

REBUTTAL

The final element of the extended model is the *rebuttal*, which acknowledges the circumstances under which the warrant does not apply (Brockriede & Ehninger, 1960; Verheij, 2005). In other words, the rebuttal provides exceptions to the inferential leap. For example, an acquaintance, Ralph, might say, "Of course dolphins give live birth. They're mammals." The unstated warrant in Ralph's argument is that all mammals give birth to live young, as opposed to fish and birds that lay eggs. There are a few exceptions, though. Monotremes are classified as mammals even though they lay eggs. As such, Ralph could offer a rebuttal to the warrant by adding, "unless we are talking about monotremes, like a platypus or an echidna, but dolphins are cetaceans, like whales."

Although adding a rebuttal is an option, it is also somewhat unusual. Instead, most arguers wait to see whether their argument is challenged before adding exceptions to the claim or warrant. A rebuttal, nonetheless, serves two useful functions. First, it helps preempt anticipated challenges to the argument, which could be especially useful in a prepared speech or written argument. Second, a rebuttal makes arguers seem more open-minded by acknowledging that they are aware of exceptions to the warrant.

EXTENDED TOULMIN MODEL: PUTTING IT ALL TOGETHER

You can find a display of the extended Toulmin model in Figure 3.4. As you study the figure, it's useful to know that the argument being made (by a lawyer, perhaps) is based on something called the "plain view" doctrine, which states that if a law officer sees contraband in plain view (e.g., on the dashboard), he or she may lawfully search and seize the items (for details see *Arizona* v. *Hicks*, 1987; Horton v. California, 1990; Stephens & Glenn, 2005; Woody, 2006).

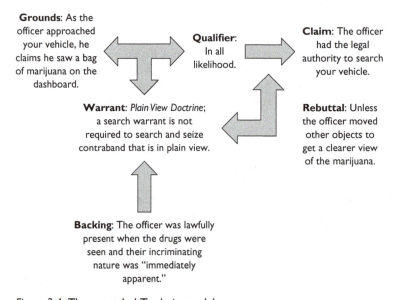

Figure 3.4 The extended Toulmin model.

Strengths and Limitations of the Toulmin Model

The Toulmin model is a valuable tool for diagramming arguments as message units, one argument at a time. Its value lies in analyzing simple, clear-cut arguments (Ball, 1994), the sort one can scribble on a chalkboard or legal pad. It does have its drawbacks, however. The first is that the Toulmin model presents a somewhat idealized view of arguments. As such, it can be frustrating when dealing with arguments that are messy, vague, or convoluted—as they often are in real life (Hitchcock & Verheij, 2005).

A second complaint is that the extended model can be unwieldy. Indeed, in ordinary conversations, we rarely encounter six-part arguments. As such, it is often more expedient to present the first triad of claim, grounds, and (implied) warrant. If one of those elements is challenged, you can then simply create a new argument featuring the challenge as the claim. Bottom line? Why go to all the extra work if the other person says "You had me at the claim"?

A third limitation of the Toulmin model is the time and effort it takes to break an argument into its constituent parts. Indeed, in the heat of an argument, you seldom have the luxury of being able to jot down diagrams, ponder your options, and weigh possible responses. More often than not you have to "shoot from the hip" as it were. If you've ever walked away from an argument and thought to yourself, "Darn, I wish I had said this . . ." or "D'oh! If only I'd thought of that . . ." you know that arguing extemporaneously can be hit or miss. Given the proper time, however, the Toulmin model can help you examine an argument carefully. You could, for example, analyze the arguments in a newspaper editorial before penning a reply. Or you could use the model to outline key arguments on a public policy controversy. You could also use the model to anticipate likely objections to your own arguments and develop effective responses before making a presentation.

A fourth drawback to the Toulmin model is that it is somewhat linear in nature. As such, it doesn't account for the give and take process of *arguing* that is more typical in everyday conversations. Suppose, for example, that Mel asks his wife, "When are you going to get around to doing the dishes?" and she responds by asking, "When are you going to get around to fixing the sink?" See what we mean? Everyday arguments aren't always as simple as claim–data–warrant. With that in mind, we turn now to a different type of model.

Dialogical Models

In contrast to monological models like Toulmin's, *dialogical approaches* are more interactive in nature. As such, they are more concerned with argument$_2$, that is, the activity of arguing, than they are with focusing on the elements within an argument. One such approach is pragma-dialectics, which we cover next.

Pragma-Dialectics

The *pragma-dialectical* approach was developed by two Dutch scholars, Frans van Eemeren and Rob Grootendorst (1984, 1992, 2004), who believed that the study of argumentation should include both descriptive and prescriptive elements (Mitchell, 2010). In other words, theirs is a practical approach to how arguments *do* function as well as how they *should* function. Although the term "pragma-dialectics" may sound a bit daunting, it simply refers to a pragmatic (pragma) approach to addressing opposing points of view (dialectic). According to this approach, an argument is a complex speech act that functions as a tool for managing disagreements.

THE OUGHTS AND SHOULDS OF ARGUING: THE 10 COMMANDMENTS OF ARGUING

According to pragma-dialectics, the goal of an argument is to eliminate or resolve a difference of opinion (van Eemeren & Grootendorst, 1984, 2004). Before entering into a critical discussion, arguers should agree to abide by a set of normative rules or conventions for arguing. Indeed, van Eemeren and Grootendorst go so far as to refer to the rules as the *10 commandments* of arguing. For instance, the *starting point rule* says that an arguer cannot introduce a new premise without first proving it, or ignore an existing premise without first disproving it (van Eemeren, Garssen & Mueffels, 2009, p. 23). By way of example, if two people were having an argument over biblical scripture, one could not begin with the assumption that the Bible should be interpreted literally, rather than figuratively, unless the other person agreed. All 10 rules can be found in Box 3.1.

Research suggests that following these 10 commandments is well advised. Indeed, in a series of investigations, van Eemeren, Garssen, and Mueffels (2009) had students read an assortment of hypothetical arguments. Some of the arguments violated one or more of the commandments, while others did not. The consistent finding was that participants rated arguments that violated the normative rules as less reasonable than arguments that did not. Although the studies can be faulted for relying on hypothetical arguments and a single dependent measure (perceived reasonableness) (see Hample, 2010), the normative standards hold up fairly well.

In addition to these 10 commandments, the pragma-dialectic approach emphasizes other rules. For instance, it suggests that arguers should state their positions explicitly without beating around the bush or engaging in obfuscation. Suppose, for example, that a mother is unhappy with her daughter's choice of a wedding venue, which is in a barn in winter, and demonstrates her displeasure by pouting and giving her daughter the "silent treatment." According to the pragma-dialectical approach, this is improper. Instead, the mother should state her position, or *standpoint*, explicitly. For example, the mother might say, "I don't think a wedding, in a barn, in Quebec City, in January, is a good idea. It will be freezing." That said, while advocates are expected to argue assertively for their standpoints, they should remain willing to revise or retract their position in light of superior arguments and evidence.

Box 3.1   Ten Commandments of Arguing

1   *Freedom rule: Discussants may not prevent each other from advancing standpoints or from calling standpoints into question.* This rule is violated if one person prevents another from speaking or declares some topics "off limits." An example would be that, as Daphne is about to make a point, Jasper shouts "shut your pie hole!"

2   *Obligation to defend rule: Discussants who advance a standpoint may not refuse to defend this standpoint when requested to do so.* An arguer who refused to accept the burden of proof or tried to shift the burden of proof would violate this rule. For example, when asked to substantiate his claim that the duck-billed platypus is venomous, Garth says, "Hey, It's a fact. Google it if you don't believe me."

3   *Standpoint rule: Attacks on standpoints may not bear on a standpoint that has not actually been put forward by the other party.* This rule is violated when one arguer is guilty of "putting words in the other person's mouth." An example would be if Ned argued that

nonviolent drug offenders should be exempted from mandatory minimum sentences, and Ralph responded, "Why would you want to release rapists and murderers before they have completed their sentences?"

4   *Relevance rule: Standpoints may not be defended by non-argumentation or argumentation that is not relevant to the standpoint.* This rule is violated if an arguer provides irrelevant reasons or plays on emotions rather than reason. An example would be if Becky told Lyle, "If you don't agree with me, I'm leaving you."

5   *Unexpressed premise rule: Discussants may not falsely attribute unexpressed premises to the other party, nor disown responsibility for their own unexpressed premises.* This rule would be violated if an arguer claimed, "I never said that," when, in fact, the arguer did say that or words to that effect. The rule is also violated if an arguer ignores unstated assumptions that follow from the standpoint being advocated. For example, suppose Tony advocates bombing a city held by Isis into oblivion. Naomi points out that many civilians would undoubtedly be killed too. Tony says, "I'm not advocating killing civilians, only radical insurgents."

6   *Starting point rule: Discussants may not falsely present something as an accepted starting point or falsely deny that something is an accepted starting point.* This rule is violated if an arguer "smuggles" a presupposition into an argument or assumes a premise is self-evident when it is not. An example would be if a couple were getting a divorce and one spouse said, "I'm getting the house, of course, so would you rather have the car or the dog?"

7   *Argument scheme rule: Standpoints may not be regarded as conclusively defended if the defense does not take place by means of appropriate argument schemes that are applied correctly.* This rule sounds more complicated than it is. There are established ways of making certain kinds of arguments. For example, when making a cause–effect argument, the effect must *follow* the cause. An effect may not precede its cause. When making an analogy, the two things being compared must be alike in their *relevant* respects, not superficial respects. An arguer who said, "bananas are like cowards because both are yellow" would be focusing on irrelevant features of the analogy.

8   *Validity rule: Reasoning that in an argumentation is presented as formally conclusive may not be invalid in a logical sense.* This rule is violated if an arguer claims a conclusion *follows logically* or has been *validly deduced* when it has not. An example would be if Larry said, "All people who text while driving endanger other motorists. Lucinda was not texting while driving. Therefore, Lucinda did not endanger other motorists." Lucinda might not have been texting, but she could have endangered other motorists by drinking and driving, speeding, tailgating, or nodding off.

9   *Closure rule or concluding rule: Inconclusive defenses of standpoints may not lead to maintaining these standpoints, and conclusive defenses of standpoints may not lead to maintaining expressions of doubt concerning these standpoints.* This rule is violated if an arguer continues to adhere to a position that lacks support or refuses to accept a position that has strong support. An example would be an arguer who said, "I don't care if all the evidence does prove childhood vaccines are not the cause of autism. I still think they are."

(continued)

(continued)

10 *Usage rule: Discussants may not use any formulations that are insufficiently clear or confusingly ambiguous, and they may not deliberately misinterpret the other party's formulations.* This rule is violated if an arguer is purposely vague, beats around the bush, or won't commit to a position. Suppose Josephine is in favor of physician-assisted suicide. Norene asks, "Do you support it only if a patient is terminally ill and, if so, how long does the person's life expectancy have to be to qualify?" Josephine says, "Hmm . . . I'm not sure." Norene then asks, "Does the terminally ill patient have to be in extreme or unbearable pain to qualify?" Josephine replies, "Maybe, but maybe not."

From Van Eemeren, Grootendorst & Henkemans (2002).

STRATEGIC MANEUVERING

According to the pragma-dialectical approach, arguers engage in *strategic maneuvering*, whereby they adapt their arguments for maximum persuasive effect (van Eemeren, 2010; van Eemeren & Houtlosser, 2002a, 2002b). By way of example, consider the argument below.

Mabel: "Marijuana's illegality makes it a 'forbidden fruit.' Teenagers are tempted to try it precisely because it's illegal. Besides, marijuana laws don't work. Anyone who wants to buy it, can."

Lars: "If anyone can buy it, then why would teens consider it a 'forbidden fruit'? And if marijuana were legalized, wouldn't there still be a legal age limit for buying it?"

Mabel: "If you tell teens they can't have something, they'll want it even more. If marijuana were legalized, it would be regulated like alcohol or cigarettes. There are no regulations now, because weed is bought and sold on the black market."

Lars: "Then wouldn't marijuana still be a 'forbidden fruit' for anyone under the age of 18? There are under-age smokers and drinkers, so it would be naïve to think there wouldn't be under-age 'tokers.' The black market in marijuana would still flourish."

In the above dialogue, Mabel has unwittingly walked into a contradiction. She took the stance that marijuana's appeal was, in part, based on its illegality, then later acknowledged that it would remain illegal for anyone under the age of 18. Lars strategically maneuvered her into the contradiction by getting her to state her premises clearly, then pointing out that her premises were incompatible.

Although strategic maneuvering is an important component of arguing, keep in mind that such maneuvering is considered fallacious if, alongside it, an arguer breaks any of the commandments that we discussed earlier (van Eemeren & Houtlosser, 2003). That's because fallacious maneuvering violates the rational pact one enters into when engaging in a dispute. In the above argument, for example, suppose Lars told Mabel, "You must be high right now. Only a weed-head would think that legalizing marijuana would decrease its use." This, according to the pragma-dialectical approach, would violate the first rule, which states that "Parties must not prevent each other from advancing standpoints or from casting doubt on standpoints" (see Box 3.1). That's right, Lars! Insulting your opponents impedes their ability to advance arguments freely (Garssen, 2009).

ARGUMENT STAGES: STEP BY STEP

The pragma-dialectical approach (van Eemeren & Grootendorst, 1984) maintains that ideal arguments proceed through four stages. During the initial *confrontation stage*, parties acknowledge their differences of opinion and agree to have a civil argument. Next comes the *opening stage* in which they launch their first argumentative salvos, stating their standpoints and engaging in strategic maneuvering. An *argumentation stage* follows, which is characterized by point, counterpoint, additional strategic maneuvering (sometimes), and refutation and rebuttal. Finally, there is a *concluding stage*, in which the arguers assess whether the disagreement has been resolved.

Although these stages reflect the *ideal sequence* for an argument, most arguments fall short of this ideal. In practice, some may end prematurely and others may skip or bypass one or more stages. For example, one person might walk out abruptly and slam the door. Whether arguments follow the ideal model or not, the basic goal of arguing, resolving disagreements while adhering to normative rules for arguing, still applies.

CRITICISMS OF PRAGMA-DIALECTICS

Pragma-dialectics is not without its detractors. Lumer (2010), for one, has faulted the approach for its reliance on "unqualified consensus" as the goal of argument. Specifically, pragma-dialectics is *resolution-oriented* (van Eemeren & Grootendorst, 2004, p. 4), but, according to Lumer, on highly controversial issues, resolution may be neither possible nor desirable. Consider, for instance, the highly charged issue of abortion. Pro-life advocates believe that life begins at conception, while pro-choice proponents believe that life begins at viability. Given that the two sides are so diametrically opposed, why expect consensus to be reached? A resolution would require that one side or the other abandon its core values. Furthermore, just because two parties reach agreement on an issue doesn't mean they are right or correct. They might have reached a false consensus.

Bonevac (2003), another critic, has faulted pragma-dialectics for its emphasis on bilateral arguments, that is, one person trying to convince another and vice versa. But what about multilateral arguments in which more than two parties are involved? When Donald Trump takes a standpoint on Israel's settlements on the West Bank, for example, he must persuade multiple audiences, including Democrats, Republicans, Israelis, Palestinians, and other foreign powers. For many controversies, there are multiple protagonists and antagonists and they must position their arguments relative to one another.

Another concern with pragma-dialectics is that, although it is highly applicable to interpersonal arguments, it is not as well-suited for arguments in other contexts. In a criminal trial, for example, there are hundreds of rules that govern attorneys' arguments and conduct. Imagine what a trial would be like if all these rules were scrapped in favor of the 10 commandments. Chaos would ensue. Moreover, some legal rules contradict the normative standards of pragma-dialectics. For example, a trial attorney must show deference to the court, but not toward a witness. An attorney may brand a witness a liar by asking, "Isn't it true, Mr. Boswell, that you are an unprepossessing liar who would say anything to avoid going to prison?" An attorney may not badger a witness, but the attorney may use sarcasm, ridicule, or mockery to impeach a witness's testimony. Like it or not, unpleasant, unfriendly, and downright hostile questions must sometimes be put to a witness.

After an attorney browbeats a witness, the jurors may judge the attorney's tactics to be unfair. Nonetheless, they may still question the veracity of the witness' testimony. In the political arena, voters may report that they dislike attack ads and that such ads are unfair. Attack ads are, nevertheless, highly effective in damaging an opponent's credibility (Seiter & Gass, 2010).

Likewise, other fields such as astronomy, medicine, and paleontology, have established rules for presenting arguments, proving claims, evaluating evidence, and so on. Yet, it is unclear how pragma-dialectics might square with these rules. Pragma-dialectics operates on the assumption that, although some arguments are specific to certain fields, people still evaluate arguments according to the 10 normative rules (see Goodnight, 2006, p. 74).

A final criticism of the pragma-dialectical approach is that it fails to specify how fallacious versus non-fallacious moves can be differentiated. Consider the dialogue below.

Ludmilla: "Laws that discriminate against transgender persons are analogous to laws permitting racial discrimination in the United States' civil rights era."

Wally: "I beg to disagree. Sexual orientation is not as immutable as race. Sexual orientation is more fluid."

Ludmilla: "Sexual orientation is not simply a choice, like saying 'I prefer pepperoni over sausage on pizza'."

Wally: "Granted, but people's sexual orientations can and do change. And it is easier to hide or disguise. A person's race does not change and not anyone can 'pass' as belonging to another race."

In this dispute, Ludmilla makes an analogy between different laws. But how suspect does an analogy have to be before it is considered faulty? Who, for example, decides what is faulty and what isn't? To remedy this problem, van Eemeren and Grootendorst invoke the concept of a *reasonable rabbi*, who serves as "a reasonable critic who judges reasonably" (2004, p. 12). The reasonable rabbi is akin to a neutral third party who adjudicates a dispute fairly and impartially. For example, in an arbitration hearing, an impartial arbitrator is appointed to settle a matter outside a court setting. The arbitrator considers both sides' arguments and evidence and renders a binding decision. The concept of the reasonable rabbi is somewhat idealistic, however. Suppose you are in the middle of an argument. Who has a reasonable rabbi or rabbi-like person on speed dial? The rabbi functions more like a *deus ex machina* device than an explanation of how close arguments should be resolved. If Ludmilla and Wally don't have a reasonable rabbi on hand, how would they make the determination among themselves?

These criticisms notwithstanding, the pragma-dialectical approach offers a constructive approach for managing arguments so they don't get out of hand. The descriptive features of the model suggest how people can argue effectively, while the prescriptive features suggest how people can argue appropriately. As you'll soon see, these twin goals of arguing effectively and appropriately are emphasized throughout this text.

Rhetorical Models

Rhetorical models of argument view argumentation as a form of persuasion that emphasizes the importance of adapting reasons to the listener's frame of reference. Two such models are presented here, Chaim Perelman's *new rhetoric* and Walter Fisher's *narrative paradigm*.

Perelman's New Rhetoric

Chaim Perelman, along with his co-author, Lucie Olbrechts-Tyteca, helped to revitalize the study of argument, which at the time was seen by many as a vehicle for discovering timeless truths. Perelman, however, argued that such discoveries were better suited to the study of formal logic or deduction, a topic for a later chapter in this book. Instead, Perelman's approach to argument was more practical in nature, emphasizing the importance of tailoring arguments to the listener's point of view. What constitutes a "good" argument, he suggested, is in the eye of the beholder. Hence, arguments must be framed with a view toward winning the listener's acceptance. More specifically, all argument seeks the *adherence of minds* (Perelman & Olbrechts-Tyteca, 1969, p. 14), which, for Perelman, meant agreement or assent on a particular issue.

In the process of seeking intellectual agreement, or what Perelman calls *communion*, with the listener, the first task is finding *common ground*. In other words, the *starting point* of any argument must be based on a shared frame of reference between the participants. Initially, the arguer must establish a premise (or premises) based on the beliefs, values, and assumptions held by the audience, and then transfer the audience's acceptance of that premise to the arguer's conclusion. As Perelman put it, "the aim of argumentation is not, like demonstration, to prove the truth of the conclusion from premises, but to transfer to the conclusion the *adherence* accorded to the premises" (Perelman, 1982, p. 21). This emphasis on adapting arguments to the audience's frame of reference is vital to Perelman's rhetorical approach.

Perelman envisioned two types of audiences; a *particular audience* and a *universal audience*. A particular audience may consist of a specific person (your boss), a demographic group (Hispanics), or a segment of a population (millennial voters). It also might be a school board, swing voters in a state, or niche groups such as home-schoolers, eco-minded consumers, or early adopters of technology.

Adapting your arguments to one particular audience can be challenging, but what happens if you find yourself arguing to several particular audiences at once? Public policy disputes and foreign policy issues, for example, often involve more than one particular audience, and each of them might have different points of view about what seems reasonable. How, then, can one go about deciding what is reasonable? For such broad, all-encompassing arguments, Perelman developed a construct that he termed the *universal audience*, which symbolizes rationale, reasonable people everywhere (Perelman & Olbrechts-Tyteca, 1969, p. 33). The universal audience is not unlike our judicial system's "reasonable man" standard. Jurors, for example, are expected to be rational and display good judgment when deliberating about a case. The universal audience is also akin to pragma-dialectic's concept of a "reasonable rabbi." The universal audience represents what any *reasonable person* would accept, agree, or assent to. Although the universal audience is an abstract construct, it can be thought of as the aggregate of all intelligent, reasonable people. An opponent of human trafficking, for example, might make his or her case to the "court of world opinion." There is no such actual court, but the advocate could write an editorial or position paper aimed at rationale people everywhere. The concept of the universal audience aids in framing arguments for all humankind or posterity.

The Narrative Paradigm

Scholars in rhetorical theory and critical studies question the traditional view that there is an objective reality, apart from a person's perceptions of things. Instead, such scholars suggest that people construct their realities using symbols. A parent, for example, might see her young son as "precocious," whereas the son's kindergarten teacher may see the kid as a "hellion," and a child psychologist may see a child suffering from ADHD. Each "sees" a different child. Were each asked to describe the child, the parent, the teacher, and the child psychologist might tell very different stories. Indeed, one way that people negotiate their differing perceptions is through the stories, or narratives, they tell. Narratives are used to shape our identity, construct our social reality, and mold the world in which we live. What's more, narratives can be viewed as arguments. With that as a foundation, Walter Fisher pioneered the narrative approach to argument (1984, 1985, 1989a, 1989b, 2000).

HUMANS AS STORYTELLERS

According to Fisher, humans are, by nature, storytellers, a.k.a. *homo narrans*. Storytelling is a cultural universal. Shared stories form society's collective memory. What's more, stories are compelling in ways that facts and statistics cannot be. Indeed, Verene (1985) maintains that arguments, by themselves, lack purpose unless and until they are incorporated into a storyline. That's because we tend to get caught up in a well-told story. We identify with the characters, their trials, and tribulations.

NARRATIVES AS ARGUMENT

In what way are narratives related to argumentation? First, every story is told from the point of view of the narrator, which makes stories inherently persuasive. Moreover, stories rely on *narrative rationality* or a "logic of good reasons," to make them believable. As Hollihan and Baaske noted, "Narrative arguments are rational arguments, and we can learn a great deal about how people reason through stories" (2005, p. 24). Narratives may include implicit or explicit claims. Stories are particularly well-suited for advancing value or judgment claims. Think, for example, of the moral principles embodied in children's fairy tales and fables.[3] Want to argue that deception has negative consequences? What better way than through a story like *The Boy Who Cried Wolf*. Compelling narratives also can advance policy claims and promote social change (Taylor, 2008). As one example, Dr. Martin Luther King's "I Have a Dream" speech helped to galvanize the Civil Rights movement in the U.S. in the 1960s.

NARRATIVE PROBABILITY AND FIDELITY

How are stories evaluated? According to Fisher (1984, 1985), they are judged by the twin standards of *narrative probability* and *narrative fidelity*. Narrative probability refers to how credible and coherent a story is; whether it "hangs together" or makes sense. A story that was internally inconsistent, for example, would lack narrative probability. Narrative fidelity, on the other hand, has to do with whether the story rings true to the listener. A character we can relate to, or a story we can identify with, possesses narrative fidelity. A story that contradicted a listener's lived experience, however, would lack narrative fidelity.

As an illustration of narrative fidelity, consider the many stories that abused women shared on Twitter, using the hashtag #WhyIStayed (https://twitter.com/hashtag/whyistayed?lang=en). Some examples are displayed below.

- "I tried to leave the house once after an abusive episode, and he blocked me. He slept in front of the door that entire night" #WhyIStayed
- "Because he told me that no one would love me after him, and I was insecure enough to believe him." #WhyIStayed
- "Because his abuse was so gradual and manipulative, I didn't even realize what was happening to me." #WhyIStayed

"If the coach and horses and the footmen and the beautiful clothes all turned back into the pumpkin and the mice and the rags, then how come the glass slipper didn't turn back, too?"

Figure 3.5 A child questions the narrative probability of the Cinderella story.

© Henry Martin/*The New Yorker* Collection/www.cartoonbank.com.

The recurring themes—powerlessness, shame, guilt, lack of resources, custody issues—rang true for hundreds of thousands of women who felt trapped in abusive relationships. Their lived experience mirrored that of the stories shared by other women.

COMPETING NARRATIVES

When one person puts forth a narrative, another person may counter it with a contrasting narrative. For example, in the United States, advocates for the Black Lives Matter (BLM) movement have decried the deaths of unarmed black people at the hands of the police, often for minor infractions. Black Lives Matter has portrayed police as harboring implicit racial bias, engaging in racial profiling, and using deadly force with impunity (Sociologists for Justice, 2014).

To counter this narrative, pro-police advocates insist that police officers have dangerous jobs, encounter all kinds of unpredictable people, and often must make split-second decisions to use deadly force. Pro-police advocates have tried to flip the narrative, claiming, as Rudy Giuliani, the former mayor of New York City did, that "Black Lives Matter puts a target on police officers' backs" (Reisman, 2016). Intimidation by BLM, said Nikki Haley, has made it harder for police to do their jobs, putting more black lives at risk (Martin, 2015).

LIMITATIONS OF THE NARRATIVE APPROACH: CAN A BAD GUY WITH A GOOD STORY BE STOPPED BY A GOOD GUY WITH A BAD STORY?

Not all scholars who study narratives agree that they function as arguments (Bochner, 1994; Gass, 1988; Rowland, 1987; Warnick, 1987). A story that *rings* true may not *be* true. Shakespeare's *Macbeth*, for example, is a compelling story, but one that is written for dramatic effect, not historical accuracy. A good anecdote may trump facts and evidence, but that doesn't mean the facts and evidence are wrong.

Perhaps you've heard of the famous stunt in the O.J. Simpson trial, when Simpson struggled to put on a leather glove found at the crime scene. "If it doesn't fit, you must acquit" Johnnie Cochran, his defense attorney, declared. The narrative swayed that particular jury, but it was little more than courtroom theatrics. In an episode of the award-winning television series *The People v. O.J. Simpson*, O.J.'s defense attorney, Johnnie Cochran, advised, "Evidence doesn't win the day. Jurors go with the narrative that makes sense. We're here to tell a story. Our job is to tell that story better than the other side tells theirs" (Cole & Singleton, 2016).

In the same way that the first teachers of persuasion—known in the fifth century BC as the sophists—were derided by Plato for "making the worse appear the better reason" (Corbett, 1971, p. 598), a skilled storyteller with a false narrative may be more believable than an unskilled storyteller with a true narrative. It was a false narrative, after all, alleging that Saddam Hussein had weapons of mass destruction and ties to Al Qaeda, that led to the U.S. invasion of Iraq. In fact, Iraq had no chemical, biological, or nuclear capability whatsoever and no ties to Al Qaeda.

Consider historical films, for example, such as *Amadeus, Titanic,* or *The Social Network.* They may spin a good yarn, but at the expense of accuracy (Carnes, 1996). Dramatic license often trumps historical facts. Similarly, the Warren Commission's report, which reviewed the assassination of President John F. Kennedy, is boring compared with Oliver Stone's film *JFK*, which takes considerable liberties with the facts (Lardner, 1991; Margolis, 1991). In short, a good story often embellishes the truth, or even sacrifices the truth for the sake of the storyline.

Finally, some narratives are not only false, they are dangerous. People sometimes respond reflexively to stories, rather than reflectively. Barbara Warnick (1987) points out that Hitler's *Mein Kampf* was a compelling story that contributed to the rise of Nazi Germany. Similarly, Robert Rowland (1987) cautions that narratives may be used to justify the oppression of minorities. As Polletta and Lee (2006) observed,

> when disadvantaged groups use narrative to challenge the status quo, they may be especially vulnerable to skepticism about the veracity, authority, or generalizability of the form. When advantaged groups use narrative, they may be less likely even to be heard as telling stories. (p. 705)

False narratives may wind up on the wrong side of history, but for historical victims of racism, sexism, and other "isms" that offers little solace.

Despite these concerns, the narrative paradigm reminds us that arguments should resonate with listeners. People don't necessarily respond well to cold, hard facts. Stories can humanize arguments and, in turn, make them more persuasive.

Summary

Argumentation is a form of persuasion that emphasizes reasoning giving. It is useful to distinguish between an argument$_1$, a message unit, and argument$_2$, the act of arguing. In addition to identifying a number of fallacies and classifying the means of persuasion into three types (ethos, logos, and pathos), Aristotle endorsed the enthymeme (an abbreviated syllogism) as the primary means of persuasion.

Monological models, such as Toulmin's, examine arguments as message units. The basic Toulmin model identifies the claim, grounds, and warrant of an argument. The warrant, which is typically unstated, serves as the link between the claim and the grounds. The extended Toulmin model adds the additional elements of qualifier, backing, and rebuttal.

Dialogical models, such as pragma-dialectics, emphasize the interactive nature of arguing. Pragma-dialectics focuses on resolving disagreements within the boundaries of a set of normative guidelines to which arguers must adhere. Strategic maneuvers that violate the guidelines are considered fallacious or unfair. An ideal argument proceeds through four stages, but in practice many actual arguments do not.

Rhetorical approaches emphasize the persuasive aspects of language and the importance of adapting arguments to the listener's frame of reference. Perelman's approach is based on trying to gain another person's adherence by tailoring arguments to that person's point of view. Fisher's narrative paradigm emphasizes the importance of stories as arguments that follow a "logic of good reasons." Stories are judged on the basis of their narrative probability (coherence) and fidelity.

Notes

1 According to one poll, 18 percent of Americans believe the sun revolves around the earth (a geocentric view), rather than the other way around (the heliocentric view) (Wang & Aamodt, 2008). Copernicus must be spinning in his grave.
2 There is some controversy over how best to conceptualize warrants (see Keith & Beard, 2008; Verheij, 2005). For our purposes, however, it is safe to say that warrants authorize the inferential leap from the claim to the grounds.
3 Fairy tales may teach unintended values as well. For example, beauty is equated with good and ugliness with evil. Females are portrayed as passive and helpless. Stepmothers don't fare well either.

References

Aristotle (1982). *The rhetoric of Aristotle* (L. Cooper, trans.). New York: Appleton-Century-Crofts.

Arizona v. Hicks, U.S. 321 (1987).

Ball, W.J. (1994). Using Virgil to analyze public policy arguments: A system based on Toulmin's informal logic. *Social Science Computer Review, 12*(1), 181–194.

Bentahar, J., Moulin, B. & Bélanger, M. (2010). A taxonomy of argumentation models used for knowledge representation. *Artificial Intelligence Review, 33*(3), 211–259, doi: 10.1007/s10462-010-9154-1.

Bitzer, L.F. (1959). Aristotle's enthymeme revisited. *Quarterly Journal of Speech, 45*(4), 399–408, doi. org/10.1080/00335635909382374.

Bochner, A. (1994). Perspectives on inquiry II: Theories and stories. In M. Knapp & G.R. Miller (Eds), *Handbook of interpersonal communication* (pp. 21–41). Thousand Oaks, CA: Sage.

Bonevac, D. (2003). Pragma-dialectics and beyond. *Argumentation, 17*(4), 451–459, doi:10.102 3/A:1026311002268.

Brockriede, W. (1975). Where is argument? *Journal of the American Forensic Association, 11*(4), 179–182, doi. org/10.1080/00028533.1975.11951059.

Brockriede, W. & Ehninger, D. (1960). Toulmin on argument: An interpretation and application. *Quarterly Journal of Speech, 46*(1), 44–53, doi.org/10.1080/00335636009382390.

Carnes, M.C. (Ed.) (1996). *Past imperfect: history according to the movies.* New York: Henry Holt and Company.

Cole, J.R. (Writer) & Singleton, J. (Director) (2016, March 1). The race card [Television series episode]. In R. Murphy, N. Jacobson, B. Simpson, S. Alexander, L. Karazewski & B. Falchuk (Executive Producers), *The People v. O. J. Simpson: American Crime Story.* Fox 21 Television Studios and FX Productions.

Corbett, E.P.J. (1971). *Classical rhetoric for the modern student* (2nd Ed.). New York: Oxford University Press.

Dunbar, R. (2010). *How many friends does one person need? Dunbar's number and other evolutionary quirks.* Cambridge, MA: Harvard University Press.

Ehninger, D. (1970). Argument as method. *Speech Monographs, 37*(2), 101–110, doi.org/10.1080/0363775 7009375654.

Fisher, W.R. (1984). Narration as a human communication paradigm: The case of public moral argument. *Communication Monographs, 51*(1), 1–22, doi.org/10.1080/03637758409390180.

Fisher, W.R. (1985). The narrative paradigm: An elaboration. *Communication Monographs, 52*(4), 347–367, doi.org/10.1080/03637758509376117.

Fisher, W.R. (1989a). Clarifying the narrative paradigm. *Communication Monographs, 56*(1), 55–58, doi. org/10.1080/03637758909390249.

Fisher, W.R. (1989b). *Human communication as narration: Toward a philosophy of reason, value, and action.* Columbia, SC: University of South Carolina Press.

Fisher, W.R. (2000). The ethic(s) of argument and practical wisdom. In T.A. Hollihan (Ed.), *Argument at century's end: Reflecting on the past and envisioning the future* (pp. 1–15). Annandale, VA: National Communication Association.

Freeman, J.B. (2005). Systemetizing Toulmin's warrants: An epistemic approach. *Argumentation, 19*(3), 331–346, doi: 10.1007/s10503-005-4420-0.

Garssen, B. (2009). Ad hominem in disguise: Strategic manoeuvering with direct personal attacks. *Argumentation and Advocacy, 45*(4), 207–213, doi.org/10.1080/00028533.2009.11821709.

Gass, R.H. (1988). The narrative perspective in academic debate: A critique. *Argumentation and Advocacy, 25*(2), 78–92, doi.org/10.1080/00028533.1988.11951386.

Goodnight, G.T. (2006). When reasons matter most: Pragma-dialectics and the problem of informed consent. In P. Houtlosser & A. van Rees (Eds), *Considering pragma-dialectics* (pp. 72–82). Mahwah, NJ: Lawrence Erlbaum Associates.

Hample, D. (2010). Review of *Fallacies and judgments of reasonableness: empirical research concerning the pragma-dialectical discussion rules,* by *F.H. van Eemeren, B. Garssen & B. Meuffel* [book review]. *Argumentation, 24*(3), 375–381, doi: 10.1007/978-90-481-2614-9.

Hitchcock, D. & Verheij, B. (2005). The Toulmin model today: Introduction to the special issue on contemporary work using Stephen Edelston Toulmin's layout of arguments. *Argumentation, 19*(3), 255–258. doi: 10.1007/s10503-005-4414-y.

Hollihan, T.A. & Baaske, K.T. (2005). *Arguments and arguing: The products and process of human decision making,* 2nd Ed. Long Grove, IL: Waveland Press.

Horton v. *California,* 496 U.S. 128 (1990).

Johnson, R.H. (2000). *Manifest rationality: A pragmatic theory of argument.* Mahwah, NJ: Lawrence Earlbaum Associates.

Jonsen, A.R. & Toulmin, S. (1988). *The abuse of casuistry: A history of moral reasoning.* Berkeley, CA: University of California Press.

Keith, W.M. & Beard, D.E. (2008). Toulmin's rhetorical logic: What's the warrant for warrants? *Philosophy and Rhetoric, 41*(1), 22–50, doi: 10.1353/par.2008.0003.

Lardner, G. (1991, May 19). On the set: Dallas in Wonderland; Oliver Stone's version of the Kennedy assassination exploits the edge of paranoia. *Washington Post,* p. D-1.

Legge, N.J. & DiSanza, J.R. (1993). Can you make an argument without being in an argument? A relational approach to the study of interactional argument. *Journal of the Northwest Communication Association, 21,* 1–19.

Lumer, C. (2010). Pragma-dialectics and the function of argumentation. *Argumentation, 24*(1), 41–69, doi. org/10.1007/s10503-008-9118-7.

Margolis, J. (1991, May 14). JFK movie and book attempt to rewrite history. *Chicago Tribune,* p. 19.

Martin, J. (2015, September 2). Nikki Haley says Black Lives Matter is endangering black lives. *New York Times.* Retrieved on December 22, 2016 from: www.nytimes.com/politics/first-draft/2015/09/02/nikki-haley-says-black-lives-matter-movement-is-endangering-black-lives/?_r=0.

Mitchell, G.R. (2010). Higher order strategic maneuvering in argumentation. *Argumentation, 24*(3), 319–335, doi.org/10.1007/s10503-009-9178-3.

O'Keefe, D.J. (1977). Two concepts of argument. *The Journal of the American Forensic Association, 13*(3), 121–128, doi.org/10.1080/00028533.1977.11951098.

O'Keefe, D.J. (1982). The concepts of argument and arguing. In J.R. Cox & C.A. Willard (Eds), *Advances in argumentation theory and research* (pp. 3–23). Carbondale, IL: Southern Illinois University Press.

Perelman, C. (1982). *The realm of rhetoric* (William Kluback, trans.). Notre Dame, IN: University of Notre Dame Press.

Perelman, C. & Olbrechts-Tyteca, L. (1969). *The new rhetoric: A treatise on argumentation* (J. Wilkinson & P. Weaver, trans.). Notre Dame, IN: University of Notre Dame Press.

Polletta, F. & Lee, J. (2006). Is telling stories good for democracy: Rhetoric and public deliberation after 9/11. *American Sociological Review, 71*(5), 699–723, doi.org/10.1177/000312240607100501.

Rapp, C. & B. Wagner, T. (2013). On some Aristotelian sources of modern argumentation theory. *Argumentation, 27*(1), 7–30, doi: 10.1007/s10503-012-9280-9.

Reisman, S. (2016, July 8). Rudy Giuliani: Black Lives Matter puts a target on police officers' backs. *Mediate*. Retrieved on December 22, 2016 from: www.mediaite.com/online/rudy-giuliani-black-lives-matter-puts-a-target-on-police-officers-backs.

Rowland, R.C. (1987). Narrative: Mode of discourse or paradigm. *Speech Monographs, 54*(3), 264–275, doi.org/10.1080/03637758709390232.

Rowland, R.C. & Barge, J.K. (1991). On argument as disagreement. *Argumentation & Advocacy, 28*(1), 41.

Seiter, J.S. & Gass, R.H. (2010). Aggressive communication in political contexts. In T.A. Avtgis & A.S. Rancer (Eds), *Arguments, aggression, and conflict: New directions in theory and research* (pp. 217–240). New York: Routledge.

Sociologists for Justice (2014, September 28). *Sociologists issue statement on Ferguson*. Retrieved on December 22, 2016 from: https://sociologistsforjustice.org/public-statement.

Stephens, O.H. & Glenn, R.A. (2005). *Unreasonable searches and seizures: Rights and liberties under the law*. Santa Barbara, CA: ABC-CLIO, Inc.

Taylor, J. (2008). The problem of women's sociality in contemporary North American feminist memoir. *Gender & Society, 22*(6), 705–727, doi.org/10.1177/0891243208324598.

Toulmin, S.E. (1958). *The uses of argument*. Cambridge: Cambridge University Press.

Toulmin, S.E. (2003). *The uses of argument* (updated Ed.). Cambridge: Cambridge University Press.

Toulmin, S.E., Rieke, R. & Janik, A. (1984). *An introduction to reasoning* (2nd Ed.). New York: Macmillan.

Van Eemeren, F.H. (2010). *Strategic maneuvering in argumentative discourse*. Philadelphia, PA: John Benjamins Publishing Company.

Van Eemeren, F.H., Garssen, B. & Mueffels, B. (2009). *Fallacies and judgments of reasonableness*. New York: Springer.

Van Eemeren, F.H. & Grootendorst, R. (1984). *Speech acts in argumentative discussions: A theoretical model for the analysis of discussions directed towards solving conflicts of opinion*. Dordrecht: Floris Publications.

Van Eemeren, F.H. & Grootendorst, R. (1992). *Argumentation, communication, and fallacies*. Hillsdale, NJ: Lawrence Erlbaum Associates.

Van Eemeren, F.H. & Grootendorst, R. (2004). *A systematic theory of argumentation: The pragma-dialectical approach*. Cambridge: Cambridge University Press.

Van Eemeren, F.H., Grootendorst, R. & Henkemans, F.S. (1996). *Fundamentals of argumentation theory*. Mahwah, NJ: Lawrence Erlbaum.

Van Eemeren, F.H., Grootendorst, R. & Henkemans, F.S. (2002). *Argumentation: Analysis, evaluation, presentation*. Mahwah, NJ: Lawrence Earlbaum Associates.

Van Eemeren, F.H. & Houtlosser, P. (2002a). Strategic maneuvering with the burden of proof. In F.H. van Eemeren (Ed.), *Advances in pragma-dialectics* (pp. 13–28). Amsterdam: SicSat.

Van Eemeren, F.H. & Houtlosser, P. (2002b). Strategic maneuvering: Maintaining a delicate balance. In F.H. van Eemeren & P. Houtlosser (Eds), *Dialectic and rhetoric: The warp and woof of argumentation analysis* (pp. 131–160). Kluwer: Dordrecht.

Van Eemeren, F.H. & Houtlosser, P. (2003). Fallacies as derailments of strategic maneuvering: The argumentum ad verecundiam, a case in point. In F.H. van Eemeren, J.A. Blair, C.A. Willard & F.S. Henkemans (Eds), *Proceedings of the fifth conference of the International Society for the Study of Argumentation*, (pp. 289–292). Amsterdam: SicSat.

Verene, D.P. (1985). Philosophy, argument, and narration. *Philosophy and Rhetoric, 22*(2), 141–144. Retrieved February 23, 2019 from: www.jstor.org/stable/40237582.

Verheij, B. (2005). Evaluating arguments based on Toulmin's scheme. *Argumentation, 19*(3), 347–371, doi. org/10.1007/s10503-005-4421-z.

Voss, J.F. (2005). Toulmin's model and the solving of ill-structured problems. *Argumentation, 19*(3), 321–329, doi.org/10.1007/s10503-005-4419-6.

Walton, D.N. (1995). *A pragmatic theory of fallacies.* Tuscaloosa, AL: University of Alabama Press.

Wang, S. & Aamodt, S. (2008, June 29). Your brain lies to you. *New York Times.* Retrieved February 23, 2019 from: www.nytimes.com/2008/06/29/opinion/29iht-edwang.1.14069662.html.

Warnick, B. (1987). The narrative paradigm: Another story. *Quarterly Journal of Speech, 73*(2), 172–182, doi.org/10.1080/00335638709383801.

Woody, R.H. (2006). *Search and seizure: The fourth amendment for law enforcement officers.* Springfield, IL: Charles C. Thomas.

Chapter 4

The Nature of Critical Thinking

Dumb and Dumberer

In fiction, criminals are often depicted as brilliant masterminds, capable of planning elaborate heists with panache and élan. In real life, however, many criminals are a bit daft. One infamous case involves a bank robber, named McArthur Wheeler, who heard that lemon juice could be used to make invisible ink. He was right too (Murphy, 2011). Then he took the idea a step further, reasoning that if he applied lemon juice to his face, his face would become invisible. He rubbed lemon juice on his face and robbed two banks in one day. Both robberies were caught on security cameras. His face was clearly visible in both. "But I wore the juice," he protested, when police arrested him that same evening.

Mr. Wheeler's errant reasoning has been featured in discussions of the *Dunning-Kruger effect*, which states that the poorest thinkers among us fail to realize that they are among the poorest thinkers (Kruger & Dunning, 1999). We delve into this cognitive deficiency in more detail later in this chapter. For now, though, let's be honest: Although most of us aren't as daffy as the bank robber, we all make foolish mistakes from time to time. One of the authors has worn pink underwear and t-shirts on more than one occasion, after combining colored with white clothes in the washer. The other singed his eyebrows and eyelashes halfway off while lighting a gas-powered hot tub. It took weeks for them to grow back. We mention this, in part, to poke fun at ourselves, but also to illustrate that everybody does dumb things. That said, using critical thinking skills and learning from our own and others' mistakes is one way of avoiding blunders. Critical thinking can also help us solve problems and make better decisions. With that in mind, this chapter explores the nature of critical thinking. First, we examine ignorance and stupidity as impediments to clear thinking. Next, we offer a definition of critical thinking along with an examination of its key characteristics. Finally, we consider the impact of digital technology on critical thinking ability.

Ignorance Versus Stupidity: No Duh!

Ignorance and stupidity are the twin enemies of critical thinking, but they are not the same thing (McIntyre, 2015). Specifically, *ignorance* involves a fundamental lack of knowledge, information, or expertise (Abbott, 2010). To be ignorant is to be uninformed or misinformed about something. For example, a child who picks up a rattlesnake and gets bitten simply doesn't know any better. On the other hand, *stupidity* refers to a person who knows better, but still engages in foolish or risky behavior. For example, a college student who grabs a rattler by the tail, while showing off for his buddies, is being stupid. Likewise, if you haven't seen the fellow who trims his hedges with a chainsaw and a rope, visit www.youtube.com/watch?v=gO9M90fdZDA.

Ignorance is forgivable to a certain extent. As Will Rogers' old adage goes, "everybody is ignorant, only on different subjects" (1924, p. 64). Ungar (2008) refers to such subject-specific ignorance as *functional cognitive deficits*, which, as you might have guessed, are typically situation dependent. Indeed, most people don't know how to amortize and depreciate assets over time, but if you are an accountant, you should know. Most people don't know how to administer CPR, but if you are an emergency medical technician (EMT) you darn well better. Neither author is familiar with gang signs, so we avoid playing "rock, paper, scissors" in tough neighborhoods.

Blissful and Willful Ignorance: Failing to See vs Turning a Blind Eye

Some people are blissfully ignorant of even the most basic nuggets of useful information. Did you know that, according to a national survey (Dewey, 2017), seven percent of American adults believe chocolate milk comes from brown cows? We wonder where they think strawberry flavored milk comes from. As another example, one in four Americans believes the sun revolves around the earth, whereas the earth, in fact, orbits the sun (Neuman, 2014).

There is a difference, though, between blissful ignorance and willful ignorance, especially when it affects the behavior of others, and particularly when the blunderer wields more influence, as celebrities often do. Actress Sienna Miller's comment on cigarettes illustrates such willful ignorance. "Love them," she said. "I think the more positive approach you have to smoking, the less harmful it is" (Hind, 2008, p. 11). In other words, smokers, if you're worried about cancer, just give your lungs a little pep talk. Willful ignorance is especially dangerous because the person actively avoids contradictory information.

Some people learn from their previous mistakes. Others don't always seem to. The actor, Shia LeBeouf, fits into the latter group. He has been caught plagiarizing more than a dozen times (Stampler, 2014). What is remarkable is that, after being exposed, he then plagiarized his apologies. Here is his *mea culpa* for lifting the words of Daniel Clowes, a graphic novelist and screen-writer (Figure 4.1a).

Figure 4.1a Shia LeBeouf's apology 1. Twitter, 6.52 am, December 18, 2013.

LeBeouf's apology is almost identical to Kanye West's apology to Taylor Swift after grabbing her microphone at the Grammys, "It starts with this . . . I'm sorry Taylor" (CNN, 2010, para. 6). Yet another of Shia's tweeted apologies was confusingly similar to one offered by Mark Zuckerberg (Figure 4.1b).

Compare LaBeouf's apology with one Mark Zuckerberg wrote at a much earlier date in response to complaints from Facebook users: "I want to thank all of you who have written in and created groups and protested. Even though I wish I hadn't made so many of you angry, I am glad we got to hear you" (Zuckerberg, 2006, para. 5).

After being called out repeatedly, it's hard to imagine that LaBeouf didn't know what was going on. There are other cases where people plead innocence by saying things like, "I didn't know any better." What's to be made of them? On the one hand, we have little doubt that *some* people who offer this excuse are being sincere, and their ignorance should be taken into account. As noted earlier, everyone makes mistakes. On the other hand, we believe it's fair to consider whether people should be expected to know and understand certain basic concepts. Take college campuses, for example. Should all college students know that "No means no" when it comes to sexual advances and that silence or a lack of resistance does not imply consent? Should they know that affirmative consent, e.g., a clear and enthusiastic "Yes," is what counts? Should they know that affirmative consent must be ongoing? A person who agrees on one occasion may not agree on another and a person who agrees to A or B may not agree to C. We think students should know these things. We also think colleges and universities have a responsibility to teach these principles to all incoming students.

Likewise, citizens should have a modicum of information about government. Democracy depends on an informed citizenry capable of choosing wisely between candidates and issues. As Iyengar, Hahn, Bonfadelli, and Marr (2009) emphasized, "informed citizenship is a fundamental premise of democratic government" (p. 341). Yet, a survey revealed that only one in four Americans could name all three branches of U.S. government (the legislative branch, executive branch, and judicial branch) (Gorman, 2016). Worse yet, that number reflects a decline in civics

Figure 4.1b Shia LeBeouf's apology 2. Twitter, 7.16 am, December 19, 2013.

knowledge. Why does knowing the three branches of government matter? As Jamieson points out, "those unfamiliar with our three branches of government can't understand the importance of checks and balances" (Annenberg Public Policy Center, 2016, para. 5).

Similarly, a *Newsweek* survey found that 29 percent of Americans could not name the vice president and 44 percent did not know what the Bill of Rights was (Romano, 2011). Another survey found that 45 percent of respondents thought that the phrase "from each according to his ability, to each according to his needs" was part of the U.S. Constitution (Goldberg, 2007). In fact, it is a quote from Karl Marx.

That said, Americans aren't alone when it comes to ignorance. An international survey revealed that the U.S. shared the top spots for public ignorance with Italy and South Korea (Gover, 2014). Moreover, one poll found that most people in Great Britain were misinformed or ignorant regarding facts related to decisions about "Brexit" (whether their country should leave the European Union) (Somin, 2016). The good news is that ignorance is treatable. We simply have to improve our knowledge and understanding of issues that affect us. Better yet, in the digital age, answers to many questions are but a few keystrokes away.

Random Acts of Stupidity: Learning From Our Mistakes

Stupidity is not so much about a class of persons as it is about a class of behaviors. As Forrest Gump's mother said, "Stupid is as stupid does." The good news is that we can learn from our mistakes, even though not everyone takes life's lessons to heart. The *Peanuts* cartoon character Charlie Brown, for example, keeps trying to kick the football, expecting a different outcome, even though Lucy always yanks the football away at the last moment. In the next few pages we present examples of individuals, groups, and organizations that acted foolishly. We offer these examples not to humiliate the people involved, but rather to show that seemingly intelligent people, including those in positions of power, sometimes fail to think before they act.

Caught Pants Down

Charlie Brown is a cartoon character. Former congressman Anthony Weiner is not. He resigned from Congress in 2011 following a sexting scandal appropriately dubbed "Weinergate." He knew better than to send explicit selfies via cellphone, but he did so anyway. In 2013 Weiner also sabotaged his comeback bid to be mayor of New York City by, once again, sexting. In 2017 he pleaded guilty to sending explicit pictures to a 15-year-old girl. He was sentenced to nearly two years in prison (Demick, 2017).

Weiner's actions illustrate what is called *nonadaptive behavior*, that is, making the same mistake over and over. He admitted that what he was doing was wrong, but said he couldn't stop himself. "I have a disease, but I have no excuses," he told the judge who sentenced him. "I'm an addict."

The American Psychological Association, however, does not acknowledge that "sex addiction" is an actual disease (O'Connor, 2014). As Dr. Joye Swan (2016), chair of psychology at Woodbury University, noted, "I'm not saying that people cannot and do not destroy their lives based on impulsive and risky sexual behavior . . . but addiction has a real meaning and a clinical definition" (para. 2). Regrettably, Anthony Weiner became the poster boy for the perils of sexting.

What can be learned from his example? If you are unable to control your impulses or find yourself engaging in self-destructive behavior, seek professional help. Weiner checked himself into rehab twice. He also could have chucked his cellphone and given up using the internet except under supervision. Better that than becoming a punchline for late-night comedians and serving prison time as a sex offender.

Cambridge Police: Don't Spray Me Bro

People in positions of authority may fail to think critically, and, sometimes, it's ethnocentric thinking that clouds their judgment. As an illustration, a spokesperson for the Cambridge, Massachusetts, police department offered the following explanation for the practice of hog-tying Hispanic suspects who became violent, rather than using pepper spray, which was standard procedure with other suspects: "Pepper spray doesn't work well on Mexican American suspects," the source said. Why? "Because Mexicans grow up eating too much spicy food, and because they spend so much time picking hot peppers in the fields" (Tobar, 1999, para. 3).

This explanation is befuddling on multiple levels. First, it doesn't follow that developing a tolerance to foods you *eat* would translate into a tolerance for having those foods sprayed *in your eyes*! One of the authors managed to get toothpaste in his eyes once. Even though he brushes his teeth every day, it stung like the dickens. The same author has experienced a similar effect with Head & Shoulders shampoo. The eyes, they burn.

Second, many cultures enjoy spicy foods. Cajun, Chinese Sichuan, Jamaican, South Indian, and Thai cuisine come to mind. Would unruly suspects from those cultures/ethnicities have to be hog-tied too?

Third, the explanation presumes that most Mexicans in Massachusetts are pepper pickers, an unlikely occupation for anyone living in the Bay State. Fourth, just in case you are wondering, there is no scientific basis for the belief that Hispanics are immune to pepper spray, this according to medical experts and pepper spray manufacturers (Hsu, 1999, p. B-2).

Flash forward 20 years, when a similar stereotype was applied by a former Border Patrol agent. After pepper spray was used to disperse immigrants, including women and children, at the U.S.–Mexico border, former chief Ron Coleman said "pepper spray is natural" and "you could actually put it on your nachos and eat it" (cited in Daugherty, 2018). As we noted earlier, however, things that might taste fine in your mouth do not feel good in your eyes, including toothpaste and pepper spray.

What, then, can be learned from this example? For one thing, public servants are not immune to *biased thinking*. Rather than thinking critically about the issue, the Massachusetts police department seemed to be relying on a false negative cultural stereotype. Thinking critically, however, requires that you move beyond such practices. In this case, increasing your cultural sensitivity could help you avoid gaffes and blunders based on cultural stereotypes. Not surprisingly, the Cambridge police department issued a formal apology once the story was publicized and promised that the erroneous information would be stricken from its police training program.

Rape-Lite? To Blurt or Not to Blurt . . .

Regardless of whether people consider themselves liberal or conservative, they are fully capable of engaging in shallow thinking. Consider the off-handed remarks made by Whoopi Goldberg on the TV show *The View*, and by former congressman Todd Akin in a TV interview. Whoopi's comment was in response to the arrest of movie director Roman Polanski, in Switzerland, for fleeing the U.S.A. after his rape conviction in 1978. The rape victim was a 13-year-old girl, whom Polanski sexually assaulted in ways too graphic to describe in a textbook. Whoopi commented, "I know it wasn't rape-rape. I think it was something else, but I don't believe it was rape-rape." What was it then? Keep in mind that Polanski had already pleaded guilty to a charge of unlawful sex with a minor (Addley & Connolly, 2009). He was awaiting sentencing when he fled the country. Other than being a celebrity, how did Polanski's actions fail to meet the requirements for rape?

What can we learn from Whoopi's mistake? To put it bluntly, make sure you know what you're talking about before putting your foot in your mouth. In her eagerness to weigh in with an opinion, Whoopi seemed to be implying that celebrities should be held to a different legal standard than the rest of us. As a result, her comment performed a disservice to rape victims everywhere. Dismissing a rape as something other than a rape further contributes to the stigmatization of victims.

In a similar vein, former congressman Todd Akin damaged his bid for a senate seat in 2012 when he offered the following reason why rape victims didn't need legal access to abortions: "Pregnancy from rape is really rare. If it's a legitimate rape, the female body has ways to try to shut that whole thing down" (Alter, 2014, para. 1). Really? Apparently, in the former congressman's eyes, some rapes are more legitimate than others. He was wrong on the facts, however, since the pregnancy rate among rape victims of reproductive age is 5 percent, the same as that for consensual sex, which translates into about 32,000 rape-related pregnancies per year (Clancy, 2012; Holmes, Resnick, Kilpatrick & Best, 1996). With that kind of reasoning, should anyone be surprised that he lost the election?

Illusory Superiority and the Dunning-Kruger Effect: They Know Not That They Know Not

We began this chapter by describing the ill-conceived crime spree of a bank robber who thought that rubbing lemon juice on his face would make him invisible. Not only was his scheme stupid, he had no idea how stupid it was. How could he be so naïve? The answer is a cognitive deficit known as the Dunning-Kruger effect (Kruger & Dunning, 1999). The poorest thinkers among us not only fail to recognize that they have poor thinking skills, they also tend to wildly overestimate their thinking ability. For example, those who scored in the bottom 12th percentile on a test of reasoning skills thought they scored in the top 68th percentile. In other words, people who got a low "F" thought they had earned a "C." Worse yet, because unskilled thinkers don't realize that they are unskilled, they do little to improve.

But wait. It's not just poor thinkers who misjudge themselves. Most people are prone to overestimate their abilities, a phenomenon called *illusory superiority*. That's right, most people consider themselves to be above average. They see themselves as smarter than the average person, better at driving than the average person, funnier than the average person, and so on. We don't say it publicly but, privately, we think we are better than everyone else.

Illusory superiority can lead to serious mistakes. A motorist might think he is a better driver than most and that he is capable of texting and driving, even though others shouldn't. A hiker might believe she has a better sense of direction than other trekkers and winds up needing to be rescued after getting lost. A poker player may think he is better at reading tells than other players and winds up losing his shirt. A stock market investor may be convinced she's savvier than the average investor and wind up losing her life savings.

By definition, not everyone can be above average. Some people have to be average, or below average, or the concept makes no sense. Not only that, giving the impression that you're superior can be off putting, even when you know what you're talking about. Thus, before making a supercilious statement, consider whether anyone asked for your advice. Before weighing in with a confident yet condescending opinion, ask yourself if you are about to engage in "mansplaining." Before telling everyone in your work group how to do their job, ask yourself if you want to come across as a "know it all."

What Is and Isn't Critical Thinking?

We hope some of the preceding examples illustrate why the ability to think critically is so vital. "There is no more central issue to education," writes Michael Peters, "than thinking and reasoning" (2007, p. 350). Indeed, if students only learned "things" in college, but not how to *think* about those things, there would be little value in earning a degree. That's because knowledge often becomes obsolete. In fact, Samuel Arbesman (2010, 2012) coined the term *mesofacts* to refer to knowledge, often learned in school, that changes. In grade school, for example, your authors were taught that dinosaurs were cold-blooded lizards. Not so, say scientists today. And you may be old enough to remember when Pluto was considered a real planet. Now it's just a dwarf planet. The shame!

While these are fun examples, the problem, according to Arbesman, is our tendency to cling to mesofacts beyond their expiration date, which can lead to poor decisions. In medical fields related to diseases of the liver, for example, Arbesman (2012) noted that half of the knowledge was obsolete within about 45 years. Imagine what might happen if a doctor were treating patients based on such knowledge!

Knowledge obsolescence is increasingly common. People change careers often. As a result, adopting a habit of thinking, developing a questioning attitude, and becoming a life-long learner is far more important. In fact, a survey of over 300 corporate executives revealed that the top three characteristics they were looking for in college graduates were "teamwork skills," "critical thinking and analytic reasoning skills," and "oral/written communication" skills (Vance, 2007, p. 30).

Thinking Outside the Box

"Critical thinking" has become a buzz term, so much so that everyone claims to be doing it, without a clear understanding of what, exactly, "it" is. The popularity of the term was illustrated by a survey of college professors, 89 percent of whom reported that teaching critical thinking was one of their primary objectives. As it turns out, however, only 10 percent were *actually* teaching critical thinking on a regular basis (Paul, Elder & Bartell, 1997).

As useful as it is to "think outside the box," there are also occasions when it is necessary to think inside the box, that is, within the practical constraints of a given situation. As Norris (1985) emphasized, "critical thinking skills are no substitute for experience, common sense, and knowledge of subject matter" (p. 44). Moreover, thinking unconventionally is no guarantee that someone will arrive at a better solution to a problem.

Critical Thinking Defined

Think for a moment about all of the ways that thinking is encouraged in our society. Students are urged to "put on their thinking caps," "think for themselves," engage in "higher level thinking,"

Figure 4.2 "He's always thinking outside the rock."
© Michael Maslin/*The New Yorker* Collection/www.cartoonbank.com.

and practice "non-linear thinking." People are advised to "think long and hard," "think straight," "think twice," "think on their feet," and "work smarter, not harder." Consumers are told to "think different," "think green," and "think outside the bun." Governments fund "think tanks" and newspapers publish "think pieces."

Given all this hoopla, what exactly *is* thinking, or, more specifically, *critical thinking*? A simple elegant definition was offered by Norris (1985) who stated that "thinking critically can be defined as rationally deciding what to do or believe" (p. 40). For the purposes of this text, *critical thinking in its most general sense involves the use of reasoning and rationality to achieve better understanding, enhanced problem-solving, and superior decision-making.* Critical thinking, then, is the antithesis of relying on reflex responses, acting on hunches, succumbing to force of habit, making snap judgments, resorting to impulse decisions, or obeying instinct. With this definition as a starting point, let's consider some important characteristics of critical thinking.

Conceptualizing Critical Thinking

Skeptical, But Not Cynical: Giving the Hairy Eyeball

Several years ago, one of the authors asked his class to "critically analyze" some form of communication. In his essay, one student focused on the author and, for several pages, proceeded to insult him. The author was taken aback. The student had always *seemed* to enjoy class. What was going on? It turns out that, stapled to the back of the paper, was a handwritten note from the student, apologizing for the insults and claiming that this was the most difficult paper he'd ever written. Why? He loved the class, he claimed, and the author was one of his favorite professors. Clearly, there had been a misunderstanding that was eventually cleared up. The student had equated the word "critical" with being disapproving, disparaging, and denigrating.

Critical thinking, however, is not synonymous with criticism. As common as this misconception may be, the word "critical" is not pejorative, either here or when used in the term "critical thinking." Any bully can kick down a sand castle. It takes effort to build one in the first place. Likewise, intellectual bullies enjoy kicking apart others' ideas, without offering insights of their own for examination. A cynic places more emphasis on the "cons," whereas a critical thinker places equal emphasis on the "pros" *and* the "cons" of an idea. A critical thinker is open to new ideas, not closed to them. But a critical thinker demands proof. Holding a "critical" attitude means adopting a questioning spirit, making assumptions explicit, testing sources and evidence, and remaining as objective and impartial as possible. As such, the "critical" part of critical thinking can be contrasted with thinking based on stereotypes, common sense, heuristic cues (e.g., brand names, celebrity endorsements), decision rules (e.g., quality costs more, size matters) obedience to authority, or gut reactions. It also can be contrasted with biased thinking, wishful thinking, superstitious thinking, and mystical thinking.

Not All Thinking Is Critical Thinking: Thoughtfulness Versus Thoughtlessness

When you roll out of bed each morning, you probably make a number of "mindless" decisions. You might have the same thing for breakfast each day. You might follow the same route on your way to work or school. You might perform some tasks on "automatic pilot" or "in your sleep." Psychologists refer to this tendency as *automaticity* (Bargh & Williams, 2006). Such habitual thinking has its advantages. It is fast, efficient, and often adequate when making simple choices. More important decisions, however, deserve careful thought and attention. Indeed, thinking critically means being rigorous in your thinking habits and is the opposite of mindless behavior.

Thinking About Thinking: Reflective Versus Reflexive

Sometimes people are thinking, but their thought process is simplistic. At other times they are biased in their thinking. They engage in denial or develop rationalizations. In contrast, critical thinkers are aware of their thought processes, understand the assumptions under which they are operating, and recognize the inferences they are making. Critical thinking is often referred to as reflective, analytical, or higher-level thinking, because it consists of more than simply grasping an idea. Critical thinking involves manipulating ideas. To think critically one must be able to analyze ideas, identify interrelationships among them, recognize applications and implications of ideas, make comparisons and contrasts among and between ideas, and test and evaluate those ideas.

Critical Thinking and Creative Thinking

Critical thinking is not synonymous with creative thinking, although the two are complimentary. As Paul and Elder (2006) noted, "imagination and reason are an inseparable team. They function best in tandem, like the right and left legs in walking or running" (p. 34). Critical thinking is often, although not always, more left-brained and textual, while creative thinking tends to be more right-brained and visual. Moreover, while critical thinking is more focused, disciplined, and systematic, creative thinking is more imaginative, uninhibited, and unstructured. Engineers and artists, for example, tend to think differently (Gridley, 2007). Nevertheless, creative thinking can be an asset to critical thinking. A chess grandmaster, for example, might use creative thinking to alter a traditional opening, causing an opponent to make a costly gambit. Albert Einstein was well known for using visual thinking in what he called "thought experiments," rather than mathematical equations, to solve physics problems (Miller, 2001).

Don't Teach and Chew Gum at the Same Time

A clear demonstration that creative thinking doesn't always involve critical thinking was demonstrated in a Rockville, Maryland, classroom. For years, students had participated in a class exercise called the "gum game" (Fisher, 2007; de Vise, 2007), which went like this: A piece of gum was chewed by one person, then passed from student to student around the classroom. Each student took a turn chewing the same wad of gum. Here's a case where it really is best to be first in line! The idea was to simulate how sexual promiscuity could result in an STD being passed from one person to another.

It took nine years for the school district to figure out that the exercise was unsanitary. When we read about it, it took us about a second to say "urp . . ." and conclude that the exercise was disgusting. It took us another five minutes to think of several *hygienic ways* of demonstrating the same principle. What if, for instance, students passed around a ball painted with fluorescent invisible ink (commonly used in nightclubs for age verification and re-entry)? Afterwards, they could look at their hands under an ultraviolet light. Any ink that was transferred from the ball onto their hands would glow under the U.V. light. The advantage, of course, is that ink is non-toxic, washes off, and isn't full of "cooties."

Critical Thinking and Intelligence

Critical thinking is also not synonymous with intelligence although, as is the case with creative thinking, the two often go hand in hand (Stanovich & West, 2008). That said, sometimes the smartest people make the dumbest mistakes (Sternberg, 2002; Tavris & Aronson, 2007; Van Hecke, 2007). Take President Bill Clinton, for example. He was and still is a smart guy, but he wasn't using his head when he chose to have an affair with Monica Lewinsky. Similarly, the book and subsequent documentary *The Smartest Guys in the Room* (McLean & Elkind, 2003) chronicles how Enron's top executives, Kenneth Lay and Jeffrey Skilling, created a financial house of cards by relying on creative accounting. Their business, however, was really a shell game. Twenty-one thousand employees lost their jobs and pensions. One hundred and eighty thousand investors were scammed out of $60 billion dollars. And let's not forget Bernie Madoff, a Wall Street financier, who ripped off investors for $65 billion. Although there were numerous clues about the Ponzi scheme, investors and the SEC didn't look into them because Madoff traveled in the right social circles and seemed like a charming fellow (Trigaux, 2009).

Why don't intelligent people always engage in critical thinking? There are a variety of explanations, one of which is *hubris* (Feinberg & Tarrant, 1995). Some brainy people have a blind spot. Because they are smart they presume they must be right. They also may engage in consensus-seeking or a phenomenon known as *groupthink* (see Chapter 2), in which people in a group presume they know everything, assume an air of infallibility, and, in turn, reinforce, rather than challenge, one another's ideas. Finally, some smart people, in I.Q. terms, may be low in *emotional intelligence* (Goleman, 2006), that is, they may be less adept at monitoring and regulating their emotions in socially appropriate ways.

Knowledge and Critical Thinking

Knowledge, like intelligence, is clearly an asset, but not an ironclad guarantee of critical thinking. It is often *necessary* for critical thinking, but not *sufficient* to produce better thinking, problem-solving, and decision-making. Knowledgeable people sometimes fail to use their knowledge.

An extreme case of knowing a lot, but being unable to apply the knowledge, involved a fellow named Kim Peek. Peek, who served as the inspiration for the movie *Rain Man*, was born without a corpus callosum, which connects the left and right hemispheres of the brain. He was diagnosed as having Savant Syndrome, which, in his case, was manifested in a phenomenal photographic memory. Among other things, he memorized 12,000 books. Even so, he could not engage in abstract thinking and scored well below average on traditional I.Q. tests. For instance, he could not understand ordinary proverbs such as "a rolling stone gathers no moss." Despite his vast knowledge his ability to think was limited.

Skill Set or Disposition?

Are you energetic? Positive? Trustworthy? If so, do these descriptors refer to an attitude, a skill, or a trait? We ask these questions as a way of illustrating the difference between skills, which are things you can do, and dispositions, which are attributes, characteristics, or inclinations that make up who you are. The same types of questions can be asked of critical thinking. Specifically, is critical thinking best understood as a skill set or a disposition?

There are at least three schools of thought. Some scholars, like Richard Paul (1982, 1993) and Robert Ennis (1992, 1996), maintain that the ability to think critically relies on a set of skills. Such skills include the ability to apply tests of evidence and source credibility, expose fallacies in reasoning, and identify unexpressed premises or inferential leaps, among other things. Others, like Jane Roland Martin (1992), suggest that critical thinking is based on an attitude or orientation. That is, some people have a disposition to ask questions, challenge ideas, and analyze issues. For them, critical thinking is a habit of mind.

We, however, like Facione (2007), embrace a third perspective, which suggests that both skills and dispositions are crucial for critical thinking. Indeed, having skills without the inclination to use them, or having a questioning spirit without any skills would be useless. This notion is consistent with a well-known theory of persuasion known as the Elaboration Likelihood Model (Petty & Cacioppo,1986), which maintains that, to engage in active mental deliberation (i.e., "*central processing*"), one must have both the *motivation* and the *ability* to do so. Take away either one, and a person cannot or will not engage in effortful thinking. For example, picture a group of senior citizens listening to a speech about birth control options or a group of preschoolers listening to a speech about reverse mortgages. While the former group most likely would lack the motivation to think critically about the speech, the latter group would probably lack the ability to do so.

Generic Ability or Subject-Specific?

Is critical thinking a generic ability that is widely applicable to all topics and issues, in the same way that being athletic might help you play multiple sports? Or is it more subject-specific such that critical thinking in one discipline is unique from that in another, in the same way that being a chessmaster will help win chess matches but not piano competitions? *Generalists*, such as Robert Ennis (1992), maintain that critical thinking skills are applicable across a wide range of subjects. Others (Quinn, 1994; Worsham & Stockton, 1986) echo this view, noting that many basic thinking skills are cross-disciplinary.

Specifists, such as John McPeck (1981), on the other hand, argue that critical thinking is domain-specific. Likewise, Bailin, Case, Coombs, and Daniels (1999a) note emphatically that "background knowledge in the particular area is a precondition for critical thinking" (p. 271). For example, a forensic pathologist might be able to determine that a stabbing victim was running away, rather than standing still, based on blood spatter patterns. To make this inference the C.S.I. would have to know that when blood drips straight down the drops form a circular pattern on impact, whereas when blood drips from a moving person the pattern tends to be elliptical.

At first glance, both of these perspectives seem reasonable. To be sure, a number of thinking processes related to problem-solving and decision-making span multiple fields and professions. At the same time, many forms of critical thinking do require specific knowledge and are wedded to specific fields (Bailin et al., 1999b; McPeck, 1981; Moore, 2004).

So how might this controversy be resolved? We suggest, as Davies (2006) did, that the generalist versus specifist debate represents something of a false dichotomy. While there is little doubt that some contexts require specific knowledge, many thinking skills are generic in nature. Analogical reasoning is common to many disciplines and to everyday life. The same holds true for causal reasoning, sign reasoning, generalization, and argument by example. Suppose a person has a good understanding of analogies as they relate to political science. Would the person have to begin all over to understand how analogies operate in law or medicine? In short, it seems reasonable to assume that at least some thinking ability would be transferable from context to context.

Critical Thinking and Culture

A final consideration about the nature of critical thinking is the extent to which different cultures share basic assumptions about reasoning and rationality. The question has been raised, then, about whether there is such a thing as universal rationality. One answer, offered by Nisbett (2003), is that culture fundamentally shapes thinking and reasoning processes. Some scholars, for example, regard Westerners as more analytic and Asians as more holistic in their thinking. People from Western cultures are more likely to view issues or objects independently, whereas people from Asian cultures tend view issues and objects in context (e.g., Choi, Koo & Choi, 2007; Varnum, Grossmann, Kitayama & Nisbett, 2010). For Westerners, reasoning tends to be rule-based and contradictions are viewed as untenable. In contrast, Easterners tend to see reasoning as contextual and contradiction is understood to be part of life (De Oliveira & Nisbett, 2017).

Such different styles of thinking may affect the ways in which people approach or avoid arguments. One study (Hample & Anagondahalli, 2015), for example, found that people in the U.S. are typically motivated to either approach or avoid argumentation. In contrast, people from India are motivated to approach *and* avoid arguments. Why? One possibility is that analytical/polarized thinkers (i.e., people in Western cultures) tend to resolve contradictions by picking one option out of two contradictory propositions (i.e., either approaching or avoiding argumentation), while holistic/dialectical thinkers (i.e., people in Asian cultures) tend to resolve contradiction by accepting both propositions (i.e., being motivated to approach and avoid argumentation) (Hample & Anagondahalli, 2015).

An alternative perspective offered by Ryan and Louie (2007) suggests that classifying Asian and Western cultures in binary terms, such as "adversarial" versus "harmonious" and "independent" versus "dependent," represents a false dichotomy. Similarly, Chan and Yan (2007) maintain that, although differences in Eastern and Western reasoning styles exist, they are largely a matter of degree, not kind. Reasoning, they suggest, is culture-bound, but the cultural differences reflect adaptations to circumstances, not inherent differences in reasoning ability. Siegel echoes this sentiment, noting that "while different cultures differ in their evaluations of the rational status of particular arguments, 'rationality itself,' is best understood as transcending particular cultures" (cited in Mason, 2007, p. 345). Along similar lines, Hornikx and de Best (2011) found that people from the U.S. and India responded similarly to different types of evidence. Likewise, a considerable amount of research suggests that although cultures differ in the way their members approach and respond to arguments, they are often more similar than they are different (e.g., Santibáñez & Hample, 2015). Perhaps the safest conclusion we can draw from this discussion, then, is that the concept of rationality is trans-cultural, but that culture accounts for differences in specific reasoning and argumentation practices.

From Tweeters to Twits? Is Technology Making Us Stupid?

Technology is our friend. But it can be a "frenemy" too. It not only permeates every aspect of our lives, it may also affect the way we think. Among teens, texting has eclipsed talking by phone in terms of popularity (Pew Research Center, 2015). Tweeting is a national pastime. Laptops and iPads are regular features of the Starbucks landscape and college classrooms. So what's to be made of all this technology use? Does digital technology affect our thinking skills? Critics, it seems, disagree. While some charge that technology hampers critical thinking, others maintain that it aids our ability to think. We examine both sides of this controversy next.

This Is Your Brain on the Web: Naysayers' Criticisms

Both authors are fans of technology. We love having the latest gadgets. That said, we have some misgivings about the effect of technology on our lives. The siren song of technology is seductive. It's shiny and new, but also relentless. Did you know, for example, that the average adult checks her or his cellphone every 6 ½ minutes (Turkle, 2015)? Or that young adults (18–24) exchange an average of 128 texts per day (Burke, 2016)? Some Twitter addicts need a fix every hour or more. Meanwhile, students text during class (c'mon, 'fess up), drivers chatter on their cellphones (hands free, hopefully), and movie goers check their messages in the dark (Argh!).

Some critics warn that technology is making us stupid. Psychologist Jean Twenge (2017), for example, notes that electronic devices seem to have an especially strong ability to deprive us of sleep, which, in turn, is related to compromised thinking and reasoning. What's more, Nicholas Carr (2008) worries that our increasing reliance on the internet actually makes us *think* differently. How so? As we flit from link to link on the web, our thinking process becomes herky-jerky. We skim quickly, rather than reading carefully. We find long tracts of text daunting. Sure, we can access information instantly, but we fail to think about it deeply. In short, Googling, according to Carr, has jumbled our brains.

Worse yet, some critics accuse electronic communication of dumbing down our ability to use language (Baron, 2008). Texting, they charge, is ruining our writing. For example, one study (Cingel & Sundar, 2012) found that the more adolescents texted, the worse their knowledge of grammar. The researchers surmised that this was because texting favors speed over grammatical accuracy. Thus, efficient texting begets poor grammar. Another study (Rosen, Chang, Erwin, Carrier & Cheever, 2010) also found a negative correlation, this time between 18–25 year olds' texting frequency and their formal writing skills.

As further evidence, some critics bemoan the quality of students' essays, which are often littered with text-speak. "Linguistic butchery while texting is one thing," writes Mary Kolesnikova, "in school assignments it is quite another" (2008, p. A-17). We tend to agree. We don't mind getting an email from a student asking "? R U gonna post a study guide ths wk? TIA, Lola" (translation: "Question, are you going to post a study guide this week? Thanks in advance, Lola."). We draw the line, however, at an essay that reads "IDK Y there iz so much RUing ovr Roe v Wade bcz iz like anshnt hstry 2 me. WSIC?" ("I don't know why there is so much arguing over Roe vs Wade because it is ancient history to me. Why should I care?"). To this we reply, "4COL PLZ COHBTLS now!" ("For crying out loud, please, crush our heads between two large stones now!").

e-Litter on the Information Highway

If it is true, as Marshal McLuhan (McLuhan & Fiore, 1967) famously remarked, that "The medium is the message," what are the implications of texting, Instant Messaging, and Twitter? In most cases, these technologies rely on efficiency, not complexity. Lost are the subtleties of language that require more than a few keystrokes. Original thought and novel expression give way to simple acronyms (LOL, OMG, TMI). The range of human emotion is reduced to emojis. Much is superficial, and little is profound. Ideas aren't nuanced, they are homogenized. Grammar and spelling are devalued over the need for speed. The comma has become an endangered species, which is fitting perhaps, considering that its purpose, after all, is to cause one to pause. Don't get us wrong. We don't want to come across as curmudgeons. We'd be hypocrites if we didn't admit to using some text-speak ourselves. It has its place. That said, it is no substitute for the written word when it comes to communicating complex ideas.

Multitasking or Multi-Muddling?

Some of us are clearly better at multitasking than others. On YouTube, for instance, you can watch a guy juggling a chainsaw and balls while riding a unicycle (www.youtube.com/watch?v=MV_Kd9OGqq8). That said, if we think we can do five tasks at once, we are probably kidding ourselves. Research by neuroscientists reveals that the human brain is poorly equipped to perform simultaneous mental tasks (Aritoni, 2007; Rosen, 2008). In fact, people who think they are multitasking are actually switching back and forth from one task to another and, in the end, taking more time, or, in some cases, crashing while texting and driving (Janowich, Mishra & Gazzaley, 2015).

By way of illustration, a BBC study (2005), carried out by the Institute of Psychiatry, found that employees who continually checked their email and phone messages suffered a 10 point drop in intelligence! That decrease, the study noted, was greater than the I.Q. loss associated with smoking marijuana. A study by Foerde, Knowlton, and Poldrack (2006) revealed that multitasking has an adverse effect on learning. They performed fMRI brain scans on people as they performed a solo task or two tasks simultaneously. Those who performed two tasks at once exhibited poorer understanding and recall afterwards.

Finally, you probably know that second-hand cigarette smoke can cause cancer, but were you aware that second-hand technology use can affect your learning? It's true! In one study reported by Gross (2014), students who used laptops in class learned less than those who took their notes in longhand. In another study, not only did the laptop users learn less, but people sitting near them did too. Presumably, Gross (2014) noted, "not only do the laptop-using students end up staring at Facebook, but the students behind them do, as well." For this reason, we know several colleagues who, like Gross, have banned laptops in their classrooms.

Technology May Be Making Us Smarter

In defense of the "always on" generation, let us say that many of technology's detractors sound like a cranky old man shouting "Hey, you kids, get off my lawn!" The disdain some people have for millennials, videogames, social media, and all things electronic may represent a culture war of sorts. People who love traditional books and newspapers may disparage digital media. Labeling the younger generation as narcissistic self-entitled airheads is fashionable among many baby-boomers nowadays.

Stephen Johnson (2005) takes the contrary view. He argues that technology is making us smarter. Television, the internet, and videogames all *enhance* cognitive functioning, according to Johnson. Modern TV shows have more complex plotlines (can you follow *Game of Thrones*?) and reality shows often function as mini-psychology experiments. Meanwhile, many computer games require problem-solving skills and sustained focus.

An important piece of evidence supporting Johnson's position is that I.Q. scores have risen roughly three points per decade, a phenomenon known as the *Flynn effect* (Flynn, 1998). If people are getting dumber, why are I.Q. scores improving? Wendy Williams (1998), a human development expert, suggests that the answer lies in the fact that *crystallized intelligence* (knowledge, facts, information) is decreasing, while *fluid intelligence* (impromptu thinking) is improving. Fluid intelligence requires more openness and flexibility in people's cognitive processes.

Perhaps technology's skeptics are the modern-day equivalents of Chicken Little, crying "the sky is falling." Technology may simply be the latest scapegoat for all of society's woes. Proponents of texting argue that text-speak is creative and liberating. Acronyms and abbreviations are simply a form of language play. Crystal (2008) maintains that texting improves overall literacy and creates opportunities for using language in novel and entertaining ways. Let's face it, people don't need to hold as many facts in their heads nowadays, given that answers to many questions are just a mouse click away. Any good college library offers access to a vast range of full text electronic articles—far more than a bricks and mortar library could ever hold. Al Gore (2007) opined in his book, *The Assault on Reason*, that "reason, logic, and truth seem to play a sharply diminished role in the way America now makes important decisions (p. 1)." An informed citizenry, he emphasized, will depend increasingly on the internet.

We think it is worth being mindful of the potential negative effects of technology. Literacy is not instinctive, it must be passed on from one generation to the next. Hence, complete illiteracy is always but one generation away. At the same time, we should remember that past generations found plenty of ways to fritter away their time; playing bingo, foosball, and Pong, or watching soap operas and reading tabloids. Such activities whiled away the hours, but they were hardly transformative. Today's students text during class. In our day, students passed notes, made paper airplanes, doodled, and lobbed an occasional spitball. Have things changed so much?

Summary

Critical thinking is essential for problem-solving and decision-making. Stupidity and ignorance are impediments to critical thinking, but they are not the same thing. Becoming knowledgeable about public policy controversies and thinking through the arguments and evidence presented on all sides of an issue is vital to a democratic society. At its core, critical thinking is about using reasoning and rationality to make decisions. Not all thinking entails critical thinking; a critical thinker is skeptical, but not overly cynical. Critical thinking is not synonymous with intelligence or creative thinking, though they are assets to one another. Critical thinking is part skill set and part disposition and it sometimes relies on domain-specific knowledge. Culture plays a role in habits of critical thinking, but such differences are matters of degree, not kind. Some have expressed grave concerns about the impact of modern technology on thinking skills. Others counter that technology may be changing our thinking for the better.

References

Abbott, A. (2010). Varieties of ignorance. *American Sociology*, *41*(3), 174–189, doi.org/10.1007/s12108-010-9094-x.

Addley, E. & Connolly, K. (2009, September 27). Roman Polanski arrested in Switzerland 31 years after fleeing trial. *The Guardian*. Retrieved February 23, 2019 from: www.theguardian.com/film/2009/sep/27/roman-polanski-arrest-switzerland-custody.

Alter, C. (2014, July 17). Todd Akin still doesn't get what's wrong with saying 'legitimate rape." *Time*. Retrieved on November 30, 2016 from: http://time.com/3001785/todd-akin-legitimate-rape-msnbc-child-of-rape.

Annenberg Public Policy Center (2016, September 13). *Americans' knowledge of the branches of government is declining*. Retrieved on February 23, 2019 from: www.annenbergpublicpolicycenter.org/americans-knowledge-of-the-branches-of-government-is-declining.

Arbesman, S. (2010, February 28). Warning: Your reality is out of date. *The Boston Globe*. Retrieved on December 12, 2016 from: http://archive.boston.com/bostonglobe/ideas/articles/2010/02/28/warning_your_reality_is_out_of_date.

Arbesman, S. (2012, November 5). Be forewarned: Your knowledge is decaying. *Harvard Business Review*. Retrieved on December 12, 2016 from: https://hbr.org/2012/11/be-forewarned-your-knowledge-i.

Aritoni, L. (2007, February 26). Teens can multitask, but what are costs? Ability to analyze may be affected, experts worry. *Washington Post*, p. A-1. Retrieved on October 18, 2008 from: Lexis-Nexis Academic database.

Bailin, S., Case, R., Coombs, J.R. & Daniels, L.B. (1999a). Common misconceptions of critical thinking. *Journal of Curriculum Studies*, *31*(3), 269–283, doi.org/10.1080/002202799183124.

Bailin, S., Case, R., Coombs, J.R. & Daniels, L.B. (1999b). Conceptualizing critical thinking. *Journal of Curriculum Studies*, *31*(3), 285–302, doi.org/10.1080/002202799183133.

Bargh, J.A. & Williams, E.L. (2006). The automaticity of social life. *Current Directions in Psychological Science*, *15*(10), 1–4, doi: 10.1111/j.0963-7214.2006.00395.x.

Baron, N. (2008). *Always on: Language in an online and mobile world.* New York: Oxford University Press.

BBC (2005, April 22). "Infomania" worse than marijuana. *BBC News.* Retrieved on October 18, 2008 from: http://news.bbc.co.uk/2/hi/uk_news/4471607.stm.

Burke, K. (2016, May 18). How many texts do people send every day? *Text Request.* Retrieved on December 2, 2016 from: www.textrequest.com/blog/many-texts-people-send-per-day.

Carr, N. (2008, July/August). Is Google making us stupid? *Atlantic Monthly.*

Chan, H.M. & Yan, H.K.T. (2007). Is there a geography of thought for East–West differences? Why or why not? *Educational Philosophy and Theory, 39*(4), 383–403, doi.org/10.1111/j.1469-5812.2007.00346.x.

Choi, I., Koo, M. & Choi, J.A. (2007). Individual differences in analytic versus holistic thinking. *Personality and Social Psychology Bulletin, 33*(5), 691–705, doi: 10.1177/0146167206298568.

Cingel, D.P. & Sundar, S.S. (2012). Texting, techspeak, and tweens: The relationship between text messaging and English grammar skills. *New Media & Society, 14*(8), 1304–1320, doi: 10.1177/1461444812442927.

Clancy, K. (2012, August 20). Here is some legitimate science on pregnancy and rape. *Scientific American.* Retrieved on November 30, 2016 from: https://blogs.scientificamerican.com/context-and-variation/here-is-some-legitimate-science-on-pregnancy-and-rape.

CNN (2010, September 6). Kanye West: I'm sorry, Taylor. *The Marquee Blog*, CNN. Retrieved on November 27, 2016 from: http://marquee.blogs.cnn.com/2010/09/06/kanye-west-im-sorry-taylor.

Crystal, D. (2008). *Txtng: The gr8 db8.* Oxford: Oxford University Press.

Daugherty, O. (2018, November 26). Former Border Patrol deputy chief defends using pepper spray: You could put it on your nachos and eat it. *The Hill.* Retrieved on February 26, 2019 from: https://thehill.com/latino/418192-border-patrol-foundation-president-defends-using-pepper-spray-you-could-put-it-on-your.

Davies, W.M. (2006). An 'infusion' approach to critical thinking: Moore on the critical thinking debate. *Higher Education Research & Development, 25*(2), 179–193, doi: 10.1080/07294360600610420.

Demick, B. (2017, September 25). Weiner tells New York judge, "I have no excuses," as he is sentenced to 21 months in sexting case. *Los Angeles Times.* Retrieved on October 2, 2017 from: www.latimes.com/nation/la-na-weiner-sentence-20170925-story.html.

De Oliveira, S. & Nisbett, R.E. (2017). Culture changes how we think about thinking: From "human inference" to "geography of thought." *Perspectives on Psychological Science, 12*(5), 782–790, doi.org/10.1177/1745691617702718.

de Vise, D. (2007, February 10). Students get lesson to chew on: Gum sharing disgusts Montgomery parents, officials. *Washington Post*, p. A-1. Retrieved February 23, 2019 from: www.washingtonpost.com/archive/politics/2007/02/10/students-get-lesson-to-chew-on-span-classbankheadgum-sharing-disgusts-montgomery-parents-officials-span/64494549-f7a0-4465-a5bc-da75740a3658/?noredirect=on&utm_term=.0542f07568da.

Dewey, C. (2017, June 15). The surprising number of American adults who think chocolate milk comes from brown cows. *Washington Post.* Retrieved on September 5, 2017 from: www.washingtonpost.com/news/wonk/wp/2017/06/15/seven-percent-of-americans-think-chocolate-milk-comes-from-brown-cows-and-thats-not-even-the-scary-part/?utm_term=.fcef9162c4b2.

Ennis, R.H. (1992). The degree to which critical thinking is subject specific: Clarification and needed research. In S.P. Norris (Ed.), *The generalizability of critical thinking: Multiple perspectives on an educational ideal* (pp. 21–37). New York: Teachers College Press.

Ennis, R.H. (1996). *Critical thinking.* Upper Saddle River, NJ: Prentice-Hall.

Ennis, R.H. (1997). Incorporating critical thinking into the curriculum: An introduction to some basic issues. *Inquiry, 16*(3), 1–9, doi: 10.5840/inquiryctnews199716312.

Facione, P.A. (2007). Critical thinking: What it is and why it counts. Milbrae, CA: California Academic Press. Retrieved on June 4, 2008 from: www.insightassessment.com/pdf_files/what&why2006.pdf.

Feinberg, M.R. & Tarrant, J.J. (1995). *Why smart people do dumb things: Lessons from the new science of behavioral economics.* New York: Fireside.

Fisher, M. (2007, February 15). Don't gum up sex-ed: Leave instruction to professional teachers. *Washington Post*, p. B-1. Retrieved on February 24, 2019 from: https://search-proquest-com.lib-proxy.fullerton.edu/docview/410095148?accountid=9840.

Flynn, J.R. (1998). IQ gains over time: Toward finding the causes. In U. Neisser (Ed.), *The rising curve: Long term gains in IQ and related measures* (pp. 25–66). Washington, DC: American Psychological Association.

Foerde, K., Knowlton, B.J. & Poldrack, R.A. (2006). Modulation of competing memory systems by distraction. *Proceedings of the National Academy of Science*, *103*(31), 1178–1783, doi.org/10.1073/pnas.0602659103.

Goldberg, J. (2007, July 25). The will of the uninformed. *National Review Online*. Retrieved on June 1, 2010 from: http://article.nationalreview.com/312999/the-will-of-the-uninformed/jonah-goldberg.

Goleman, D. (2006). *Emotional intelligence: 10th anniversary issue, why it can matter more than IQ*. New York: Bantam.

Gore, A. (2007). *The assault on reason*. New York: Penguin Press.

Gorman, N. (2016, September 14). New survey on civic knowledge finds one-third of respondents cannot name all three branches of government. *Education World*. Retrieved February 23, 2019 from: www.educationworld.com/a_news/new-survey-civic-knowledge-finds-one-third-respondents-cannot-name-all-three-branches.

Gover, D. (2014, October 29). Ignorance index reveals most uninformed nations: Italy, U.S., and South Korea top the oblivious list. *International Business Times*. Retrieved on December 11, 2016 from: www.ibtimes.co.uk/ignorance-index-reveals-most-uninformed-nations-italy-us-south-korea-top-oblivious-list-1472319.

Gridley, M.A. (2007). Differences in thinking styles of artists and engineers. *Career Development Quarterly*, *56*(2), 177–182, doi.org/10.1002/j.2161-0045.2007.tb00030.x.

Gross, T. (2014, December 30). This year, I resolve to ban laptops from my classroom. *Washington Post*. Retrieved on December 13, 2016 from: www.washingtonpost.com/posteverything/wp/2014/12/30/this-year-im-resolving-to-ban-laptops-from-my-classroom/?utm_term=.63efb90e496d.

Hample, D. & Anagondahalli, D. (2015). Understandings of arguing in India and the United States: Argument frames, personalization of conflict, argumentativeness, and verbal aggressiveness. *Journal of Intercultural Communication Research*, *44*(1), 1–26, doi: 10.1080/17475759.2014.1000939.

Hind, J. (2008, November 9). Up front: Did I say that? Sienna Miller. *The Observer*, p. 11. Retrieved on August 19, 2010 from: the Lexis-Nexis Academic database.

Holmes, M.A., Resnick, H.S., Kilpatrick, D.G. & Best, C.L. (1996). Rape-related pregnancy. Estimates and descriptive characteristics from a national sample of women. *American Journal of Obstetric Gynecology*, *175*(2), 320–325, doi: 10.1016/S0002-9378(96)70141-2.

Hornikx, J. & de Best, J. (2011). Persuasive evidence in India: An investigation of the impact of evidence types and evidence quality. *Argumentation and Advocacy*, *47*(4), 246–257, doi.org/10.1080/00028533.2011.11821750.

Hsu, K. (1999, August 14). Cambridge police apologize for pepper-spray comments. *The Boston Globe*, p. B2. Retried February 23, 2019 from: http://articles.latimes.com/1999/aug/14/news/mn-70.

Iyengar, S., Hahn, K.S., Bonfadelli, H. & Marr, M. (2009). "Dark areas of ignorance" revisited: Comparing international affairs knowledge in Switzerland and the United States. *Communication Research*, *36*(3), 341–358, doi.org/10.1177/0093650209333024.

Jamieson, K.H. (2016, September 13). American's knowledge of the branches of government is declining. Retrieved on November 27, 2016 from: www.annenbergpublicpolicycenter.org/americans-knowledge-of-the-branches-of-government-is-declining.

Janowich, J., Mishra, J. & Gazzaley, A. (2015). A cognitive paradigm to investigate interference in working memory by distractions and interruptions. *Journal of Visual Experience*, (101), e52226, doi: 10.3791/52226.

Johnson, S. (2005). *Everything bad is good for you*. New York: Penguin Group.

Kolesnikova, M. (2008, May 13). OMG, KMN before my head asplodes. *Los Angeles Times*, p. A-17. Retrieved February 23, 2019 from: http://articles.latimes.com/2008/may/13/news/OE-KOLESNIKOVA13.

Kruger, J. & Dunning, D. (1999). Unskilled and unaware of it: How difficulties in recognizing one's own incompetence lead to inflated self-assessments. *Journal of Personality and Social Psychology*, 77(6), 1121–1134, doi.org/10.1037/0022-3514.77.6.112.

Martin, J.R. (1992). Critical thinking for a human world. In S. Norris (Ed.), *The generalizability of critical thinking: Multiple perspectives on an educational ideal*. New York: Teachers College Press.

Marx, K. (1875/1978). *Critique of the Gotha program*. In R.C. Tucker (Ed.), *The Marx-Engels reader* (2nd Ed., pp. 525–541). New York: W.W. Norton.

Mason, M. (2007). Critical thinking and learning. *Educational Philosophy and Theory*, *39*(4), 339–349, doi.org/10.1111/j.1469-5812.2007.00343.x.

McIntyre, L. (2015). *Respecting truth: Willful ignorance in the internet age*. New York: Routledge.

McLean, B. & Elkind, P. (2003). *The smartest guys in the room: The amazing rise and scandalous fall of Enron*. New York: Portfolio.

McLuhan, M. & Fiore, Q. (1967). *The medium is the massage* [sic]. New York: Random House.

McPeck, J. (1981). *Critical thinking and education*. Oxford: Martin Robinson.

Miller, A.I. (2001). *Einstein, Picasso: Space, time, and the beauty that causes havoc*. New York: Basic Books.

Moore, T. (2004). The critical thinking debate: How general are general thinking skills? *Higher Education Research & Development*, *23*(1), 3–18, doi.org/10.1080/0729436032000168469.

Murphy, L.E. (2011). Invisible ink reveals cool chemistry. *Scientific American*. Retrieved on September 27, 2017 from: www.scientificamerican.com/article/bring-science-home-invisible-ink.

Neuman, S. (2014, February 14). 1 in 4 Americans thinks the sun goes around the earth, survey says. *The Two-Way*, NPR. Retrieved on October 2, 2017 from: www.npr.org/sections/thetwo-way/2014/02/14/277058739/1-in-4-americans-think-the-sun-goes-around-the-earth-survey-says.

Nisbett, R.E. (2003). *The geography of thought: How Asians and Westerners think differently . . . and why*. New York: Free Press.

Norris, S.P. (1985). Synthesis of research on critical thinking. *Educational Leadership*, *42*(8), 40–45.

O'Connor, P. (2014, May 1). Is sex addiction real? *Psychology Today*. Retrieved on September 2, 2017 from: www.psychologytoday.com/blog/philosophy-stirred-not-shaken/201405/is-sex-addiction-real.

Paul, R. (1982). Teaching critical thinking in the 'strong sense': A focus on self deception, world views, and a dialectical mode of analysis. *Informal Logic Newsletter*, *4*(2).

Paul, R.W. (1993). *Critical thinking: What every person needs to survive in a rapidly changing world*. Santa Rosa, CA: Foundation for Critical Thinking.

Paul, R. & Elder, L. (2006). Critical thinking: The nature of critical and creative thought. *Journal of Developmental Education*, *30*(2), 34–35.

Paul, R.W., Elder, L. & Bartell, T. (1997). *California teacher preparation for instruction in critical thinking: Research findings and policy recommendations*. Sacramento, CA: California Commission on Teacher Credentialing, State of California.

Peters, M.A. (2007). Kinds of thinking, styles of reasoning. *Educational Philosophy and Theory*, *39*(4), 350–363, doi.org/10.1111/j.1469-5812.2007.00344.x.

Petty, R.E. & Cacioppo, J.T. (1986). *The Elaboration Likelihood Model of persuasion*. New York: Academic Press. Retrieved on August 19, 2010 from: http://people-press.org/report/645.

Pew Research Center (2015). *Teens relationships survey, Sept. 25–29, and Feb 10–March 2015*. Retrieved on December 2, 2016 from: www.pewresearch.org/fact-tank/2015/08/17/for-teens-phone-calls-are-reserved-for-closer-relationships.

Quinn, V. (1994). In defence of critical thinking. *Journal of Philosophy of Education*, *28*(1), 101–111, doi.org/10.1111/j.1467-9752.1994.tb00316.x.

Rogers, W. (1924). *Illiterate digest*. New York: McNaught Syndicate.

Romano, A. (2011, April 4). How dumb are we? Newsweek gave 1,000 Americans the U.S. citizenship test—38 percent failed. The country's future is imperiled by our ignorance. *Newsweek*, *157*(14), 56.

Rosen, C. (2008, Spring). The myth of multitasking. *The New Atlantis*, *20*, 105–110.

Rosen, L.D., Chang, L.E., Erwin, L., Carrier, L.M. & Cheever, N.A. (2010). The relationship between "textisms" and formal and informal writing among adolescents. *Communication Research*, *37*(3), 420–440, doi: 10.1177/0093650210362465.

Ryan, J. & Louie, K. (2007). False dichotomy? 'Western' and 'Confucian' concepts of scholarships and learning. *Educational Philosophy and Theory*, *39*(4), 401–417, doi.org/10.1111/j.1469-5812.2007.00347.x.

Santibáñez, C. & Hample, D. (2015). Orientations toward interpersonal arguing in Chile. *Pragmatics*, *25*(3), 453–476, doi: 10.1075/prag.25.3.06san.

Somin, I. (2016, June 14). Brexit and political ignorance. *The Washington Post*. Retrieved on September 1, 2017 from: www.washingtonpost.com/news/volokh-conspiracy/wp/2016/06/14/brexit-and-political-ignorance/?utm_term=.c1c8acc9c6e4.

Somin, I. (2017, September 15). Public ignorance about the Constitution. *Washington Post*. Retrieved on September 27, 2017 from: www.washingtonpost.com/news/volokh-conspiracy/wp/2017/09/15/public-ignorance-about-the-constitution/?utm_term=.e05f92cc01f9.

Stampler, L. (2014, February 10). A brief history of Shia LaBeouf copying the work of others. *Time*. Retrieved on November 26, 2016 from: http://time.com/6094/shia-labeouf-plagiarism-scandal.

Stanovich, K.E. & West, R.F. (2008). On the relative independence of thinking biases and cognitive ability. *Journal of Personality and Social Psychology*, *94*(4), 672–695, doi: 10.1037/0022-3514.94.4.672.

Sternberg, R.J. (Ed.) (2002). *Why smart people can be so stupid*. New Haven, CT: Yale University Press.

Swan, J. (2016, September 8). Anthony Weiner is not a sex addict, neither is anyone else. *Psychology Today*. Retrieved on September 2, 2017 from: www.psychologytoday.com/blog/close-and-personal/201609/anthony-weiner-is-not-sex-addict-neither-is-anyone-else-0.

Tavris, C. & Aronson, E. (2007). *Mistakes were made (but not by me): Why we justify foolish beliefs, bad decisions, and hurtful acts*. Orlando, FL: Harcourt.

Tobar, H. (1999, August 14). Cambridge police apologize over pepper spray remark. *Los Angeles Times*. Retrieved February 23, 2019 from: http://articles.latimes.com/1999/aug/14/news/mn-70.

Trigaux, R. (2009, September 27). Madoff, minions feasted on naiveté. *St. Petersburg Times*, p. 1-D. Retrieved February 24, 2019 from: https://search-proquest-com.lib-proxy.fullerton.edu/docview/264343331?accountid=9840.

Turkle, S. (2015). *Reclaiming conversation: The power of talk in a digital age*. New York: Penguin Books.

Twenge, J.M. (2017, September). Has the smartphone destroyed a generation? *The Atlantic*, *320*, 58–65.

Ungar, S. (2008). Ignorance is an under-identified problem. *British Journal of Sociology*, *59*(2), 301–326, doi: 10.1111/j.1468-4446.2008.00195.x.

US Weekly (2009, December 2). Tiger Woods: I have let my family down. *US Weekly*. Retrieved on November 26, 2016 from: www.usmagazine.com/celebrity-news/news/tiger-statement-2009212.

Vance, E. (2007). Graduates lack key skills, report says. *The Chronicle of Higher Education*, *53*(22), 30.

Van Hecke, M.L. (2007). *Blind spots: Why smart people do dumb things*. Amherst, NY: Prometheus Books.

Varnum, M.E.W., Grossmann, I., Kitayama, S. & Nisbett, R.E. (2010). The origin of cultural differences in cognition: The social orientation hypothesis. *Current Directions in Psychological Science*, *19*(1), 9–13, doi: 10.1177/096372140935930.

Williams, W.M. (1998). Are we raising smarter children today? School-and-home-related influences on IQ. In U. Neisser (Ed.), *The Rising curve: Long-term changes in IQ and related measures* (pp. 125–154). Washington, DC: American Psychological Association Books.

Worsham, A.M. & Stockton, A.J. (1986). A model for teaching thinking skills: The inclusion process. *Phi Delta Kappa Fastbacks*, *236*, 7–41. Bloomington, IN: Phi Delta Kappa Educational Foundation (ED 268 532).

Zuckerberg, M. (2006, September 8). *An open letter from Mark Zuckerberg*. Facebook inscription, para. 5. Retrieved February 23, 2019 from: https://fr-fr.facebook.com/notes/facebook/an-open-letter-from-mark-zuckerberg/2208562130.

Chapter 5

Building Blocks of Argument

Don't Build Your Arguments Out of Straw

In the story of the "three little pigs," the quality of the building materials played a crucial role in the porkers' survival. Unlike the houses built of straw and sticks, the house built of bricks withstood the wolf's huffing and puffing. Similarly, the quality of the materials or "building blocks" of an argument affect its integrity. If the basic elements are flimsy, an argument can be demolished easily.

In Chapter 3 we briefly introduced the basic building blocks of arguments: claims, grounds, and warrants. With that chapter as a basis, we turn now to a deeper examination of these concepts, and, in so doing, provide a foundation for constructing solid arguments. Because claims are the starting points of argument, we begin with them.

Claim Spotting: What's Your Point?

Consider the somewhat dubious claims below.

- "During my service in the United States Congress, I took the initiative in creating the Internet" (Al Gore, in a CNN interview with Wolf Blitzer, March 9, 1999).
- "A glass of red wine is equivalent to an hour at the gym . . ." (Daisy Mae Sitch, digital and social media manager at the *Huffington Post*, U.K., July 23, 2015).
- "HIV is not the cause of AIDS" (Peter Duesberg, molecular biologist, 1988).
- "An 'extremely credible source' has called my office and told me that @BarackObama's birth certificate is a fraud" (Tweet by Donald Trump on August 6, 2012).

How much stock would you place in such claims? Are some more suspect than others? Why or why not?

Evaluating claims such as these is essential to being a critical thinker. However, before you can scrutinize claims, you must first be able to identify them. How, then, do you spot a claim? As noted in Chapter 3, a *claim* is the point an arguer is trying to make. It may be a fact a person states, an opinion someone expresses, a request an individual makes, or a course of action an advocate recommends.

One way of recognizing claims is to think about which part of an argument *is the claim* and which part of an argument *supports the claim*. Suppose a cowpoke cautions a greenhorn at a dude ranch about a testy horse. "Buddy may be fixin' to bite you. His ears are pinned back."

The cowpoke's claim or point is "Buddy may be fixin' to bite you." The statement "His ears are pinned back" provides support for this claim.

Another method for spotting claims is to look for "clue words," such as *thus, therefore*, and *hence*. Suppose the cowhand said, "Zeke's had nothing but beans for supper, hence I ain't sleepin' next to him in the bunkhouse." In this case, the claim is in the last part of the sentence. The word "hence" indicates that *the claim follows*. Other clue words and phrases that can help you identify the claim include:

- consequently
- therefore
- thus
- accordingly
- *ergo* (Latin for therefore)
- so . . .
- In sum . . .
- We may conclude that . . .
- It follows that . . .
- The bottom line is . . .
- Which proves that . . .
- The truth of the matter is . . .
- The most likely explanation is . . .
- It is clear that . . . .

Sometimes, however, claims are trickier to identify, especially when they are unstated or implicit. For example, a parent might tell a teenager who has missed a curfew, "Billy, it's 2 am. You know what that means," implying that the teen is grounded. On occasion, arguers will make oblique claims, sometimes purposefully so. Toward the end of a date, for instance, one person might tell another, "The night is young. I've got a nice bottle of wine back at my place." The invitation might be for a glass of wine and friendly conversation, or something more.

When you can't find clue words or have trouble identifying an unstated claim, you can simply ask the arguer for clarification. For instance, in the previous example, the date might clarify the other's intention by asking, "What did you have in mind? Just a glass of wine or something more?" Other questions for clarifying the claim include:

"What exactly is your point?"

"What are you driving at?"

"Get to the point" or "Cut to the chase"

"What's the bottom line?"

"Stop beating around the bush."

Types of Claims: Different Claims for Different Aims

While identifying claims is essential to analyzing arguments, it is only a first step. You also need to be able to distinguish between different types of claims. Let's examine four common types of claims.

Factual Claims: Just the Facts, Jack

John F. Kennedy, the 35th President of the United States, was assassinated on November 22, 1963. That is a fact. You can see it on the 8 mm film shot by Abraham Zapruder, a citizen who happened to be filming the motorcade. It is also a fact that a specific person or persons shot him, even if people disagree on who was responsible. The conclusion of the Warren Commission, which investigated the assassination, is that Lee Harvey Oswald acted alone when he killed JFK. Conspiracy theorists, however, have advanced a number of alternative theories arguing variously that the CIA, the KGB, the Mafia, the Federal Reserve, the Illuminati, and space aliens were to blame.

When it comes to facts, people don't always agree. And, like it or not, when two people are engaged in a factual dispute, at least one of them, and perhaps both, must be wrong. The parties to a factual dispute may not be able to resolve the disagreement then and there. Otherwise, there would be no need for the argument.

A key feature of factual claims is that they are *empirically verifiable*. In other words, there is an objectively true or false answer. Did you know, for example, that the letter "e" is the most frequently used letter in the English language? Cryptographers rely on this fact. Or did you know that approximately 1 in 50 people has a third nipple? Now you do! The claim "a zombie cannot be killed by a stake through the heart" is not empirically verifiable, because zombies don't exist. The same applies to claims about the Easter Bunny or other fictitious characters.

Faux Facts

Even a false claim of fact is, nevertheless, a factual claim. A person who said, "It took 105 years for the Chicago Cubs to win their second World Series" would be making a false factual claim (it took 108 years). If an arguer claimed that Tom Cruise won an Oscar, the arguer would be making a factual claim, but would be mistaken.

Alternative Facts

The year 2016 ushered in a new era of fake news and "alternative facts." Alternative facts, though, are simply falsehoods unless they are empirically verifiable. The use of double-speak, dissembling, spin, and loaded language is not new. However, some factual claims are provably false. When an advocate continues to repeat a claim after it has been proven false, we would argue that the advocate is advancing a lie.

Fortifying Facts

What constitutes a fact in everyday argument often boils down to expert opinion. Unless two arguers can verify a fact for themselves, they have to rely on an authority. For example, Egyptologists generally agree that the Great Pyramid of Giza was built around 2560 BC (Brier & Houdin, 2008). They may be wrong, but the Great Pyramid was built at one time or another. Their expert opinion, for all intents and purposes, provides the best factual estimate available.

To strengthen a factual claim, then, you should identify a qualified source for the claim. If Hank claimed "There are 11 million undocumented immigrants living in the United States," he could be challenged by some other estimate. However, if Hank said "the *Pew Research Center*

Figure 5.1 The New Yorker, 3/7/1977, SKU 116530.
© Dana Fradon/*The New Yorker* Collection/www.cartoonbank.com.

reports that in 2016 there were 10.7 million unauthorized immigrants living in the United States," his claim would be harder to dispute (Pew Research Center, 2018).

Factual claims also can be strengthened by pointing to a *consensus of experts* on the issue. A consensus of opinion represents the unanimity, or near unanimity of experts' views on a subject. For instance, HIV cannot be transmitted casually. This represents the consensus view of epidemiologists (see, for example, the Centers for Disease Control, 2016). An advocate can also point to the *preponderance of evidence* for one side of an issue. A preponderance of evidence refers to the majority or weight of the evidence falling on one side of an issue.

Past, Present, and Future Facts

It's fairly obvious that factual claims can be made about the past (e.g., "Four American presidents have been assassinated while in office") or present (e.g., "Boanthropy is a disorder in which people believe they are cows or oxen"). But did you know that factual claims can also be made about the future? A meteorologist who states "We can expect to see snow this weekend" would be making such a claim. Indeed, by the weekend's end, it will or will not have snowed. Likewise, economists offer forecasts about inflation and sports fans predict scores in upcoming games.

Of course, while such factual claims *will be* empirically verifiable at some point in the future, those about past events can also be "iffy." Consider, for example, the story of Pheidippides. According to some accounts, in 490 BC, this Athenian messenger ran a great distance to report the Greeks' victory over Persia in the Battle of Marathon (hence, the modern-day sporting event). Having delivered his message, he died. Although such a historical event either did or did not take place, verifying it could prove quite difficult. Indeed, Plutarch and Herodotus both wrote about Pheidippides' feat, but modern historians believe that the evidence is doubtful (de Sélincourt & Burn, 1972; Frost, 1979; Marton, Benario & Gynn, 1997).

Factual Estimates

An arguer also can state the probability of a fact. An oncologist might tell a patient, "based on remission rates, there is a one in three chance your cancer will return." An arguer also can offer an average. A person might claim, for instance, that "a typical apple contains 55 calories." If an arguer is plucking numbers out of thin air, however, then the claim is pure conjecture. Claims such as "men think about sex every seven seconds" or "the average person swallows four spiders per year" have no basis in fact (Dixit, 2007; Snopes, 2002, 2014; The Straight Dope, 2000).

Hypothetical Facts?

Consider the following hypothetical claims:

> "If Hitler hadn't tried to fight a war on two fronts (Europe and Russia), Germany would have won World War II."

> "If the *Titanic* had hit the iceberg head on, it wouldn't have sunk."

> "If it weren't for Russian meddling in the 2016 presidential election, Hillary Clinton would have won."

Such "what if" statements are common, but are they *factual* claims? The answer lies in a point we made earlier. Remember, factual claims must be empirically verifiable. To the extent that a hypothetical claim is based on conjecture, it is really a *judgment* claim (which we consider next). In the legal arena, for example, a judge might ask a hypothetical question of a lawyer to clarify a legal issue. The lawyer's answer represents his or her interpretation of the law, but opposing counsel may disagree.

People sometimes argue about hypothetical scenarios just for fun. In such cases, *opinions* may be offered, but no factually correct answer is possible. How many more home runs would the baseball player Ted Williams have hit had he not missed three seasons during World War II and almost two seasons during the Korean War? There is no correct answer to such questions. If you are speculating about what *didn't happen*, you could just as easily speculate that Williams might have suffered a career-ending injury and retired prematurely.

Hypothesis Contrary to Fact

Other hypothetical arguments are more problematic, especially when a fallacy known as *hypothesis contrary to fact* is involved. This fallacy is committed when people begin an argument with an assumption that they already know to be false. If the initial premise is false, any inference drawn from the premise is meaningless. A factual premise that is false presumes a world that doesn't exist. Such a premise can only lead to an intellectual exercise about an imaginary world. In Philip Roth's novel *The Plot Against America*, for example, Charles Lindbergh, the anti-Semitic aviation hero, defeats Franklin Delano Roosevelt in the 1940 presidential election. As a result, a peace pact is signed with Germany and Jewish people in the U.S. are widely persecuted.

In a related vein, some factual claims may posit a premise that can never be proven. The age-old question "How many angels can dance on the head of a pin?" illustrates this problem. Because the existence of angels cannot be proven, disputes over what they might or might not do are pointless. Should someone pose this question to you, simply respond by asking "Are they fat angels or thin angels?" or "What type of dance?"

Fact–Inference Confusion

People frequently confuse facts with inferences or opinions. An example serves to illustrate this point: Several years ago, after having dinner with another couple, one of the authors and his wife had an interesting conversation.

"Your friend is having an affair," the author's wife declared. "He's cheating on his wife." The author was caught off guard. He'd been friends with the couple for years. They seemed so happy. "Did she *tell* you?" he asked. "I just know," his wife insisted. "You can tell by looking. He's lost weight. He's got a new hairstyle. Did you see the Tommy Bahama shirt he was wearing?" The author couldn't deny that she had her facts straight. But did the facts justify an inference about an affair? The author's wife seemed to be confusing facts with inferences, and making a big inference at that. And she's not alone. People often confuse the two.

To clarify, a fact is empirically verifiable ("your tires have less than 2/32 of an inch of tread depth"), whereas an *inference* goes beyond the available facts to reach a conclusion ("your tires are unsafe"). Of course, the interpretation reached may or may not be true. As it turns out, the author's wife was right—the friend *was* having an affair. Inferences, however, are not always so reliable.

A key skill you should develop to become a more critical thinker and effective arguer is to recognize the distinction between facts and inferences. That way, when someone you are arguing with makes an inference as if it were a fact, you can point it out. Don't allow someone to smuggle in opinions posing as facts. Ask for empirical proof when an arguer presents a claim as a fact. For practice, try distinguishing facts from inferences in Box 5.1.

Box 5.1   Fact or Inference?

Consider the series of claims below. Which are facts and which are inferences? Remember, a false claim about a fact is nonetheless a factual claim.

The sun rises in the east and sets in the west.

Pisces are artistic, intuitive, and musical.

This painting is a forgery.

Approximately 14 percent of Americans live in poverty.

In chess, a bishop may only move diagonally.

Nature is neither cruel nor kind, nature is indifferent.

The Pacific Ocean is the largest of the five oceans.

Cigarettes are more dangerous than marijuana.

There is intelligent life elsewhere in the universe.

(Note: the correct answers can be found at the end of the chapter.)

Facts Matter, Even in a "Post-Fact" Society

In 2008, Farhad Manjoo proclaimed that we live in a "post-fact society" (Manjoo, 2008), a theme that was echoed during the 2016 presidential election when media pundits called this the "post-truth" era. Much to our dismay, the *Oxford Dictionary* joined in, declaring "post-truth" the word of the year for 2016 (Wang, 2016). And, sadly, perhaps they're right. To be sure, some arguers play fast and loose with the truth. In the U.S., consultants and lobbyists can be hired to create disinformation campaigns. In fact, Rabin-Havt, of Media Matters, warned of "a growing industry that exists to create and disseminate fictitious public policy 'facts' on behalf of business and ideological interests willing to pay for them" (2016, p. xi). Outside the U.S., fake news is propagated by paid trolls, not a few of whom work for foreign governments (Chen, 2016). Their goal, as noted by Adrian Chen, is to "overwhelm social media with a flood of fake content, seeding doubt and paranoia, and destroying the possibility of using the Internet as a democratic space" (2016, para. 4).

Why Do People Ignore the Facts?

In 2005, comedian Stephen Colbert coined the term "truthiness" to refer to claims that people believe, not because they are true but because they want them to be true. And he might have been on to something. Research suggests that people ignore facts as a type of defense mechanism. One study (Campbell & Friesen, 2015), for example, found that when evaluating arguments on controversial issues, people tend to embrace facts that suit their side and ignore those that do not. In addition, when the facts are against them, people are more inclined to say, "It's a question of morality, not facts." As the study's authors observed, "When people's beliefs are threatened, they often take flight to a land where facts do not matter" (Campbell & Friesen, 2016, para. 10).

Ignoring Facts Doesn't Change Them

Ignoring facts in an ostrich-like fashion, however, doesn't make them go away. The earth is not flat, even though members of the Flat Earth Society claim that it is (http://theflatearthsociety.org). The Holocaust occurred, even if Holocaust deniers refuse to believe it. Abortion is not the cause of California's drought, even though assemblywoman Shannon Grove of Bakersfield claimed that was the case (White, 2015).

Consequences for Ignoring Facts: Measles and Pizza

Sometimes, as the old sayings suggest, "ignorance is bliss" and "the truth hurts," but what about the alternative? When people ignore facts or succumb to fake news, there can be serious negative consequences. Take vaccinations, for example. What happened when rumors suggested that childhood immunizations lead to autism? Scores of parents refused to have their children vaccinated. The result: the worst outbreak of measles in 20 years and the worst epidemic of whooping cough in 70 years (Salzberg, 2015).

As another example, a fellow named Edgar Welch followed stories on Twitter (#PizzaGate) about a pizza parlor that was supposedly a front for a child sex trafficking operation (Fisher, Cox & Hermann, 2016). According to the fake stories, the pedophile ring was being secretly run by Hillary Clinton! Welch drove cross-country, stormed the pizza parlor with an AR-15, and fired several rounds before being arrested.

Facts Still Matter

If you bemoan the decline of fact-based reasoning, as we do, don't count facts out just yet. Alex Mantzarlis, of the International Fact-Checking Network, admits that although facts have taken a beating, they still matter. As evidence, the proliferation of fact-checking websites suggests that people do care about the veracity of public figures' claims. Better yet, a study by Nyhan and Reifler (2015a) revealed that politicians who were reminded that they would be subject to fact-checking were less likely to make false claims. These same researchers found that the public views fact-checking quite favorably (Nyhan & Reifler, 2015b). Not surprisingly, more educated, more informed people held the most favorable attitudes toward fact-checking. What's more, the way in which information is presented (i.e., graphical versus textual) may diminish misperceptions of facts (Nyhan & Reifler, 2018). As such, Nyhan (2016) concluded optimistically that "despite all the hand-wringing, we do not seem to have entered a post-truth era" (para. 11).

That said, more real-time fact checking of claims would help. Fortunately, some networks are moving in this direction by incorporating fact-checking into chyrons (scrolling text at the bottom of the screen). Google, Facebook, and other platforms have agreed to crack down on fake news, but users bear responsibility for distinguishing fake from real stories too. Just because a friend shared a post or a tweet doesn't mean it's true. (For more advice on avoiding faux news, see Box 5.2.)

Box 5.2   Evaluating News in the Post-Truth Era

What do these news headlines have in common? "Hillary Sold Weapons to ISIS." "Kim Jong Un Voted Sexiest Man Alive." "Pope Francis endorsed Donald Trump for President." First, all three were reported by at least one major news outlet. Second, all three are fake. Made up news stories have been around a long time, but the 2016 presidential election ushered in a new era of counterfeit journalism. Some fake news sites describe themselves as satirical, others bill themselves as fantasy news. Some stories are created by trolls in foreign countries (Timberg, 2016). They have an impact too. As an example, in the months leading up to the presidential election in 2016, fake news stories were read and shared more than legitimate news stories (Lee, 2016).

When it comes to online news, it is important to be able to separate the wheat from the chaff. Regrettably, many people lack what is called "news literacy." Most people can't distinguish between real news and sponsored (paid) content. Indeed, a Stanford University study (Stanford History Education Group, 2016; also see Crook, 2016) described the ability of students to differentiate the quality of news sources as "dismaying" and "bleak." News recipients bear some responsibility for testing the veracity of news stories before accepting them or passing them along. Here are some suggestions for distinguishing real from fake news.

- Beware of shocking headlines. Legitimate news outlets don't rely on incredulous headlines to attract eyeballs. Do a Google search of a sensational headline to see if other serious news sources are reporting the same thing.
- Just because your friend or family member shares a link or forwards a message doesn't mean it's true. Your friend or family member may be uninformed or a victim of trolling. Ask who the primary source for a news story is. Second-hand and third-hand sources may be unreliable.
- Don't trust the headline. Never "like" or "share" a story without first reading the actual article. According to a study by Gabielkov, Ramachandran, Chaintreau, and Legout (2016) "59% of the shared URLs are never clicked" (p. 7).
- Look for slanting. The more biased and one-sided the point of view being offered, the less likely it is that you are dealing with a serious journalistic outlet.
- Click the "About" tab on a website's homepage to learn more about the source, site, or organization.
- Don't get all your news from one place. Incorporate variety into your news reading or viewing habits. Don't rely on just one medium, such as radio or social media, for news content. Similarly, don't depend exclusively on one network or website. Check out the BBC, Al Jazeera, or other foreign news channels to get a fuller picture of events. See how different newspapers, such as the U.K.'s *The Guardian* or India's *Times of India*, cover an international story.
- Don't rely on social media exclusively for news. Social media news feeds are selective. They don't provide you with the whole picture. Facebook, Instagram, and Twitter rely on sophisticated algorithms to provide content *you want to see* that is *consistent with your point of view* to ensure you keep coming back for more (Kolowich, 2016).

- Check the suffix (.com, .org) at the end of a website's name. If the suffix is ".co" that is a red flag. For example, abcnews.com is genuine, but abcnews.com.co is not. Most legitimate news sites will have .com, .org, .gov, .net, or .edu as their suffix.
- Pay attention to the site's name too. For instance, cnn.com is real, cnn-channel is not. Some well-known fake news sites include Empire News, National Report, World News Daily Report, and the News Examiner website.
- When questioning the authenticity of images, use reverse image searching. Google Image Search (https://images.google.com) and TinEye (www.tineye.com) can be used to check on a particular image. Just drag and drop an image into the search bar.
- Rely on fact-checking websites to determine whether factual claims are true or not. There are now more than 100 fact-checking outlets (Adair, 2016). Here are some of our favorites:

  o FactCheck.org is a nonpartisan nonprofit site run by the University of Pennsylvania's Annenberg Public Policy Center.
  o Fact Checker is operated by the Washington Post and awards 1–4 "Pinocchios" based on a statement's veracity.
  o GossipCop.com is useful for fact-checking celebrity gossip.
  o www.hoax-slayer.com focuses on debunking email scams, spam, and phishing schemes.
  o Opensecrets.org monitors campaign contributions and the role of money in politics.
  o Politicfact.com is known for its "truth-o-meter." The site, which was awarded a Pulitzer Prize in 2009, is hosted by the *Tampa Bay Times*, whose reporters and editors fact-check news stories.
  o Snopes.com is dedicated to debunking urban myths and legends along with pop culture phenomena.
  o Truthorfiction.com examines the veracity of various rumors, viruses, and hoaxes.

Even the fact-checkers get it wrong from time to time (Mantzarlis, 2015). There have also been accusations that the fact-checkers themselves harbor biases (Hemingway, 2011; Marietta, Barker & Bowser, 2015).

Value and Judgment Claims

A second type of claim that occupies center stage in many disputes is a *value* or *judgment* claim. Such claims involve matters of taste and opinion (e.g., "Macs are better than P.C.s" or "Chimpanzees make terrible pets."). Value claims can also reflect judgments about what is moral or immoral ("human trafficking is abhorrent"), wise or unwise ("censorship is un-American"), or beautiful or ugly ("Victoria Falls is the most magnificent waterfall in the world"). Consider the following brief argument.

Lloyd: "I love rap music."
Jane: "Rap music endorses drug use, condones violence, encourages misogyny, and promotes crass materialism."
Lloyd: "I know. That's why I love it!"

As you can see, both arguers are offering judgments about rap music. A key feature of value or judgment claims is that they possess an *evaluative dimension*. That is, they reflect a *positive or negative attitude* toward a specific idea, person, or thing. And, unlike factual claims, value or judgment claims always rely on some sort of inference. All of the following are value claims:

- Tammy's prom dress is ugly.
- Democracy is the worst form of government except for all those others that have been tried (Winston Churchill).
- 60 is the new 40.
- Jon Hamm is dreamy.
- Child molesters are the scum of the earth.

Because value claims may be supported by facts, it is important as critical thinkers to differentiate the claim from the proof for the claim. If, for example, an arguer said, "By virtue of her 20 Oscar nominations, Meryl Streep is the greatest actress in the world," the *value claim* is that she is the greatest actress in the world. The factual *support for the claim* is that she has received 20 academy award nominations.

All Opinions Are Not Equal

Everyone, as they say, is entitled to his or her opinion. That doesn't mean, however, that everyone's opinion is equally good. If all opinions are equal, what if it is one person's opinion that *not all* opinions are equal? If you think Jonah Hill is better looking than Ryan Gosling or that Whoopi Goldberg is more attractive than Kerry Washington, you are entitled to your opinion, but you are in a club of one. Just because opinions are subjective, doesn't mean that all opinions carry the same weight.

Sometimes news shows dredge up marginally qualified pundits to represent one side or the other in a controversy. They do so because they feel obliged to present both sides of the issue. In doing so, however, they may lend more credence to a dissenting view than it deserves. For example, when news media discuss climate change, they usually feature a pro-warming and an anti-warming expert. Yet, according to a Stanford University study, 97 percent of climatologists who regularly publish articles in scholarly journals agree that man-made climate change is a very real phenomenon (Anderegg, Prall, Harold & Schneider, 2010).

Wimping Out on Value Disputes

People often avoid value disputes by saying "I suppose we'll just have to agree to disagree." But they *don't* have to. Instead, they can argue meaningfully about their subjective preferences. Granted, some opinions aren't worth arguing about because they are purely subjective, e.g., "I like Coke, you prefer Pepsi." When it comes to taste buds, each to his or her own. But some value disputes matter. Suppose, for instance, that Roy and Dale are redecorating their living room and they need to agree on a color scheme. Not all colors go equally well together. Based on the color wheel, opposite colors tend to be complimentary. Thus, green and tan would be a better match for their room than green and gray. That values are subjective is no reason to avoid value disputes. In Chapter 13 we delve into how to build and refute a value case. For now, it is enough to understand the difference between value claims and other types of claims.

Policy Claims

A dentist tells a patient, "You should brush and floss your teeth more regularly."

The patient asks, "All of them?"

"No," says the dentist, "only the ones you want to keep."

In this conversation, the dentist starts by making a policy claim. Policy claims advocate courses of action such as legislative changes, revisions to a company's policies, or alterations in an individual's behavior. When you hear someone complain, "There oughta be a law . . ." or "Don't just stand there—do something!" the person is advocating a policy claim. For our purposes, policy claims also include commands and directives. A sign on a restaurant door that states "No shirt, no shoes, no service" tells diners what they must do if they want to eat there.

Notice that, often, the presence of the word *should* signifies a policy proposition. Thus, while "Tattoos are made with ink" is a factual claim and "Tattoos are cool" is a value claim, "You should get a rib tattoo" is a policy claim. Also notice that, in addition to advocating that someone should take an action, policy claims might advise against a particular course of action. For example, "Never sign a contract without reading it first" is a policy claim. The statement "Never wear flip flops to a job interview" is a policy claim as well.

As with fact and value claims, policy claims may be qualified or conditional. For example, a person could be in favor of drone strikes, but only against targets that represent a clear immediate threat to their country or its citizens.

Values Are Implicit in Policy Claims and Vice Versa

Although value claims and policy claims are distinct, the two are intertwined. Specifically, when an arguer advocates a policy claim, he or she is tacitly endorsing a value claim. For instance, to say that "Capital punishment should be abolished" also implies that it is wrong or immoral. To claim that "state laws should be enacted prohibiting parents from spanking their children," suggests that spanking children is physically and/or emotionally harmful.

The reverse is also the case; value claims often tacitly endorse policies. A person who stated "Abortion is murder" would, in all likelihood, favor a ban on abortion. An animal rights activist who believed eating animals was immoral would probably advocate a vegan diet as well. It would be difficult, indeed, to have a policy dispute that did not entail value concerns or a value dispute without policy implications.

Definitional Claims

A fourth and final type of claim is a *definitional* claim, which centers on the proper classification of things. By way of illustration, what is the difference between a vegetarian and a vegan? Is it cut and dried? One of the authors once met a woman who claimed she was a "vegetarian." The following polite, yet perplexing conversation ensued.

Author: "Do you ever eat dairy products or eggs?"
Vegetarian: "Well, sometimes I have eggs, or cheese, and I like cream in my coffee."

Author:	"So you're more of a lacto-ovo vegetarian—dairy products and eggs are okay but you don't eat meat?"
Vegetarian:	"Actually, I eat fish. And I have chicken once in a while, but not very often."
Author:	"I thought that vegetarians didn't eat anything 'with a face'."
Vegetarian:	"I don't. At least, not very often."

In short, the woman wasn't so much a vegetarian as she was an infrequent meat eater.

Although definitional disputes are less common than fact, value, or policy disputes, they are important nonetheless. That's because it is often necessary to agree on definitions before a value or policy argument can proceed. If arguers don't agree on what they are arguing about, the argument serves little purpose.

Race: It's Not a Black or White Issue

An illustration of a definitional controversy surrounds the concept of "race" and what it does or does not represent. To what does "race" refer? The highly charged nature of the construct is exemplified by clashes over casting decisions in Hollywood. The choice to cast Zoe Saldana, a multi-ethnic actress, to play Nina Simone in a biopic about the late singer's life prompted outrage by some who felt Saldana was not "black enough" for the role (@NinaSimoneMusic). Conversely, others complained that a black actor, John Boyega, should not have been cast as a storm trooper in *Star Wars: The Force Awakens*. Some went so far as to call the choice "white genocide" (@BoycottStarWarsVII). In an

"It all depends on how you define 'chop.'"

Figure 5.2 The New Yorker 10/5/1998, SKU:117721.

© Tom Cheney/*The New Yorker* Collection/www.cartoonbank.com.

even more bizarre twist, Rachel Dolezal, the former head of the NAACP in Spokane, resigned following the revelation that she was white, not black, as she had claimed to be. While Dolezal acknowledged that she was born white, she said she identified as black.

Why is race such a vexing construct? While race was once considered a biological characteristic, most scientists now agree that it is a social construct (Gannon, 2016). Nevertheless, many people still believe that race refers to distinct biological groups. Many subscribe to an artificial definition of race, dubbed the "single-drop" theory. If a person has any African ancestry, so the theory goes, the person is considered African-American. Geneticists, however, have traced all human DNA back to an ancestral "Adam" and "Eve" who emerged from the Rift Valley, in Africa, some 50,000 years ago (Wade, 2006). Thus, according to the single-drop theory, all humankind is African.

Alas Pluto, You Will Be Missed

In the scientific realm, an example of a definitional controversy involved demoting Pluto from a full-fledged planet to a "dwarf planet." Pluto had been considered a planet since its discovery in 1930. In 2006, however, the International Astronomical Union kicked Pluto to the curb of the solar system (Bartlett, 2006). Why ditch Pluto? Because to meet the new definition of a planet, an object in our solar system must a) orbit the sun, which Pluto does, b) have sufficient mass or gravity to form a spherical shape, which Pluto has, and c) sweep up asteroids, comets, and other debris in its orbit—which Pluto, sadly, does not do (Morring, 2006). Pluto is only one of many objects residing in the Kuiper Belt, some of which are nearly the size of Pluto. Pluto is unable to absorb these other objects in its path. That didn't seem to bother politicians in Illinois and New Mexico, however, who voted that Pluto is an official planet every time it passes over their respective states. Why? Clyde Tombaugh, born in Illinois, discovered Pluto while residing in New Mexico. What's more, he did it on March 13th, known as "Pluto Day" in Illinois and "Pluto Planet Day" in New Mexico (Wheedleton, 2010). Meanwhile, it's possible that Pluto might, once again, orbit the sun with dignity. Indeed, some scientists have proposed new definitions, hoping to bring Pluto back into the fold (see Bowerman, 2017).

Everyday Definitions Versus Specialized Fields

Quite often what passes for a fact in everyday life is actually open to definition in specialized fields. What is the tallest mountain in the world? Most people would say "Mt. Everest" without giving it another thought. Measured from *sea level* to its summit, Everest is the *highest* mountain on Earth at 29,028 feet. However, measured from its *base* to its summit, Mauna Kea near Hawaii is *taller* at 33,476 feet. Here's the catch; much of Mauna Kea's height lies below the surface of the ocean. Complicating the definition even more, a mountain in Ecuador, Chimborazo, has the distinction of being even taller, when measured from the *center of the Earth* to its summit. The Earth is not a perfect sphere. It bulges at the equator. As a result, if one ran a tape measure from the Earth's exact center to the summit of Chimborazo, the distance would be greater than that for Everest or Mauna Kea measured in the same way. Another way of putting it is that Chimborazo sticks out farther into space. The point is that it all depends on one's definition. Geologists might parse such a definition.

Other examples of definitional disputes involve distinguishing between "nudity" and "obscenity," whether water-boarding is a form of torture, and what constitutes "art." Ambiguity surrounding definitions creeps into many discussions. When people say they favor a "flat tax" is it clear what they mean? With respect to health care coverage, is everyone clear on what a "single payer" or "public option" means? Do people who favor a ban on "assault weapons" know exactly which weapons fit the definition? If someone favors "euthanasia" or assisted suicide, exactly what would he or she support; *passive* euthanasia, which involves withholding extraordinary life-saving measures, or *active* euthanasia, such as administering a lethal injection? Time spent clarifying definitions at the outset of an argument may prevent a good deal of frustration later on.

Confusing Claims

We hope you now have a better grasp of different types of claims that might be advanced in an argument. As we noted earlier, being able to distinguish between factual, value, policy, and definitional claims can help you avoid problems. By way of example, a common error involves confusing factual claims (what *is* the case) with policy claims (what *should* be the case). Consider the following exchange:

Mona: "I think handguns should be banned in all 50 states."

Zach: "That'll never happen."

Mona: "I didn't say it *would* happen, I said it *should*. Guns kill almost 10,000 people per year in the U.S., compared with about 40 gun deaths per year in England."

In this example, Zach has committed what is known as a *should/would fallacy* by responding to a *policy* claim ("I think handguns should be banned in all 50 states") as if it were a *factual* claim ("Handguns will be banned in all 50 states"). Had Zach recognized that Mona's argument was based on a policy claim, he could have countered her argument more effectively. He could have argued, for example, that Chicago has some of the toughest gun laws in the U.S., and it also has one of the highest murder rates.

Another common mistake involves confusing a *factual* claim with a *value* or *judgment* claim. Consider the dialogue below:

Betty: "Abortion is murder, plain and simple, because human life begins at the moment of conception."

Roy: "How do you know when human life begins? And what do you define as human life?"

Betty: "If a fetus is *human*, and it's *alive*, then it's a living human being. It's just an earlier stage of human life."

Roy: "But there *isn't* a fetus at the moment of conception. There is a one-celled zygote. Cell division and cell specialization haven't occurred. There is no brain, no heart, no central nervous system. There isn't a person."

Betty: "A zygote already has its own unique DNA. All the ingredients necessary for human life are present in a zygote."

Roy: "The necessary ingredients may be present, but they aren't sufficient to guarantee human life. The zygote has to form an embryo, and the embryo has to attach itself to the uterine wall before there is a fetus. And the fetus still wouldn't possess conscious awareness."

Betty: "Those are all stages of human life, just as childhood or adolescence are stages of human life. As for awareness, an infant lacks the cognitive development of an adult, but it is no less human."

In this example, both Roy and Betty are arguing *as if* they are stating facts, but a decision about when human life begins is a matter of judgment. The judgment may be based on facts, but the interpretation of those facts requires judgment. Accordingly, to make coherent arguments or refute others' arguments, one must respond to the specific type of claim being made.

Proof: The Grounds for Arguments

Now that you understand what claims are, let's examine the second part of an argument: grounds. A helpful way to understand the relationship between claims and grounds is to think about a house and its foundation. Specifically, in the same way that a house needs a solid foundation, a claim requires solid support. When someone asks you, "What's your proof?" or "Who says?" or "How do you know?" the person is asking about *grounds* or support for the claim you are making. Grounds, then, are synonymous with proof. If you find yourself presenting an argument, there are a number of ways you might prove your claim (see Hitchcock, 2005). You might, for example, use studies, reports, eyewitness accounts, facts and figures, expert opinion, nonverbal cues, controlled experiments, physical evidence or other artifacts to prove your case. In addition, demonstrations or your own personal experience can function as proof, as well as examples drawn from others' experiences. Importantly, premises that have previously been accepted by your target audience can also serve as grounds. For instance, if your audience agrees that chess is a sport, you might convince them that chess should be in the Olympics too. Don't laugh. Did you know that the Olympics used to award medals for painting, literature, and music?

As noted in Chapter 3, grounds, like claims, can often be spotted using "clue words." Specifically, grounds often follow words such as "because," "since," "according to . . ." "given that . . ." and "based on . . .." Of course, if you are unsure about another person's grounds you can always ask the person, "Why do you think so?" or "And you know this how?" or "Got any evidence to back that up?"

Multi-Grounded Arguments

It also bears repeating that some arguments contain multiple grounds. Imagine, for a moment, that Sonia and Gigi are roommates. Sonia has been out on a string of bad dates. They have the following conversation:

Sonia: "My last dinner date was a disaster. The guy was wearing a fanny pack, talked about his old girlfriend, ate food off my plate without asking, and both of his credit cards were declined."

Gigi: "No way!"

Sonia: "Guess who paid? Not Mr. Overdrawn."

Gigi: "You should try an online dating service. You'll have a bigger selection of guys, you can screen out losers without having to meet them face to face, and it's a lot safer."

Notice that Sonia provided four different reasons why her last dinner date was a nightmare (i.e., the fanny pack, the topic of conversation, food pilfering, and the overdrawn credit cards). Likewise, Gigi provided three different grounds to support her recommendation that Sonia try an online dating service (i.e., more choices, pre-screening, and safety). Clearly, arguers often have more than one reason for advocating a claim.

Have You Got a Warrant?

With a firm grasp of claims and grounds behind us, let's now examine the third part of an argument: the warrant. To help understand what a warrant is and does, consider an example from the world of law enforcement. Specifically, in the same way that a search warrant gives police the right to search a person's residence, providing authorization to cross the threshold from door to domicile, you might think of the warrant in an argument as authorizing the inferential leap that listeners make when connecting the claim to the grounds. A similar thing happens in the world of humor. For example, when the comedian Tim Vine says "Velcro . . . what a rip off!"—you need to know that Velcro makes a ripping sound. Otherwise, you won't get his joke. In a nutshell, then, understanding an argument "entails a cognitive process of *moving* from the grounds to the claim (Brockriede & Ehninger, 1960, p. 44). It takes some time, even if it is milliseconds, to grasp the warrant. A person hears an argument, the brain starts whirring, then the person thinks "Oh . . . I get it."

Of course, when making arguments, an arguer can state the warrant explicitly, in which case the listener doesn't have to connect the dots. In most cases, however, warrants are unstated (Brockriede & Ehninger, 1960). To make sense, they must be implicitly understood by the recipient of an argument. That is, the receiver must decipher the connection between the grounds and the claim. Interestingly, people are better at understanding warrants than they are at articulating them. What's more, an argument often "sounds" like a good one, or a bad one, even if a person can't clearly identify the warrant. This suggests that making sense of arguments occurs at a "deep" level of consciousness. It also suggests that people are innately rational, but not strictly logical in their thinking.

Deciphering Warrants

Of the three basic elements of an argument, the warrant is the most difficult to identify. Claims and grounds, as we've seen, can be spotted by looking for clue words. In contrast, because warrants are usually unstated, they lack these linguistic markers or "clue words" (Keith & Beard, 2008). As such, the implicit nature of warrants often leads to confusion in everyday arguments. If you can't grasp the warrant, you might be left saying, "Huh? I don't get it." Imagine, for example, that someone told you, "The Boswells probably believe in ghosts because they drive a hybrid car." If you're like us, you'd be left scratching your head. In contrast, consider the statement, "The Boswells must be environmentally conscious because they drive a hybrid car." In this case, you would have no trouble making the connection.

A receiver might fail to grasp the inferential leap for a variety of reasons. To name a few, the warrant might be based on a value assumption that the receiver does not share, a belief the receiver does not hold, or a cultural norm about which the receiver is unaware. In China, for example, belching can indicate an appreciation for good food. If you didn't know that, however, imagine what you'd think if a Chinese person told you, "Zhang is a wonderful guest. He burped at the dinner table." For these reasons and others, it is not uncommon for a listener to draw the *wrong* inference by making a different connection than the one that the arguer intended. The following exchange illustrates this problem.

Mabel: "Our town recently added a dozen more police officers and reports of breaking and entering increased by 50 percent."

Chuck: "Wow, so the new cops are committing a lot of burglaries."

Mabel: "No, citizens are more willing to report break-ins because they believe the police will be able to do something about it."

Chuck: "Or maybe your town hired a lot of bad cops."

The recipient of an argument *needn't agree* with the warrant in order to make sense of it, but a person must be able to make sense of another's warrant to disagree effectively.

All-Purpose Warrants

Some tools, like a hammer, are general-purpose tools. Others, such as a torque wrench, have more specialized functions. Warrants are like tools in this respect. Some are fairly generic, others more specific, as you'll see in the sections that follow.

Warrants Based on Reasoning

Among the most common warrants are those based on *inductive reasoning*, which simply refers to ordinary reasoning as opposed to formal logic or deduction. *Analogies*, for example, are quite

"The DNA sample from the mink fibres found in the suspect's car matched

the DNA sample from the mink coat found at the scene of the crime,

so I'm thinking, maybe these minks were twins?"

Figure 5.3 The New Yorker, 3/16/2009, SKU:132616.
© Zachary Kanin/*The New Yorker* Collection/www.cartoonbank.com.

common in everyday reasoning. People readily identify similarities between things. As an illustration, a pro-life advocate might claim that abortion is wrong by making an analogy to the Holocaust. Just as the Holocaust involved exterminating Jewish lives on a massive scale, she or he might argue, the practice of abortion destroys infant lives on an immense scale. The warrant hinges on the extent to which the two are analogous or comparable with one another.

Sign reasoning is another form of inductive reasoning. Medical symptoms, for example, may signify certain ailments. Jaundice, or yellowing of the eyes and skin, dark urine, and excessive fatigue are indicators of liver damage. As such, by observing such symptoms or signs, a doctor might be able to make a preliminary diagnosis.

Yet another type of inductive reasoning involves *cause–effect* inferences. A causal inference assumes that one thing or event (cause or antecedent) brings about another (effect or consequent). A coroner, for example, must determine whether a person died of natural causes or as a result of foul play. When an airplane crashes, investigators try to determine the cause of the crash. Was it pilot error, a mechanical failure, or an act of terrorism?

Still another form of reasoning involves *generalization*. People have a natural tendency to recognize patterns. If a kindergartner named Billy bites a kid on the first day of class, then bites another kid on the second day of class, it won't be long before the other kids start calling him "Billy the Biter." Similarly, a prosecuting attorney might argue that repeated offenses indicate that a criminal is unredeemable.

Although all of these forms of reasoning can be convincing, keep in mind that they are also subject to error. An analogy, for example, might be a *faulty analogy*, and signs can be fallible. Likewise, causal reasoning is subject to error. For example, a person might mistake coincidence for causation. Most superstitions operate this way. Finally, while some generalizations are highly dependable, others are not. False cultural stereotypes, for example, are based on a fallacy called a *sweeping generalization*. We'll have more to say about these and other types of reasoning in Chapter 6. For now, it is enough to know that analogies, signs, causal inferences, and generalizations often serve as warrants.

Other Common Warrants

Folk wisdom and proverbs, such as "look before you leap," "half a loaf is better than none," and "a stitch in time saves nine," can also serve as warrants. Of course, folk wisdom is sometimes contradictory. The advice "look before you leap" seems at odds with the advice "he who hesitates is lost." Similarly, the proverb, "Don't look a gift horse in the mouth" seems counter to the adage "Beware of Greeks bearing gifts."

Social norms also can function as warrants. If, for example, Shirley tells her friends, "Reggie is a cheapskate. He never leaves a tip," she is assuming that her friends will fill in the missing warrant; that leaving a gratuity is the proper thing to do. Leaving a tip, not cutting in front of another person in line, and giving up one's seat to an elderly person on a bus or train are all customary norms in the U.S. Suppose that, rather than raising his hand, a student snapped his fingers repeatedly to get a teacher's attention in class. Most students would perceive this as a norm violation.

Ethical principles often function as warrants. Suppose Howard tells Norma, "I can't marry you, you're my sister." The claim, I can't marry you, is connected to the grounds, you're my sister, via the assumption that "incest is wrong." Having sex with animals is also a universal no-no. Slavery and human trafficking, while they persist, are condemned by all official governments. Genocide, too, is universally frowned upon.

Shared values that are held by society, such as the importance of freedom, liberty, justice, and equality can also connect claims and grounds. For example, a female manager might complain to her boss, "I deserve the same salary as Ned is getting. I'm doing the same job, I'm just as productive, and I've been with the company just as long." In this case, the warrant would be based on the value of "equal pay for equal work."

Authorities can serve as warrants too. An arguer might cite an expert source on a topic or issue. For example, Tyree might say, "Dr. Mohan Munasinghe, one of the world's foremost experts on climate change, and a Nobel Peace Prize recipient, maintains that in order to combat global warming, nations must emphasize sustainable development" (see Munasinghe, 2001). The warrant is that a renowned expert and Nobel Prize winner is a reliable, trustworthy source. There are few universally admired sources, however. Credibility is in the eye of the beholder.

Finding Warrants in Fields

Up to this point, the warrants we've discussed are said to be *field invariant*. That's because they are not limited to a specific argumentative arena. They are found in all walks of life. Other warrants, however, are more specialized. They tend to operate in specific fields or contexts. As such, these types of warrants are said to be *field specific*. To illustrate, let's consider two such field-dependent warrants.

BLUE SHIFT, RED SHIFT

In astronomy, "blue shift" in the visible light spectrum means a celestial object is moving toward Earth, while "red shift" means the object is moving away from Earth. This is a result of the Doppler effect: Light from an approaching object has shorter, compressed wavelengths, which translates into a blue shift. Light from a receding object has longer wavelengths, which translates into a red shift. When astronomers observe blue or red shift in the visible light spectrum it functions as a warrant, a commonly accepted principle, for determining an object's motion relative to Earth. Thus, demonstrating red shift in a galaxy would support the inference that the galaxy was accelerating away from our solar system. Indeed, all distant galaxies show red-shift, indicating they are moving away from Earth and each other (Appenzeller, 2009). The universe is expanding.

TO DRAW OR NOT TO DRAW?

In poker, most players learn—perhaps the hard way—that the odds of completing an "inside straight" (also known as a "gutshot draw" or "belly buster draw") are quite low. Suppose, for example, that you've got a 4, 5, 7, and 8 (we'll ignore suits for now) and, with one card left to be dealt, you need a 6 to complete your straight. There are, of course, only four 6s in a standard deck of cards, so your chances of catching one are pretty slim. With that in mind, if your opponent makes a bet—say, $1—should you fold (surrender) or call (put in $1 yourself) to try to hit that 6? The answer, it turns out, depends on how much you can win if a 6 is dealt. Imagine, as an extreme example, that if a 6 comes, you'll win a million dollars. In other words, your odds of catching a 6 are slim (close to 11 to 1 against you), but the reward is so huge (1,000,000 to 1) that the risk is worth it. On the other hand, if you catch your 6 and can only win $2, clearly a fold is in order. Hence the axiom one of the author's uncles taught him—"never draw to an inside straight"—is usually true, but not always. This axiom functions as a warrant specific to the game of poker.

As these examples illustrate, some warrants apply to specific fields or contexts. Arguing within such fields therefore requires considerable knowledge and expertise about the assumptions, rules, standards, and practices governing those fields. A good poker player might be a lousy astronomer and vice versa.

Multi-Warranted Arguments

Just as some arguments have multiple grounds, so some arguments also have multiple warrants. This could be the result of an arguer supplying more than one warrant, or the result of different listeners interpreting the warrant in different ways. The Surgeon General's warning on a pack of cigarettes, for example, could be perceived as a *cause–effect inference* (smoking causes cancer) or as an *authoritative warrant* (the Surgeon General is an authority figure). As another example, suppose Walter said, "My horse has been acting skittish lately. That could mean there is going to be an earthquake." The warrant, or inferential leap, would likely be based on *sign reasoning*; the horse's quirky behavior portends a possible earthquake. Another possible warrant, though, is *cause–effect reasoning*. Walter could mean that his horse senses minor tremors (cause), unnoticeable to humans, which precede an earthquake (effect). Two different listeners, then, might process the argument in two different ways. To resolve differing interpretations, a listener who was unsure about the warrant could ask for clarification. The listener might ask Walter, "Are you saying that nervous behavior by animals is a reliable sign of an impending earthquake?" Or the listener could ask, "Whenever your horse acts skittish, is it always followed by an earthquake?"

Summary

Well-reasoned arguments require clearly stated claims. Ordinary arguers often mix and match claims. This can lead to confusion because different types of claims require different kinds of proof. Four types of claims were identified. Factual claims are empirically verifiable, value or judgment claims express an attitude toward something and are not empirically verifiable, policy claims advocate a specific course of action, and definitional claims argue about classifications and categories into which things belong. All four types of claims are interrelated.

Grounds function as an arguer's proof. A claim might be supported by a single form of proof, or multiple pieces of evidence. Warrants, which are often unstated, supply the inferential leap that connects the claim and grounds. Warrants can be based on inductive reasoning, such as analogy, sign, cause–effect, and generalization. Warrants also can be based on folk wisdom, social norms, ethical principles, shared values, and authorities. Many warrants are specialized and function only in specific fields.

Answers to Types of Claims from Box 5.1

1. Fact: The earth rotates toward the east, so the sun appears to move from east to west. Viewed from the North Pole, the earth's rotation is counter-clockwise. 2. Inference: An astrologer has to interpret what the arrangement of stars in the night sky means and how they might affect a person's personality. 3. Fact: A painting either is or isn't a forgery. Someone painted it. That someone either was or

wasn't the artist who signed the painting. 4. Inference: What constitutes "poverty" depends on one's definition. The U.S. Census bureau provides poverty statistics based on its own definitions (www. census.gov/topics/income-poverty/poverty.html). 5. Fact: assuming one is following the rules of chess. Anyone can look up the rules for how pieces move on a chessboard. 6. Inference: Indifference, like cruelty and kindness, are human qualities that one is projecting onto nature. 7. Fact: You can verify this by looking at a globe, or looking in a geography text. The Pacific Ocean is larger than the entire land mass of the world. 8. Inference: Dangerous to whom and in what way? If you were a passenger on a train or plane, wouldn't you prefer that the engineer or pilot were smoking a cigarette rather than a joint? 9. Inference: It is a fact that there is or isn't life elsewhere in the galaxy. However, whether that life is "intelligent" requires some sort of conjecture. On Earth, is a starfish intelligent? Is life in a petri dish intelligent? Is reality TV?

References

Adair, B. (2016, August 15). It's time to fact-check all the news. St. Petersburg, FL: *Poynter*. Retrieved on August 27, 2016 from: www.poynter.org/2016/its-time-to-fact-check-all-the-news/426261.

Anderegg, W.R.L., Prall, J.W., Harold, J. & Schneider, S.H. (2010, online early edition). Expert credibility in climate change. *Proceedings of the National Academy of Sciences*. Retrieved on August 22, 2010 from: www.pnas.org/content/early/2010/06/04/1003187107.full.pdf+html.

Appenzeller, I. (2009). *High-redshift galaxies: Light from the early universe*. Heidelberg: Springer Verlag.

Bartlett, S. (2006, September 2). Pluto left out in the cold. *The Lancet*, p. 828.

Bowerman, M. (2017, February 21). NASA scientists want to make Pluto a planet again. *USA Today Network*. Retrieved February 23, 2019 from: www.usatoday.com/story/tech/nation-now/2017/02/21/pluto-have-last-laugh-nasa-scientists-wants-make-pluto-planet-again/98187922.

Brier, B. & Houdin, J. (2008). *The secret of the great pyramid: How one man's obsession led to the solution of ancient Egypt's greatest mystery*. New York: HarperCollins.

Brockriede, W. & Ehninger, D. (1960). Toulmin on argument: An interpretation and application. *Quarterly Journal of Speech*, 46(1), 44–53, doi.org/10.1080/00335636009382390.

Campbell, T. & Friesen, J. (2015, March 3). Why people "fly from facts." *Scientific American*. Retrieved February 23, 2019 from: www.scientificamerican.com/article/why-people-fly-from-facts.

Centers for Disease Control (2016). *HIV transmission*. Atlanta, GA: Centers for Disease Control. Retrieved December 1, 2016 from: www.cdc.gov/hiv/basics/transmission.html.

Chen, A. (2016, July 27). The real paranoia-inducing purpose of Russian hacks. *The New Yorker*. Retrieved February 23, 2019 from: www.newyorker.com/news/news-desk/the-real-paranoia-inducing-purpose-of-russian-hacks.

Crook, J. (2016, November 22). Most students can't tell fake news from real news, study shows. *TechCrunch*. Retrieved December 02, 2016 from: https://techcrunch.com/2016/11/22/most-students-cant-tell-fake-news-from-real-news-study-shows.

de Sélincourt, A. & Burn, A.R. (1972). *Herodotus: The histories* (Book VI, pp. 105–106. London: Penguin Classics.

Dixit, J. (2007, June 4). Shocking stats about men and sex. *Psychology Today*. Retrieved October 27, 2009 from: www.psychologytoday.com/articles/200706/five-shocking-stats-about-men-and-sex.

Duesberg, P.H. (1988). HIV is not the cause of AIDS. *Science*, *241*(4865), 514–517, doi: 10.1126/science.3399880.

Fisher, M., Cox, J.W. & Hermann, P. (2016, December 6). Pizzagate: From rumor, to hashtag, to gunfire in D.C. *Washington Post*. Retrieved February 23, 2019 from: www.washingtonpost.com/local/pizzagate-from-rumor-to-hashtag-to-gunfire-in-dc/2016/12/06/4c7def50-bbd4-11e6-94ac-3d324840106c_story.html?utm_term=.eb57a1dca856.

Frost, F.J. (1979). The dubious origins of the marathon. *American Journal of Ancient History*, *4*(2), 159–163.

Gabielkov, M., Ramachandran, A., Chaintreau, A. & Legout, A. (2016). Social clicks: What and who gets read on Twitter? Paper presented at CCSD ACM SIGMETRICS / IFIP Performance conference, June, Antibes Juan-les-Pins, France. HAL-Inria. Retrieved on December 10, 2016 from: https://hal.inria.fr/hal-01281190.

Gannon, M. (2016, February 5). Race is a social construct, scientists argue. *Scientific American*. Retrieved on January 8, 2017 from: www.scientificamerican.com/article/race-is-a-social-construct-scientists-argue.

Hemingway, M. (2011, December 19). Lies, damned lies, and 'fact-checking'. *The Weekly Standard*. Retrieved on August 18, 2016 from: www.weeklystandard.com/lies-damned-lies-and-fact-checking/article/611854.

Hitchcock, D.L. (2005). Good reasoning on the Toulmin model. *Argumentation*, *19*(3): 373–391, doi.org/10.1007/s10503-005-4422-y.

Hoax-Slayer (2015, August 25). Identifying fake-news articles and websites. *Hoax-Slayer*. Retrieved February 23, 2019 from: www.hoax-slayer.com/identifying-fake-news-articles.shtm.

Keith, W. & Beard, D. (2008). Toulmin's rhetorical logic: What's the warrant for warrants? *Philosophy & Rhetoric*, *41*(1), 22–50, doi: 10.1353/par.2008.0003.

Kolowich, L. (2016, April 14). How the news feed algorithms work on Facebook, Twitter, and Instagram. *Hubspot*. Retrieved on January 7, 2017 from: https://blog.hubspot.com/marketing/how-algorithm-works-facebook-twitter-instagram#sm.000p2wrqu15x5fl3r0f11lr4j8kxy.

Lee, T.B. (2016, November 16). The top 20 fake news stories outperformed real news at the end of the 2016 campaign. *Vox*. Retrieved on December 1, 2016 from: www.vox.com/new-money/2016/11/16/13659840/facebook-fake-news-chart.

Manjoo, F. (2008). *True enough: Learning to live in a post-fact society*. Hoboken, NJ: Wiley.

Mantzarlis, A. (2015, October 28). Fact-checking the fact-checkers. St. Petersburg, FL: *Poynter*. Retrieved on August 27, 2016 from: www.poynter.org/2015/fact-checking-the-fact-checkers/381458.

Marietta, M., Barker, D.C. & Bowser, T. (2015). Fact-checking politics: Does the fact-check industry provide consistent guidance on disputed realities? *Forum*, *13*(4), 577–596, doi: 10.1515/for-2015-0040.

Marton, D.E., Benario, H.W. & Gynn, R.W.H. (1997). Development of the marathon from Pheidippides to the present, with statistics of significant races. *Annals of the New York Academy of Sciences*, *301*(1), 820–852, doi.org/10.1111/j.1749-6632.1977.tb38250.x.

Morring, F. (2006, September 4). Dwarf Pluto. *Aviation Week & Space Technology*, *165*(9), 16.

Munasinghe, M. (2001). Exploring the linkages between climate change and sustainable development: A challenge for transdisciplinary research. *Conservation Ecology*, *5*(1) art.14, doi: 10.5751/ES-00239-050114.

Nyhan, B. (2016, November 5). Fact-checking can change views? We rate that as mostly true. *New York Times*. Retrieved on August 1, 2018 from: www.nytimes.com/2016/11/06/upshot/fact-checking-can-change-views-we-rate-that-as-mostly-true.html.

Nyhan, B. & Reifler, J. (2013). The effects of fact-checking threat. *New America Foundation*. Retrieved on August 1, 2018 from: www.dartmouth.edu/~nyhan/nyhan-reifler-report-naf.pdf.

Nyhan, B. & Reifler, J. (2015a). The effect of fact-checking on elites: A field experiment on U.S. state legislators. *American Journal of Political Science*, *59*(1), 628–640, doi.org/10.1111/ajps.12162.

Nyhan, B. & Reifler, J. (2015b). *Estimating fact-checking effects: Evidence from a long-term experiment during campaign 2014*. American Press Institute and Democracy Fund. Retrieved on January 5, 2017 from: www.americanpressinstitute.org/wp-content/uploads/2015/04/Estimating-Fact-Checkings-Effect.pdf.

Nyhan, B. & Reifler, J. (2018). The roles of information deficits and identity threat in the prevalence of misperceptions. *Journal of Elections, Public Opinion and Parties* (published online), doi: 10.1080/17457289.2018.1465061.

Pew Research Center (2018, November 27). *Unauthorized immigrant population trends for states, birth countries and regions*. Washington, DC: Pew Research Center. Retrieved on February 23, 2019 from: www.pewhispanic.org/interactives/unauthorized-trends.

Rabin-Havt, A. (2016). *Lies, incorporated: The world of post-truth politics*. New York: Anchor Books.

Salzberg, S. (2015, February 1). Anti-vaccine movement causes worst measles epidemic in 20 years. *Forbes*. Retrieved February 23, 2019 from: www.forbes.com/sites/stevensalzberg/2015/02/01/anti-vaccine-movement-causes-worst-measles-epidemic-in-20-years/#30dd7bec6069.

Snopes (2002, April 18). Daydream deceiver. *Snopes*. Retrieved October 26, 2009 from: www.snopes.com/science/stats/thinksex.asp.

Snopes (2014, April 28). Spiders inside her. *Snopes*. Retrieved October 26, 2009 from: www.snopes.com/science/stats/spiders.asp.

Stanford History Education Group (2016, November 22). *Evaluating information: The cornerstone of civic online reasoning*. Stanford History Education Group. Retrieved December 02, 2016 from: https://sheg.stanford.edu/upload/V3LessonPlans/Executive%20Summary%2011.21.16.pdf.

The Straight Dope (2000, September 8). Does the average person consumer four spiders per year in his sleep? *The Straight Dope*. Retrieved October 26, 2009 from: www.straightdope.com/columns/read/1828/does-the-average-person-consume-four-spiders-per-year-in-his-sleep.

Timberg, C. (2016, November 24). Russian propaganda held spread 'fake news' during election, experts say. *Washington Post*. Retrieved on December 4, 2016 from: www.washingtonpost.com/business/economy/russian-propaganda-effort-helped-spread-fake-news-during-election-experts-say/2016/11/24/793903b6-8a40-4ca9-b712-716af66098fe_story.html?utm_term=.d18c1cf97f08.

Wade, N. (2006). *Before the dawn: Recovering the lost history of our ancestors*. New York: Penguin Press.

Wang, A.B. (2016, November 16). 'Post-truth' named 2016 word of the year by Oxford Dictionaries. *Washington Post*. Retrieved February 23, 2019 from: www.washingtonpost.com/news/the-fix/wp/2016/11/16/post-truth-named-2016-word-of-the-year-by-oxford-dictionaries/?noredirect=on&utm_term=.925fd90fe9b2.

Wheedleton, K. (2010, March 11). March 13th is Pluto and Planet Day [Blog post]. Retrieved February 23, 2019 from: http://bugsandbunnies.blogspot.com/2010/03/march-13th-is-pluto-is-planet-day-and.html.

White, J.B. (2015, June 12). Shannon Grove under fire for linking drought to abortion. *The Sacramento Bee*. Retrieved February 23, 2019 from: www.sacbee.com/news/politics-government/capitol-alert/article23868907.html.

Chapter 6

Evidence and Proof

Where's Your Proof?

Don't believe everything you read or hear. One of the authors has a scar on his right leg because he failed to heed this advice. As a kid, he scraped his leg. A buddy informed him that dog saliva had healing powers, so he gladly let the family pooch lick away at the abrasion. That's when the infection developed. He learned the hard way that dog drool has no antiseptic qualities whatsoever.

Unfortunately, the author's childhood friend is not the only one handing out bad advice. It's not uncommon to hear people support their claims with statements such as:

"I read somewhere that . . .."

"Hey, trust me on this."

"They couldn't say it, if it weren't true."

"I know a guy, who knows a guy, who told him that . . .."

When a person offers proof for a claim by *asserting* that there is proof for the claim, be wary. Just because someone claims to have seen "Bigfoot," as some do (see www.bigfootencounters.com), doesn't make it true. The same caution applies to tabloid gossip. For example, in 2017, actress Rebel Wilson won a $4.56 million defamation suit against an Australian publisher who branded her as a "serial liar." The judge ruled that Bauer media had engaged in a "calculated, baseless and unjustifiable" attack that cost the actress movie roles (Ackerman, 2017, para. 1). Even legitimate news sources get their facts wrong—more often than one might think. For example, in a segment on CBS' *60 Minutes* that aired in 2004, Dan Rather relied on faked documents suggesting that George W. Bush shirked his duties while serving in the National Guard (Krauthammer, 2005; Memmott, 2004). Four producers were fired over the scandal and Rather left the show soon after. Since then, the incident has been called "a watershed moment in American TV journalism" (Anderson, 2015).

Prove It to Me

The problem is that we can't always get our information first-hand. We must rely on media reports, government agencies, and social networks to find out what is going on in the world. But how can

"It's a bedtime story. It doesn't __need__ corroboration."

Figure 6.1 Budding skepticism
© Michael Maslin/*The New Yorker* Collection/www.cartoonbank.com.

we know if such information is accurate? What tests might we use to assess the quality of evidence that is offered by others or that we might want to use in our own arguments? Learning to evaluate such information is not always easy. Indeed, Sadler (2004) noted that people of all ages "have difficulty in constructing well-substantiated arguments" (p. 516). With that in mind, this chapter examines the nature of evidence and how it is used, and abused, to support claims. In it, you'll learn important tests for evaluating source credibility and evidence, including statistical proof.

Field Dependent and Field Invariant Proof

Some forms of evidence are *field invariant*, meaning that the standards for evaluating evidence can be understood by the general public, without special knowledge or training. A *reasonable person* standard is often applied in such cases. The reasonable person standard asks how an ordinary, reasonable person would judge the proof that is presented. The kinds of evidence found in Op-Ed pieces, offered by pundits on news shows, and included in position pieces in popular magazines fall into this category.

Other forms of evidence are *field dependent*, meaning that what constitutes acceptable proof is specific to a particular context, field, or discipline. In some specific fields, standards for collecting, presenting, and evaluating evidence are quite specific. In criminal law, for example, the *exclusionary rule* bars evidence obtained from an illegal search from being presented at trial. In journalism, reputable news organizations abide by a "two-source" rule, whereby two independent sources must corroborate a story before it can be published. In social science research, statistical significance (often at the $p < .05$ level) is commonly recognized as the threshold for proof. This means a researcher is 95 percent confident the results obtained are not due to chance. With the distinction between field invariant and field dependent standards for evidence in mind, we turn to some of the most basic field invariant tests of evidence next.

Tests of Evidence

Source Credibility: Who Says So?

Some products' names, such as Dr. Pepper, Doc Marten, and Dr. Scholl, suggest a certain level of expertise. Did you know, for example, that Dr. Pepper was invented by a pharmacist working at a drug store in Waco, Texas? Or that Doc Marten's shoes are named after Dr. Klaus Märten, a physician in the German Army during World War II? Or that Dr. William Scholl received his medical degree from the Illinois Medical College? Of course, the fact that these products are named after real doctors doesn't necessarily make them superior. The "doctor" moniker, however, does add psychological prestige. Perhaps that's why Dr. Dre (Andre Romelle Young), Dr. Demento (Barry Eugene Hansen), Dr. J (Julius Irving), Dr. Seuss (Theodore Seuss Geisel), and Doc Rivers (Glenn Anton Rivers) adopted the title, even though none of them attended medical school.

The proof for many claims, not just those made by doctors, hinges on the credibility or authority of the claim's source. In technical terms, such proof is called an *authoritative warrant*. That is, the claim is linked to the grounds by the *authority* of the source (see Figure 6.2). For example, if Oprah Winfrey, considered by many to be an authoritative source, so much as mentions a product, sales of the product can soar, a phenomenon dubbed the *Oprah Effect*. Given the frequency with which bloggers, celebrity endorsers, infomercial spokespersons, movie critics, political pundits, and TV hosts endorse things, it is worth knowing how to apply basic tests of source credibility. We explain how in the sections that follow.

Who's Who: Is the Source Known?

The first test of source credibility has to do with whether the source is clearly identified. Sometimes the source of a claim is unknown. Consider the banter below:

Hank: "There really are vampires, you know."
Newt: "Oh really?"
Hank: "I read it on the web."
Newt: "*Just . . .* on the web?"

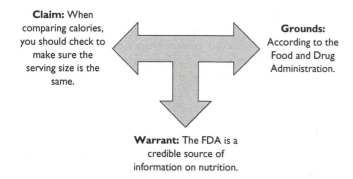

Figure 6.2 Illustration of an authoritative warrant.

Hank:	"It was one of those question–answer search engines, like www.Ask.com, or www.WikiAnswers.com."
Newt:	"But who posted the answer on the search engine?"
Hank:	"I don't know, some vampire expert I guess."
Newt:	"So if you read the same thing in a bathroom stall, would you believe it?"
Hank:	"No way. I never trust bathroom graffiti. Not since that one time."

People might say "I heard somewhere . . ." or "They say that . . ." which really isn't a source at all. Moreover, a vague source (e.g., "According to a government study . . .") is little better than no source at all. In fact, if people can't recall the source of their information, how can you be sure that they recall the content of the information correctly? For all you know, they might even be confusing a fictional source with an actual source, which happens from time to time. It turns out, for example, that medical students have employed flawed treatments that they learned by watching television shows like *Grey's Anatomy, House,* or *Scrubs* (Blackwell, 2009).

Confidential Sources: Don't Quote Me on That

We've suggested that you should be wary when people do not provide sources for their evidence. There are exceptions, however. Consider investigative journalists, who often rely on unnamed sources to get a story out. Such sources might be mob informants, corporate insiders, government moles, or other whistleblowers, who help fulfill the "watchdog" function of the press. If reporters had to identify these sources, it could have a chilling effect on such disclosures. At the same time, it's important to keep in mind that a source's reasons for not going on the record matter. Is the source afraid of reprisals? Uncertain about the information being disclosed? Using anonymity for revenge or to spread misinformation? Will the source profit from the revelations?

Who's Who Online?

When people evaluate the credibility of websites, they often base their evaluation on extraneous cues, such as the look or design of a website (Flanagin & Metzger, 2007; Metzger, Flanagin &

Medders, 2010), which, if you ask us, is akin to judging a book by its cover. Even so, it's hard to blame them. Indeed, identifying online sources can be especially tricky because it isn't always clear who's responsible for the content. Not only can information be added anonymously, trolls and bots may post misinformation to confuse you. And even when a source is provided, it may not be the original source. Considering this, if no author is provided, no institutional affiliation given, no sponsoring group or organization identified, you would be well-advised to steer clear of the information, no matter how glitzy it appears.

Who Do You Trust? Is the Source Qualified?

That said, just because a source is *known* doesn't necessarily mean the source is knowledgeable. Hence, in addition to asking yourself whether a source is identified, a second useful test of credibility is to ask yourself whether a source is *qualified*. By way of example, there are numerous infomercial spokespersons selling fitness equipment, nutritional supplements, and other health aids. But what are their actual qualifications? Labels such as "fitness expert" or "nutritionist" have no agreed-upon meaning. One way of recognizing qualified sources, then, is to look for official degrees, credentials, or certifications, such as M.D., Ph.D., C.P.A., or R.N. A surgeon who is board certified, for example, is generally preferable to one who is not. When choosing a mechanic, you are better off picking one who is A.S.E. certified, even if your cousin knows a guy who can fix your car on the cheap.

It's also important to remember that a source may have expertise in one area, but not another. Serena Williams, the highest-paid female athlete in 2017, is an expert at tennis, which would justify her endorsements of Nike and Wilson (Badenhausen, 2017). However, she's not an expert on investing (JP Morgan) or computers (IBM, Intel), which she also endorses. Gwyneth Paltrow's website www.Goop.com offers loads of advice on nutrition and peddles a lot of diet and food wares. But the actress has no degree in dietetics, health science, or nutrition science. In fact, she never completed college.

Scholarly Refereed Journal Articles: It's All Academic

For many types of disputes the best evidence comes from peer-reviewed journal articles, which are written by experts in a particular field. Importantly, most articles undergo *blind review*, which means the reviewers, who are also experts in the field, don't know the author's identity. This peer review process is designed to ensure that articles are evaluated rigorously and fairly by multiple experts on the subject. For many subjects, then, peer reviewed represents the "gold standard" of proof.

Anecdotal Evidence: Be Wary of Fish Tales

Humans are, by nature, storytellers. As such, we tend to prefer stories over statistics (Kida, 2006). The problem, of course, is that anecdotal evidence can be extremely unreliable. People who report seeing alien spaceships, the ghost of Elvis, or the Loch Ness Monster may provide vivid accounts, but that doesn't make their stories true. As an illustration, consider the case of actress, model, and television host Jenny McCarthy, who became a vocal advocate for a theory that childhood vaccines cause autism. Her proof was her own son's experience. In other words, a *sample of one.* The theory she supports has been soundly rejected by medical researchers (Hornig et al., 2008; Hudson, 2009; Miller & Reynolds, 2009), but that didn't stop McCarthy from appearing on talk shows, peddling her anti-immunization views. The problem is that McCarthy has no scientific background or medical expertise. As one pediatrician put it, "If your child had a brain tumor, would you want Jenny McCarthy's advice? Then why is this any different?" (McDonald, cited in Senger, 2009, p. A-3). Worse yet, if McCarthy succeeds in convincing parents not to vaccinate their children, millions of children may be put at risk. "Anti-vaxxers" like McCarthy have already been blamed for measles outbreaks throughout the U.S., which is troubling considering that "vaccination," according to experts, "is the single greatest medical intervention that has saved the most lives over the past century" (Kruskal & Allen, 2008, p. A-11).

Testimonials: Beware the Average Joe or Jill

Closely related to anecdotal evidence is the use of testimonials. Anecdotes may be about someone else's experience, but testimonials come "straight from the horse's mouth." A testimonial typically consists of an ordinary person who liked a particular product. "After I tried the Wonder Mop T-1000," an infomercial customer might say, "I threw all my other mops away." The problem with testimonials is that the advertiser is free to "cherry pick" a few success stories. That is why disclaimers, such as "results not typical" or "individual results may vary," appear in the fine print of such ads (FTC, 2009).

Source Bias: What's in It For You?

Even if you know better than to rely on unknown sources, unqualified sources, anecdotal evidence, or testimonials, there's another concern. A source may be biased. While it's easy to forgive the grandmother with a bumper sticker that reads, "My grandchildren are cuter than yours," we should expect others to be impartial. For example, based on the principle that "justice is blind," judges should be fair minded. Likewise, researchers should maintain "scientific objectivity" when conducting experiments just as professors should be fair when grading students' essays.

Media Bias: Unfair and Unbalanced?

There is an old joke about an imaginary headline in the *New York Times* that reads, "Giant Meteor to Destroy Earth! Poor, Minorities Hit Hardest." To get the joke, you have to understand that, to some people, the media has a liberal bias. Indeed, a recent poll found that 84 percent of Republicans believe in such a bias (PEW Research Center, 2017). No wonder some conservatives refer to mainstream media as "fake news," "lamestream media," or "drive-by media." Yet the same poll found that 64 percent of Democrats also perceived there was media bias—*but in the other direction.* How can mainstream media have both a liberal *and* a conservative bias? The answer may lie in a phenomenon known as the *hostile media effect* (HME), which refers to the tendency for people to perceive media coverage as being biased *against* their position (Gunther & Liebhart, 2006; Perloff, 2015). The more opinionated they are, the greater they tend to perceive media bias. This makes sense, because where you sit on the political spectrum determines how many viewpoints fall to the left or right of you. If you are a "left-wing, tree-hugging, bleeding heart" liberal, most media coverage will appear conservatively biased to you. Conversely, if you are a "right-wing, die-hard, tea party" conservative, most media coverage will seem to have a liberal bent. (See Box 6.1.)

Box 6.1   Is There a Liberal Media Bias?

Is there a liberal media bias? More journalists are Democrats than Republicans so, critics claim, they tend to approach stories from a liberal point of view (Goldberg, 2002; Lichter, Rothman & Lichter, 1991). However, empirical studies reveal that the press is not nearly so left-leaning as its detractors claim. For instance, a study that examined newspaper stories from 1991–2004 found that there was an absence of bias in the labeling of senators and congresspersons (Eisinger, Veenstra & Koehn, 2007).

In a similar vein, during the 2008 presidential campaign, two researchers (Butler & Schoefield, 2010) examined editorial bias by mailing fictitious letters to the editors of major U.S. newspapers. Half the letters were pro-Obama, half were pro-McCain. If editors harbor a liberal bias, one would expect more of the pro-Obama letters to have been published. Counter to the "liberal media" conspiracy theory, however, editors were 13–16 percent more likely to publish the pro-McCain letters. Similarly, in a meta-analysis of studies on news bias, D'Alessio and Allen (2007a, 2007b) found that there was a slightly, yet statistically significant pro-Republican bias in coverage by newspapers. These findings tend to debunk the notion that the press favors liberal over conservative points of view.

Overcoming Source Bias

As a critical thinker, you can combat source bias in several ways. The first is to become more aware of your own biases. Strive to be open-minded, rather than insisting on being right. Be willing to play devil's advocate with your own ideas: Ask yourself why *you* might be wrong and why the *other person* might be right.

Second, recognize that the information you receive, especially from social media newsfeeds, is often filtered. Did you know, for example, that Facebook and other social media sites use algorithms to sift through news stories? Why? To determine which stories a person will find most engaging and include them in the person's newsfeed. The algorithm relies on the person's previous likes, comments, and shares to predict preferences (*Forbes*, 2017). A byproduct of getting information this way is that people tend to remain in bubbles, reading about stories that reinforce their beliefs.

What can you do to become less insulated? Don't get all your news from social media. Watch news on TV, read a newspaper, even if it's online, listen to radio programming that isn't your

Figure 6.3 The media bias continuum.

usual fare. Don't let social media curate stories for you. You can do this by actively seeking out stories on current events, rather than waiting for a news feed to deliver them to you. Diversify your news sources; see what the BBC, Al Jazeera, Reuters, the Associated Press, or other international news sources have to say.

Third, when evaluating sources, ask what the source's primary motivation is. Is there a profit motive at stake? Is the source trying to score political points? Is the source seeking the media spotlight? Is there an underlying motivation besides the one offered? The good news is that some professionals have a *fiduciary responsibility*, meaning that it's their duty to act in the best interests of their clients. They cannot line their own pockets at their clients' expense. The bad news is that not all goods and services come with such a guarantee. Did you know, for example, that many financial advisors have no legal obligation to steer your investments in a direction that benefits you as opposed to them (Olen & Pollack, 2016)? Likewise, if you are buying a car, a wedding dress, printer ink or, yes, even a textbook, it's *caveat emptor* or buyer beware.

A fourth tack is to investigate whether sources have potential conflicts of interest. For example, when researchers submit manuscripts to scholarly journals, they are required to disclose any funding sources or financial interests related to the study. In contrast, politicians often support legislation that benefits themselves financially (Hill, Ridge & Ingram, 2017). The website www. opensecrets.org does an excellent job of identifying political conflicts of interest. Should it worry you, for example, that senators who tend to vote against bills to regulate prescription drug prices receive nearly twice as much in campaign donations from the pharmaceutical industry as those who support legislation to regulate drug prices (Sultan, 2017)?

Fourth, even in cases where unbiased experts are scarce, you can *triangulate* where the truth may lie by comparing various biased sources. Suppose, for instance, that a neo-conservative argued that the U.S. should initiate a preemptive strike on Iran's nuclear facilities (as Alan Kuperman did in an Op-Ed piece in the *New York Times* (Kuperman, 2009)). Rather than taking one pundit's word for it, see what Op-Ed rebuttals were printed in reply. What's more, look beyond U.S. media to see what foreign correspondents and diplomats think. If you rely on a single media outlet for your information, you will get only a small slice of the informational pie.

A fifth strategy is to make use of fact-checking websites to verify sources' claims. One of our favorites is *Snopes.com*, which is especially useful for checking on urban myths and legends. As just one example, it's not true that a college student was so stressed about grades that he committed suicide during a test by shoving pencils up his nostrils (www.snopes.com/college/exam/pencils.asp). In Chapter 5, we identified a variety of useful fact-checking websites. We supplement that list with other useful websites in Box 6.2 below.

Box 6.2   Fact-Checking Websites

- AltNews, www.altnews.in, an Indian fact-checking website that "debunks misinformation, disinformation, and malinformation."
- ClarkHoward.com and Scambusters.org (for consumer information).
- EU vs Disinformation, https://euvsdisinfo.eu/about, a website devoted to exposing Kremlin disinformation.
- Full Fact, https://fullfact.org, a nonprofit U.K. fact-checking website.

(continued)

(continued)

- Media Research Center (mrc.org) and Newsbusters.org (conservative websites that expose liberal media bias).
- MediaMatters.org (liberal website that exposes conservative media bias).
- Opensecrets.org.
- StraightDope, www.straightdope.com, a fact-checking website that focuses on science-related topics.
- Truthorfiction.com.

Context Is Key

It is easy to take statements out of context in the Twittersphere. For instance, during his confirmation hearings to become the Secretary of Housing and Urban Development, Dr. Ben Carson fielded questions about how he would manage the agency. A testy exchange with Senator Elizabeth Warren ensued. To see how Joe Scarborough, host of MSNBC's *Morning Joe*, tweeted about one of Dr. Carson's answers, see Figure 6.4a.

The tweet, as you can see, ignores the context in which the answer was given. Here is the actual back and forth between Dr. Carson and Senator Warren: www.youtube.com/watch?v=CoB0BhQaw-w.

Warren:	"My concern is whether or not, among the billions of dollars that you will be responsible for handing out, in grants and loans, can you just assure us that not one dollar will go to benefit either the President elect or his family?"
Carson:	"It will not be my intention to do anything to benefit any American, particularly. It's for all Americans, everything that we do."
Warren:	"Do I take that to mean you may manage programs that will significantly benefit the President elect?"
Carson:	"You can take it to mean that I will manage things in a way that benefits the American people."

Figure 6.4a Joe Scarborough's tweet.
Twitter.com.

Clearly, when considered in context, Dr. Carson's position was that he did not intend to make policies that would benefit President Donald Trump in particular.

Another example of tweeting out of context targeted Jake Tapper, host of CNN's *The Lead*. The tweet by Fox News implied that Tapper sympathized with a terrorist who reportedly yelled "Allahu Akbar" after running down 18 pedestrians and cyclists with a truck in Manhattan, killing eight of them (see Figure 6.4b).

The paraphrase, however, was taken out of context. What Tapper actually said about the tragedy was, "the Arabic chant 'allahu akbar'—'God is great'—sometimes said under the most beautiful of circumstances, and too often we hear of it being said in moments like this." The phrase itself is an affirmation of faith. It might be heard at a Muslim wedding, the birth of a Muslim child or, unfortunately, by a jihadist detonating an explosive vest. Fox News later removed the tweet.

Considering these examples, when evaluating quotations or other evidence, context counts. The key test is whether the quote has been selected or edited in such a way as to distort its original meaning. To determine this, an arguer is well-advised to research both sides of an issue. The more familiar you are with the evidence on all sides of an issue, the more readily you can determine whether a quotation is being taken out of context.

Suppressed Evidence

The test for *suppressed evidence* examines whether sources are purposely withholding information that could be damaging to their side. For example, for decades tobacco manufacturers suppressed evidence about the health risks associated with smoking. They also withheld evidence that they manipulated nicotine levels in cigarettes to maximize their addictiveness. When it was no longer possible to deny the direct harms of smoking, they shifted their attention to denying the harms of second-hand smoke (Rogue Industry, 2009).

Spotting suppressed evidence is difficult, precisely because it is being withheld. Once again, this highlights the importance of researching both sides of an issue. Indeed, what one person withholds, another may divulge. In some cases, however, the person who is keeping the evidence secret may be the only person aware of its existence. As such, you may have to think like a detective by reading between the lines and asking focused questions to find out as much information as you can.

Fox News ✓
@FoxNews

.@CNN 's Jake Tapper Says 'Allahu Akbar' Is 'Beautiful' Right After NYC Terror Attack

Figure 6.4b Tweet by Fox News.
Twitter.com.

Consensus of Expert Opinion: Four Out of Five Dentists Agree

Imagine that your foot were crushed by a falling piano. Your surgeon explains that the foot will have to be amputated before infection sets in. Would you want a second or third opinion? If three different surgeons gave you the same answer, would you accept their recommendation? What if a fourth surgeon said your foot could be saved?

When experts are at odds over a controversial issue, one approach is to rely on the *consensus of expert opinion*, giving greater weight to their combined expertise. Of course, the consensus view may be mistaken, but the collective wisdom of most experts is usually a better bet than the judgment of a few. Take the issue of climate change, for example. Because the media tries to represent both sides, it may appear that climatologists are divided on the issue of global warming. In fact, there is striking agreement among climate experts that global warming is a very real phenomenon. Indeed, a Stanford University study found that, among climatologists who publish frequently in scholarly journals, there is 97 percent agreement on the basic tenets of anthropogenic (man-made) climate change (Anderegg, Prall, Harold & Schneider, 2010). Moreover, the study found that the expertise of the climatologists who favored man-made climate change "vastly overshadows that of the climate change skeptics and contrarians" (Anderegg et al., 2010, p. 2).

Preponderance of Evidence: Tipping the Scales

The preponderance of evidence standard is based on the quantity of proof for a particular side. Specifically, in some cases, the sheer weight of evidence favors one side or another. For example, when claims of sexual abuse by Catholic priests began to emerge in the 1980s, many Catholics were skeptical. But, as more and more charges were filed, it became harder and harder to deny the evidence of serious misdeeds. The Catholic Church now acknowledges that about four percent of priests were accused of sexually abusing a minor (Bono, 2004). That represents 10,600 victims in the U.S. alone. Numbers like that are hard to ignore.

Although some people imagine that a preponderance of evidence represents an overwhelming quantity, that's not always the case. Instead, preponderance may reflect a simple majority of the evidence, wherein more than 50 percent of the evidence favors one side. In other words, based on the available evidence, a claim is more probable than not (Redmayne, 1999). This approach, which is also known as a "balancing test," is the standard of proof in civil litigation. There are limitations to this approach, however (Kaye, 2006). Basing an argument on the quantity, rather than the quality, of evidence is a weaker standard of proof.[1]

In other cases, however, the preponderance of evidence need not be limited to a "> 50 percent" standard. In fact, the preponderance of evidence may reflect multiple converging forms of proof from separate sources that strongly point to a particular conclusion. For example, despite large sums of money allocated to the Drug Abuse Resistance Education program (DARE) in schools, a ten-year study revealed that "the preponderance of evidence suggests that DARE has no long-term effect on drug use" (Lynam, Milich, Zimmerman, Novak, Logan, Martin, Leukefeld & Clayton, 1999, p. 590). Consistent with other studies, no significant decreases in cigarette, alcohol, or marijuana use were found (Sherman, Sommers & Manno, 2000).

Relevance: Beside the Point?

Ordinary arguers sometimes assume that "the evidence speaks for itself." We think it is better to assume that evidence is mute, or at least mumbles. To argue effectively, you need to explain *what* the evidence means and *how* it supports your claim. Likewise, when evaluating evidence, the test of relevance basically asks, "does this evidence even matter?" and "If so, why?"

Imagine, for example, that you're the judge in a criminal trial. The prosecutor wants to show jurors gruesome photographs of a crime scene. The defense attorney objects, arguing that the grisly photos are immaterial and will only prejudice the jury. As the judge, you would have to determine whether the *probative value* of the evidence, e.g., its relevance in proving some point of contention, outweighed its prejudicial effect (see Bright & Goodman-Delahunty, 2006).

As another example, imagine that you're a U.S. Senator evaluating proposed legislation that grants consumers basic protection from credit card companies. Sound like a good idea? What would you think if another lawmaker proposed an amendment to your bill that allowed people to carry loaded weapons into national parks? Would you wonder what in the world guns in parks had to do with protection from credit card companies? The good news is that, according to parliamentary procedure, an amendment to a motion must be *germane*, that is, directly related to the motion in question. The bad news is that, in the U.S. Congress, you would hardly know the requirement exists.[2] Indeed, legislators frequently add riders, earmarks, "pork barrel" provisions, and "poison pills" to legislation. In fact, it turns out that our example was not hypothetical. According to Hulse (2009), a bill granting basic protections from credit card companies was actually amended to allow people to carry loaded weapons onto national parks (Hulse, 2009). The legislation, which was signed into law by then president Obama, overturned an earlier, Reagan era, ban on weapons in national parks.

Recency of Evidence: Out with the Old, In with the New

Recent evidence is vital on many issues. The stock market, for example, can swing hundreds of points in a matter of minutes. Political candidates who commit verbal gaffes on a Monday may see their polling numbers plummet by Tuesday. All else being equal, recent evidence is preferable to dated evidence. The caveat "all else being equal" is an important one, however. Bad evidence, no matter how recent, is still worthless. An infamous case involved the presidential election in 2000, when major TV networks began "counting chickens" based on early returns. After projecting Al Gore as the winner over George W. Bush, they had to recant their predictions. Consider the chronology of then CBS News anchor Dan Rather's comments.

7:00 pm: "Let's get one thing straight from the get-go. We would rather be last in reporting a return than be wrong."

8:00 pm: "Excuse me one second. I'm so sorry to interrupt you. Mike (Wallace), you know I wouldn't do this if it weren't big. Florida goes for Al Gore. Now, folks, the equation changes."

8:30 pm: Bush's lead is "shakier than cafeteria Jell-O."

10:00 pm: "Bulletin: Florida pulled back into the undecided column. Computer and data problem."

11:00 pm: "If you're disgusted with us, frankly I don't blame you."

Of course, we now know that the difference in the number of votes cast for Bush or Gore in 2000 was smaller than the margin of error in the vote counting procedure. The networks were so eager to project a winner that they "put their socks on over their boots."

Recency and Fact Versus Value Claims

Generally speaking, recency is more important when arguing about factual claims than value or judgment claims. Facts can change quickly. Values tend to be more enduring. For example, execution rates vary from year to year, but people's attitudes toward capital punishment are more entrenched. Because facts are transitory, citing a 2009 source to document the annual number of executions in the U.S. would be misleading. The number of executions has declined since then (Death Penalty Information Center, 2019). However, because value claims are more enduring, a quotation from a Supreme Court justice saying that capital punishment was morally justifiable or unjustifiable would be as valid if it were made in 1960 or 2020.

Reliability: You Can Count on Me

Imagine that you stepped on a bathroom scale to check your weight. You step off, then right back on. You gained five pounds! You try again, only to discover you've lost seven pounds! Clearly, if your scale is not reliable, you cannot trust it. The same applies to evidence. To say that evidence is reliable means that the source has an excellent track record and the evidence itself is consistently accurate.

The reliability of evidence is a key consideration in arguing, reasoning, and thinking. Indeed, if you were choosing a stockbroker, you would want one with a solid history of producing favorable returns. If you were an undercover cop who was relying on a snitch to find out when a drug deal was going down, you'd want reliable information. If you were conducting a public opinion poll, you would want a small margin for error.

Rumor Mills: I Heard It Through the Grapevine

In everyday life we are often faced with information based on gossip, rumor mills, and whisper campaigns. In fact, some reports suggest that 43 to 63 percent of employees get all or most of their information about their companies around the "water cooler" (Fisher, 2005; Lorenzo, 2002). How reliable is such information? While the office grapevine may distort information, there is often some element of truth behind such rumors (Newstrom, Monczka & Reif, 1974). The problem, of course, is figuring out what's true and what's not.

How can you tell if such information is reliable? If a co-worker claims that a new round of lay-offs is coming, rather than panicking or feeding the rumors yourself, do some fact-checking. You could go to the person who is in the best position to know whether the rumor is true. You could also look for signs that pink slips might be coming. Has there been a recent merger? Has the company's stock value suddenly changed? Has there been turn-over in top-level management? Such steps may save you a good deal of angst in deciding whether to dust off your resume or not.

Is Wikipedia a Reliable Source?

Wikipedia is often the first source students turn to when looking up information. Hopefully, it is not their last. To give Wikipedia its due, a study reported in the journal *Nature* found that Wikipedia was almost as accurate as the prestigious *Encyclopedia Britannica* on scientific matters (Giles, 2005). That said, Wikipedia's open source architecture poses new challenges to traditional epistemology or "ways of knowing." That's because anyone can post information or misinformation. As such, Wikipedia's reliability is based on the collective wisdom of its users. But the "knowledge of the commons" can also become a "tragedy of the commons." According to *Rasmussen Reports*, "25 percent of those who have visited Wikipedia have read something they know to be inaccurate" (Glanfield, 2009, p. 7). For example, David Beckham's bio temporarily listed him as an 18th-century goalkeeper.

Fortunately, Wikipedia has developed methods for detecting cyber-vandalism. New pages are checked for suspect material. Repeat vandals are blocked and frequently vandalized pages are locked. Mistakes are corrected, usually quickly (Schiff, 2006). Even so, as Glanfield surmised,

> there is no way that every page can be fact-checked every minute of every day, and therefore as a serious research tool the website is flawed. Although Wikipedia is underpinned by noble principles, its sheer size ensures that it will remain a vast collection of knowledge, fact and fiction. (2009, p. 7)

Considering this, our advice when using Wikipedia is the same as Ronald Reagan's when making nuclear arms agreements with the former Soviet Union; trust, but verify.

Statistical Proof

Sorry, You've Got the Wrong Number

The last type of evidence we consider is statistical proof, about which people are often highly suspicious. They may dismiss such proof by saying "figures lie and liars figure" or "statistics can be made to prove anything." In order to argue, think, and reason well, you need to know how to evaluate statistical proof. As Ben-Zvi and Garfield (2004) noted, "quantitative information is everywhere, and statistics are increasingly presented as a way to add credibility to advertisements, arguments, or advice" (p. 3). Although a comprehensive examination of statistical literacy is beyond the scope of this text, we offer some general rules of thumb to use when testing quantitative proof.

Beware the WAG

When people don't know an actual number, they sometimes make one up. Such conjecture is known as a *WAG* or *Wild Ass Guess* (Figure 6.5). In fact, 93.2 percent of all statistics, including this one, are made up on the spot! All kidding aside, some arguers tend to play fast and loose with numbers. A sports fan might assert, "I'll bet half of all athletes take performance-enhancing drugs" or a boss might surmise that "90 percent of employees pilfer office supplies from work."

Wilt Chamberlain was one of the greatest centers in basketball history. He still holds multiple NBA records today. In his autobiography, *A View From Above*, he claimed to have set a different sort of record. Specifically, he claimed to have slept with 20,000 women! That sounds like a WAG to us. The "Big Dipper," as Chamberlain liked to be called, was born in 1936. If he became sexually active at the early age of 15, and remained so until his death in 1999, he would have had 48 years of "scoring" potential. That works out to 416 women per year, or 1.14 women per day (or night). Mathematically, it is possible. But how did he come up with the nice round number of 20,000? Did he make a notch in his bedpost every night? We suspect he came up with the number the same way he got rebounds; he grabbed it out of thin air.

Figure 6.5 "Dilbert makes a WAG." Scott Adams, www.dilbert.com, May 8, 2008.
© Scott Adams/Dilbert.com.

Survey Says . . .

Opinion polls are a vital source of information. Based on polls, we can determine, among other things, how much confidence consumers have in the economy, how much they approve of the president, and what they think about immigration laws. That said, when evaluating evidence from polls and surveys, there are caveats to consider.

First, it is important to determine whether the poll was scientific or not. How so? A scientific poll relies on a random sample of people, controls for bias in the wording of questions, and reports the margin of error. Of course, not all polls are scientific. If a TV show asks viewers to text in their answers to a question, such as "Do you think that ex-felons who have served their sentence should have their voting rights restored?", the sample is neither random nor representative of the general population. Only some viewers watch a particular show and only some of those viewers are sufficiently motivated to text in an answer. Not only that, the wording of the question may affect viewers' responses. Does "served their sentence" mean no longer on parole or probation? Finally, the margin of error may not be reported. Sampling error, which is typically plus/minus 3–5 points in a scientific poll, refers to how well the responses of a sample group reflect the true sentiments of the larger population. What's more, even a well-conducted scientific poll only provides a static "snapshot" of respondents' perceptions at a particular point in time.

Unknowable Statistics: Sex and Lies

Some statistics are unknowable. For instance, how many sexual assaults go unreported or how many immigrants are in the U.S. illegally? Experts can estimate, but no one can know the true numbers. By way of example, a statistic that is readily available on the web is that "the average male thinks about sex every seven seconds!" That works out to more than 7,000 sex thoughts per day. Furthermore, one sex thought every seven seconds leaves only 57 seconds for thinking about food and sports which, of course, are the only other things men ever think about. More credible sources place the number from 1–19 sex thoughts per day for men (Stafford, 2014).

Although there are studies on how often men and women have erotic thoughts, they rely on self-reports. If the information is unknown to the respondents, however, they cannot accurately report it to the researcher.

What's more, the respondents may not *want* to report it, especially if the information involves embarrassing, illegal, or questionable behavior. According to one survey, for example, "the average person tells four lies a day" (*WorldNetDaily.com*, 2008, para. 1). Hmm. But what if the respondents *lied* to the interviewer(s) who conducted the survey? A study by several experts on deception found that people tell, on average, two lies per day (DePaulo, Kashy, Kirkendol & Wyer, 1999). Another claims that the average person tells three lies per ten minutes of conversation (Ekman, 2009). Such estimates vary widely because people have different conceptions, motives, habits, and opportunities for lying, among other things. In addition, the methodology used in a particular study has a lot to do with the results obtained (Serota, Levine & Boster, 2010).

Erroneous Extrapolations

Sometimes people make statistical projections that are unwarranted. For example, suppose a new company made a 5 percent profit in its first year, a 10 percent profit in its second year, and a 20 percent profit in its third year. Based on this trend, would it be safe to assume that the company will double its profits every year? Probably not. Indeed, doubling a smaller number, like $100 into $200, may be easier than doubling a larger number, like $500,000 into a million dollars. Plus, demand may level off, competitors may appear, and the economy could sour. In other words, the company might remain profitable, but it would be foolish to assume profits would continue to double indefinitely. Hence the stock market adage, "past performance is no guarantee of future results."

Keep the Numbers in Perspective

Startling statistics can be used for fear-mongering. For instance, a TV show on food allergies, titled "One Bite and You're Dead," may proclaim that 200 people—mostly children—die every year from allergic reactions to food (see, for example, Broussard, 2009). No wonder peanuts are banned in school lunches. Even one death from an allergic reaction to food is too many. Nevertheless, kids are more likely to choke to death on food than die from an allergic reaction. Big bites, not peanuts, pose a greater risk. Other risks pose a greater danger too, including deaths from car accidents, handguns, drownings, burns, poisonings, and pedestrian fatalities. So yes, perhaps grade school teachers should carry an EpiPen, but they would do even better by learning the Heimlich maneuver.

Considering this, when you are presented with a scary statistic, it helps to put the numbers in perspective. For instance, people may worry about road rage, but they are far more likely to die in a traffic accident because they failed to wear their seatbelt. Rabies, mad cow disease, and leprosy might sound scary, but the odds of contracting these diseases are extremely remote. Fewer than two people per year in the U.S. die from rabies (CDC, 2010a). No one in the U.S. has died from mad cow disease. Leprosy, or Hansen's disease, is difficult to contract and highly treatable. In comparison, some 10,000 or more people die each year in the U.S. from the flu (CDC, 2010b), yet many people don't even bother to get a flu shot.

Summary

People believe all sorts of weird things; that a flying saucer crashed in Roswell, New Mexico, that the moon landing was faked, that Bigfoot is alive and well, that black helicopters are monitoring U.S. citizens, that September 11th was an inside job, and that Barack Obama's birth certificate was faked. In order to navigate the maze of "proof" for such claims, you must be able to apply tests of evidence. For field-dependent disputes, arguers should apply evidentiary standards appropriate to a particular field. For everyday disagreements, arguers often have to negotiate the criteria for evaluating evidence themselves. Evidence is often incomplete. The key is to use the best available evidence, whatever it happens to be.

A number of tests of sources were discussed, including whether the source is known, qualified, and unbiased. Generally speaking, anecdotal evidence and testimonials are suspect forms of evidence and should be accepted cautiously or avoided altogether. Relying on scholarly journal articles and the consensus of expert opinion is a better way to go. The preponderance of evidence is a weaker standard, but can be applied more rigorously than a simple balancing test.

Despite widespread claims of a liberal media bias, empirical studies show that mainstream news sources generally do not exhibit favoritism toward left-leaning stories. In order of least to most biased are: scholarly journals, newspapers, television network news, radio, and the blogosphere. Five strategies for overcoming bias were discussed.

In addition to applying tests of sources, evidence should be evaluated in terms of its context, relevance, recency, and reliability. New technologies, such as Wikipedia, Twitter, and social media, have complicated the task of evaluating evidence. At the same time, fact-checking has been made easier by new technology..

When statistical proof is offered in support of a claim, you should ask whether the numbers make sense on their face. Determine whether the statistic is even knowable and how the statistic was calculated. Watch for faulty extrapolations and keep the numbers in perspective. Finally, don't rely on non-scientific polls that depend on atypical samples, include biased questions, or have large (or unknown) sampling error. Critical thinking is not based on how strongly one holds one's beliefs, but on how well one's beliefs are supported by evidence. Pay attention to the proof.

Notes

1 To illustrate the limitations of relying on a simple balancing test, suppose a woman buys ten apricots, six from "Moe's Grocery Store" and four from "Penny's Produce Stand." After eating all 10 apricots she develops food poisoning. Lab tests show there was salmonella in at least one of the apricots, but there is no way of determining which one(s). Based on a simple balancing test, should the woman be able to file a civil suit and win a judgment against Moe's Grocery Store? After all, the odds that the apricots came from his store are greater than not (60 percent versus 40 percent).
2 The rules regarding germane and non-germane amendments vary in the House of Representatives and the Senate. In the Senate, for instance, an amendment need not be germane unless the bill involves appropriations and budgets, or the bill is under cloture, or there is a consent agreement in place.

References

Ackerman, P. (2017, September 14). Rebel Wilson wins record $4.5m defamation payout. *The Australian*. Retrieved on October 23, 2017 from: www.theaustralian.com.au/news/nation/rebel-wilson-wins-45m-defamation-payout/news-story/e0168d8ffe74d4ac99946990861f0947.

Anderegg, W.R.L., Prall, J.W., Harold, J. & Schneider, S.H. (2010, online early edition). Expert credibility in climate change. *Proceedings of the National Academy of Sciences*. Retrieved on August 22, 2010 from: www.pnas.org/content/early/2010/06/04/1003187107.full.pdf+html.

Anderson, J. (2015, October 16). Dan Rather vs. George W. Bush: 'Truth' comes out. *Fortune*. Retrieved on January 11, 2018 from: http://fortune.com/2015/10/16/truth-cbs-rather-bush.

Badenhausen, K. (2017, August 14). Serena Williams heads the highest paid female athletes 2017. *Forbes*. Retrieved on January 11, 2018 from: www.forbes.com/sites/kurtbadenhausen/2017/08/14/the-highest-paid-female-athletes-2017/#364564763d0b.

Ben-Zvi, D. & Garfield, J. (Eds) (2004). *The challenge of developing statistical literacy, reasoning, and thinking*. New York: Kluwer Academic Publishers.

Blackwell, T. (2009, March 23). Young doctors learn bad habits from TV medical dramas. *The National Post*. Retrieved November 27, 2009 from: www.nationalpost.com/news/story.html?id=1419824.

Bono, A. (2004). John Jay study reveals extent of abuse problem. Retrieved September 20, 2010 from: www.americancatholic.org/news/clergysexabuse/johnjaycns.asp.

Bright, D.A. & Goodman-Delahunty, J. (2006). Gruesome evidence and emotion: Anger, blame, and jury decision-making. *Law and Human Behavior*, *30*(2), 183–202, doi: 10.1007/s10979-006-9027-y.

Broussard, M. (2009, January 17). Food allergy deaths: Less common than you think. *Huffington Post*. Retrieved on January 10, 2018 from: www.huffingtonpost.com/meredith-broussard/food-allergy-deaths-less_b_151462.html.

Butler, D. & Schoefield, E. (2010). Were newspapers more interested in Pro-Obama letters to the editor in 2008? Evidence from a field experiment. *American Political Research*, *38*(2), 356–371, doi.org/10.1177/1532673X09349912.

Callins v. *Collins*, 510 U.S. 1141, 1145 (1994). (Blackman, J., dissenting).

Centers for Disease Control and Prevention (2010a). *Rabies*. Atlanta, GA: Centers for Disease Control and Prevention. Retrieved August 30, 2010 from: www.cdc.gov/rabies/location/usa/index.html.

Centers for Disease Control and Prevention (2010b). *Estimating seasonal influenza-associated deaths in the United States: CDC study confirms variability of flu*. Atlanta, GA: Centers for Disease Control and Prevention. Retrieved August 31, 2010 from: www.cdc.gov/flu/about/disease/us_flu-related_deaths.htm.

D'Alessio, D. & Allen, M. (2007a). Media bias in presidential elections: A meta-analysis. *Journal of Communication*, *50*(4), 133–156, doi: 10.1111/j.1460-2466.2000.tb02866.x.

D'Alessio, D. & Allen, M. (2007b). On the role of newspaper ownership on bias in presidential campaign coverage by newspapers. In R.W. Preiss, B.M. Gayle, N. Burrell, M. Allen & J. Bryant (Eds), *Mass media effects research: Advances through meta-analysis* (pp. 429–454). Mahwah, NJ: Lawrence Erlbaum Associates.

Death Penalty Information Center (2019). Facts About the Death Penalty. Washington, DC: Death Penalty Information Center. Retrieved February 23, 2019 from: https://deathpenaltyinfo.org/documents/FactSheet.pdf.

DePaulo, B.M., Kashy, D.A., Kirkendol, S.E. & Wyer, M.M. (1999). Lying in everyday life. *Journal of Personality and Social Psychology*, *70*(5), 979–995, doi.org/10.1037/0022-3514.70.5.979.

Eisinger, R.M., Veenstra, L.R. & Koehn, J.P. (2007). What media bias? Conservative and liberal labeling in major U.S. newspapers. *Harvard International Journal of Press/Politics*, *12*(1), 17–36, doi.org/10.1177/1081180X06297460.

Ekman, P. (2009). *Telling lies: Clues to deceit in the marketplace, politics, and marriage*. New York: W.W. Norton.

Federal Trade Commission (FTC) (2009, October 5). *FTC publishes final guides governing endorsements, testimonials*. Washington, DC: Federal Trade Commission. Retrieved June 27, 2010 from: www.ftc.gov/opa/2009/10/endortest.shtm.

Fisher, A. (2005, December 12). Psst! Rumors can help at work. *Fortune*, *152*(12), 202.

Flanagin, A.J. & Metzger, M.J. (2007). The role of site features, user attributes, and information verification behaviors on the perceived credibility of web-based information. *New Media & Society*, *9*(2), 319–342, doi.org/10.1177/1461444807075015.

Forbes (2017, May 15). Your social media newsfeed and the algorithms that drive it. *Forbes*. Retrieved on January 11, 2018 from: www.forbes.com/sites/quora/2017/05/15/your-social-media-news-feed-and-the-algorithms-that-drive-it/#4e45650b4eb8.

Giles, J. (2005). Internet encyclopedias go head to head. *Nature, 438*(7070), 900–901, doi: org/10.1038/438900a.

Glanfield, T. (2009, November 25). Giant vulnerability to misinformation, mischief, and malice. *The Times* (London), p. 7.

Goldberg, B. (2002). *Bias: A CBS insider exposes how media distort the news*. Washington, DC: Regnery Publishing.

Gunther, A.C. & Liebhart, J. (2006). Broad reach or biased source? Decomposing the hostile media effect. *Journal of Communication, 56*(3), 449–466, doi: 10.1111/j.1460-2466.2006.00295.x.

Hill, A.D., Ridge, J.W. & Ingram, A. (2017, February 24). The growing conflict-of-interest problem in the Congress. *Harvard Business Review*. Retrieved on January 6, 2018 from: https://hbr.org/2017/02/the-growing-conflict-of-interest-problem-in-the-u-s-congress.

Hornig, M., Briesse, T., Buie, T., Bauman, M., Lauwers, G., Siemetzki, U., Hummel, K., Rota, P.A., Bellini, W.J., O'Leary, J.J., Sheils, O., Alden, E., Pickering, L. & Lipkin, W.I. (2008). Lack of association between measles virus vaccine and autism with enteropathy: A case-controlled study. *PloS One, 3*(9): e3140.doi:10.1371/journal.pone.0003140. Retrieved December 2, 2009 from: www.plosone.org/article/info%3Adoi%2F10.1371%2Fjournal.pone.0003140.

Hudson, A. (2009, February 13). Autism claims denied due to lack of evidence. *Washington Times*, p. A-3.

Hulse, C. (2009). Bill changing credit card rules is sent to Obama with gun measure included. *New York Times*. Retrieved on January 10, 2018 from: www.nytimes.com/2009/05/21/us/politics/21cards.html.

Kaye, D. (2006). The limits of the preponderance of evidence standard: Justifiably naked statistical evidence and multiple causation. *Law & Social Inquiry, 7*(2), 487–516, doi.org/10.1111/j.1747-4469.1982.tb00464.x.

Kida, T.E. (2006). *Don't believe everything you think: The 6 basic mistakes we make when thinking*. Amherst, NY: Prometheus Books.

Krauthammer, C. (2005, January 14). Rather biased. *Washington Post*, p. A-19.

Kruskal, B. & Allen, C. (2008, January 31). Perpetrating the autism myth. *The Boston Globe*, p. A-11.

Kuperman, A.J. (2009, December 24). There's only one way to stop Iran. *New York Times*, p. A-23.

Lichter, R., Rothman, S. & Lichter, L. (1991). *The media elite*. New York: Hastings House.

Lorenzo, S. (2002). Tell it to the grapevine. *Communication World, 19*(4), 28, 48.

Lynam, D.R., Milich, R., Zimmerman, R., Novak, S.P., Logan, T.K., Martin, C., Leukefeld, C. & Clayton, R. (1999). Project DARE: No effects at 1-year follow-up. *Journal of Consulting and Clinical Psychology, 67*(4), 590–593.

Memmott, M. (2004, September 22). Bloggers keep eye on the news. *USA Today*, p. 8-A.

Metzger, M.J., Flanagin, A.J. & Medders, R.B. (2010). Social and heuristic approaches to credibility evaluation online. *Journal of Communication, 60*(3), 413–439, doi: org/10.1111/j.1460-2466.2010.01488.x.

Miller, L. & Reynolds, J. (2009). Autism and vaccination—the current evidence. *Journal for Specialists in Pediatric Nursing, 14*(3), 166–172, doi.org/10.1111/j.1744-6155.2009.00194.x.

Newstrom, J.W., Monczka, R.E. & Reif, W.E. (1974). Perceptions of the grapevine: Its value and influence. *Journal of Business Communication, 11*(3), 12–20, doi.org/10.1177/002194367401100303.

Olen, H. & Pollack, H. (2016). *The index card: Why personal finance doesn't have to be complicated*. New York: Portfolio/Penguin.

Perloff, R.A. (2015). A three-decade retrospective of the Hostile Media Effect. *Mass Communication and Society, 18*(6), 701–729, doi.org/10.1080/15205436.2015.1051234.

Pew Research Center (2017, May 9). Americans' attitudes about the news media deeply divided along partisan lines. Washington, DC: PEW Research Center. Retrieved February 23, 2019 from: www.journalism.org/2017/05/10/americans-attitudes-about-the-news-media-deeply-divided-along-partisan-lines/pj_2017-05-10_media-attitudes_a-07.

Redmayne, M. (1999). Standards of proof in civil litigation. *Modern Law Review*, *62*(2), 167–195, doi. org/10.1111/1468-2230.00200.

Rogue Industry (Editorial) (2009, May 31). *New York Times*, p. WK-7.

Sadler, T.D. (2004). Informal reasoning regarding social scientific issues: A critical review of research. *Journal of Research in Science Teaching*, *41*(5), 513–536, doi.org/10.1002/tea.20009.

Schiff, S. (2006, July 31). Know it all: Can Wikipedia conquer expertise? *The New Yorker*, *82*(23), 36.

Senger, E. (2009, May 19). Vexation over vaccines: Doctors fear Oprah deal with actress will renew inoculation hysteria. *The National Post* (Canada), p. A-3.

Serota, K., Levine, T. & Boster, F.J. (2010). The prevalence of lying in America: Three studies of self-reported lies. *Human Communication Research*, *36*(1), 2–25, doi.org/10.1111/j.1468-2958.2009.01366.x.

Sherman, L.W., Sommers, C.H. & Manno, B.V. (2000). The safe and drug-free schools program. *Brookings Papers on Education Policy*, *3*, 125–171, www.jstor.org/stable/20067221.

Stafford, T. (2014, June 18). How often do men really think about sex? *BBC*. Retrieved on January 11, 2018 from: www.bbc.com/future/story/20140617-how-often-do-men-think-about-sex.

Sultan, N.V. (2017, January 18). Senate vote on prescription drug price legislation calls loyalties into question. *www.opensecrets.com*. Retrieved on January 7, 2018 from: www.opensecrets.org/news/2017/01/a-senate-vote-on-prescription-drug-price.

WorldNetDaily.com (2008, January 21). No lie: People average 4 fibs a day. *WorldNetDaily.com*. Retrieved August 30, 2010 from: www.wnd.com/?pageId=45642.

Chapter 7

Informal Reasoning

Ordinary, Everyday Reasoning

Upon arriving at the scene of an apparent suicide, detective Keesha Kane observes a dead man slumped over his computer keyboard, a bullet hole in his right temple. A pistol lays within easy reach of his hand. Over the din of two barking dogs, the man's wife is hysterical. "I was asleep in the bedroom when I heard a pop or a bang," she explains. "I hurried downstairs, where I found my husband, exactly as you see him here. He's been depressed lately, but I never imagined . . .."

Detective Kane studies the scene, clicks a few computer files, and announces, "This was no suicide. The gun is near his right hand, the wound is to his right temple, and yet, his computer's mouse is set up for a southpaw."

"So?"

"Your husband was left-handed, suggesting that someone else shot him, then placed the gun near his right hand to make it *appear* like a suicide."

"But . . .." The wife hugs herself, shivering. "Who could have done such a thing?"

"Not an intruder. Just listen to your dogs. The way they're baying at me, no doubt they'd have gone crazy over an intruder. Surely, they'd have wakened you before a shot was fired. And yet, you claim that . . .."

"Duke! Bosco! Shut up! I'm trying to concentrate!"

The detective leans forward. "Mrs. Chandler, were you *truly* asleep when the shot was fired?"

"I loved my husband! If you're insinuating that . . .." The wife's eyes narrow into thin lines. Her voice goes deadly calm. "Why would I want him dead?"

"Better question: Why were some of his files deleted *after* you called 911? Perhaps we'll know better when we restore them," Kane declares. "In the meantime, you have the right to remain silent . . .."

In making the victim's wife a prime suspect, Detective Kane is relying on what's called *inductive reasoning*. She bases her initial suspicion on a *generalization* that left-handed people tend to hold guns with their left hands. She also makes a *causal inference* that murder, not suicide, was the cause of death, based on the inconsistency between the deceased's hand preference and the location of the gun. Furthermore, she relies on *sign reasoning* to infer that the dogs didn't bark because no stranger was present, and again on sign reasoning to infer that the files deleted after the husband's death provide clues to motives for the crime. Of course, Detective Kane may be wrong. She has made multiple assumptions and inferences. Nevertheless, her reasoning accounts for all the available evidence.

After reading this chapter, we hope you'll agree with us that being able to use informal reasoning, as the detective does, is essential for arguing and reasoning well. Understanding these types of inductive reasoning will improve your ability to make and refute arguments. With that in mind, in this chapter we'll take a look at several kinds of inductive reasoning, including cause–effect, analogy, sign, generalization, and example. First, however, let's examine inductive reasoning more broadly.

Inductive Reasoning Defined: Take a Leap

Inductive reasoning, otherwise known as informal reasoning, isn't just for detectives. Ordinary people use inductive reasoning all the time. It is the *lingua franca* of everyday argument. In fact, informal reasoning is so ubiquitous that we usually grasp arguments without even being aware of doing so. Simply stated, inductive reasoning is any form of reasoning that requires an inference. In the process of such reasoning, an arguer reaches a conclusion about something that is unknown on the basis of something that is known. For example, if you saw a woman's eyes tear up, you might infer that she was sad. Keep in mind, however, that although we use inductive reasoning regularly, we don't always use it well. Instead, we often jump to the wrong conclusions. For example, the woman in question might be crying with joy or cutting an onion. Whatever the case, her example illustrates an important characteristic of inductive reasoning. Specifically, inductive reasoning is *probabilistic* in nature, meaning that, when making an inference, we cannot be certain that we are correct.

Causal Reasoning: But Why?

Cause–effect reasoning attempts to answer questions that ask "why?" As such, causal reasoning is based on an inference that some cause, or *antecedent*, produces an effect, or *consequent*. As you might have guessed, causal inferences can be made about physical phenomena; e.g., a well-placed kick to the groin (cause) can leave a would-be assailant doubled over in pain (effect). Causal inferences also can be made about internal mental states; e.g., Lars' girlfriend dumped him (cause), which explains why he's so upset (effect). Causal inferences also may be made about social problems or circumstances; e.g., in the Great Recession, subprime mortgages and predatory lending (causes) led to the collapse of the housing market (effect). All the questions below center on causal controversies.

- Does frequent use of "earbuds" cause hearing loss?
- What causes autism?
- Did foreign bots or trolls affect the outcome of the 2016 presidential election?
- What makes some people gay?
- Are human activities the primary cause of global warming?
- Is marijuana a "gateway" drug?
- Does excessive exposure to TV impair infants' cognitive development?

Bases for Inferring Causation

How do people make causal inferences? The philosophers David Hume and John Stewart Mill suggested that people make causal inferences in a variety of ways (see Buehner, 2005; Ducheyne,

2008; Young, 1995). First, causation based on *temporal proximity* refers to our tendency to infer a cause–effect relationship when we observe that one event follows another closely in time. Imagine, for example, that you ate some "sofa" pizza, which you found under a couch cushion, and became ill soon afterwards. You might be tempted to infer that the pizza was the cause of your food poisoning. Keep in mind, however, that inferences such as these can be iffy. Studies have shown that even slight changes in the duration between antecedent and consequent can affect observers' judgments about causation (Shanks, Pearson & Dickinson, 1989).

Second, causation based on *physical contiguity* refers to our tendency to infer causation if one thing is close to, or contacts, another thing. For example, if you bit into a hot slice of pizza and burned the roof of your mouth, you might infer that scalding cheese produces seared flesh.

Finally, causation based on *constant conjunction*[1] refers to our tendency to infer causation when the relationship between one event and another is highly consistent or reliable. For example, if you develop heartburn every time you eat pizza with pepperoni, you might put "two and two together," inferring that pepperoni is responsible for your indigestion. Of these three mechanisms, constant conjunction appears to hold more sway as a basis for making causal inferences (Buehner & McGregor, 2009).

Tenets of Causal Reasoning

Causation Is Inferred, Not Directly Observed: Connecting the Dots

As we've already seen, one important feature of causal reasoning is that cause–effect relationships cannot be directly observed, they *must be inferred*.[2] People don't always realize when they make causal inferences, however. Instead, their initial inference is often remembered as if it were a fact. In one study, for example, when research participants were shown pictures of a shopper who picked up an orange from the floor of a supermarket, they assumed the shopper had dropped the orange (Hannigan & Reinitz, 2001). Subsequently, when the participants were shown a picture of the same shopper dropping an orange, they believed they had seen it before.

What's more, people often make causal inferences without thinking about them critically. This is especially true where controversial public policy issues are involved. Suppose, for example, that a high school adopted a policy requiring all students to wear uniforms (alleged cause). Afterwards, imagine that the same school witnessed a decrease in bullying (alleged effect). It would be easy to infer that the uniforms caused the decrease in violence. But what if other factors were responsible? For instance, what if the school had adopted, at the same time, a zero tolerance policy? Or hallway monitors? Or imagine that violence declined at all the other schools in the district too, even those that didn't require uniforms. We hope you see our point. Careless causal inferences can, in and of themselves, lead to all sorts of problems!

Causation Isn't a Sure Thing: Some Doubt About It

That said, you needn't be 100 percent certain of causal inferences to make use of them. To be sure, observed regularities between two events are often imperfect. Take a cause such as studying hard, for example. Burying your nose in a book (even this one!) won't *always* produce the desired effect (a high score on a test). Because cause–effect relationships are inferred, the strength of such inferences varies, meaning that some inferences leave more room for doubt than others.

For example, did you know that wearing a seatbelt (cause) improves your likelihood of surviving a car crash (effect) by about 48 percent (Glassbrenner, 2003)? While not perfect, that's still a pretty good reason to buckle up. On the other hand, did you know that the odds of drowning (1 in 1,073) are greater than the odds of being shot and killed (1 in 5,981) (according to the National Safety Council, 2010)? Although death from either cause is unlikely, you would be well-advised to take precautions to minimize such risks; e.g., don't swim alone in the ocean and don't go bird hunting with a clumsy friend. An arguer, then, need not be certain of a causal connection in order to advance a causal argument.

A Cause Must Precede Its Effect: First Things First

A third tenet of causal reasoning is that the cause, or antecedent, must occur *before* the effect, or consequent. Otherwise, the wrong cause has been identified. This seems fairly obvious. Lightning, for example, causes thunder, not the reverse. In some cases, however, it may be difficult to determine the sequence of causality. Is urban blight caused by businesses moving away, or do businesses move away because of urban blight? Does playing violent video games make kids more aggressive or are more aggressive kids drawn to violent video games? In such "chicken vs egg" questions, determining cause and effect can be difficult.

Correlation Does Not Prove Causation: Casual Not Causal

A final tenet of causal reasoning says this: Correlation does not equal causation. Two events may be correlated without being causally connected. A well-known example is that ice cream sales correlate strongly with drowning deaths. Specifically, as ice cream sales increase, so do drownings and, as ice cream sales decrease, drownings decrease too. No one is suggesting that ice cream causes people to drown, or that after seeing someone drown, people crave ice cream. Both are effects of hot weather. When temperatures soar, people head for the water and for ice cream vendors.

As another example, a preliminary study (Karpinski & Duberstein, 2009) found that frequent Facebook users had lower grades in college. As a result of the study, some media outlets erroneously reported that using Facebook *caused* students to have lower grades (Young, 2009). But the authors of the study never made such a claim. Instead, they stressed that students who fancy Facebook may spend more of their free time enjoying leisure activities of all kinds; seeing movies, going to concerts, hanging out with friends. In other words, Facebook may not be the culprit. When a strong correlation between two phenomena is observed, it is worth looking into the possibility of a causal connection, however one shouldn't jump to conclusions.

Types of Causation: All Shapes and Sizes

Complex Causes: It's Complicated

Complex social problems rarely have a single cause. Childhood obesity, for example, has reached epidemic proportions. Although some people find it convenient to blame the fast food industry for making kids fat—as several civil suits brought by parents have alleged—the cause is not so simple. Sure, some Happy Meals exceed 500 calories, 23 percent of which comes from fat. Even so, you could just as easily indict parents for not preparing healthy meals at home. You could also blame TV, cell phones, and computers for making kids more sedentary. You could fault schools as well for decreasing time spent in physical education. The list goes on, but, hopefully, we've made our point: As an arguer and critical thinker, you should avoid over-simplifying issues and recognize when someone else is doing so. One way of avoiding oversimplification is to acknowledge a cause as only a contributing factor, a point we examine next.

Partial or Contributory Cause: Joining Forces

In music, three or more distinct notes must be played together to produce a chord. Each individual note forms part of the chord. Similarly, different causes may combine to bring about an effect. A *partial cause* or *contributory cause* helps produce an effect, but only with the help of other causes. A three-car pile-up, for example, might be the result of contributory negligence on the part of all the drivers involved. The first might have been tailgating, the second might have been texting, and the third might have had faulty brakes. Each driver's behavior, by itself, might not have resulted in an accident, but, taken together, their combined errors allowed the accident to occur. As another example, a physician might tell a patient with heart disease, "Your weight, your smoking, and your sedentary lifestyle are all contributing factors to your heart problems. You're going to have to diet, exercise, and stop smoking if you want to avoid another heart attack."

Necessary Cause: It's a Must

There is an old joke in which a tourist asks a New York City cabdriver, "How do you get to Carnegie Hall?" "Practice," answers the cabbie, "practice."

That practicing is a must if you want to become a concert performer illustrates what is known as a *necessary cause*. As its name implies, a necessary cause *must be present* in order for the effect to occur. Remove the cause, and there won't be an effect. For example, adequate vitamin C intake is necessary to prevent scurvy. Unlike most mammals, the human body does not produce its own vitamin C. Even a moderate shortage of vitamin C can increase susceptibility to bruising or impede the healing of wounds. As another example, it is necessary to prepare *fugu*, or puffer fish, very carefully to avoid lethal poisoning. A single bite of an improperly cleaned fish can prove fatal. For additional examples, consider the statements below. They all exemplify a necessary cause inasmuch as a specific requirement or condition must be met in order to bring about a specific effect.

- No pain, no gain.
- It takes money to make money.
- No shirt, no shoes, no service.
- You snooze, you lose.
- It takes two to tango.
- Nothing ventured, nothing gained.

Although a necessary cause must be present for the effect to occur, it's important to understand that the mere presence of a necessary cause is no guarantee that the effect will occur. To be inducted into the Baseball Hall of Fame, for example, a player must have played for at least 10 seasons and been retired for at least five years. Satisfying those necessary requirements, however, is still no guarantee of getting in. The player has to be pretty darn good too. Only a few elite players are enshrined into the Hall of Fame each year.

Another key point to remember is that while a necessary cause *must be present* for the effect to occur, it *may not be sufficient* to bring about the effect all by itself. To start a car, for instance, you need a working battery, but that's not all you need (got gas?). The bottom line is that your causal inferences will be stronger if you keep in mind that *a* cause is not necessarily *the* cause of a particular effect.

Sufficient Cause: Enough Is Enough

A second type of cause, known as a *sufficient cause*, is one that is capable of producing an effect all by itself. For instance, the saying "an apple a day keeps the doctor away" implies that eating apples regularly is sufficient to avoid illness. Conversely, the saying "money can't buy happiness" suggests that being rich, in and of itself, is insufficient to guarantee contentment. A real-life example of a sufficient cause is that, for a child with a severe peanut allergy, ingesting even a small amount of peanut butter is sufficient to cause anaphylactic shock. As another example, based on the 14th Amendment, being born in the United States is sufficient for being considered a U.S. citizen.

Although a sufficient cause will produce an effect, in and of itself, it is not the *only means* of producing the effect. Indeed, a person can become a naturalized U.S. citizen without being born in the U.S., and a child who is allergic to peanuts might also be allergic to bee stings, either of which could produce anaphylactic shock. As another illustration, consider the variety of means fiction writers have invented for killing a vampire. To kill a vampire, it would be sufficient to drive a wooden stake through his/her/its heart. There are other ways of offing a vampire though, including direct exposure to sunlight, crosses and holy water, and removal of native soil.[3] Nevertheless, a wooden stake through the heart will do the trick. In short, your causal inferences will be stronger if you remember that *a* cause is not necessarily the *only* cause of a particular effect. We examine the latter type of cause next.

Sole Cause: The One and Only

The real estate axiom "location, location, location" suggests that location is the one and only thing that matters when buying a home. If that were true, location would be an example of a third type of cause, known as a *sole cause*. Specifically, a sole cause is the *only cause* that produces a particular effect. A sole cause therefore satisfies *both* the necessary *and* sufficient tests. That is, the cause must be present for the effect to occur (necessary), and, if present, the cause will produce the effect by itself (sufficient). For example, the sole cause of Down Syndrome is a genetic abnormality involving chromosome 21.[4] As another example, an autopsy might determine that electrocution was the sole cause of a person's death. True, there are many ways to die, but for a particular person, say, a golfer who insisted on playing golf during a thunderstorm, electrocution might be the one and only cause of death.

Root Cause: What Lies Beneath?

As we noted earlier, complex social problems rarely have a sole cause. Because social problems are thorny, some arguers offer what they consider to be the *root cause* of a problem instead. A root cause is viewed as the fundamental underlying cause of a number of effects. Sure, other causes may play a role, but the root cause, or *proximate cause* as it's known in legal reasoning, is the most direct primary cause that can be identified. The expression "the love of money is the root of all evil" identifies a root cause. Marxists maintain that the root cause of oppression is the division of society into social classes, in which the few control the means of production for the many. Radical feminists argue that the root cause of female inequality is a patriarchal society. Foreign policy experts suggest that poverty and injustice are the root causes of terrorism. Advocates of family values argue that the root cause of many social problems is the decline of the traditional two-parent family.

Identifying a root cause can be tricky because there is always the risk of oversimplification. For instance, poverty and injustice may be breeding grounds for terrorism, but religious extremism plays a role as well. What's more, attempts to identify root causes are subject to what's known as *reductionism* or an infinite regress, which occurs when a sequence of reasoning never stops. By way of example: If the decline of the traditional two-parent family is the source of all of society's woes, then what is responsible for the decline of the two-parent family? And so on . . ..

Effect-to-Cause Inference: Reasoning Backwards

Arguers sometimes reason backwards, by first observing an effect and then inferring its likely cause. This sort of reasoning, known as *effect-to-cause reasoning*, is actually a form of *sign reasoning*, which we consider later in this chapter. For now, here's how it works. Suppose Zelda noticed that Navi had a black eye and, as a result, inferred that Navi had gotten into a fistfight. Zelda would be using effect-to-cause reasoning, but can you see where Zelda might be wrong? If you're thinking that the shiner could be due to any number of causes—say, eye surgery, taking a line drive to the face, or falling off a beanstalk—good for you! To infer that a fight was the most likely cause, Zelda would have to know something else about Navi, for example, that she is hot-headed or prone to fisticuffs. Even then, she could be wrong.

That's not to say that effect-to-cause reasoning is something to avoid. In fact, we often use effect-to-cause reasoning when making inferences about people's internal mental states. If a classmate passed you on campus and failed to say hello, you might try to guess why. Did she not see you? Was she preoccupied? Is she mad at you? In this respect, we are all amateur psychologists who go about inferring why people say the things they say or do the things they do. This is why perception checking (discussed in Chapters 1 and 2) is such a valuable skill. It prevents us from jumping to the wrong conclusions.

Reciprocal Causation

Imagine the following conversation between a motorist and a passenger:

Earl: "Stop telling me how to drive!"
Trudy: "If you paid closer attention to your driving, I wouldn't need to say anything!"
Earl: "I could pay closer attention if you'd stop bugging me about my driving!"

In this example, each person sees the other's behavior as the cause and their own reaction as the effect. The example illustrates that two things may be *both* causes and effects of one another. In such cases, cause and effect are bidirectional. As another example, one country's foreign policy may affect another country's foreign policy and vice versa. When North Korea makes threatening statements toward the U.S., the U.S., in turn, engages in more saber rattling, which only provokes North Korea into more blustering, which causes the U.S. to engage in more military posturing, and so on. You can improve your causal reasoning by remembering that sometimes causation is a two-way street.

Causal Chains: One Thing Leads to Another

Edward Lorenz, who is often referred to as the father of chaos theory, presented a lecture in 1972 with the provocative title, "Does the flap of a butterfly's wings in Brazil set off a tornado in Texas?" His idea, dubbed the *butterfly effect*, was that even the smallest of changes in a complex dynamic system could produce huge unintended effects. Arguments based on causal chains embody this principle. A causal chain involves a sequence of events in which an initial cause produces an effect, and that effect, in turn, acts as a cause that produces its own effect, and so on. Such arguments are often referred to as a "snowball effect," "domino theory," a "slippery slope," or a "ripple effect." For example, at some point, HIV/AIDS jumped from a chimpanzee in West Africa to humans and mutated into a worldwide pandemic (Sharp & Hahn, 2011).

Along these same lines, did you know that the development of Viagra may have helped protect a number of endangered species? No, zookeepers aren't giving blue pills to pandas to increase their libido. It's more complicated than that. Here's the explanation: One of the major threats to endangered species is poaching. Poachers kill exotic animals for a variety of reasons, one of which is that some species are coveted for their aphrodisiac properties (Prusher, 2001). Powdered rhinoceros horn and tiger-penis soup, for example, are believed to enhance virility (*The Economist*, 1998). Trading in endangered species is illegal, which makes aphrodisiacs sold on the black market expensive. What's more, there is no proof that the concoctions actually work. Viagra's effectiveness, on the other hand, has been demonstrated in clinical trials. It's also relatively inexpensive and it's readily available. So, why pay $500 for a black market potion, when you can get a Viagra prescription for $20? Viagra's effectiveness has decreased the demand for black market aphrodisiacs, which, in turn, has reduced the profit motive for poaching endangered species. As weird as it may seem, then, Viagra and other erectile dysfunction pills are a link in the causal chain that is helping protect endangered species (von Hippel, von Hippel, Chan & Cheng, 2005).

Faulty Cause

People are so adept at perceiving causal relationships that they perceive them even where none exist. For example, a superstitious person might believe it's bad luck (effect) if a black cat crosses his or her path (cause). This particular fallacy, confusing coincidence with causation, is just one type of fallacious causal reasoning. We'll examine it and other types of faulty causal reasoning in the next chapter, but, now, let's turn to another type of reasoning.

Reasoning by Analogy: Life Is Like a Box of Chocolates

Analogies are one of the most common forms of inductive reasoning. At its most basic, an analogy makes a comparison between two things, events, or phenomena and argues that they are comparable in some important respect(s).[5] For example, analogies to life compare it with a "bowl of cherries," a "rat race," "a winding river," and a "roller coaster." As with all inductive reasoning, analogies may be flawed. Comparing life with a box of chocolates, for example, offers a rather rosy view of human existence. Whatever surprises await, the analogy suggests, they will be yummy.

Flawed yet Persuasive

From a purely logical standpoint, analogies are a weaker form of inductive reasoning. At some level, all analogies break down. After all, if two things were alike in every respect, they would be the same thing. That said, although analogies are not strictly logical, they can be highly persuasive. Their logical weakness is also their rhetorical strength: They reconceptualize something into terms that are easier to comprehend. For example, a doctor who compares "high cholesterol" to "hair that clogs your drain" might persuade patients to eat healthier by helping them understand health risks in ways they hadn't before (Osborne, 2003).

How Analogical Reasoning Works

Most analogies involve a *source domain*, e.g., something that is familiar, and a *target domain*, something that is less familiar. The key features of the source domain must be transferable to the target domain. For example, in aeronautics, a bird's wing (source domain) can be likened to an airplane's wing (target domain). The curvature of a bird's wing corresponds with the camber of an airplane wing. Both are curved, which causes air to pass more quickly over the wing than beneath it. The faster air above has less air pressure than the slower air below, which provides lift. Of course, a bird's wing is covered in feathers; an airplane wing is not. Birds also flap their wings; planes do not. These features of the source and target are non-transferable.

As another example, Charles Darwin applied knowledge about the breeding of domesticated animals to develop insights into processes governing natural selection among other species (Holyoak, 2005). In the same way that breeders select tamer species for domestication, nature "selects" fitter species for survival. Controlled studies demonstrate that people are successful at analogical transfer anywhere from 12 to 79 percent of the time, depending on the nature and difficulty of the problem (Koenig & Griggs, 2004).

Analogies and Critical Thinking

Analogies aid critical thinking. How? In the process of moving from the source to the target domain, new insights can be generated (Krawczyk, McClelland, Donovan, Tillman & Maguire, 2010). As such, analogies help us solve problems by allowing us to think about solutions in new and creative ways. As an illustration, a classic study by Glick and Holyoak (1980) demonstrated that people were able to use knowledge from one problem-solving situation, involving a general attacking a fortress from multiple directions, to a new problem-solving situation, requiring the use of lasers, aimed from multiple directions, to destroy a tumor.

Literal and Figurative Analogies: Explaining a Joke Is Like Dissecting a Frog

Analogies may be literal or figurative. Literal analogies compare similar things in similar classes. For example, you might compare a prolific home run hitter, such as Barry Bonds, with Roger

Maris or Babe Ruth. Likewise, some critics argued that Hurricane Maria was President Donald Trump's "Katrina," drawing a literal analogy between President George W. Bush's mishandling of relief efforts to New Orleans following Hurricane Katrina, and Trump's sluggishness in responding to the devastation that hit Puerto Rico in 2017. Not surprisingly, President Barack Obama's less than speedy response to an oil spill in the Gulf of Mexico drew similar comparisons. As you might have imagined, literal analogies are usually easier to grasp and contest, since the comparison involves similar phenomena.

Other analogies are figurative: They make comparisons across different classes of things. Explaining a joke isn't *literally* like dissecting a frog, but as White and White observed (1941), neither the frog nor the joke is better off afterward. As another example, comparing someone to a "fish out of water" relies on a figurative analogy. The person isn't *literally* a fish, but rather is out of his or her natural element. Likewise, a task that is so easy it's "like taking candy from a baby," doesn't require an *actual* baby, but rather the imagination to understand that babies are (wait for it!) sitting ducks, yet another figurative analogy. Figurative analogies involving sports are common in politics, business, and other fields. A politician might say, "This bill is a slam dunk," or "my opponent fumbled the ball on Social Security." Likewise, a CEO might say, "We're going to play hardball with the competition." Generally speaking, figurative analogies are harder to grasp and challenge because the bases for comparison are less obvious.

Two-Part and Four-Part Analogies

Some analogies involve only two elements, that is, a comparison between A and B. Comparing Lady GaGa with Madonna, for example, involves a two-part analogy. During his confirmation hearing to become Chief Justice of the U.S. Supreme Court, John Roberts used the following two-part analogy to compare the role of a judge with that of an umpire.

> Judges and justices are servants of the law, not the other way around. Judges are like umpires. Umpires don't make the rules; they apply them. The role of an umpire and a judge is critical. They make sure everybody plays by the rules. But it is a limited role. Nobody ever went to a ball game to see the umpire. (Roberts, 2010, cited in AmericanRhetoric.com, 2017)

Other analogies, known as arguments based on *parallel case*, involve four elements, wherein the relationship of A to B is analogous to the relationship between C and D. Here are two examples:

- "Beethoven is to classical music what van Gogh is to impressionistic painting."
- "The Bible is to Christianity what the Koran is to Islam."

Yet another example of a four-part analogy can be found in American columnist Michael Hiltzik's explanation of why he thinks good CEOs do not necessarily make good politicians. Although he notes that some leadership qualities overlap, he cautions that

> Many qualities that make a good CEO are necessary, but not sufficient, to make a good politician, in the same sense that a concert violinist and a neurosurgeon need supple fingers—but that doesn't mean you'd want a violinist to perform your surgery. (Hiltzik, 2010, p. B-12)

Stare Decisis: Analogy in Law

Analogies play a key role in jurisprudence. The doctrine of *stare decisis* relies on the use of legal precedents as a basis for interpreting the law. Simply put, judges make decisions based on comparisons between prior cases and current ones. For example, the U.S. Supreme Court has a long history of supporting the right to bear arms, based on the Second Amendment. Thus, it isn't surprising that the Court overturned a ban on handguns enacted in Washington, D.C. in 2008 (*District of Columbia* v. *Heller*, 554, U.S.) and a ban on handguns in the home that Chicago adopted in 2010 (*McDonald* v. *Chicago*, U.S.). As Justice Alito wrote in the majority opinion, "It is clear that the Framers . . . counted the right to keep and bear arms among those fundamental rights necessary to our system of ordered liberty" (Barnes & Eggen, 2010).

Box 7.1   The Overworked Hitler Analogy

Dave Barry, one of our favorite satirists, suggests that winning any argument is as easy as telling your opponent, "That sounds suspiciously like something Adolf Hitler might say" or "You certainly do remind me of Adolf Hitler" (as cited in Adler & Proctor, 2011, p. 353). He's joking, of course, but, let's face it, some analogies are overworked, and the Hitler analogy is a case in point. In fact, invoking the name of Adolf Hitler as a catch-all for any-one held in disdain tends to short-circuit rational thinking. If your professor doesn't allow texting during class, your professor is not Adolf Hitler. If your step-mom doesn't approve of an outfit you are wearing, she is not Adolf Hitler. Once someone plays the Hitler card, the tone and tenor of an argument turns ugly. Moreover, using the Hitler analogy tends to trivialize the true heinousness of Hitler's crimes against humanity.

Hitler analogies are also downright unoriginal. Why not be more creative and find a better historical parallel? Consider some lesser evil character from history, literature, or cinema. You could go with a fictitious evil prison warden, such as Warden Norton from *The Shawshank Redemption*. Other options include Simon Legree from *Uncle Tom's Cabin* or William Bly from *Mutiny on the Bounty*. Or how about Al Capone, Benedict Arnold, the Joker, Lex Luthor, Moriarty, or Vlad the Impaler? If the target of your analogy is a female, consider lesser evil *femme fatales* such as Beverly Gail Allit (The "Angel of Death"), Helen Grayle (a.k.a VelmaValento from Raymond Chandler's *Farewell My Lovely*), Lizzie Borden, Mary Anne Cotton (the "Black Widow"), *Apprentice* contestant Omerosa, Nurse Ratched (from *One Flew Over the Cuckoo's Nest*), or Ursula (from the *Little Mermaid*). If you are going to be mean-spirited (and we hope you won't!), at least be original. Better yet, when feeling snippy, you could always reread Chapter 2. Invoking Hitler's name tends to provoke defensiveness rather than dialogue. To promote reasoned argument, avoid playing the Hitler card.

Structural Versus Superficial Features

Some analogies are more fitting than others and being able to understand why is crucial to becoming a critical thinker and effective arguer. The key is whether an analogy's points of comparison are similar in their *relevant important respects*. According to Blanchette and Dunbar

(2001; Dunbar, 2001), an essential skill involves the ability to differentiate the *superficial features* from the *structural features* of a comparison. Specifically, superficial features involve trivial or surface points, while structural features focus on substantive aspects of the comparison (Gentner, Rattermann & Forbus, 1993). For example, if someone were comparing the human eye with a camera, the fact that one requires a battery would involve a superficial point of comparison. On the other hand, the structural features of the analogy would focus (pun intended) on the optical functions performed by each. For example, the pupil is analogous to a camera's aperture (f-stop), and the cornea and lens of the eye are analogous to a camera's lens. A structural difference in the analogy is that the retina is an active system, sending information to the brain, whereas an analog camera's film or a digital camera's sensor and pixels are not.

Sign Reasoning: If It Walks Like a Duck, and Talks Like a Duck . . .

The comedian Jeff Foxworthy has made a comfortable living by telling jokes based on sign reasoning; e.g., "You might be a redneck if . . . ." So what, specifically, is sign reasoning? It is an inference based on the assumption that the presence of one thing is a reliable indicator or predictor of another thing. The saying "where there is smoke, there is fire" is based on such reasoning. Likewise, Hallmark's slogan, "When you care to send the very best," suggests that sending their brand of card signifies that you really care about someone.

   As you might have imagined, people rely on sign reasoning on a daily basis. Your doctor, for example, might look for medical symptoms (like a fever or sore throat), which are a type of sign, to make a preliminary diagnosis about an illness. Police detectives might rely on circumstantial evidence (e.g., threats made recently by a suspect before a victim was slain), which is also a type of sign, to help solve crimes. Economists use a variety of economic indicators to make predictions about the economy. In relationships, too, people use sign reasoning. On a first date, for example, two people may be looking for signs of compatibility or incompatibility. "She's into composting," he thinks to himself, "I'm all about living green as well." "He didn't flinch when I mentioned that I own 30 cats," she notes, "That's a plus." If she orders the most expensive item on the menu, however, he may infer that she is "high maintenance." And if he drinks way too much, she may see a "red flag," indicating alcoholism.

Signs Signify What, But Not Why

Although signs establish that a relationship exists between two things, sign reasoning itself doesn't explain *why* the relationship exists. If you saw a student rushing to class, you might take it as a sign that the student was late, but you wouldn't know why the student was late. As we've already seen, to answer why questions one must rely on cause–effect reasoning.

Fallible and Infallible Signs

The old saying "Don't judge a book by its cover" suggests that signs vary in their reliability. Some signs, like the groundhog's shadow, are highly *fallible*, even if fun. Other examples, however, are not so innocuous. Consider the practice of "racial profiling" by police (Barnum &

"The killer had to be a man. Not only is the knife still bloody—it wasn't even put in the sink."

Figure 7.1 Sign reasoning suggests the killer was a male. Cartoon by Kim Warp, *The New Yorker*, January 4, 2010.
© Kim Warp/The New Yorker Collection/www.cartoonbank.com.

Perfetti, 2010). Many African-Americans report being pulled over for an infraction facetiously dubbed as "DWB," or "driving while black." A black person driving an expensive car, or a clunker, in an affluent neighborhood may be stopped because he or she "looks suspicious." In fact, 85 percent of African-Americans believe that racial profiling by police is common (Warren, 2010). But does race alone make a person more suspicious? Relying on race as a reliable sign of illegal activity undermines the very principle of fairness and equality under the law (Miller, 2007) (for more on faulty sign reasoning, see Box 7.2).

Box 7.2   Bull's-Eye of the Hurricane

Given the choice of fighting someone named Rocco or someone named Tiffany, whom would you pick? What if Tiffany and Rocco were not people, but hurricanes? If this sounds like a silly question, think again, because hurricanes with female names kill more people than hurricanes with male names. That's according to a study that examined over 60 years of hurricane-related deaths (Jung, Shavitt, Viswanathan & Hilbe, 2014; also see Rice, 2014). But what's really going on here? It turns out that a combination of sexism and faulty sign reasoning may be the culprit. According to the study's authors, people may not take hurricanes with feminine names as seriously as those with masculine names. As a result, they fail to take warnings to prepare or evacuate for a hurricane "Hanna" as seriously as for a hurricane "Harvey."[6] Of course, the hurricane has no idea what its name is.

Not only is the likelihood of fearing a hurricane related to its name, but so is the willingness of people to donate to relief efforts following a hurricane. One study found that people whose first or last names shared an initial with a hurricane's name were more likely to donate to disaster relief in the aftermath of a storm (Chandler, Griffin & Sorensen, 2008). That's right, Betty, Bill, and Bob would be more likely to donate to disaster relief following a hurricane "Bruce" than would Annie, Jessica, or Sally.

Not content with anthropomorphizing tropical storms, some people have gone on the offensive. How so? According to one report, Florida authorities had to warn people *not* to fire their weapons at Hurricane Irma. "To clarify," a sheriff's office tweeted, "DO NOT shoot weapons @ #Irma. You won't make it turn around & it will have very dangerous side effects" (Porter, 2017, para. 2).

So what, we ask, is the solution? One possibility is to stop naming hurricanes after people. At one time, hurricanes were referred to by letters of the alphabet, e.g., Able, Baker, Charlie, Delta, Echo, Foxtrot, etc. Hurricanes could also be assigned numbers. Another option would be to assign names based on the predicted need for disaster relief. Adam Alter (2013) suggested giving the most serious tropical storms, ones that were expected to become major hurricanes, more popular names to increase charitable donations. As a point of comparison, over 4 million Americans are named James, compared with only 65,000 who are named Wade (https://names.mongabay.com/male_names.htm). Similarly, nearly 4 million women in the U.S. are named Mary, compared with only 12,000 Celinas (https://names.mongabay.com/male_names.htm). Another approach is for people to start thinking more critically about names and labels. Regardless of their names, hurricanes are neither male nor female. So, rather than ignore them or shoot it out, seek shelter instead.

That said, some signs are more reliable, such as the field sobriety test in which motorists are asked to track a moving object (pen, finger) with their eyes. According to the National Highway Traffic Safety Administration (NHTSA), the test is 77 percent accurate in determining intoxication when properly administered (Busloff, 1993). Diagnostic tests for STDs also are highly reliable, but not infallible. A person might get tested too early to manifest an infection, there are occasional false positives and false negatives, and there is also the possibility of a lab error.

A few signs are *infallible*, or nearly so, although most of these are found in the natural sciences. One example is DNA testing as a means of establishing paternity. For example, DNA tests have shown with 99 percent certainty that Thomas Jefferson fathered children with Sally Hemings, one of his slaves (Lander & Ellis, 1998; Lewis, 2004). Another infallible sign was featured on one of our favorite old television shows, *House, M.D.* (Mankiewicz & Medak, 2004). In it, a woman who appears to be schizophrenic collapses in the E.R. Following a series of misdiagnoses, the irascible Doctor House confirms, unequivocally, that the woman is suffering from Wilson's disease, a rare genetic condition in which the body is unable to metabolize copper. How so? House notices distinctive copper-colored circles—known as Kayser-Fleischer rings—around her corneas. Now, that's impressive sign reasoning!

Although all signs are not so reliable, many are practical and useful nonetheless. For example, if a person is wearing a wedding ring, we tend to assume that she or he is married. Most of the time, we're right. However, an unmarried female might wear a wedding ring to discourage others from "hitting on her" at the gym. A married male, who also was a philanderer, might remove his wedding ring while "playing the field" at a bar or club. See what we mean? Signs are often fallible, yet functional. A good poker player must be proficient at spotting "tells," e.g., nonverbal cues that are leaked by other players, and discerning which are genuine and which are fake. Reading tells isn't foolproof, but it is still an important aspect of the game. Besides that, signs might provide the only information available. If you saw a person walking toward you with a glazed look in the eyes, wielding a knife, and muttering "Must have . . . fresh blood," would you stand there and think, "Hey, I shouldn't jump to conclusions"?

Signs Add Up: Plus Signs and Minus Signs

One sign, by itself, may not mean much, but the impact of signs is cumulative. The more signs present, the more likely the inference that is being made. Suppose that a teen becomes depressed, expresses feelings of hopelessness, withdraws from family and friends, and starts giving away prized possessions. These could all be signs that the teen is suicidal and loved ones would be foolish to ignore them before intervening. As another example, if a woman missed her period, that alone wouldn't prove she was pregnant. But if she also experienced morning sickness, strange food cravings, and weight gain, she would be foolish to ignore the signs. A home pregnancy test would provide a nearly infallible sign of pregnancy, and a follow-up visit to a gynecologist could confirm the result.

Conversely, the presence of *negative signs* can refute an inference based on sign reasoning. If a suspect had the means and motive for committing a crime, but lacked the opportunity (the suspect has an iron-clad alibi), the lack of opportunity would be a negative sign of guilt. If a girlfriend didn't call or text her boyfriend as much as she used to, it could signify that she was losing interest in the relationship. It could be the case, however, that she received a "ginormous" phone bill and had to cut back on her cell phone use. If she emailed her boyfriend regularly that would be a negative sign that she was falling out of love.

Generalization: White Men Can't Jump

A fourth type of inductive reasoning is known as generalizing. When engaging in it, we use multiple instances, recurring patterns, or repeated observations to form inferences about an entire class or category. In short, we're forming and/or applying general rules.

"What makes you think I wouldn't be up for sushi?"

Figure 7.2 Sign reasoning in action. Cartoon by Leo Cullum, *The New Yorker*, November 17, 2008.
© Leo Cullum/*The New Yorker* Collection/www.cartoonbank.com.

Women Are From Venus, Men Are From Mars

For instance, comedians often segue into a joke by saying, "Men and women are different . . .." Generally speaking, they are right. For example, men are much more willing than women to engage in casual sex. In fact, according to one series of studies (Clark & Hatfield, 1989, 2003), when college students were approached by a stranger of the opposite sex who asked to engage in casual sex, males consented more than half the time. Females rarely consented. What's more, college males and females hold different beliefs about romance. Males, for example, are more likely to believe that "bars are good places to meet a potential mate" (Abowitz, Knox, Zusman & McNeely, 2009, p. 276).

Of course, not all females and males think and act this way. Generalizing is a risky business. Yet, life would be impossible if all knowledge were fragmented and particularized and we could not form generalizations. How could you set your alarm clock if you couldn't generalize about how long it took you to get ready in the morning? How could you get from home to work if you couldn't reasonably estimate the time required for your commute? Once at work, how could you interact with co-workers if you couldn't generalize about social norms governing communication? We hope you see our point. The key is to form accurate generalizations, qualify them appropriately, and articulate them to varying degrees, rather than seeing the world in black and white.

Universal Generalizations: All Unicorns Are White

Universal generalizations use terms such as "all," "every," "never," and "always." For example, one partner might tell the other "You never listen to me" or "You always have to get your way." A friend once told one of the authors "Every year, an Indian kid (meaning a child whose family is from the Indian subcontinent) wins the national spelling bee." "Every year?" the author asked. "What about Evan O'Dorney?" (who won in 2007). As a matter of fact, in 2017 Ananya Vinay became the 13th consecutive South Asian-American (including co-champs from 2014–2016) to win the Scripps National Spelling Bee (Harper, 2017), which is a long way from "every year" yet still consistent with the generalization.

Whatever the case, as critical thinkers, we'd be well-advised to regard universal generalizations with suspicion. The saying "there's an exception to every rule" acknowledges this guideline. Those who don't run the risk of committing a fallacy known as a *sweeping generalization*, by lumping everyone together in the same group. Cultural and ethnic stereotypes, for example, often entail this fallacy, which we'll return to in the next chapter. For now, however, it's enough to know that, technically speaking, *a single exception disproves a universal generalization*. Imagine, for instance, that a business owner claimed, "We haven't had a single case of sexual harassment in the workplace." By documenting one instance of harassment, you would refute the claim. Practically speaking, however, a single exception may not be that damaging, hence the saying "the exception that proves the rule." Suppose, for example, that a wife tells her husband, "We've been married 10 years, but you never remember our anniversary!" Would the husband be off the hook if he replied, "Not so, I remembered our 1st anniversary"?

Contingent Generalizations: It Depends

Considering this, generalizations that are qualified are a much safer bet. Specifically, by qualifying generalizations with words like "most," "often," and "many," you reduce the odds that your claim will be contested. Thus, instead of saying, "We *always* spend Thanksgiving with your parents," a spouse might say, "We've spent the last three Thanksgivings with your family." And instead of telling a student "You *never* come to class on time," a professor might say, "You've been tardy four of the last six class meetings."

Another way to qualify generalizations is to make them contingent on a particular set of circumstances. For example, when spelling words, the letter "i" usually comes before the letter "e," however the guideline, "'i' before 'e,' except after 'c'," specifies the conditions under which this is not the case. Even this general rule has exceptions, however. In the word "science," for example, the rule is broken. As another example, a pediatrician might tell a parent, "Aspirin is generally safe for children over the age of four, unless they have a fever, virus, or flu-like symptoms, in which case they may develop Reye's syndrome." Clearly, specifying the conditions under which a generalization holds true makes for a stronger argument.

Statistical Generalizations: Say It with Numbers

Another way of avoiding the pitfalls of universal generalizations is to provide statistical generalizations or averages. For example, an arguer might say "76% of felons are recidivists" (meaning that they commit crimes after being released from prison), rather than "all felons are recidivists." Similarly, an arguer might say "America ranks ninth in obesity worldwide and first among industrialized nations," rather than "America is a nation of fatsoes."

Two Types of Generalizations

From the Whole to the Part

In the process of making an argument, there are two ways you can advance a generalization. In the first, you start from a general rule and then apply it to a specific case. For example, a father might advise his young son, "Being left-handed is an advantage in some sports. As a lefty, you might think about taking up baseball, fencing, soccer, or tennis." The general rule, about left-handers having an edge in some sports, is applied to a specific case, his son. Of course, the son may or may not excel in these sports, but the father is trying to stack the odds in his son's favor by relying on a general rule.

From the Part to the Whole

In the second way to advance a generalization, you start with examples or a sample case and then form the generalization. Suppose Rita meets an LDS (Mormon) mom who loves to make casseroles, Jell-O desserts, and drink hot chocolate. Then she meets another LDS mother who also bakes casseroles, makes Jell-O, and drinks hot chocolate. When she meets a third LDS mom who does the same, she may form the generalization that "LDS moms have a thing for casseroles, Jell-O and hot chocolate." Of course, forming a generalization about a group based on a sample of three members could entail a fallacy known as a *hasty generalization*, which we discuss in the next chapter. That is why when pollsters survey people and conduct opinion polls they use a large sample of people, who are selected at random, and who represent a true cross-section of the larger class of people about whom they wish to generalize.

Example: Gimme a For Instance

A final type of inductive reasoning that we consider is argument by example, which involves offering anecdotal evidence about your own experience, or that of another, to prove a point. Arguments based on example are actually a sub-set of generalization, in which one or a few examples are offered as support for a claim about a larger class or category. Each example serves as proof for the larger generalization. Argument by example is so pervasive, however, that we believe it deserves its own place within the taxonomy of inductive reasoning.

When offering an example, the assumption is that the example is typical or representative of some larger class. If not, the arguer might be accused (or guilty) of "cherry picking" examples to suit his or her purpose. Testimonials, for instance, that accompany ads for weight loss products are subject to such bias. But how typical is their experience? How about the buff ripped models in fitness commercials? Do you really believe their physiques were ordinary before going to that gym or buying some exercise equipment?[7] Nyet! Logically speaking, a single example doesn't prove much. However, from a persuasive standpoint, a single example can be quite compelling. Statistics can be abstract, confusing, or daunting, but a single well-developed example can put a name or a face on a problem. Indeed, anecdotal evidence can be so powerful that people may give more weight to stories than they deserve (Kida, 2006). When using examples, then, a useful approach is to begin with an example, then provide statistics to show that it is not an atypical case (see Gass & Seiter, 2018). When challenging another arguer's example, you can offer negative or counter-examples of your own. You also can show that the examples offered are neither typical nor representative.

Summary

Inductive reasoning is the stuff of which everyday arguments are made. The types of informal reasoning discussed in this chapter are part and parcel of ordinary arguments. Inductive arguments always require some sort of inferential leap and some leaps are more probable than others. A variety of types of cause–effect reasoning were presented. Among these types, a necessary cause should not be confused with a sufficient cause and vice versa. Sole causes are somewhat rare in public policy controversies. Most social problems have complex causes. Analogies draw comparisons between a source domain and a target domain. They are useful for fostering critical and creative thinking and are highly persuasive. Analogies may be literal or figurative. The latter pose more difficulties for arguers because they compare different classes of things. When evaluating analogies, the focus should be on structural rather than superficial features. Sign reasoning is based on indicators whose presence predicts something else. Sign reasoning, however, cannot explain why one thing predicts another. Signs may be fallible or infallible. The latter are less common in ordinary arguments. Signs are also cumulative; the more signs the more likely that they mean something. Generalizing, while risky, is also inevitable. Contingent generalizations and statistical generalizations are preferred over universal ones. Generalizations may operate by applying a general rule to a specific case, or by forming a general rule based on a specific case or cases. Argument by example is a subset of generalization, with a sample of one. Although offering a single example is logically suspect, a well-developed example can resonate with people. People respond to stories and examples can be compelling.

Notes

1 *Constant conjunction* is also referred to as *concomitant variation* or *cause–effect contingency* (Buehner & McGregor, 2009).
2 There may be real physical cause–effect relationships, but humans still must infer their existence. With respect to physical phenomena, cause–effect relationships may be so direct that inferences are easy to draw. For example, if a person turns a light switch on and off, the person is closing and opening an electrical circuit. The flow of electricity (cause) makes the bulb glow (effect), while an interruption in the circuit makes the bulb dim (effect). This seemingly obvious causal connection must still be inferred, however. Suppose a light switch was not working. Instead, the circuit is connected to a motion detector. If a person enters a room and flips the switch on, the person would likely infer that flipping the switch turned the light on. In actuality, it is the person's movement that activated the motion detector and turned on the light.
3 For you vampire aficionados, we recognize that the ways a vampire can be killed depend on whether one is reading Bram Stoker, Anne Rice, Stephanie Meyer, or some other source. We're not sure Count Chocula can be killed!

4 There are actually three types of Down Syndrome; Trisomy 21, Mosaic Down Syndrome, and Translocation Down Syndrome, but all three are the result of abnormal cell division in chromosome 21.

5 For convenience sake, we've grouped all arguments based on comparisons, including metaphors, similes, parables, and precedents, under the rubric of analogy.

6 Some critics (e.g., Rudy, 2014) have suggested that, although the results of the hurricane study are interesting and may be correct, additional research is necessary. Specifically, because almost all hurricanes before 1979 had female names, it's possible that the study's results are due to improvements in forecasting hurricanes rather than the masculinity/femininity of names. If this is the case, the author's conclusions are a good example of faulty causal reasoning.

7 As an example, Bowflex holds casting calls for fitness models. For example, Gregg Pitt, one of the Bowflex models, has graced more than 100 magazine covers. Another, Andrew Brown, also endorses numerous other fitness products. Kristia Knowles, one of the females in the Bowflex commercials, is also a spokesperson for other fitness products.

References

Abowitz, D.A., Knox, D., Zusman, M. & McNeely, A. (2009). Beliefs about romantic relationships: Gender differences among undergraduates. *College Student Journal, 43*(2/Part A), 276–284.

Adler, R.B. & Proctor, R.F. (2011). *Looking out, looking in* (13th Ed.). Boston, MA: Wadworth.

Alter, A. (2013). *Drunk tank pink: And other unexpected forces that shape how we think, feel, and behave.* New York: Penguin Books.

AmericanRhetoric.com (2017). *John G. Roberts, opening statement to the Senate Judiciary Committee.* Retrieved on November 1, 2010 from: www.americanrhetoric.com/speeches/johnrobertsenatejudiciaryaddress.htm.

Barnes, R. & Eggen, D. (2010, June 29). Supreme Court expands gun rights. *Washington Post*, p. A-1.

Barnum, C. & Perfetti, R.L. (2010). Race-sensitive choices by police officers in traffic stop encounters. *Police Quarterly, 13*(2), 180–208, doi: 10.1177/1098611110365690.

Blanchette, I. & Dunbar, K. (2001). Analogy use in naturalistic settings: The influence of audience, emotion, and goals. *Memory and Cognition, 29*(5), 730–735, doi: 10.3758/BF03200475.

Buehner, M.J. (2005). Contiguity and covariation in human causal inference. *Learning & Behavior, 33*(2), 230–238, doi.org/10.3758/BF03196065.

Buehner, M.J. & McGregor, S.J. (2009). Contingency and contiguity trade-offs in causal induction. *International Journal of Comparative Psychology, 22*(1), 19–22, doi: 10.1037/a0020976.

Busloff, S.E. (1993). Comment: Can your eyes be used against you? The use of the horizontal gaze nystagmus test in the courtroom. *Journal of Criminal Law & Criminology, 84*(1), 203–238, doi: 10.2307/1143891.

Chandler, J., Griffin, T.M. & Sorensen, N. (2008). In the "I" of the storm: Shared initials increase disaster donations. *Judgment and Decision Making, 3*(5), 404–410, doi: 2008-09227-005.

Clark, R.D. & Hatfield, E. (1989). Gender differences in receptivity to sexual offers. *Journal of Psychology and Human Sexuality, 2*(1), 39–55, doi: 10.1300/J056v02n01_04.

Clark, R.D. & Hatfield, E. (2003). Love in the afternoon. *Psychological Inquiry, 14*(3), 227–231, doi: 10.1207/S15327965PLI1403&4_8.

Ducheyne, S. (2008). J.S. Mill's canons of induction: From true causes to provisional ones. *History and Philosophy of Logic, 29*(4), 361–376, doi: org/10.1080/01445340802164377.

Dunbar, K. (2001). The analogical paradox. Why analogies are so easy in naturalistic settings, yet so difficult in the psychology laboratory? In D. Gentner, J.K. Holyoak, & B.N. Kokinov (Eds), *The analogical mind perspectives from cognitive psychology* (pp. 313–334). Cambridge, MA: MIT Press.

Gass, R.H. & Seiter, J.S. (2018). *Persuasion, social influence, and compliance gaining* (6th Ed.). New York: Routledge.

Gentner, D. (2003). Analogical reasoning, psychology of. In L. Nadel (Ed.), *Encyclopedia of cognitive science* (pp. 106–111). London: Nature Publishing Group.

Gentner, D., Rattermann, J. & Forbus, K. (1993). The roles of similarity in transfer: Separating retrievability from inferential soundness. *Cognitive Psychology*, *25*(4), 524–575, doi: org/10.1006/cogp.1993.1013.

Glassbrenner, D. (2003). *Estimating the lives saved by safety belts and air bags.* National Center for Statistics and Analysis, National Highway Traffic Safety Administration, Paper no. 500. Retrieved April 2, 2005 from: www-nrd.nhtsa.dot.gov/pdf/nrd 01/esv/esv18/CD/Files/18ESV-000500.pdf.

Glick, M. & Holyoak, K.J. (1980). Analogical problem solving. *Cognitive Psychology*, *12*(3), 306–355, doi: org/10.1016/0010-0285(80)90013-4.

Hannigan, S.L. & Reinitz, M.T. (2001). A demonstration and comparison of two types of inference based memory errors. *Journal of Experimental Psychology: Learning, Memory, and Cognition*, *27*(4), 931–940, doi: 10.1037/0278-7393.27.4.931.

Harper, B. (2017, June 2). Why have Indian-Americans won the last 10 national spelling bees? *Fatherly.* Retrieved on December 14, 2017 from: www.fatherly.com/love-money/indian-americans-dominate-scripps-spelling-bee.

Hiltzik, M. (2010, October 31). Why big-time CEOs make terrible politicians. *Los Angeles Times*, p. B-12.

Holyoak, K.J. (2005). Analogy. In K.J. Holyoak & R.G. Morrison (Eds), *The Cambridge handbook of thinking and reasoning* (pp. 117–142). New York: Cambridge University Press.

Jung, K., Shavitt, S., Viswanathan, M. & Hilbe, J.M. (2014). Female hurricanes are deadlier than male hurricanes [Abstract]. *Proceedings of the National Academy of Sciences of the United States of America*, *111*, 8782–8787, doi: 10.1073/pnas/140278611.

Karpinski, A.C. & Duberstein, A. (2009, April 16). A description of Facebook use and academic performance among undergraduate and graduate students. In poster presented at the meeting of the American Educational Research Association, San Diego, CA.

Kida, T. (2006). *Don't believe everything you think: The 6 basic mistakes we make in thinking.* Amherst, NY: Prometheus Books.

Koenig, C.S. & Griggs, R.A. (2004). Analogical transfer in the THOG task. *Quarterly Journal of Experimental Psychology*, *57A*(3), 557–570, doi: 10.1080/13546780342000070.

Krawczyk, D., McClelland, M.M., Donovan, C.M., Tillman, G.D. & Maguire, M.J. (2010). An fMRI investigation of cognitive stages in reasoning by analogy. *Brain Research*, 1342, 67–73, doi: org/10.1016/j. brainres.2010.04.

Lander, E.S. & Ellis, J.J. (1998, November 5). Founding father. *Nature*, *396*, 13–14, doi: 10.1038/23802. Retrieved February 23, 2019 from: www.nature.com/nature/journal/v396/n6706/full/396013a0. html.

Lewis, J. (2004). Thomas Jefferson and Sally Hemings redux. *William and Mary Quarterly*, *57*(1), 121–124, doi: hdl.handle.net/10822/504513.

Lorenz, E.N. (1972). *Predictability: Does the flap of a butterfly's wings in Brazil set off a tornado in Texas?* Presentation to the American Association for the Advancement of Science, Washington, DC.

Mankiewicz, J. (writer) & Medak, P. (producer) (2004, December 21). The Socratic method. *House, M.D.*, Fox TV.

Miller, K. (2007). Racial profiling and postmodern society: Police responsiveness, image maintenance, and the left flank of police legitimacy. *Journal of Contemporary Criminal Justice*, *23*(3), 248–262, doi. org/10.1177/1043986207306868.

National Safety Council (2010). *Odds of dying from.* Itasca, IL: National Safety Council. Retrieved September 26, 2010 from: www.nsc.org/news_resources/Documents/nscInjuryFacts2011_037.pdf.

Osborne, H. (2003). It's like what you already know: Using analogies to help patients understand. *The Boston Globe's On Call Magazine.* Retrieved December 14, 2017 from: http://healthliteracy. com/2003/01/01/analogies.

Porter, T. (2017, September 10). Don't fire guns at Hurricane Irma, Florida police warn. *Newsweek.com.* Retrieved on October 30, 2017 from: www.newsweek.com/dont-fire-guns-hurricane-irma-florida-police-warn-662494.

Prusher, I.R. (2001, May 29). Some unexpected relief for endangered species. *Christian Science Monitor*, p. 7.

Rice, D. (2014, June 2). Ladykillers: Hurricanes with female names deadlier. *USA Today*. Retrieved on December 27, 2017 from: www.usatoday.com/story/weather/2014/06/02/hurricane-female-names-deadly/9868413.

Rudy, K. (2014, June 6). Do the data really say female-named hurricanes are more deadly? [blog post]. *The Minitab Blog*. Retrieved on December 27, 2017 from: http://blog.minitab.com/blog/the-statistics-game/do-the-data-really-say-female-named-hurricanes-are-more-deadly.

Shanks, D.R., Pearson, S.M. & Dickinson, A. (1989). Temporal contiguity and the judgment of causality by human subjects. *Quarterly Journal of Experimental Psychology Section B: Comparative and Physiological Psychology*, *41*(2), 139–159, doi: 10.1080/14640748908401189.

Sharp, P.M. & Hahn, B.H. (2011). Origins of HIV and the AIDS pandemic. *Cold Spring Harbor Perspectives in Medicine*, 1(1), a006841, doi: 10.1101/cshperspect.a006841. Retrieved February 23, 2019 from: http://perspectivesinmedicine.cship.org.

The Economist (1998, May 30). Why rhinos recommend Viagra. *The Economist*, *347*(8070), p. 76.

von Hippel, W., von Hippel, F.A., Chan, N. & Cheng, C. (2005). Exploring the use of Viagra in place of animal and plant potency products in traditional Chinese medicine. *Environmental Conservation*, *32*(3), 235–238, doi:10.1017/S0376892905002353.

Warren, P.Y. (2010). The continuing significance of race: An analysis across two levels of policing. *Social Science Quarterly*, *91*(4), 1025–1042, doi.org/10.1111/j.1540-6237.2010.00747.x.

White, E.B. & White, K.S. (Eds) (1941). *A subtreasury of American humor*. New York: Coward-McCann.

Young, J.R. (2009, April 24). Facebook, grades, and media hype. *Chronicle of Higher Education*, *55*(33), p. A-13.

Young, M.E. (1995). On the origin of personal causal theories. *Psychonomic Bulletin & Review*, *2*(1), 83–104, doi: 10.3758/BF03214413.

Chapter 8

Fallacies in Reasoning, Part I
The "Big Five"

When Good Arguments Go Bad

Fallacies are the "black sheep" of the argumentation family. The black sheep shows up at get togethers, causes a stir, and embarrasses everyone. At best, he or she seems awkward or out of place. At worst, the black sheep is a degenerate or reprobate. This could be due to a character flaw or a failure to conform to the family's expectations. Either way, the black sheep is still part of the family. It's difficult to ignore or exclude the person entirely.

So it is with fallacies. Like 'em or not, they are part of the argumentation fold. Fallacies are arguments, but, practically speaking, they tend to short-circuit critical thinking. They are flawed in some way or violate normative standards for reasoning. They often make unwarranted inferential leaps.[1] What's more, whether they are committed intentionally or not, fallacies often masquerade as cogent arguments. As such, it's easy to be taken in by their charms. Using our sheep analogy, you shouldn't let another person use fallacious reasoning to pull the wool over your eyes. At the same time, don't be a wolf in sheep's clothing. Avoid committing fallacies yourself.

To dodge fallacies, you must first be able to spot them. With that in mind, this chapter, and the one that follows, examines some of the most common or egregious fallacies that you're likely to encounter in everyday argument. Unfortunately, we don't have sufficient space to include the myriad of fallacies known to humankind. There are simply too many. As Hansen and Pinto (1995) observed, "since the ways of error are infinite, no list of the mistakes or fallacies can be complete" (p. 113). That said, this chapter and the next provide you with a solid foundation for understanding fallacious arguments. In addition, this pair of chapters focuses on fallacies that are *inductive* or *informal* in nature.[2] As you'll recall from Chapter 7, informal reasoning always relies on inferences. As such, the conclusions reached are probabilistic in nature.

Friends or Foes? A Pragmatic Approach to Fallacies

Like the black sheep in a family, fallacies are often misunderstood.[3] Some arguers operate on the mistaken assumption that fallacies can be judged as "black or white." That is, they believe an argument either is or is not fallacious, with no in-between. Yet, just as natural wool is neither purely white nor black, inductive arguments are neither purely valid nor invalid. Informal argument lives in the gray area between. Strictly speaking, every inductive argument is *potentially* fallacious, because, as we noted above, every inductive argument contains an inferential leap. In short, then, fallaciousness is more a matter of degree.

Some people also assume that once an argument has been labeled a fallacy, it is dismissed from further consideration. Making fallacious arguments, however, is not anathema to rational thinking. In fact, under the right circumstances, some fallacies are perfectly acceptable (Ulrich, cited in Benoit, Hample & Benoit, 1992; Walton, Reed & Macagno, 2008). Not only that, but, in some cases, committing a fallacy might be the most reasonable option available.

Suppose, for example, that you are driving through a small town and decide to stop for a quick bite to eat. You are unfamiliar with the restaurants and there aren't any Yelp reviews. You ask the first person you see, "Where is a good place to eat?" The person responds, "Try the *Blue Sky* diner. They make a great lamb chop." If you take only one person's word for it, you're committing what's known as a *hasty generalization*, e.g., relying on a small, atypical sample to reach a conclusion. On the other hand, what are your alternatives? Do you really need to poll 100 local residents at random? Given the circumstances, relying on one person's opinion is perfectly reasonable. Taking time to research numerous dining establishments would defeat the purpose of stopping for "a quick bite to eat."

As another example of the acceptability of certain fallacies, consider the *ad hominem* fallacy, which involves insults, put-downs, name-calling, and character attacks. Calling a physician a "quack" or a lawyer a "shyster" is considered libelous at face value. But truth is a legal defense against libel. If a doctor *really is* a quack, e.g., has never attended medical school and has no legal license to practice medicine, it is perfectly legal to label him or her as such. Similarly, a lawyer who encourages a witness to lie or who embezzles a client's money may rightly be dubbed a shyster. Thus, although personal attacks are generally frowned upon, if a source is unqualified it makes good sense to point it out (see Walton, 1998; Seiter & Gass, 2010).

When evaluating fallaciousness, then, sometimes you should be more persnickety and other times less so. This view is consistent with what can best be described as a *pragmatic* approach to fallacies, along the lines established by Douglas Walton (1995, pp. 237–238). A pragmatic approach suggests that arguments are not fallacious simply because of their form or because they are labeled as such. Instead, we must evaluate their potential for fallaciousness within the real-world contexts in which they appear. Arguments should be considered fallacious when they sidetrack meaningful dialogue and rational discussion about an issue.

Based on this pragmatic perspective, the topic or issue, the context for the discussion, time constraints, and what's at stake all figure into the seriousness of a fallacy. As Tinsdale (2007) observed,

> it is not a matter of simply applying a fallacy label to a piece of text and then moving on. What is involved is a careful sifting of claims and meanings against a backdrop of ongoing debate, and within a wider context. (p. 5)

With these caveats in mind, we turn to the fallacies themselves.

The Usual Suspects: The Big Five

Although there are a variety of taxonomies for organizing fallacies,[4] for simplicity's sake we've chosen to present these wayward arguments in clusters of related types. This chapter focuses on what we'll call the *Big Five* fallacies; faulty cause, faulty analogy, faulty sign, hasty generalization, and sweeping generalization. Sound familiar? If so, you may have noticed that these five categories correspond with the major types of inductive reasoning covered in the previous chapter.

Depending on the circumstances, any of the fallacies could be quite egregious or fairly benign. Let's begin with fallacies based on causal inferences.

Faulty Cause: The Devil Made Me Do It

When people engage in faulty causal reasoning, they erroneously assume that an *antecedent* event (cause) is responsible for a *consequent* event (effect). As you'll see, this category includes several variations, including the *post hoc* fallacy, which we examine next.

The Post Hoc Fallacy: It's a Lost Cause

The *post hoc ergo proptor hoc* fallacy (or, if your Latin is rusty, the "after this, therefore because of this" fallacy) is one of the most common types of faulty causal reasoning. The name is usually abbreviated to the *post hoc* fallacy. Simply stated, when one event follows soon after another, a person may confuse such *temporal proximity*, or closeness in time, with a cause–effect relationship. For example, Mark Twain (a.k.a. Samuel Clemens) was born the month that Halley's comet made its appearance in 1835 and he died in the same month, 75 years later, when the comet returned in 1910. To assume that the comet's appearance caused the writer's birth or death, however, would be to confuse *coincidence* with *causation*. Superstitious thinking, such as the belief that walking under a ladder brings bad luck, is based on this fallacy. Roughly half of all Americans subscribe to some superstitious beliefs (Ravn, 2010).

NAKED SELFIES: AN ALL NATURAL DISASTER

Another example of the *post hoc* fallacy comes from a deputy chief minister in Malaysia who alleged that a 6.0 magnitude earthquake that killed dozens of people on Mt. Kinabalu was caused by tourists who posed naked for photos on the sacred mountain's summit (Pak, 2015). "Whether other people believe this or not," the official said, "it's what we believe" (Wagner, 2015, para. 4). Rest assured, we don't endorse indecent exposure, but we are pretty sure the earthquake was caused by tectonic activity, not exposed body parts.

Following the angry Mother Nature theme, a California legislator alleged that the state's enduring drought was linked to the practice of abortion (White, 2015). Not to be outdone, radio preacher Rick Wiles declared that Hurricane Harvey, which devastated Houston in 2017, was due to the city's support of gays and lesbians (Milbank, 2017).

Countering a Post Hoc Fallacy

If you're ever confronted with a *post hoc* fallacy, there are several ways you might expose it. First, you can argue that the alleged cause is *not necessary* to produce the alleged effect. Using the earthquake example, earthquakes happen even when tourists keep their clothes on. In 2011, for example, a 9.0 quake struck northeastern Japan. The quake and ensuing tidal wave killed tens of thousands. It was winter at the time, so outdoor nudity was not a factor.

Second, you can argue that the alleged cause is *not sufficient* to produce the alleged effect. For instance, if public nudity causes earthquakes, there should be more earthquakes where people take their clothes off frequently, such as clothing-optional beaches and nude resorts. The danger that awaits at a nudist colony, however, is not seismic activity, but sunburn.

"A non-virgin would have had a devastating effect on crop yield."

Figure 8.1 The *post hoc* fallacy hard at work. Published in *The New Yorker*, 12/3/2001, SKU:121352.
© Frank Cotham/The New Yorker Collection/www.cartoonbank.com.

Third, you can posit an *alternative cause* that you think provides a better explanation of cause and effect. As we noted above, geology and plate tectonics, not boobs and buns, offer a far better explanation of why earthquakes occur.

Correlation vs Causation: The More I Drink, the Better You Look

Another faulty type of causal reasoning occurs when people *confuse correlation with causation*. This type of reasoning is considered fallacious because, as we saw in Chapter 7, two phenomena may be associated without being causally connected. For example, there is a high correlation between the number of Baptists who live in certain parts of the U.S. and the frequency of tornadoes in those same areas. That's right, the more Baptists, the more tornadoes. In fact, the correlation is statistically significant ($r = .68$, $p < .0001$) (Walworth, 2001). Yet no reasonable person would assume that Baptists *cause* tornadoes. Instead, the association is what is known as an *accidental* or *spurious correlation*. It just so happens that Baptists are concentrated in a region of the United States known as the "Bible Belt." Much of the Bible Belt happens to be located in "tornado alley," which includes Texas, Oklahoma, Nebraska, Kansas, and other states that lie in the path of tornadoes. If Baptists suddenly picked up and moved to Delaware, tornadoes wouldn't follow them there.

Another example of a spurious correlation is that when an American president is a Republican, more zombie movies tend to be released, whereas when the president is a Democrat, more vampire movies tend to be made (*Mrscience.com*, 2009). Yet another dubious correlation illustrates the perils of confusing correlation with causation. Specifically, since the late 1800s, there has been a strong *negative* correlation between the number of pirates (the sea-faring kind) and climate change. That's right, as temperatures have gotten warmer, pirates have become scarcer (Anderson, 2012), suggesting that, if you want to halt global warming, plunder some ships matey! (and if you're not yet tired of strange and spurious correlations, see Box 8.1).

Box 8.1 Fun with Spurious Correlations

Did you know that the number of movies Ben Affleck has appeared in each year correlates with the number of people who have been poisoned by pesticides? It's true, and also a great illustration of how correlations do not necessarily point to causal connections. In fact, to illustrate how misleading (and entertaining) spurious correlations can be, Tyler Vigen (2015) analyzed hundreds of variables, searching for oddball correlations like the Affleck/pesticide one above. Here are some of our favorites:

- Margarine consumption is correlated with the divorce rate in Maine.
- Books published about religion are correlated with bathtub drownings.
- Undergraduate enrollment at U.S. universities is correlated with injuries related to falling TVs.
- The value of the Victoria Secret's Fantasy Bra is correlated with U.K. men who smoke cigarettes.
- Tea consumption is correlated with people killed by misusing a lawnmower.

- Money spent on pets is correlated with alcohol sold in liquor stores.
- Letters in the winning word in the Scripps National Spelling Bee are correlated with deaths due to venomous spiders.
- Nicolas Cage movie appearances is correlated with the number of people who drowned by falling into swimming pools.

Countering a Spurious Correlation

If you ever need to refute a spurious correlation, you should invoke the mantra that "correlation does not equal causation." In other words, two or more phenomena may coexist without being causally connected. What's more, when two phenomena appear to be correlated, you may be able to show that both are related to a third factor. Audience size, for example, explains the correlation between a rock band's fame and the number of Porta Potties you find at their concerts. A key difference between correlations and cause–effect relationships is that correlations are *bilateral* or two-way; "if A is correlated with B, then B is likewise correlated with A" (Murray & Kujundzic, 2005, p. 308). In contrast, causal relationships are *unilateral* or one-way. A may cause B, but that does not mean B causes A. A mail carrier's presence, for instance, may cause a dog to bark, but a dog's barking does not cause the mail carrier to appear.

Slippery Slope: If You Don't Stop Doing That, You'll Go Blind

A final causal fallacy that we consider is the *slippery slope* argument. Also referred to as a *snowball argument* or a *domino effect*, a slippery slope argument alleges that a chain reaction of cause and effect events will take place, culminating in some calamity. As an example, one of the authors and his wife once had an argument over their five-year-old son. It went something like this:

Author: "Let's get a jump on vacation by taking him out of school for a couple of days."
Wife: "In other words, let's raise a degenerate. It's always been a dream of mine."
Author: "C'mon. It's kindergarten. What's he gonna miss? Finger painting?"
Wife: "He can make that up in prison. They've got art classes, you know?"
    They both laugh.
Wife: "But seriously. Next thing you know, he's ditching high school, flunking college, looking for handouts . . . who knows what else?"

It's possible, of course, that the worst-case scenario might have come true. Playing hooky from kindergarten might be a stepping stone to a life of depravity, but the author will never know. Fallacy or not, his wife prevailed. Their son got a Master's degree. But to this day he is a terrible finger painter!

On a more serious note, some people claim that marijuana is a "gateway" drug or "stepping stone" to harder drugs. Smoking marijuana, they maintain, leads to experimentation with drugs such as ecstasy or MDMA. Using ecstasy increases the likelihood of trying cocaine, meth, or PCP. Before you know it, you're a heroin addict living on skid row. Advocates of the "stepping stone" theory point to the fact that most heroin addicts began their decline into a drug-induced oblivion by smoking marijuana. However, while most heroin addiction might be preceded by marijuana use, most marijuana users don't go on to become heroin addicts.

Countering a Slippery Slope

There are three effective ways you can counter a slippery slope fallacy. First, you can argue that the slope is not that steep or slippery. In other words, you can demonstrate that the first step can be taken, or already has been taken, without leading to the dire consequence envisioned. For example, your high school, like many in the United States, might have had a traditional "ditch day," on which seniors skipped their classes. Both authors participated in their school's respective ditch days, but did not become career criminals.

Second, you can refute a slippery slope by drawing a "bright line." When doing this, you argue that a clear distinction can be made between one step and the next, making the next step much less likely. Keeping with our example, playing hooky for a day seems rather innocent, at least to us. It's certainly poles apart from a crime spree, especially those involving victims, that lead to prison sentences. In short, drawing a bright line between one step and the next can illustrate just how far apart the steps are.

A third approach is to point out that the first step down the slope has already been taken. If the slope is that slippery then the horrible consequence is inevitable anyway. For example, a number of states have already legalized recreational marijuana use. The slippery slope scenario therefore guarantees that thousands more heroin addicts should already be roaming the streets. Having examined common fallacies in causal reasoning, let's turn our attention to another culprit in errant reasoning: the faulty analogy.

Faulty Analogy: Apples Versus Oranges

Another black sheep in the argumentation flock is the *faulty analogy*. As we saw in Chapter 7, an analogy is a comparison. Thus, when people use a faulty analogy they allege that two things are similar when, in fact, the things are not comparable in important or relevant respects. A faulty analogy may be based on *superficial features*, which involve trivial or surface points, rather than *structural features*, which focus on substantive aspects of the two things being compared. Consider the exchange below.

Dotty:	"Professor Von Schlepp, how come lawyers are allowed to refer to their briefs when making arguments in court, but we can't use our notes when we are taking an exam in class?"
Professor Von Schlepp:	"Because in a courtroom, a lawyer is practicing law, not being tested on his or her knowledge of the law."

Dotty offers an analogy of lawyers consulting briefs to students using notes. Superficially, the two might seem similar. As the professor points out, however, at a structural level the two activities are not equivalent. Lawyers refer to briefs when practicing law, but not when taking the bar exam.

It Ain't Rocket Science

Arguers often pose questions such as, "If we can put a man on the moon why can't we end poverty? Or prevent crime? Or fix Donald Trump's hair?" The problem with such "apples versus oranges" comparisons is that the Apollo mission was largely a scientific and engineering feat. Social problems pose fundamentally different challenges. Indeed, while overcoming gravity is a matter of physics, overcoming human frailties such as envy, fear, greed, jealousy, and prejudice is far more daunting. Human problems entail psychological, emotional, social, and cultural dimensions that are more difficult to predict and control. One might as well ask, "If we can put a man on the moon, why can't we avoid bad analogies?"

Anthropomorphic Analogies: You Dirty Rat

Have you noticed that people are fond of using animal analogies? Think, for example, of all the animal terms used to describe men (pig, rat, snake, jackass, chicken) and women (cow, dog, bat, bitch, shrew). True, some animal terms for men (bear, stallion) and women (chick, fox) *might* be perceived favorably, but most animal nicknames are derogatory. In fact, previous scholarship points to the ways in which women especially are portrayed as subordinate or inferior through the use of such terms (Rodriguez, 2009).

Faulty though they may be, history is replete with examples of the vile ways in which animal nicknames have been used, particularly when describing out-groups. In war time, for instance, language has been used to dehumanize people, characterizing them as vermin, jackals, monkeys, or monsters, and, in the process, making them easier to enslave or destroy. Try Googling "dehumanizing propaganda," for example, and you'll find an array of images depicting humans as beasts. Similarly, animal analogies can also be used to make people or nations seem dangerous. Consider, for example, the way a state-run news agency in North Korea recently described the United States: "Packs of wolves are coming in attack to strangle a nation" (Quinn, 2017). As far as animal comparisons go, we agree that wolves seem predatory. Then again, when's the last time you saw a wolf strangle anybody?

Countering a Faulty Analogy

To lay bare a bad analogy, you can show that the arguer is making an unfair comparison, e.g., "comparing apples with oranges." For example, during arguments before the Supreme Court on the constitutionality of the Affordable Care Act (a.k.a. Obamacare), the late Justice Antonin Scalia offered an analogy between making people purchase mandatory health insurance and requiring them to buy broccoli. If the government can impose an individual mandate to buy health-care insurance, he asked, why can't the government require a person to buy broccoli? Broccoli is good for you too.

The "health-care-is-like-broccoli" analogy is flawed because health care is a necessity, but broccoli is not. Access to medical care is, literally, a matter of life or death. Not so for broccoli. Every person will need health care at some point in his or her life. We all get sick. Indeed, every American has *already received* some form of health care, whether it was a simple childhood vaccination, a prescription antibiotic, or treatment for a more complicated and expensive medical condition. A person can live an entire lifetime without eating broccoli, however. Sure, people need to eat some healthy foods, but not broccoli in particular.

Furthermore, if your neighbor refuses to buy broccoli, it will not affect your access to broccoli. In fact, if enough people avoid broccoli, it will become *less expensive* for you to buy, according to the laws of supply and demand. Medical care is different. If your neighbor refuses to buy health insurance, it will impede your access to health care (Klein, 2012). That's because people who have insurance foot the bill for those who don't. As such, if your neighbor shows up at the emergency room without insurance, your premiums—and those of everyone else with health insurance—*will increase.*

A faulty analogy also can be countered by offering a superior analogy. For example, a federal mandate to buy health insurance is more analogous to requiring that everyone pay taxes for federal disaster relief. Broccoli has little impact on interstate commerce, but health care and natural disasters do. No one knows when the next natural disaster will strike or where. What we do know is that there will be natural disasters and they will affect everyone directly or indirectly. Sharing the risk, by having everyone pay for disaster relief, is analogous to sharing the risk for medical care via health insurance.

Faulty Sign: Don't Judge a Book by Its Cover

When people engage in *faulty sign* reasoning they mistake one thing as a reliable indicator for another thing. Like a glitchy "check engine" light on a car, a sign may not mean anything. A sign also may signify something else. For example, a poker player may *think* a "tell" by another player indicates he or she is bluffing when, in fact, that player has a great hand.

Only Gangstas Wear Hoodies?

In Florida in 2012, George Zimmerman, a neighborhood watch captain, began following a black teenager, Trayvon Martin, because the teen looked suspicious. He was wearing a hoodie. Martin, who was unarmed, was walking home after buying Skittles and Arizona Iced Tea at a convenience store. A confrontation ensued during which Zimmerman shot and killed Martin. Afterwards, the talk-show host and news commentator Geraldo Rivera opined, "I think the hoodie is as much responsible for Trayvon Martin's death as George Zimmeran was" (Banks, 2012, p. 2).

Really Geraldo? Is wearing a hoodie a reliable sign that a person is up to no good? We think not. A sweatshirt with a hood is a common item of clothing. A person armed only with snack food, as Trayvon Martin was, hardly poses a clear and present danger. Unfortunately, African American males are the frequent objects of racial profiling based on such faulty sign reasoning. Even "Gangsta" clothing, such as baggy pants or a head bandana, does not a gangster make. Youth culture may favor Gangsta, Rap, or Hip Hop attire, but that doesn't make them a menace to society. There are numerous cases in which a non-gang member has been shot or stabbed by gang members for wearing the wrong colors in the wrong place. So perhaps even gang members have trouble discerning who is a "straight up Gangsta" and who is not.

"It's Your Watch That Tells the Most About Who You Are" (Seiko Watch Slogan)

As another example of faulty sign reasoning, advertisers would like you to believe that conspicuous consumption is a sign of wealth. We are led to believe that a person who wears an expensive watch, drives a high-priced car, and drinks pricey wines must be rich. In reality, such status symbols are *faulty signs*. For instance, the type of car a person drives is *not* a reliable indicator of wealth. Some people who drive exotic cars are up to their eyeballs in debt. In point of fact, millionaires are more likely to drive Toyotas than BMWs. Thomas Stanley, a Ph.D. and expert on wealth, reported that the median price of cars driven by millionaires was $31, 367 (2009). That's far less than what a Ferrari, Maserati, Rolls Royce, or other exotic car costs.

Countering a Faulty Sign

To expose faulty sign reasoning, you should first explain why a particular sign may be *fallible* or mistaken. For example, if your parents declare that the person you are dating is a "loser" because he or she has tattoos, point out that some highly successful people sport body art. Theodore Roosevelt, Winston Churchill, Janet Napolitano, Angelina Jolie, and David Beckham all have, or had, tattoos. Second, point out that one sign proves very little. Signs add up. Can your parents identify additional signs that the person you are dating is of questionable character (e.g., the person is on probation, in rehab, or has a dozen ex-spouses)? Third, identify any *negative signs* that point to a different conclusion. For instance, if the person you are dating is a pre-med student, volunteers for a worthwhile charity, is well-liked, and is completing an M.B.A. degree, he or she would appear to be on a path toward success. Fourth, keep in mind that signs only indicate that a relationship exists between two things, but not *why* the relationship exists. The person you're dating may be unemployed, but that could be due to a bad economy, not his or her personal shortcomings.

Hasty and Sweeping Generalization

The last two "Big Five" categories of faulty reasoning both involve the practice of generalizing. Specifically, in the sections that follow, we examine fallacies known as hasty and universal (or sweeping) generalizations.

Hasty Generalization: Jumping to Conclusions

A *hasty generalization*, known by its Latin name *secundum quid*, involves jumping to a conclusion based on limited information. An arguer who commits a hasty generalization doesn't have all the facts or information needed to form a reliable conclusion. For example, arguers on both sides of the climate change debate often cite a single weather event as proof of an overall trend. "It's 90 degrees in the middle of November. How can anyone deny climate change is real?" a proponent of climate change asks. "How can there be global warming?" an opponent argues. "It's April and there is snow in my yard." A day, or even a season, of local weather, however, provides too little information to make reliable generalizations either way.

As another example, testimonials in infomercials and magazine ads often make astounding claims. A particular diet, supplement, or exercise routine reportedly transformed a person overnight. The problem with such *anecdotal evidence* is that it is not based on a *random representative sample* of people. For all we know, the transformed person could be the only success story from among many people who have used the product. That's why the before and after photos in such ads are usually accompanied by a disclaimer; "results not typical" or "individual results may vary." If you want to know whether a particular health remedy really works, look for a carefully controlled clinical trial that employs something known as a *double-blind procedure*. Specifically, in a double-blind study, neither the participants (in this case, the dieters) nor the investigator measuring the outcome (in this case, the physician or dietician overseeing the diets and weigh-ins) know the particular conditions being studied (for more on the value of double-blind experiments, see Box 8.2).

Box 8.2   The Beauty of Double-Blind Experiments

Imagine you wanted to learn whether eating Nutrageous candy bars improved people's self-esteem. How might you do it? Simple, right? Get people who've never eaten Nutrageous candy bars to eat one and then follow up by asking how they feel about themselves. What could go wrong?

The answer is "plenty." First, if people reported feeling better, it could be due to all the attention they were getting, not the candy bars. To alleviate this problem, you could include a comparison (or control) group. Specifically, from a large pool of people, you could flip a coin, randomly assigning one half to the "Nutrageous" group and the other half to a group that ate something else disguised in a Nutrageous wrapper. Both groups, however, would be "blind" to what they were really being fed. Afterwards, if the Nutrageous group had higher self-esteem, you'd feel more confident that it was because the candy bar caused it. Correct?

Not so fast! What if the Nutrageous group reported higher self-esteem because you—a huge fan of the candy bar—acted happier when feeding that group than you did when feeding the comparison group? This is where the double-blind study comes in handy. Specifically, if you, the experimenter, were "blind" to the study's conditions (i.e., you didn't know who was eating what), you'd presumably behave the same way toward both groups. Thus, if the Nutrageous group had higher self-esteem, you'd feel more confident that it was because of the candy bar and not because of you (or simple blind luck).

Phone or Text Your Vote in Now

Hasty generalizations also cause mischief in unscientific polls. Such polls are common among cable news shows and internet sites. For example, a news show may post a question, such as "Did Russia try to influence our election?", and ask viewers to phone or text in their replies. Seems simple enough, until you understand that such polls are subject to *self-selection bias*. Specifically, the sample is limited to viewers who watch that particular show. Even then, it might be that only viewers who are most ego-involved bother to participate. Such poll results may mislead less fanatical viewers who may perceive the skewed results as anchor points when forming their own opinions. A caveat such as "this is not a scientific poll" may be included when reporting the results, but it would be clearer if the source simply stated "These results may be waaaaaay wrong!"

I Hated It, but I Didn't Actually Read It

Online ratings and reviews by consumers represent a mixed bag insofar as their generalizability is concerned. For example, a book on Amazon.com might receive a five-star rating, but how many raters does that represent? If only a handful of people provide ratings, they may be the author's most ardent fans or even family members. What's more, some people provide negative ratings when they haven't actually read the book! Consider the following one-star rating of a book on Amazon.com.

> I'd like to add my name to the list of people who are very disappointed that this book does not have a Kindle edition. No, I haven't read the book, but I want to — on my Kindle! If all these one star reviews lead to fewer sales, I think that would be a great result and an excellent lesson for the author/publisher. (cited in Carr, 2010, para. 6)

Clearly, the one-star rating has nothing to do with the content of the book, only the medium in which it is available.

He's an Easy A, But No Chile Pepper

We aren't saying you should ignore online reviews entirely. Ratemyprofessor.com, for example, can provide useful insights about an instructor's classroom performance. Student ratings, however, are also subject to *self-selection bias*. Students who really loved or hated an instructor are more likely to go online and submit a rating. As a result, the ratings tend to be bi-modal, with peaks of high and low ratings rather than average ratings. The number of ratings tends to be small too. In a class of 30 students, only a few may submit an online rating. When using ratemyprofessor.com, then, we suggest that you look for common themes across multiple classes. If students consistently praise a professor for being friendly and approachable, there's probably something to it. If students uniformly complain that a professor is late in returning students' work, that's worth considering too.

Earlier in this chapter we noted that there are times when committing a hasty generalization is perfectly acceptable. For example, if you were searching for a good movie, you might accept a friend's recommendation, especially if you share similar tastes in films. At worst, you would be out the price of a ticket. The same would apply to a book or restaurant recommendation. Also, as suspect as it may be, anecdotal evidence is still better than no evidence at all.

Countering a Hasty Generalization

You can expose a hasty generalization in several ways. First, it pays to beware of anecdotal evidence. If the person you are communicating with relies on it, point out that too few examples are provided. Second, if the examples provided are atypical or unrepresentative, point it out. Underscore the fact that the person is "cherry picking" examples to suit his or her needs. Third, offer counter-examples of your own. Better yet, show that your counter-examples are more typical or representative than those of the other person. Fourth, cite averages where possible to show what is normal or typical. Finally, ask for results from a scientific poll or controlled clinical trial to ensure that a random representative sample was involved in reaching the conclusion.

Sweeping Generalization: White Men Can't Jump

"We never do anything fun." "You always get your way." "All you ever do is pout." "None of what you say makes sense." Such universal statements constitute sweeping generalizations.

Simply stated, a *sweeping generalization*, known by the Latin name *dicto simpliciter*, makes a universal claim that is unfounded. A general rule or principle is applied to an entire class or group. A sweeping generalization typically includes words such as "all," "every," "never," and "none." Cultural stereotypes, such as "All Muslims hate Jews" or "Every Christian is homophobic," represent sweeping generalizations.

A sweeping generalization may be fallacious in one of two ways. First, the general rule on which the stereotype is based may be mistaken. By way of illustration, the negative stereotype that "women are bad drivers" is simply not true. In fact, compared with female drivers, male drivers are more than three times as likely to receive violations for reckless driving and DUIs. What's more, males are responsible for more fatal crashes than females (*Statistic Brain*, 2017).

Second, even if the general rule were true, it would not apply in every specific instance. Suppose, for the sake of argument, that women were worse drivers in general. There are numerous exceptions to the general rule. Danica Patrick, Ashley Force, Courtney Force, Jamie Chadwick, Jutta Kleinschmidt, Karen Chandhok, Katherine Legge, Shirley Muldowny, Kitty O'Neil, and Michèle Mouton, and many other women have proven their driving skills in motor sports by beating numerous male drivers. Within any particular family, the mother might be the better driver or the worst compared with the father. The bottom line, then, is that before serving up stereotypes of your own, be ready to back them up with evidence, not assumptions or assertions.

Better yet, consider qualifying your generalizations with adjectives such as "many," "most," or "often." Such *contingent generalizations* tend to be more reliable because they acknowledge that the general rule depends on the particular circumstances. *Statistical generalizations*, which are expressed as a percentage, also tend to be more reliable. Indeed, claiming that "All Republicans are Bible beaters" is a sweeping generalization. Instead, claiming that "41 percent of Republicans report that they are born again or evangelicals" is not. When advancing arguments, try to avoid universal statements and qualify your claims appropriately.

Countering a Sweeping Generalization

To rebut a sweeping generalization, you can first demonstrate that the general rule is untrue. For example, suppose someone claimed that "all Christians are homophobic." You could counter this claim by pointing out that, depending on countries and denominations, many Christian churches bless same-sex unions. And, of course, many gays and lesbians consider themselves Christians. Second, you can also point out that even if the general rule applies in most cases, it doesn't apply to every specific case. There are exceptions to almost every rule (note, we said *almost every* to avoid a sweeping generalization). By way of illustration, the Catholic Church officially opposes same sex unions, but many individual Catholics favor them (CatholicCulture. org, 2011). A poll by the Public Religion Research Institute in 2011 revealed that "74 percent of American Catholics surveyed supported the rights of same-sex couples to marry or form civil unions" (Considine, 2011, p. 6).

Summary

Although fallacies are arguments that violate normative standards for reasoning, under the right circumstances they are perfectly acceptable. That said, competent arguers should typically avoid them and be able to recognize them. This chapter presented what we called the *Big Five* fallacies: faulty cause, faulty analogy, faulty sign, hasty generalization, and sweeping generalization. First, *faulty causal reasoning*—which includes committing the *post hoc fallacy, the slippery slope argument*, and/or *confusing correlation with causation*—erroneously assumes that an antecedent event (cause) is responsible for a consequent event (effect). Second, the *faulty analogy* alleges that two things are similar when, in fact, the things are not comparable in important or relevant respects. Third, *faulty sign* reasoning occurs when people mistake one thing as a reliable indicator for another thing. Fourth, making *hasty generalizations* involves jumping to conclusions based on limited information. Finally, making *sweeping generalizations* involves making unfounded universal claims. This chapter also discussed how each type of fallacious reasoning could be countered.

Notes

1 Some fallacies, such as false dilemma, involve cognitive errors (Wreen, 2009), other fallacies, such as begging the question, entail faulty premises. Still others, such as ad hominem, violate normative standards for what is considered socially acceptable argument.
2 A discussion of formal logical fallacies can be found in Chapter 11. We've separated the discussion of informal and formal logical fallacies here because the former violate pragmatic norms for arguing, while the latter violate the rules of deduction. Interestingly, there is some evidence that skill in identifying formal fallacies correlates with skill in identifying informal fallacies (Ricco, 2007).
3 Hamblin (1970) roundly criticized what he referred to as the "Standard Treatment" of fallacies for being superficial, unsystematic, and atheoretical in nature.
4 Aristotle (1955) divided fallacies into two types; fallacies involving language and fallacies involving things other than language. Schlecht (1991) classified fallacies into three types; unacceptable premises, irrelevant premises, and insufficient premises. Many other classification schemes can be found.

References

Anderson, E. (2012). True fact: The lack of pirates is causing global warming. *Forbes*. Retrieved on December 15, 2017 from: www.forbes.com/sites/erikaandersen/2012/03/23/true-fact-the-lack-of-pirates-is-causing-global-warming/#3214cc2e3a67.

Aristotle (1955). *On sophistical refutations* (E.S. Forster, trans.) Cambridge, MA: Harvard University Press.

Banks, S. (2012, March 27). Troubled fashion statement: Slaying of Florida teen Trayvon Martin casts a spotlight on the hoodie. *Los Angeles Times*, p. A-2.

Benoit, W.L., Hample, D. & Benoit, P.J. (Eds) (1992). *Readings in argumentation: Pragmatics and discourse analysis*. New York: Walter de Gruyter & Co.

Carr, P. (2010, May 22). Amazon: You need to change your idiotic customer reviews policy right now. *TechCrunch*. Retrieved on June 7, 2011 from: http://techcrunch.com/2010/03/22/im-not-kidding-do-it-now.

CatholicCulture.org (2011, March 23). Practicing Catholics more likely than general public to back homosexual unions. Retrieved on June 29, 2011 from: www.catholicculture.org/news/headlines/index.cfm?storyid=9702.

Considine, A. (2011, April 22). For Catholics, open attitudes on gay issues. *New York Times*, Section ST, p. 6.

Hamblin, C.L. (1970). *Fallacies*. London: Meuthuen & Co.

Hansen, H.V. & Pinto, R.C. (1995). *Fallacies: Classical and contemporary readings*. University Park, PA: Pennsylvania State University Press.

Klein, J. (2012, March 28). Of broccoli and broken bones. *Time*. Retrieved on August 27, 2012 from: http://swampland.time.com/2012/03/28/of-broccoli-and-broken-bones.

Milbank, D. (2017, September 8). Did lesbians cause hurricanes Irma and Harvey? *Washington Post*. Retrieved on January 2, 2018 from: www.washingtonpost.com/opinions/did-lesbians-cause-hurricanes-irma-and-harvey-god-knows/2017/09/08/638efbca-94bf-11e7-89fa-bb822a46da5b_"story.html?utm_term=.a90199df53c0.

Mrscience.com (2009, May 23). Where science meets pop culture. *Mrscience.com*. Retrieved on December 15, 2017 from: www.mrscienceshow.com/2009/05/correlation-of-week-zombies-vampires.html.

Murray, M. & Kujundzic, N. (2005). *Critical thinking: A textbook for critical reflection*. Quebec: McGill-Queen's University Press.

Pak, J. (2015, June 8). Malaysia official blames nude tourists for deadly quake. *BBC News*. Retrieved December 28, 2017 from: www.bbc.com/news/world-asia-33058692.

Quinn, M. (2017, August 9). North Korea threats draw comparisons to Cuban missile crisis. *Washington Examiner*. Retrieved on December 21, 2017 from: www.washingtonexaminer.com/north-korea-threats-draw-comparisons-to-cuban-missile-crisis/article/2631083.

Ravn, K. (2010, October 25). A little superstitious? You're not alone. *Los Angeles Times*. Retrieved on May 29, 2011 from: www.latimes.com/health/la-he-superstition-20101025,0,1186650,full.story.

Ricco, R. (2007). Individual differences in the analysis of informal reasoning fallacies. *Contemporary Educational Psychology*, *32*(3), 459–484, doi.org/10.1016/j.cedpsych.2007.01.001.

Rodriguez, I.L. (2009). Of women, bitches, chickens and vixens: Animal metaphors for women in English and Spanish. *Culture, Language, and Representation*, 7, 77–100.

Schlecht, L.F. (1991). Classifying fallacies logically. *Teaching Philosophy*, *14*(1), 53–64, doi: 10.5840/teachphil19911411.

Seiter, J.S. & Gass, R.H. (2010). Aggressive communication in political contexts. In T.A. Avtgis & A.S. Rancer (Eds), *Arguments, aggression, and conflict: New directions in theory and research* (pp. 217–240). New York: Routledge.

Stanley, T.J. (2009). *Stop acting rich and start living like a real millionaire*. Hoboken, NJ: John Wiley & Sons.

Statistic Brain (2017). Male and female driving statistics. *Statistic Brain*. Retrieved on December 16, 2017 from: www.statisticbrain.com/male-and-female-driving-statistics.

Tinsdale, C.W. (2007). *Fallacies and argument appraisal*. New York: Cambridge University Press.

Vigen, T. (2015). *Spurious correlations: Correlation does not equal causation*. New York: Hachette Books.

Wagner, M. (2015, June 8). Malaysia blames deadly earthquake on naked tourists who dissed mountain's spirits, plans ceremony to appease gods. *New York Daily News*. Retrieved August 12, 2017 from: www.nydailynews.com/news/world/malaysia-blames-deadly-earthquake-naked-tourists-article-1.2250340.

Walton, D. (1995). *A pragmatic theory of fallacy*. Tuscaloosa, AL: University of Alabama Press.

Walton, D. (1998). *Ad hominem arguments*. Tuscaloosa, AL: The University of Alabama Press.

Walton, D., Reed, C. & Macagno, F. (2008). *Argumentation schemes*. Cambridge: Cambridge University Press.

Walworth, J. (2001). Does God punish gays? A statistical approach. *Gay & Lesbian Review Worldwide*, *8*(5), 5.

White, J.B. (2015, June 12). Shannon Grove under fire for linking drought to abortion. *Sacramento Bee*. Retrieved on January 2, 2018 from: www.sacbee.com/news/politics-government/capitol-alert/article23868907.html.

Wreen, M. (2009). Look before you leap. *Social Epistemology*, *23*(2), 89–104.

Chapter 9

Fallacies in Reasoning, Part 2

In the previous chapter we covered the Big Five fallacies. Now that you have a grasp of faulty cause, faulty analogy, faulty sign, hasty generalization, and sweeping generalization, let's consider some additional fallacies. While slightly less common, they are nevertheless important to know before wading into an argument. In the case of the Big Five, the arguments are usually flawed because an unwarranted inferential leap is being made. Other fallacies, however, involve different flaws, such as suspect premises or warrants. The first four fallacies we examine in this chapter—*begging the question, bifurcation, false dilemma,* and *hypothesis contrary to fact*—all attempt to smuggle assumptions into an argument based on unstated, unproven, biased, or flawed premises. Later, we'll examine arguments that are flawed in other ways.

Iffy Assumptions: Fallacies Involving Questionable Premises

Begging the Question

An older man asks his much younger wife, "Would you have married me if my grandfather hadn't left me a fortune?" "Don't be silly," the wife replies, "I would have married you no matter who left you a fortune."

What makes this joke funny? We understand that nothing ruins a good joke like explaining it, yet here we go. This joke works because the husband's question contains two premises, one obvious and one not so obvious. The obvious premise is whether wealth entered into his wife's decision to marry him. The less obvious premise is whether *the source* of his wealth was a factor in her decision. The punch line is not only unexpectedly amusing, it also illustrates how tacit premises may be taken for granted.

When people commit the fallacy of *begging the question* or, if you prefer Latin, *petitio principi,* they take a premise for granted that has yet to be proven (Ikuenobe, 2002; Walton, 1994). In essence, an arguer who begs the question is slipping a presupposition into an argument. For example, a shoe salesperson who says, "Shall I box those up for you or would you prefer to wear them?" is assuming the customer has already agreed to buy the shoes that she or he just tried on. Another classic example is a reporter who asks a politician, "Have you stopped beating your wife?" The question presumes a history of spouse abuse, so if the politician answers "Yes," it implies he was formerly a wife beater, and if he answers "No," it suggests he's still a wife beater. Rather than answer yes or no, the politician might respond, "I have never beaten my wife. Are you still a bed wetter?"

Incidentally, in everyday life, people often misuse the term "begs the question." They assume it is synonymous with saying "raises the question" or "invites the question," which is understandable considering that question begging may occur in question form, as the above examples illustrate. However, the fallacy does not require asking a question at all. In fact, "to beg the question" is to take a claim for granted without any proof that it is true. Consider, for example, the following dialogue:

Chuck: "Wayne Gretsky is the greatest athlete of all time."
Darnell: "How do you figure?"
Chuck: "Because he is the greatest player of the greatest sport in the world; hockey."
Darnell: "Gretsky's prowess notwithstanding, you're assuming that hockey is the greatest sport in the world."
Chuck: "Because it is!"

As you can see in this dialogue, Chuck begs the question by making a declarative statement, not by asking a question. What's more, fans of America's pastime (baseball), the sweet science (boxing), the gentleman's game (cricket), and the beautiful game (soccer), among other sports, might dispute his premise that hockey is the best sport of all.

Countering Question Begging

Suppose that an eyewitness to a crime testifies that the defendant was not the perpetrator. On cross-examination, the district attorney asks, "So you're saying that the officer was lying?" The witness responds, "No, I'm saying the officer may be mistaken. I don't share the officer's recollection of the events." In this case, the witness exposes the prosecutor's assumption that because there is conflicting testimony, someone must be lying.

In ordinary settings, question begging can be difficult to spot, but, once recognized, it is one of the easiest fallacies to refute. To do so, simply point out the unstated or unproven assumption an arguer has made. Some classic pickup lines illustrate how this might be accomplished. For example, if the local Don Juan at a club asks, "Shall we go back to your place or mine?" you might say, "Who says we are going anywhere together? *You* go back to *your* place and *I'll* go back to *mine.*" If a would-be Lothario asks, "Shall I call you for breakfast tomorrow or nudge you?" you might reply, "You're assuming I'll be eating breakfast, but this conversation is making me nauseous."

As another illustration of how to counter question begging, suppose Fifi is choosing a major. She tells Loretta, "I want a great job when I graduate. Which degrees pay the most?" Loretta might reply, "You're assuming the best jobs are the highest paying ones. Why not consider which jobs are the most fulfilling, regardless of pay?" Sometimes question begging involves an arguer's claim, in which case you might say, "I think you are asking the wrong question to begin with." Sometimes question begging involves the warrant or inferential leap, in which case you might say, "You're making a big assumption there, which is . . . ."

Bifurcation and False Dilemma: Between a Rock and a Hard Place

When an arguer insists that you have only two choices, as in pearls of wisdom that begin "There are two kinds of people in this world . . .," the arguer is committing a *bifurcation* fallacy. Robert Benchley put it best when he wrote, "There may be said to be two classes of people in the world; those who constantly divide people into two classes, and those who do not" (Benchley, 1920, p. 69). Similarly, during disagreements, the father of one author was fond of saying, "There are two kinds of people in this world—you and everyone else."

Also known as a *false dichotomy, either–or* fallacy, or *black or white* fallacy, the assumption being made is that there are two, and only two, options and they are mutually exclusive. Suppose someone asked you "Are you pro-choice or pro-life?" The question presumes that you must be in one camp or the other. But what if you are largely opposed to elective abortions, especially late-term abortions, while also believing that exceptions should be permitted in cases of rape or incest?

As another example, consider an argument made by Federico Demaria, an ecological economist, who claimed that efforts to increase economic growth invariably trade-off with efforts to protect the environment.

> Economic growth is presented as the panacea that can solve any of the world's problems; poverty, inequality, sustainability, you name it. However, there is an uncomfortable scientific truth to be faced: economic growth is environmentally unsustainable . . . economic growth is not compatible with environmental sustainability. (Demaria, 2018, paras 2–3, para. 12)

The tradeoff posed by Demaria, however, assumes that nonrenewable sources of energy continue to be used to achieve growth. As fossil fuels give way to renewable energy sources, a better balance between growth and environmental sustainability may be achieved. For example, the International Energy Association reported that renewable energy accounted for two-thirds of worldwide new power generation in 2016 (IEA, 2017). Abandoned coal mines are now being repurposed as solar farms worldwide (Chameleon, 2017).

A variation of the bifurcation fallacy is known as the *false dilemma* (Tomić, 2013). Here, the arguer also contends that you have only two options, e.g., the horns of the dilemma, and *both are bad*, e.g., you'll be gored either way. In other words, you're "darned if you do and darned if you don't." This is often referred to as a "Catch 22" situation, based on the paradox posed in Joseph Heller's novel. The flight surgeon said only a crazy man would agree to fly dangerous missions, thus any airman asking to be grounded must be sane. The catch? The only way to be grounded was to ask the flight surgeon to declare the flier mentally unfit, but the mere act of asking proved the flier was sane.

There are true dilemmas as well. Often, people must choose between the lesser of two evils. For instance, a spouse may be faced with a decision to leave an alcoholic partner or stay and, perhaps, become an enabler. Legislators who advocate deporting illegal immigrants must wrestle with the problem of what to do about their children who were born in the U.S. and therefore have every right to remain as U.S. citizens. Increasing government transparency or the public's right to know may increase accountability and trust, but it may also encourage pandering and hinder behind-the-scenes negotiating.

Countering Bifurcation and False Dilemma

First, if an arguer insists that you have only two options, you can point out that a third or fourth option exists. "Who was the best James Bond" your friend asks, "Roger Moore or Daniel Craig?" "Neither," you might reply, "Sean Connery was the best."

Second, you can show that the options are not mutually exclusive by arguing that it is possible to strike a balance or find a happy medium between the two extremes. For example, suppose you are touring an art exhibit featuring works by Marlene Dumas. Your friend declares, "That's not art. It's pornography!" Many laypersons and some art critics (Uidhir, 2009) adhere to the view that pornography and art are separate and distinct. Asked to define obscenity, Supreme Court Justice Potter Stewart once famously declared "I know it when I see it" (*Jacobellis* v. *Ohio*, 1964). But can't a work of art be aesthetically pleasing and sexually arousing at the same time (see Maes, 2011)? Consider paintings such as Goya's *La Maja Desnuda* (1797–1800), or Monet's *Olympia* (1863). Is the line between art and pornography that distinct? Rather than an either–or approach, why not consider a *both–and* perspective?

A third way you can counter a false dilemma is to choose one of the "horns" and present it as a positive rather than a negative. Suppose someone argues that when it comes to the war on terror, you can favor human rights or you can favor national security, but you can't have both. Providing due process for suspected terrorists, the person maintains, trades off with efforts to thwart terrorism. To rebut this dilemma, you could grab the human rights "horn" and argue that suspending civil liberties in the name of national security only makes matters worse. You could point out that, more often than not, violating human rights breeds terrorists. The prisoner abuse scandal at Abu Ghraib became a recruiting tool for al Qaeda. The indefinite detentions at Guantanamo have radicalized many Muslims, turning them into jihadists (Bergen & Tiedemann, 2009). What's more, the Supreme Court has consistently ruled in favor of due process in cases involving the civil liberties of detainees versus government claims for national security (*Rasul* v. *Bush*, 2004; *Hamdi* v. *Rumsfeld*, 2004; *Hamdan* v. *Rumsfeld*, 2006). If we abandon core principles of democracy, such as due process guarantees, to combat terrorism, then perhaps we've defeated ourselves.

Hypothesis Contrary to Fact: When Pigs Fly

According to Hendrickson, *counterfactual reasoning* is "the process of evaluating conditional claims about alternate possibilities and their consequences" (Hendrickson, 2008, p. 6). For example:

> "If Russia hadn't meddled in the 2016 presidential election," a Democrat might suggest, "Hillary Clinton would have won."

or

> "The Cubs would've gone on to win the 2003 World Series," a Chicagoan might muse, "if some stupid fan hadn't interfered with Moises Alou catching that foul ball in game 6 of the National League Championship."

In each of these examples, a person posits that events are other than what they are or were. The person assumes that changing one element in the process would have produced a different outcome. Such reasoning is not necessarily fallacious. In fact, counterfactual reasoning is common and can be quite useful in historical arguments, scientific disputes, and controversies in the social sciences. Such reasoning can encourage free thinking by removing presumed constraints on problem solving. For example, counterfactual reasoning about a historical blunder may suggest ways of preventing history from repeating itself.

The problem is that all *retrospective hypotheticals* are just that, hypothetical. What happened, happened. What didn't, didn't. Counterfactual reasoning may help prevent a problem from recurring in the future, but it cannot alter the past. Lamenting that "except for this," "if only . . .," or "but for that," things would have turned out differently doesn't achieve much. The important point is to translate hindsight into foresight to prevent the same mistake from being made again.

When engaging in counterfactual reasoning, it helps to understand the difference between what Lebow (2000) calls *plausible counterfactuals*, which are at least conceivable, and *miracle counterfactuals*, which are highly inconceivable. To illustrate the difference, suppose that Babbs, a game show contestant, must choose between two safes, one that contains $100 and another that contains $1,000,000. If Babbs picks the $100 safe, she could reasonably say, "If only I'd picked the other safe, I'd be a millionaire." This is a plausible counterfactual.

Now let's suppose that Biff, on another game show, is asked to name the capitals of 10 nations. If he gets them all right, he wins a million dollars. Otherwise, he takes home a scented candle. Later, as Biff strikes a match to his consolation prize, he muses,

> If only my parents hadn't divorced when I was 10 years old, I would have concentrated on school more, done better in geography, and known that Ouagadougou is the capital of Burkina Faso! That divorce cost me a million bucks! Thanks a bunch, mom and dad!

The latter example illustrates a miracle counterfactual. That's because it is rather farfetched to believe that changing one distant event would have produced 10 correct answers. The example illustrates one of the primary liabilities of counterfactual reasoning, which is the problem of *interconnectedness*. Specifically, when positing a counterfactual, arguers often make the assumption that one and only one thing is, was, or would be different. Such reasoning tends to be self-serving because causes and effects are usually interrelated with other causes and effects. Why pretend that if things had been different, *only one thing* would have been different? Indeed, Biff could just as easily have surmised that if his folks had stayed married, he'd have been killed in a bar fight in Addis Ababa, the capital of Ethiopia.

A second liability to counterfactual reasoning involves *compound probabilities*, in which not just one event, but multiple events would have to occur in succession for the hypothesized outcome to occur (Lebow, 2000). In this case, for example, even if Biff's parents stayed together, knowing the correct capitals might have also depended on having good geography teachers.

Finally, a third liability involves *proximity* (Chwieroth, 2009; Fearon, 1996), which suggests that counterfactuals are only worth considering when the antecedent event and the consequent event happen closely in time. The larger the time gap, the greater the chance for confounding variables to intervene.

Countering a Hypothesis Contrary to Fact

If you ever need to counter fallacious hypotheticals, you can do so in a variety of ways. First, you can note that while such conjecture may offer an interesting intellectual exercise, it doesn't change the facts. Such "shoulda, coulda, woulda" thinking doesn't really get you anywhere. For any given event that did take place, there are an endless number of scenarios that didn't occur.

Second, you can argue that hindsight is biased. It is easy to look back and imagine how things might have been. For example, Mark Wahlberg was originally scheduled to be on board one of the September 11 flights that crashed into the World Trade Center. During an interview in *Men's Journal* he boasted:

> If I was on that plane with my kids, it wouldn't have went down like it did. There would have been a lot of blood in that first-class cabin and then me saying 'OK, we're going to land somewhere safely, don't worry'. (Hedegaard, 2012, p. 56)

Looking back, Wahlberg had the benefit of knowing the terrorists' true intentions. The passengers on board had no idea the hijackers planned on flying the planes into buildings. Would he have intuited the hijackers' motives more accurately than the actual passengers? Would he really have been braver than the other passengers? After complaints by the victims' families, Wahlberg issued an apology.

Third, you can employ standard tests of causal reasoning to evaluate the likelihood of a hypothetical scenario. For instance, you can ask whether the arguer is hypothesizing a *sole cause*, e.g., if one and only one antecedent event were different, would the consequent have been different as well? Or is the arguer hypothesizing a *sufficient* cause? That is, would changing one specific antecedent be sufficient, in and of itself, to produce the hypothesized consequent? Because causation is often complex, a change in one event might produce changes in ways unanticipated by the arguer.

Diversionary Tactics: Verbal Sleight of Hand

Some arguers are like pickpockets. They try to distract you from what's really happening. In the same way that pickpockets might pat you on the back while lifting your wallet from your pocket, arguers might try to divert your attention away from the real issue by sidetracking the discussion. How? With the help of five fallacies that we consider next: *ad hominem, tu quoque, red herring, straw man*, and *appeal to extremes* (see also, Walton, 2004).

Ad Hominem: *Only an Ignoramus Would Believe That*

If you've ever been called a jerk, moron, loser, or "a carbuncle on the behind of society," you're familiar with our next fallacy, the *ad hominem* (van Eemeren, Meuffels, & Verburg, 2000). All too frequently, arguers resort to *ad hominem* attacks when they are frustrated. There are different forms of this fallacy,[1] but the *abusive ad hominem*, the most common, impugns a person or the source of an argument, rather than the substance of an argument itself. *Ad hominems* include insults, put-downs, ridicule, and other demeaning remarks.

The media is rife with personal attacks. An arguer may resort to *verbal aggression* (see Chapters 1 and 2) in the form of racist, sexist, homophobic, or xenophobic remarks. As an example, Leslie Gibson, a candidate for Maine's legislature, disparaged Emma Gonzalez, one of the outspoken students who survived the Parkland, Florida, mass shooting. Rather than countering the student's statements about the need for stronger gun laws, however, Gibson punched below the belt by tweeting, "There is nothing about this skinhead lesbian that impresses me and there is nothing that she has to say unless you're a frothing at the mouth moonbat" (Brammer, 2018, para. 2).

Not all character attacks are fallacious, however. Sometimes questioning a person's character or integrity is relevant to the issue. Douglas Walton (Walton, 1998) and others distinguish between *abusive ad hominems*, which are illegitimate personal attacks, and *circumstantial ad hominems*, in which "a character critique is directly or indirectly related to the point being articulated" (Raley, 2008, para. 3). Similarly, we have noted that, in political contexts, attacks on candidates' personal attributes may be appropriate as long as such attacks are characterized by veracity, relevancy, and decorum (Seiter & Gass, 2010). But what about attacks on politicians' wives? Attacking Michelle Obama for wearing a sleeveless dress, as David Brooks did, or Melania Trump for her accent, as Jimmy Kimmel and Chelsea Handler did, seems out of line, at least to us. Similarly, claiming that Tom Cruise is a terrible actor because he's a Scientologist, for example, is an abusive *ad hominem*. Claiming that he's a bad actor because his acting is always "over the top," however, is a circumstantial *ad hominem* (see Raley, 2008).

Countering an Ad Hominem

In grade school, you might have learned that countering *ad hominem* attacks was as simple as saying, "I know you are but what am I?" or "It takes one to know one!" But playground comebacks may not serve you well in adulthood. Instead, to defuse a personal attack, try to get the discussion back on track. You might say, for example, "There's no need to get personal," or "Let's focus on issues rather personalities, okay?" Other responses might include:

- "I'm sure I have personal flaws, but what is your objection to my argument?"
- "You seem to have reverted to name calling. Is that supposed to convince me?"
- "Instead of explaining what's wrong with me, please explain what's wrong with my argument."

If you are the one questioning another person's character, examine your motives. Are you simply exchanging insults? If so, you're probably escalating the situation, so stop. On the other hand, if questioning the person's character is relevant to the issue at hand, explain its relevance to the issue at hand. If another person's argument is self-serving or hypocritical, it is worth pointing that out. And be on guard for a comeback known as the *tu quoque* fallacy, which we examine next.

Tu Quoque: *Two Wrongs Don't Make a Right*

People who commit the fallacy of *tu quoque* (essentially, "you too" in Latin) accuse another person of a similar wrong (Aikin, 2007; Govier, 1984; Parker, 1984). This form of errant reasoning is often referred to as "the pot calling the kettle black" or "look who's talking?" Representative James Sensenbrenner, for example, criticized former First Lady Michelle Obama's "Get Moving" campaign by saying, "She lectures us on eating right while she has a large posterior herself" (Snead, 2011, para. 2). He later apologized for the remark.

Governments also commit the *tu quoque* fallacy when criticizing other nations' policies while defending their own. For example, when the U.S. denounces other nations, such as Iran and Syria, for jailing and torturing political prisoners, those countries retort that the U.S. does the same thing with the detainees at Guantanamo.

A rejuvenated version of the *tu quoque* fallacy is known as *whataboutism*. During the Cold War, whataboutism was a common refrain whenever Russia was denounced by the U.S. for human rights violations. "What about the lynchings of minorities in America?" a Kremlin spokesperson might ask. In its modern form, whataboutism is used by liberals and conservatives alike to avoid tackling arguments head on. "What about Nazis and white supremacists?" one side might ask. "What about Antifa?" the other side might counter. "What about the Trump campaign's collusion with Russia?" one side asks. "What about Hillary Clinton's deal to sell Uranium One to the Russians?" the other side replies.

Of course, the problem with whataboutism and the *tu quoque* fallacy is that they sidetrack meaningful argument by changing the subject. Effective problem solving often requires focusing on one problem at a time, and saving other problems, related or not, for another day. That said, it is perfectly acceptable to point out when other people are being hypocritical, for example, when they say one thing while doing another. If a politician extolls family values while engaging in adultery, it is fine to call him or her out on it. Consider the apparent inconsistency between Senator Elizabeth Warren's words and her deeds when it comes to equal pay for women.

> Today is Equal Pay Day, and by the sound of it, you would think that it's some sort of historic holiday . . . But that's not what it's about. Not even close. Because in the year 2016, at a time with self-driving cars and computers that sit on your wrist, women still make only 79 cents for every dollar a man makes. (Fang, 2016)

Warren's point is well taken. Women *should* earn equal pay for equal work! However, a report revealed that Warren herself paid full-time female members less than full-time male staff members (Scher, 2017). To be fair, some of the pay disparity was because males held different titles and positions than females (Palma, 2017). One might reasonably ask, though, why couldn't Warren find equally qualified women for the higher-paid positions?

Countering a Tu Quoque

How, then, might you counter the *tu quoque* fallacy? Using the above example, if a reporter from the *New York Times* asked Warren about the gender pay gap on her staff and Warren retorted, "There is a gender pay gap at your newspaper too. Get your own house in order before attacking me," she would be committing a *tu quoque*. The reporter might counter by asking, "How does the fact that my employer pays women less absolve you from any wrongdoing? Two wrongs don't make a right."

As another example, imagine that two parents found ecstasy (MDMA) in their adolescent son's jacket pocket. How might they respond if their son said, "You guys smoke cigarettes and they cause cancer." To counter their son's remark, the parents might reply, "We wish we had never started smoking. Our poor choice doesn't justify another poor choice by you." In other words, to counter the *tu quoque* fallacy, try not to let the other person deflect blame. If he or she says, "You're a fine one to talk," respond by saying "Yes, perhaps I'm blameworthy too, but how do you defend your own actions?" Emphasize that if an action is wrong, it doesn't matter whether others commit the same wrong.

Red Herring: Don't Change the Subject

A *red herring* (a.k.a. *ignoratio elenchi*) is a diversionary tactic designed to distract attention away from the real issue at hand. In a mystery novel, a red herring is a clue that points the reader in the wrong direction. There are a number of explanations for the origin of the term, but the basic idea is that dragging a smelly fish across the path of pursuing hounds will throw them off the scent. You might also hear of this as a *smoke and mirrors* strategy or *beating around the bush*. Consider the case of a prowler who has been nabbed by the police after burglarizing a home. The burglar says, "Hey, it's a good thing I was in their house. They left the iron on. If I hadn't unplugged it before I left, the entire place might have burned down." Claiming he did the homeowners a favor is a ploy aimed at diverting attention away from the real issue: the crime of breaking and entering.

Another example can be seen in the Oscar-nominated film *The Social Network*, which finds Mark Zuckerberg's character facing a disciplinary hearing. An administrator notes, "Mark, your site Face Mash crashed the Harvard network, objectified women, and was just plain mean." Mark replies, "Really, you should be thanking me for pointing out gaps in the security of the Harvard server." Can you see why this defense is a red herring? Since Zuckerberg could have exposed flaws in the server's security and brought them to the university's attention without having students rate each other's physical appearance, his argument is clearly diversionary.

Countering a Red Herring

If you ever sniff out a red herring argument, the most effective way to deal with it is to expose it for the diversionary tactic that it is. Tell the other person, "Please stop trying to change the subject" or "let's not lose track of the real issue." Suppose, for example, that a motorist is pulled over for drunk driving. If the motorist says, "Wait, I donated to the policeman's ball! I supported a bond initiative for a new police station," the officer might reply, "That's all well and good, yet irrelevant to whether you are driving under the influence . . . ."

Straw Person: Don't Put Words in My Mouth

Miguel de Cervantes' character Don Quixote tilted at windmills, imagining them to be angry giants that needed slaying. Arguers sometimes behave this way too. They misrepresent an opposing position, the better to defeat it. Put differently, they contrive what is known as a *straw man* (or *straw person*) argument simply so they can tear it down.[2] An arguer who commits a traditional *straw man* fallacy[3] misrepresents another's position through distortion, exaggeration, or caricature. For example, the Bush administration's argument for invading Iraq was premised largely on a straw man fallacy. Specifically, the argument assumed that Saddam Hussein possessed weapons of mass destruction, even though no such chemical, biological, or nuclear weapons were ever found. Did Bush officials use the specter of WMDs as a pretext for invading Iraq or did they genuinely not know? Knowingly or unwittingly, the White House distorted the threat posed by Saddam Hussein.

There are, of course, several variations of the straw man. First, rather than distorting or exaggerating an opponent's position, an arguer could attack only the weakest argument(s) presented. This approach is termed the *weak man*[4] (Aikin & Casey, 2011; Talisse & Aikin, 2006). Yet another variation is known as the *hollow man*. As Aikin and Casey explain, the hollow man "consists of fabricating both an opponent and the opponent's view, merely in order to defeat them" (Aikin & Casey, 2011, pp. 92–93). The hollow man is often prefaced with, "There are those who claim . . ." or "Some might say that . . .." By attributing the position to an unnamed source, the arguer avoids taking responsibility for the argument. If challenged, the arguer can claim, "I never made such a claim myself."

Countering a Straw Person

If the person with whom you are arguing is trying to "make hay" with a straw person, you can explain that your position is being misrepresented. You might say, "I don't know if it was your intention or not, but you have mischaracterized my stance on this issue." If the other person offers a weak man, focusing on a lesser issue, explain that the person is arguing about trifles. You might say, "Let's get back to the heart of the issue." Finally, if the other person offers a hollow man, you can state that she or he is attacking an argument that you are not even making. And if the other person relies on the preface "Some have argued . . ." or "there are those who say . . ." point out that she or he is attacking an imaginary argument made by a fictitious arguer. Ask that the "ghost" arguer to whom she or he is referring be identified.

Appeal to Extremes: You've Gone Too Far

People are appealing to extremes when they exaggerate an opponent's position, taking it beyond what's actually being advocated. For example, at a campaign rally during the 2016 election, Donald Trump declared, "Hillary Clinton wants to abolish the Second Amendment. She wants to abolish it. Hillary Clinton wants to take your guns away, and she wants to abolish the Second Amendment!" (Diamond, 2016). While it is true that Clinton supported background checks and keeping guns out of the hands of domestic abusers and the mentally ill, she never called for an across-the-board ban on gun ownership.

An appeal to extremes may bear a resemblance to the slippery slope fallacy discussed earlier. However, a slippery slope is based on a series of causes and effects leading up to some calamity. The appeal to extremes does not rely on causal reasoning.

There is nothing wrong with extending another person's argument to a logical conclusion, so long as the extension is reasonable. Exaggerating another's argument to the point of absurdity, however, is problematic. If a couple were getting divorced, they could argue about dividing things up. Suppose, however, that the husband said, "Well if you want to be completely fair, you should get one of my testicles and I should get one of your ovaries." The husband would be appealing to extremes.

Countering an Appeal to Extremes

If a person claims that an absurd scenario represents a "logical extension" of your position, note that there is nothing logical about the extension. Clearly state the limits of your position, so it is clear where you draw the line. Take the dialogue below, for example.

Mom:	"I think we should cut back on dairy and meat. We don't need all that saturated fat in our diet."
Son:	"Give up milk? No way!"
Mom:	"I didn't say *give up* milk. I said cut back. We could have 'green tea Tuesdays,' with no dairy products."

Daughter: "I hate green tea. Plus, there's a reason we domesticated cows, you know? It's not like we're going back to being hunter-gatherers anytime soon."

Mom: "I'm not saying we should become hunter-gatherers. I'm saying we should reduce our meat consumption. We could have 'meatless Monday' meals, for example."

Although the children try to cast their mother's position in an extreme light, the mother emphasizes that she is not in favor of banning dairy or meat altogether. She exposes their exaggerations of her position.

Appeals to Emotion: You're Not Using Your Head

Emotional appeals are common. A person may urge you to follow your heart, go with your gut, or trust your feelings. What happens, though, when we let our emotions cloud our judgment? It often pays to think twice, as Wray Herbert points out in his book, *On Second Thought* (2010). Although there are a wide range of emotional appeals—such as appeals to pity, fear, or pride—in this section, we focus on two of the most common: appeal to the crowd and appeal to tradition.

Appeal to the Crowd: Everybody's Doing It

A mother tells her teenage son, "I don't care if vaping is all the rage, nicotine is still addictive no matter how you inhale it into your lungs." A husband tells his wife, "I have to wear my stormtrooper outfit to Comic-Con. Everyone will be in costume!" A taxpayer tells an I.R.S. auditor, "Everyone cheats on their taxes. Why pick on me?" People sometimes justify their behavior by claiming, "Everyone's doing it." When they do so, they are *appealing to the crowd* or, as it's known in Latin, making an *ad populum* appeal. In some cases, popular support or public enthusiasm is an important consideration. Hence not all popular appeals are fallacious (Walton, 1980). But what if the majority is wrong? At one time, a majority of people believed the earth was flat and that the earth was the center of the solar system.

The phenomenon of *jumping on the bandwagon*, as it is also called, is quite common. Consider as an example the Great Recession of 2007–2009, which was brought about by foolhardy subprime mortgages. Hordes of people bought houses they knew they could not afford. They hoped to "flip" the houses a short time later and turn a tidy profit. But when their balloon payments became due, they found themselves "underwater," owing far more than their homes were worth. A cascade of mortgage defaults ensued. The lesson to be learned is clear: Before jumping on the bandwagon, make sure you know where it is headed. For all you know, it may be careening toward a cliff.

Countering an Appeal to the Crowd: Against the Grain

There are a variety of ways to rebut an appeal to the crowd. First, you can point out that "counting heads" is ill-advised if ordinary people lack knowledge or expertise on an issue. Widely-held beliefs are often mistaken. The average person, for example, knows little about climatology, so asking the "person on the street" whether climate change is a real phenomenon or not serves little purpose other than to gauge public opinion on the issue. Climatologists are the folks to ask about climate change.

Figure 9.1 Roz Chast cartoon, July 11, 1988, people waiting for the next bandwagon.
© Roz Chast/*The New Yorker* Collection/www.cartoonbank.com.

A second way to counter this fallacy is to point out that what's popular isn't always what's right. At various times throughout history, a majority of the population endorsed slavery, opposed women's suffrage, and favored forced sterilization of people with intellectual disabilities. Relying on majority rule can lead to a "tyranny of the majority." One can counter majority rule by arguing for the preeminence of human rights or inalienable rights regardless of majority will.

Appeal to Tradition: Set in Our Ways

How many politicians does it take to change a light bulb?

"Two; one to change it and one to change it back again."

There's some truth to this old joke. Indeed, when it comes to doing things differently, people often flinch. As the old saying goes, "Traditions die hard." Some traditions make sense.

Others do not. Some, for example, regard the circumcision of newborn males as an important cultural and religious ritual, while others see it as a barbaric practice. Some parents believe that telling their children about fictional characters (spoiler alert) like Santa, the Easter bunny, and the tooth fairy, is part of the joy of childhood. Others believe parents set a bad example by lying to their children.

Regardless of their conviction, people commit the fallacy of *appeal to tradition* when they endorse a custom, practice, or ritual that no longer serves a useful purpose. The tradition may even be counterproductive. The Chinese practice of footbinding, for example, once considered a status symbol, proved to be dysfunctional once women were expected to join the workforce. Is the practice that different from some of the extreme forms of cosmetic surgery that women undergo in the name of beauty in contemporary society?

Countering an Appeal to Tradition: Force of Habit

The best way to counter an appeal to tradition is to ask what beneficial purpose is being served, other than adherence to the tradition. Sometimes, the obverse of tradition is progress. For example, following a bridal or baby shower, traditional etiquette dictates that the bride or expectant mother sends written thank you notes to everyone by mail. Not doing so, the argument goes, shows a lack of appreciation. But is it the medium or the message that really counts? An email or text message is eco-friendlier. And if the electronic thank you is thoughtful, sincere, and heart-felt, does it really matter if the sender licks an envelope and affixes a stamp? To demonstrate that she wasn't taking the lazy way out, a new bride or mother could follow-up an electronic thank you with an electronic image of the gift being put to good use.

Fallacies of Presumption: Shifting the Burden of Proof

In the previous section we compared people who use diversionary fallacies with pickpockets. In contrast, those who commit the fallacies in this section might be compared with shirkers. That's because they try to foist the burden of proof onto other people rather than meeting it them-selves. As we noted in Chapter 3, however, an advocate for a position normally has the *burden of proof*, that is, an obligation to provide reasoning and evidence in support of a claim (Walton & Koszowy, 2018). Shifting that burden of proof violates one of the 10 commandments of arguing (van Eemeren & Houtlosser, 2002).

Appeal to Ignorance: You Can't Prove I'm Wrong, So I Must Be Right

When a person commits the *appeal to ignorance* fallacy, also known as *ad ignorantium*, he or she shifts the burden of proof by essentially saying, "I don't have to prove my argument is true, you have to prove it is false" (Walton, 1999). To illustrate, consider this exchange:

Liam: "Why do you have an owl's foot hanging from your rear-view mirror?"
Otto: "It keeps the mole people who live below the earth away."
Liam: "What are you talking about? I don't see any mole people. I've never seen any mole people."
Otto: "That's because the owl's foot is working!"

In this example, Otto assumes that the owl's foot is working because he sees no evidence that it is *not* working.[5] The problem, of course, is that a lack of evidence that a claim is false does not prove the claim is true.

A real-life example of this fallacy involved a spate of sexual harassment claims against Bill O'Reilly, then at Fox News. Speaking in O'Reilly's defense, a Fox spokesperson said, "No current or former Fox employee ever took advantage of the 21st Century Fox hotline to raise a concern about Bill O'Reilly, even anonymously" (cited in Scheiber, 2017). Of course, an absence of calls to the hotline doesn't prove an absence of sexual harassment in the workplace. Female employees may have been afraid to use the hotline, or unaware there was a hotline. Whatever the case, O'Reilly was subsequently ousted from the network.

Conspiracy theorists are also fond of this fallacy. "No one," they might say, "has proven that Bigfoot doesn't exist," or, "I say September 11th was an inside job, until someone proves otherwise." Of course, it is difficult, if not impossible, to prove a negative. Conspiracy theorists rely on this. If Chuck says, "There are invisible snakes wriggling around your feet," Irma might reply, "I don't see any," to which Chuck would respond, "Exactly."

Countering an Appeal to Ignorance

It is reasonable to point out that an arguer has failed to meet her or his burden of proof and tried to shift it onto others. If an arguer insists that you must prove his or her claim is false, point out the difficulty, or impossibility, of proving a negative. For instance, no one has proven there isn't a "fountain of youth" somewhere in Florida, as Ponce de Leon believed. However, if such a magical fountain existed, someone should have stumbled upon it by now. People have traipsed all over Florida. None have come back 10 years younger.

Tautology: It's Called an Elephant Because It Looks Like One

Tautological arguments are constructed in such a way that they cannot be disproved. Rather than proving the premise for a claim, a *tautology* reiterates the premise in different terms. You can often spot tautologies based on their use of circular reasoning. Saying, for example, that "Timmy is afraid of heights because he has acrophobia" is the same as saying "Timmy has acrophobia because he is afraid of heights." Suppose a friend tells you, "I'm psychic." You reply, "Oh yeah, prove it." "I knew you wouldn't believe me," your friend says, "which proves I'm psychic."

Many grand theories, such as Marxism, Freudian psychology, and Skinnerian behaviorism, are subject to this fallacy. Neo-Marxists, for instance, claim that capitalism is at the root of all of society's woes. However, if someone points out that planned economies, such as Cuba and North Korea, are much worse off, Marxist apologists claim, "Those aren't true examples of Marxist states." Or consider a Freudian example; suppose Mimi invites Pierre over for dinner. He brings a bottle of wine and a loaf of French bread. The following conversation ensues.

Mimi: "You know, French bread is a phallic symbol."
Pierre: "I happen to like thick crust."
Mimi: "You only *think* you like thick crust. That's *not* why you chose French bread."
Pierre: "The shape of the bread has nothing to do with it."
Mimi: "I'd expect you to say that. Freudian urges are subconscious."

It may be possible to explain every decision in Freudian terms, but that doesn't mean every urge is based on a subconscious desire. Even if Pierre brought a round loaf of bread, Mimi could still insist, "You repressed your urge to buy French bread."

Countering a Tautology

Because tautologies rely on circular assumptions, they are difficult to refute. No matter the outcome, the tautologist will claim it supports his or her position. To counter such reasoning, you can point out that the other person's position is *nonfalsifiable*. That is, no set of circumstances, should they occur, would disprove the person's argument *if* the person's argument were false. In the preceding example, is there any food or drink Pierre could have brought that Mimi would agree is free of Freudian implications? Ask the other person to identify a specific outcome that would prove his or her position false if, in fact, it were false. If the person responds by saying "There is no way to prove my position is false, because it is true" you know you are dealing with a tautology.

Fallacies Involving Ambiguity: It's Not Cheating if You Don't Remember

Although there are a number of fallacies based on vague, imprecise, or confusing language (such as *amphiboly, accent, composition*, and *division*), we focus on one primary offender here; equivocation.

Equivocation: Between the Lines

Equivocation relies on the inherent ambiguity of language (Woods & Walton, 1989). Equivocators use language in an evasive, misleading way. Consider the brief dialogue that follows:

Lois: "Are you cheating on me?"
Ralph: "I swear I'm not seeing anyone else."
Lois: "But are you having an affair with someone? Are you involved with someone else?"
Ralph: "Trust me, I'm not sleeping with anyone else."
Lois: "How about online? Are you having an online affair?"
Ralph: "An online affair? How can you have an affair without any physical contact?"
Lois: "How? You could be texting intimate messages, sexting pictures of each other, or having phone sex. Are you doing any of those things?"
Ralph: "Well . . . I wouldn't call that 'cheating'."

In this example, Ralph is equivocating. First, he is dodgy with language (e.g., not *seeing* anyone, not *sleeping with* anyone). Second, he hedges on what he considers to be an affair. Lois deftly calls him on this.

It Depends on What Your Definition of "Is" Is (Bill Clinton's Grand Jury Testimony)

An iconic moment of real-life equivocation occurred on January 26, 1998 when then president Bill Clinton addressed the nation about his alleged sexual dalliance with White House intern Monica Lewinsky. Clinton wagged his finger at the cameras, and proclaimed:

I want to say one thing to the American people. I want you to listen to me. I'm going to say this again: I did not have sexual relations with that woman, Miss Lewinsky. I never told anybody to lie, not a single time; never. These allegations are false. And I need to go back to work for the American people. (Clinton, cited by Bennet, 1998, p. A-1)

Clinton equivocated in his use of the term "sexual relations" because he did have oral sex with Monica Lewinsky on multiple occasions, according to her testimony before the Independent Counsel (Starr Report, 1998). The DNA evidence (e.g., the infamous stain on her cocktail dress) corroborated her testimony (Starr Report, 1998). When Clinton proclaimed that he "did not have sexual relations with that woman . . ." he apparently meant sex in the "missionary" position, as opposed to other forms of sex. His parsing of language was clearly meant to be evasive.

Euphemisms: But She Has a Great Personality

Equivocation often relies on *euphemisms*, which are polite, diplomatic terms that are substituted for more offensive, distasteful terms. The practice of using euphemisms is also referred to as *double-speak*. George Orwell likened euphemisms to a cuttlefish spurting out ink in an effort to distract and confuse (Orwell, 1950). For example, in response to charges that the U.S. was torturing detainees at "black sites" in other countries, George W. Bush responded that, "this government does not torture people" (Ward, 2007, p. A-1). Yet the Bush administration approved what it called "enhanced interrogation techniques" including waterboarding, freezing, and withholding medical care (Thomas et al., 2005). Then vice president Dick Cheney maintained that if a technique did not result in organ failure or death it was not torture. Human rights advocates labeled Cheney's policy as "torture-lite."

Other examples of euphemisms abound. When telemarketers interrupt your dinner with a "courtesy call," a dentist says, "you may experience some discomfort," a power company claims to use "clean coal," or a politician presents "alternative facts," you know you are dealing with euphemisms.

Reframing: I Didn't Steal the Car, Officer, I Liberated It!

People can also use equivocation to reinterpret or reframe their actions. For example, a meth addict who told his grandmother "I wasn't *stealing* money from your purse, I was only *borrowing* it" would be equivocating. A husband who racked up huge credit card bills might tell his wife, "I did it all for you, baby."

Countering Equivocation

One strategy for dealing with equivocation is to ask people to define their terms clearly, which makes it harder for them to waffle back and forth from one meaning to another. If a key term can be used in different senses, make sure the other person isn't hedging. A motorist who is involved in a traffic accident may say, "I wasn't *talking* on my cell phone while driving," but may fail to mention that he or she was texting.

A second strategy is to avoid high-level abstractions and get down to specifics. For example, a politician might say, "I'm for family values. The family unit is the backbone of our nation." When asked about specific types of families, e.g., same sex families who adopt or use surrogates, families with undocumented members or "Dreamers," or unmarried cohabitating families, the politician might begin to waffle.

As another example, when companies and organizations tout themselves as being "eco-friendly" or "environmentally conscious," it is difficult to know exactly what those labels mean. When a hotel asks you to reuse your towels, for example, is management really trying to save the Earth or just lower their utility bills? Cynics have dubbed this type of marketing "greenwashing" (Dahl, 2010).

A third approach is to point out that equivocation in the form of euphemisms can trivialize the importance of an issue. By way of example, saying that two people engaged in "non-consensual sex" minimizes the fact that one person *raped* or *sexually assaulted* the other. Likewise, calling a murder an "honor killing" belies the immorality of allowing males to murder female family members because the latter were victims of rape, refused an arranged marriage, dated someone from a different village, or associated with non-familial males in public. The phrase "honor killing" implies that it is a virtuous act, rather than a backward, misogynistic practice in which women are treated like property.

Non-Sequitur: If You Don't Eat Your Vegetables, the Terrorists Have Won

In Chapter 3 we saw that a warrant connects the claim of an argument to its grounds. But if that connection makes no sense, there is a good chance that a *non sequitur* fallacy has been committed. Specifically, a person commits a *non sequitur* fallacy by advancing a claim that appears to lack any connection to the grounds. In Latin, *non sequitur* simply means "does not follow." In practical terms, a *non sequitur* offers an *irrelevant reason* as proof for a claim. Suppose a movie buff said, "Harvey Weinstein can't be that loathsome. The guy produced or distributed 81 films that won Oscars." Weinstein's talent as a movie producer, however, has no bearing on the veracity of the charges of sexual assault for which he was indicted.

As another example, when Julia Louise Dreyfus' character Christine was accused of being a racist in the TV show *The New Adventures of Old Christine*, she defended herself by saying, "I'm not a racist, I drive a Prius for God's sake" (Season 1, episode 1). The former doesn't follow from the latter, however. The humor rests on her convoluted inference that a) she drives a Prius, b) a Prius is an eco-friendly car, c) people who drive eco-friendly cars tend to be liberal and racially tolerant, hence, d) she cannot be a racist. There are a lot of dots to connect in this argument.

A real-life example of this fallacy was committed by Nancy Pelosi, the Speaker of the House, when she argued for passage of the Health Care Reform Act, often referred to as Obamacare. "We have to pass the bill," she said, "So we can find out what's in it" (www.youtube.com/watch?v=hV-05TLiiLU). In some cases, the listener may be able to fashion a connection of sorts from two seemingly unrelated statements, but not always. Consider the statements below. Do the claims seem increasingly irrelevant to the grounds?

"I can't date you because you have the same first name as my brother."

"My car's radio is broken, so I'm going to have to sell it."

"I'll never get a tattoo. I like golf too much."

"I'm hungry. Let's play *Scrabble*."

Of course, any argument could be labeled a *non sequitur* if the inferential leap were found wanting. We recommend using this label only when there is *no apparent connection* between the claim and grounds, as opposed to a weak connection that can be classified as another fallacy. That is, if the missing warrant involves a faulty analogy, a faulty cause, a faulty sign, or some other errant inference, label it as such. Otherwise, every bad argument will wind up being called a *non sequitur*.

Countering a Non Sequitur

When faced with a *non sequitur*, our first impulse might be to say "Huh?" or scratch our head. If we cannot divine how the arguer got from A to B, however, we should ask him or her to connect the dots for us. Suppose that Roy and Dotty have just started dating. When Roy buys her perfume, the following conversation ensues:

Dotty: "Thanks, but I don't wear perfume. I'm a strong believer in animal rights."
Roy: "Am I missing something? What's perfume got to do with animal rights?"
Dotty: "Try asking a beaver or sperm whale."
Roy: "I'm still not getting it."
Dotty: "Animal secretions are harvested to make fragrances. Did you know, for instance, that castor is secreted from under beavers' tails and that ambergris comes from the bile ducts of sperm whales?"
Roy: "Yuck."
Dotty: "Not to mention musk. Why should animals suffer so I can smell good?"
Roy: (Looking at the perfume's label) "It says here that this cologne is animal free and vegan approved."
Dotty: "You're so sweet."

Because Roy failed to see any connection between refusing to wear cologne and support for animal rights, Dotty's original comment appeared to be a *non sequitur*. Once she explained the connection, Roy was able to respond to her objection by noting that the fragrance he gave her was non-animalic.

You can do likewise when you encounter an apparent irrelevant reason. First ask, "What does _____ have to do with _____?" If you aren't satisfied with the answer, ask for proof of the alleged connection and, if proof is provided, offer counter arguments or evidence of your own. Suppose, for example, that a mother is convinced that her son couldn't be a bully because he's kind to the family's pets. The school's principal might respond,

> We have eyewitness accounts from students and teachers. Just because a person is nice to animals, doesn't prove the person is nice to people. And just because a child is well-behaved at home doesn't guarantee that he or she acts the same way at school.

Summary

In this chapter we examined a variety of fallacies that are common in every-day argument. Some involve faulty premises, while others involve diversionary tactics. Still others involve unfair attempts to shift the burden of proof, and some rely on the inherent ambiguities of language. In addition to offering clues for identifying each fallacy, we also offered suggestions on how to counter them. Although argumentation scholars have catalogued many more fallacies than the ones covered here, we have reviewed some of the most common and egregious fallacies in reasoning.

Notes

1 Another type, the *circumstantial ad hominem*, focuses on a contradiction between what a person says and what the person does. We cover this under the heading of the *tu quoque* fallacy. Some other types of ad hominem arguments we don't have space to cover include the *genetic fallacy, guilt by association* and *poisoning the well* (Walton, 1998).
2 Yes, we realize that the term "straw man" may be perceived as sexist, since women are just as capable as men at committing this fallacy. We chose to go with straw man, rather than straw person, not because it is the more traditional label but because this is how modern scholars refer to the fallacy as well. We were concerned that students who tried to look up the term "straw person," to seek more information on their own, would be less successful.
3 Talisse and Aikin (2006) refer to this type as a *representational* straw man, although we think the term *misrepresentational* is a better descriptor.
4 Talisse and Aikin (2006) call this the *selection* straw man, because the arguer is selective about the arguments she or he chooses to rebut.
5 This particular example also entails a *post hoc* fallacy, since Otto presumes the owl's foot (cause) is what is keeping the mole people away (effect). Fallacies often overlap in this way and the same argument may entail multiple fallacies.

References

Aikin, S.F. (2007). Tu quoque arguments and the significance of hypocrisy. *SSRN Electronic Journal, 28*(2), 1–9. doi.org/10.2139/ssrn.1012620.

Aikin, S.F. & Casey, J. (2011). Straw men, weak men, and hollow men. *Argumentation, 25*(1), 87–105, doi.org/10.1007/s10503-010-9199-y.

Aristotle (1955). Sophistical refutations (translated by E. S. Forster & D. J. Furley). Loeb Classical Library 400. Cambridge, MA: Harvard University Press.

Benchley, R. (1920). *The most popular book of the month: An extremely literary review of the latest edition of the New York City telephone directory*, p. 69. New York: Conde Nast.

Bennet, J. (1998, September 27). The president under fire: The overview; Clinton emphatically denies an affair with ex-intern: Lawyers say he is distracted by events. *New York Times*, p. A-1.

Bergen, P. & Tiedemann, K. (2009, May 5). Inflating the Guantanamo threat. *New York Times*, p. 25.

Brammer, J.P. (2018, March 13). "Skinhead lesbian": GOP candidate attacks Parkland teen Emma Gonzalez. *ABC News*. Retrieved on March 14, 2018 from: www.nbcnews.com/P.feature/nbc-out/skinhead-lesbian-gop-candidate-attacks-parkland-teen-emma-gonzalez-n856311.

Carr, P. (2010, May 22). Amazon: You need to change your idiotic customer reviews policy right now. *TechCrunch*. Retrieved on June 7, 2011 from: http://techcrunch.com/2010/03/22/im-not-kidding-do-it-now.

CatholicCulture.org (2011, March 23). Practicing Catholics more likely than general public to back homosexual unions. *CatholicCulture.org*. Retrieved on June 29, 2011 from: www.catholicculture.org/news/headlines/index.cfm?storyid=9702.

Chameleon, K. (2017, December 12). Dead coal mines everywhere are being reincarnated as solar farms. *Quartz*. Retrieved on March 4, 2018 from: https://qz.com/1153672.

Chwieroth, J.M. (2009). Counterfactuals and the study of the American presidency. *Presidential Studies Quarterly, 32*(2), 293–327, doi.org/10.1111/j.0360-4918.2002.00222.x.

Dahl, R. (2010). Greenwashing: Do you know what you're buying? *Environmental Health Perspectives*, *118*(6), A246–A252, doi: 10.1289/ehp.118-a246.

Demaria, F. (2018, February 22). Why economic growth is not compatible with environmental sustainability. *Ecologist*. Retrieved on March 4, 2018 from: https://theecologist.org/2018/feb/22/why-economic-growth-not-compatible-environmental-sustainability.

Diamond, J. (2016, May 7). Trump says Clinton wants to abolish the 2nd amendment. *CNN*. Retrieved on March 26, 2018 from: www.cnn.com/2016/05/07/politics/donald-trump-hillary-clinton-second-amendment/index.html.

Fang, M. (2016, April 12). Elizabeth Warren: Equal pay day "is a day of embarrassment." *Huffington Post*. Retrieved on March 27, 2018 from: www.huffingtonpost.com/entry/elizabeth-warren-equal-pay-day_us_570d62e5e4b0836057a2b8b8.

Fearon, J.D. (1996). Causes and counterfactuals in social science: Exploring an analogy between cellular automata and historical processes. In P.E. Tetlock and A. Belkin (Eds), *Counterfactual thought experiments in world politics: Logical, methodological, and psychological perspectives* (pp. 39–67). Princeton, NJ: Princeton University Press.

Govier, T. (1984). Worries about tu quoque as a fallacy. *Informal Logic*, *3*(3), 2–4. doi: 10.22329/il/v3i1.2720.

Hamdan v. *Rumsfeld*, 548 U.S. 557 (2006).

Hamdi v. *Rumsfeld*, 542 U.S. 507 (2004).

Hedegaard, E. (2012, February). Mark Wahlberg: How a street fighting kid became a master of self-discipline. *Men's Journal*, *21*(1), 53–56, 94.

Hendrickson, N. (2008). Counterfactual reasoning: A basic guide for analysts, strategists, and decision makers. *Proteus Monograph Series*, *2*(5). Retrieved on August 27, 2018 from: www.au.af.mil/au/awc/awcgate/army-usawc/csl_counterfactual_reasoning.pdf.

Herbert, W. (2010). *On second thought: Outsmarting your mind's hard-wired habits*. New York: Crown Publishers.

Ikuenobe, P. (2002). In search of criteria for 'fallacies' and 'begging the question.' *Argumentation 16*(4), 421–441. doi:10.1023/A:1021158632437

International Energy Association (IEA) (2017). *Solar leads the charge in another record year for renewables*. Paris: International Energy Association. Retrieved on March 29, 2018 from: www.iea.org/publications/renewables2017.

Jacobellis v. *Ohio*, 378 U.S. 184 (1964).

Lebow, R.N. (2000). What's so different about a counterfactual? *World Politics*, *52*(4), 550–585, doi: org/10.1017/S0043887100020104.

Maes, H. (2011). Drawing the line: Art versus pornography. *Philosophy Compass*, *6*(6), 385–397,doi.org/10.1111/j.1747-9991.2011..00403.x.

Orwell, G. (1950). *Politics and the English language*. Evansville, IN: Herbert W. Simpson.

Palma, B. (2017, April 6). Does Elizabeth Warren pay female staffers less than their male counterparts? *Snopes*. Retrieved on March 27, 2018 from: www.snopes.com/fact-check/elizabeth-warren-staff-pay.

Parker, R. A. (1984). Tu quoque arguments: A rhetorical perspective. *Journal of the American Forensic Association*, *20*, 123–132.

Raley, Y. (2008, June 1). Character attacks: How to properly apply the *Ad Hominem*. *Scientific American Mind*. Retrieved on July 9, 2018 from: www.scientificamerican.com/article/character-attack.

Rasul v. *Bush*, 542, U.S. 466 (2004).

Scheiber, N. (2017, April 21). Anonymous harassment hotlines are hard to find and harder to trust. *New York Times*. Retrieved on August 27, 2018 from: www.nytimes.com/2017/04/21/business/media/fox-sexual-harassment-hotline-bill-oreilly.html.

Scher, B. (2017, April 4). Elizabeth Warren's female staffers made 71% of male staffers' salaries in 2016. *Washington Free Beacon*. Retrieved on March 27, 2018 from: https://freebeacon.com/issues/elizabeth-warrens-female-staffers-made-71-less-male-staffers-earnings-2016.

Seiter, J.S. & Gass, R.H. (2010). Aggressive communication in political contexts. In T.A. Avtgis & A.S. Rancer (Eds), *Arguments, aggression, and conflict: New directions in theory and research* (pp. 217–240). New York: Routledge.

Snead, E. (2011, December 2). Republican congressman Jim Sensenbrenner overheard talking about Michelle Obama's "large posterior" (update). *The Hollywood Reporter*. Retrieved on January 11, 2012 from: www.hollywoodreporter.com/fash-track/jim-sensenbrenner-michelle-obama-75983.

Starr Report (1998, September 8). There is substantial and credible information that President Clinton committed acts that may constitute grounds for impeachment. Office of the Independent Counsel. *New York Times*. Retrieved on August 4, 2011 from: www.nytimes.com/specials/starr/7grounds_1.html.

Talisse, R. & Aikin, S.F. (2006). Two forms of the straw man. *Argumentation*, *20*(3), 345–352, doi.org/10.1007/s10503-006-9017-8.

Talisse, R. & Raley, Y. (2008, February). Getting duped: How the media messes with your mind. *Scientific American Mind*, *19*(1), 16–17.

Thomas, E., Hirsh, M., Wolffe, M.H., Isikoff, M., Klaidman, D., Barry, J., Taylor Jr., S. & Tuttle, S. (2005, November 21). The debate over torture; right after 9/11, Cheney said "we have to work . . . the dark side if you will." *Newsweek*, p. 26.

Tomić, T. (2013). False dilemma: A systematic exposition. *Argumentation, 27*(4), 347–368. doi:10.1007/s10503-013-9292-0

Uidhir, C.M. (2009). Why pornography can't be art. *Philosophy and Literature*, *33*(1), 193–203, doi: 10.1353/phl.0.0036.

van Eemeren, F. H., Meuffels, B., & Verburg, M. (2000). The (un)reasonableness of Ad Hominem fallacies. *Journal of Language and Social Psychology*, *19*(4), 416–435. doi.org/10.1177/0261927X00019004002

van Eemeren, F.H. and Houtlosser, P. (2002). Strategic maneuvering with the burden of proof. In F.H. van Eemeren (Ed), *Advances in pragma-dialectics* (pp. 13–28). Amsterdam: SicSat.

Walton, D. (1980). Why is the 'ad populum' a fallacy? *Philosophy and Rhetoric*, *13*(4), 264–278.

Walton, D. (1994). Begging the question as a pragmatic fallacy. *Synthese*, *100*(1), 95–131. doi.org/10.1007/BF01063922

Walton, D. (1995). *A pragmatic theory of fallacy*. Tuscaloosa, AL: University of Alabama Press.

Walton, D. (1998). *Ad hominem arguments*. Tuscaloosa, AL: The University of Alabama Press.

Walton, D. (1999). The appeal to ignorance, or argumentum ad ignorantiam. *Argumentation*, *13*(4), 367–377. doi:10.1023/A:1007780012323.

Walton, D. (2004). Classification of fallacies of relevance. *Informal Logic*, *24*(1), 71–103. doi: 22329/il.v24i1.2133

Walton, D. & Koszowy, M. (2018). Whately on authority, deference, presumption and burden of proof. *Rhetorica*, *36*(2), 179–204. doi:10.1525/rh.2018.36.2.179.

Ward, J. (2007, October 6). Bush denies approving torture: interrogation adheres "to U.S. law." *Washington Times*, p. A-1.

Woods, J. & Walton, D. (1989). Equivocation and practical logic, in J. Woods and D.N. Walton (Eds.), *Fallacies: Selected Papers 1972–1982* (pp. 195–207). Dordrecht: Foris.

Further Reading on Fallacies in Reasoning

Arp, R., Barbone, S., & Bruce, M. (Eds.) (2019). *Bad arguments: 100 of the most important fallacies in Western Philosophy*. Hoboken, NJ: Wiley Blackwell.

Bennett, B. (2012). *Logically fallacious: The Ultimate collection of over 300 logical fallacies*. Sudbury, MA: ArchieBoy Holdings.

Capps, J. & Capps, D. (2009). *You've got to be kidding! How jokes can help you think*. West Sussex: Wiley-Blackwell

Cavender, N.M. & Kahane, H. (2018). *Logic and contemporary rhetoric: The use of reason in everyday life* (13th Ed.). Belmont, CA: Cengage.

Clark, J. & Clark, K. (2005). *Humbug! The skeptic's guide to spotting fallacies in thinking*. Capalaba, Australia: Nifty Book.

Copi, I.M., Cohen, C., & McMahon, K. (2016). *Introduction to logic* (14th Ed.). New York: Routledge.

Damer, T.E. (2009). *Attacking faulty reasoning* (6th ed.). Belmont, CA: Wadsworth.

Hamblin, C.L. (1970). *Fallacies*. London: Meuthuen & Company.

Tindale, C.W. (2007). *Fallacies and argument appraisal*. New York: Cambridge University Press.

van Eemeren, F., Garssen, B., & Mueffels, B. (2009). *Fallacies and judgments of reasonableness: Empirical research concerning the pragma-dialectical discussion rules*. New York: Springer.

Walton, D.N. (1998). *Ad hominem arguments*. Tuskaloosa, AL: University of Alabama Press.

Walton, D.N. (1999). *Appeal to popular opinion*. Pennsylvania, PA: Pennsylvania State University Press.

Walton, D.N. (1996) *Fallacies arising from ambiguity*. Dordrecht, Kluwer: Springer-Science & Business Media.

Walton, D.N. (1987). *Informal fallacies: Towards a theory of argument criticisms*. Amsterdam, PA: John Benjamins Publishing Company.

Chapter 10

Judgment, Decision Making, and Problem Solving

A Curious Rule of Thumb (. . . and Fingers)

Some time ago, while giving a test, one of the authors became aware of faint recurring thuds coming from the center of his classroom. He noticed a student doing something odd. Every so often the student would pause, smack his fingers on the edge of his desk, consider his hand for a moment, and then scribble something on his test. At first, the author wondered if the student was sending signals to someone, perhaps about the correct answers to the test. When it was clear, however, that no funny business was going on, the author waited for the student to finish the test and then asked what all the thumping was about. The student smiled, explaining that each of his fingers represented an answer to a multiple-choice question. "So, for example, if I can narrow the correct answer down to *a*," the student said, holding up his index finger, "*c*," holding up his ring finger, "and *d*," holding up his pinky, "I smack the desk and whichever finger hurts the most is the answer I mark on my test." Not surprisingly, the student earned a poor grade on the test, but, hey, we give him props for creativity!

Multiple Choices

Although all of us have resorted to questionable decision-making tactics, it is clear that flipping coins, reading tea leaves, or pulling petals off daisies leaves much to be desired, especially when making important decisions. Although the prospect of "eeny-meeny-miny-moeing" our way into a career path, a happy marriage, or an investment decision seems absurd, the task of making decisions and solving difficult problems can be daunting. While most of us can probably identify with this sentiment, the reality is that problems and choices bombard us daily. What's more, when you consider the possible negative consequences of making poor choices and bad decisions, we hope you agree that exploring the topics of decision making and problem solving is not only a worthwhile endeavor but also essential to success in life. With that in mind, the purpose of this chapter is to investigate these topics. Along the way, we'll consider rational models of decision making, impediments to good judgment and critical thinking, and guidelines for being an effective decision maker and problem solver, alone and in groups. First, we should note that volumes of literature in multiple disciplines have been written on each of these topics. We can only hope to cover the basics here. Even so, we believe this introduction will help you think more critically and effectively about the choices and problems you will encounter throughout your life.

Figure 10.1 Paper, scissors, rock cartoon by John Seiter.

Rational Models of Decision Making: Tapping into Your Inner Math Geek

Traditional approaches to decision making, rooted in economics and mathematics, propose that good decisions are based on laws of logic and probability (Hastie & Dawes, 2010). These approaches suggest that "life is a gamble, and the better you understand the odds, the more likely you are to prosper" (McKenzie, 2005, p. 321). Understanding such approaches is important because, as Hastie and Dawes (2010) point out, they are dominant in professional evaluations of good decision making. Here, we'll discuss two key concepts from such approaches: expected value and expected utility.

Expected Value: Weighing the Odds and Outcomes

Did you ever watch the popular television show *Deal or No Deal*? Several scholars in the field of economics have pointed out that the show is a useful tool for understanding principles of decision making. (e.g., see Aissia, 2016; de Roos & Sarafidis, 2010; Hogarth, Karelaia & Trujillo, 2012; Kahyaoglu & Ican, 2017; Post, van den Assem, Baltussen & Thaler, 2008). If you've never seen the show, you might consider watching an old episode on YouTube or playing a free online version yourself. Otherwise, here's how it works. As a contestant, you are shown 26 closed briefcases, each containing some monetary value ranging from one penny to $1,000,000. You are asked to pick one briefcase, which is given to you, but you are not allowed to see what is inside. Then, in round after round, with a live audience cheering, the host shows you the amount of money in the remaining briefcases, one or two at a time. After each round, a "banker" offers you some amount of money to buy your briefcase and you have to decide whether to accept the offer or go on to another round. If you continue and the next briefcase contains a little bit of money, the banker's offer increases. However, if the next case contains gobs of money, the offer decreases.

Given this, let's imagine you are a contestant facing the following quandary. You are down to four cases, including your own, and you know that these remaining cases contain $100, $400, $10,000, and $500,000. As suspenseful music swells in the background, the banker offers you $112,500 to buy back your briefcase. If you reject the offer, the game continues. Specifically, you'll be shown the amount of money in *one* more case before the banker makes another offer. Of course, if you reject the offer and the next case contains heaps of money (e.g., $500,000), the banker's next offer will obviously go down. If, on the other hand, you are shown a low value (e.g., $100), the banker's next offer will go up. Before reading on, stop and think for a moment. What would you tell the banker? Deal or no deal?

It turns out that, if you are ever faced with a situation like this, you can use probability theory and something called expected value to help you make your decision. *Expected value* is simply the average amount of money you stand to win or lose if faced with the same situation again and again. In this situation, you already know the value of taking the banker's deal is $112,500. But how much value can you expect if you decide to say "No deal!" instead? To find out, you can work out the solution mathematically, as shown in Box 10.1. Otherwise, if you prefer to skip the math for now, it all works out to $127,625. In other words, if you were faced with this same decision every day for the rest of your life and decided to say "No deal" every day, you would average $127,625 a day. Since that's more than the measly $112,500 the banker is offering, the rational decision, based on expected value, would be to kindly tell the banker to go jump in a lake. No deal!

Box 10.1   Deal or No Deal? How to Calculate Expected Value

To figure out whether you should accept the banker's $112,500 offer to buy back your briefcase, you can calculate the expected value of turning the offer down. First, ask yourself how many possible outcomes there are. In this situation, there are four briefcases remaining, and, thus, four possible outcomes. In other words, if you reject the offer and play another round, you will end up selecting either the 1) $100, 2) $400, 3) $10,000 or 4) $500,000 case. Second, ask yourself what the probability is of each outcome occurring. In this situation there are four briefcases, so your chance or probability of selecting each case is ¼ (or, if you prefer percentages, your chance is 25 percent). Finally, if you multiply each of these outcomes by their probability of occurring and then add them up, you get an expected value of: (¼)($100) + (¼)($400) + (¼)($10,000) + (¼)($500,000) = $25 + $100 + $2,500 + $125,000 = **$127,625**, which is more than the banker's offer.

The problem, of course, is that, if you really were a contestant on the game show, you wouldn't be making this decision *every* day. Indeed, being on a game show happens rarely if at all. Knowing that, would you accept the offer? Before deciding, let's consider another concept known as expected utility.

Expected Utility: Now That I Need!

A contestant who based a decision only on expected value would focus on the amount of cash he or she stood to win. Another way to decide, however, takes into account *expected utility*, which is based not just on the size of the payout, but on the amount of pleasure or happiness that the money would bring (von Neumann & Morgenstern, 1947; Savage, 1954). To illustrate the concept of expected utility, let's consider another game show, *The Price Is Right*. Contestants try to guess the price of a variety of prizes including merchandise and vacations. Imagine you are one of several contestants on the show. You are trying to guess the price of a riding lawnmower. Whichever contestant comes closest, without going over, wins the mower.

Here is where expected utility comes into play. What if you live in a 5th-floor apartment, have no yard or grass to mow, and no place to stow a large contraption? You wouldn't derive much pleasure from making the winning guess, especially once you learned that you would have to pay income tax on the value of the mower. Sure, you could always sell the prize and buy something else, but the mower itself would be as useful as a rear-view mirror on a bowling ball. Another contestant, however, might be thrilled to win a riding mower. A contestant with a huge yard, lots of grass, and no working mower, might click his or her heels thrice in the air upon making the winning guess.

Likewise, in the *Deal or No Deal* example, whom do you suppose would value the $112,500 offer more: a multi-zillionaire or a person who desperately needed money to go to college or to avoid losing a home? Clearly, from the desperate person's perspective, the offer has more expected utility. In other words, in some cases, people can decide against expected value and still be considered rational. As such, accepting the banker's offer might not be a bad idea.

According to Barsalou (1992), one advantage of using expected utility (versus expected value) as a tool for making decisions is that you can apply it in situations beyond those involving monetary values. You might use it, for example, to choose careers, vacation spots, and so on. One way to do this is to weigh the utility of each choice's outcomes alongside each outcome's probability of occurring, just like we did earlier. For a specific example, see Box 10.2.

Box 10.2 Putting Expected Utility to the Test

Imagine that Hortense is a personnel manager trying to decide whether to hire Bucky or Buster for a new job. Rather than flip coins, Hortense can assess the expected utility of each job candidate. How? She starts by looking for possible and important outcomes of the hire. For simplicity, let's say she identifies three, which include hiring a person who is 1) amiable, 2) hard working, and 3) competent. She then subjectively assesses the importance or utility of each outcome. For example, on a scale of 1–10, let's say she estimates that, for her, amiability gets a rating of 9, work ethic gets a rating of 8, and competence gets a rating of 6. In other words, for her, hiring an amiable person is most important, followed by hiring a hard worker, followed by hiring a competent person. She then estimates the probability that hiring a particular candidate will result in each outcome. Let's say that, after weighing the evidence, she decides that Bucky has an 80 percent chance of being amiable, a 60 percent chance of being a hard worker, and a 70 percent chance of being competent. If she multiplies the importance or utility rating that she has subjectively assigned to each possible outcome (amiability = 9, work ethic = 8, competence = 6) by its probability of occurring (amiability = .80, work ethic = .60, competence = .70) and then adds everything up, she can find the expected utility of hiring Bucky: .8(9) + .6(8) + .7(6) = **16.2**. If she does the same for Buster and then compares the scores, it should make her hiring decision easier.

Heuristics and Biases: Decision-Making Snags

Expected value and utility are routinely used as benchmarks against which to compare human decision making (McKenzie, 2005). They are often referred to as normative or prescriptive models because they suggest how decisions *should* be made if people seek to be rational. People, however, are not innately logical. We don't always resort to math and rationality to make optimal decisions. Instead, Herbert Simon (1956) suggested that we rely on *bounded rationality*—that is, we use rules of thumb or shortcuts to help us make reasonable decisions most of the time. Although such short cuts, also known as *heuristics*, can be quick, easy, and lead to positive outcomes (see Box 10.3), a program of research led by psychologists Amos Tversky, Daniel Kahneman, and their colleagues (Gilovich, Griffin & Kahneman, 2002; Tversky & Kahneman, 1974; Kahneman, Slovic & Tversky, 1982) indicates that such heuristics are replete with biases. These biases, in turn, can produce errors in judgment and decision making. Although we don't have room to examine all of the heuristics and biases, in the following sections we discuss some that we find most interesting and useful to know about.

Box 10.3   Just a Hunch: The Role of Emotions and Intuition in Decision Making

Several years ago, a friend of one of the authors answered her front door and was greeted by a man selling magazine subscriptions. He acted nice enough, but, even so, she got a weird feeling. Something about him didn't seem right. When she tried to send him away, he persisted with his "sales pitch," until, eventually, she had to be rude and closed the door on him. Later, she learned that the man had raped one of her neighbors.

Examples like this suggest that good decisions are not always the result of logical reasoning. Sometimes they are based on common sense and emotions. In fact, a fair amount of both popular (e.g., Gladwell, 2005; Kahneman, 2011) and scholarly (e.g., McKenzie, 2005) literature suggests that the heuristics and hunches people use to make decisions can

(continued)

(continued)

be adaptive and efficient, perhaps even more so than logical reasoning. Consider, as an example, "logic machines" such as computers. As McKenzie (2005) noted, although computers are able to outperform humans in highly constrained environments such as playing chess, attempts to have them perform "real-world" tasks have been plagued by failure because they lack emotions and common sense. In other words, "depending on a purely logical analysis will not get you very far in the real world, where context, meaning and relevance, rather than pure structure, are crucial" (McKenzie, 2005, p. 334).

The case against logical and deliberative decision making becomes even stronger when you consider research showing how much it can trip you up. In a classic study (Wilson & Schooler, 1991), for example, students were asked to taste and rate a variety of strawberry jams. While some of the students provided a quick and intuitive rating, others were asked to analyze and provide reasons for their ratings. Can you guess which group came closer to matching ratings provided by experts? It turns out that those who thought carefully about their choices performed the worst!

Outside of the laboratory, you can also find cases where intuition seems to prevail over logic. For example, in his bestselling book *Blink: The Power of Thinking without Thinking*, Malcolm Gladwell (2005) tells how the Getty Museum in Los Angeles got bamboozled. Apparently, after scientific tests verified the authenticity of an ancient Greek statue, the museum purchased it for almost $10 million. That, however, didn't prevent several art historians from getting a bad intuitive sense about the statue. It turns out they were right. The thing was a fake!

If stories such as this make you wonder whether you'd be better off tossing this book in a dumpster and sticking purely with your intuition, not so fast! Chabris and Simons (2010; Simons & Chabris, 2010) note that opposing stories are easy to find. That is, it's fairly common in the art world for science to find fake pieces that seemed intuitively real. In other words, relying on one case to decide that intuition trumps reason, while, at the same time, ignoring counter examples, is a mistake (and a recurring theme in this book!).

So what, then, is to be made of all this? Should intuition be trusted? Is systematic reasoning and logic at all useful? The answer to these questions, we suspect, is "it depends." Intuitive, unconscious decision making may be better in some situations than others. For instance, Hastie and Dawes (2010) noted that, when making decisions about things like jam that are consumed in a simple automatic sensory manner, intuitive reasoning may be best. Moreover, some laboratory research suggests that if time is limited, people perform better when using heuristics than when using more complex approaches to decision making (e.g., Payne, Bettman & Johnson, 1988). Likewise, in the "real world," we imagine that extensive deliberations can be counterproductive, or even dangerous. If you are ever confronted by an icky salesperson at your front door or a growl in the wilderness, don't waste time trying to decide if you need to be polite or to calculate the probability that you are in mountain lion territory. Trust your intuition and get out of there. On the other hand, for other types of decisions, it is clear, as we hope this chapter demonstrates, that relying on intuitions and heuristics can lead you to make serious mistakes. In cases such as these, a more conscious, deliberative, and logical approach is best.

Framing and Sunk Costs: Throwing Good Money After Bad

Let's return, for the last time, to *Deal or No Deal*. Imagine a contestant who, after selecting a "bad" briefcase, is presented with an offer much lower than he or she was previously offered. Have you ever been in a similar situation? Perhaps you bought a used car that turned out to be a lemon. You paid for one repair after another, hoping each would be the last. Then something else would break. Perhaps you spent years preparing for a climbing expedition and then had to decide whether "to go for it" or turn back when the weather turned nasty. Perhaps you stayed in a bad relationship too long because you'd already put in so much time and effort into working things out.

When outsiders are looking in, it is easy to scoff at motorists stranded on the roadside, mountain climbers (like many on Everest) who lose their lives, and battered spouses who stick around. Such behavior, although irrational, becomes more understandable when we realize that people tend to be risk averse. They have an extreme aversion to losses. In fact, *prospect theory* (Kahneman & Tversky, 2013)—which replaces the notion of "utility" with "value"—argues that people are, by nature, risk averse. They place a higher value on *not* losing something than they do on gaining something. As such, the price people name for selling something they own is often higher than what they claim they would pay for it (Barberis, 2013; Kahneman, Knetsch & Thaler, 1990).

Sunk Costs: In Too Deep

One manifestation of our aversion to losses is known as the *sunk cost effect*, which was illustrated in the examples at the start of this section. It occurs when we persist in an endeavor even after we've made an investment that cannot be recovered (Arkes & Blumer, 1985). Some time ago, one of the authors caught himself making this very mistake. After purchasing an entire season of a particular television show and watching several episodes, the author's wife decided the show was "stupid" and stopped watching. The author agreed with his wife's evaluation, but stuck with the show for several more episodes. After all, he didn't want to waste money. Plus, he'd invested so much time watching! Worse yet, the author received several more seasons of the show as a gift from his brother, who assumed the author must love the show if he watched it so often! Of course, not wanting to waste a generous gift, the author convinced himself that he was stuck watching and did.

Message Framing: Seeing Things From a Different Angle

A second way that people's aversion to loss leads them astray occurs when they react irrationally to how messages are *framed*. For example, imagine that a deadly virus is threatening the lives of 600 people in your town. For whatever reason, you are in charge of deciding what to do. Take a moment to think about which of the following actions you would choose: Action 1, which guarantees that 200 of the 600 people will be saved; or Action 2, which gives a 33.3 percent chance that all 600 people will be saved and a 66.6 percent chance that no one will be saved. If you are like the majority of people in a classic study (Tversky & Kahneman, 1981), you picked Action 1. Curiously, however, when the exact same actions were slightly reworded (i.e., "Action 1: guarantees that 400 of the 600 people will die. Action 2: gives a 33.3 percent chance that no one will die and a 66.6 percent chance that everyone will die."), the majority of people picked Action 2. In short, by reframing Action 1 so that it guaranteed deaths, research participants, like most people who fear losses, ignored expected value and picked Action 2 instead.

An unusual disease is expected to kill 600 people.

To fight it, which action would you choose?

Some participants were given these two choices:

Action A	or	**Action B**
200 people will be saved.		There is a 1/3 probability that 600 people will be saved and a 2/3 probability that none will be saved.

And some participants were given these two choices:

Action A	or	**Action B**
400 people will die.		There is a 1/3 probability that nobody will die and a 2/3 probability that 600 people will die.

Results: The first group of participants picked Action A, and the second picked Action B, even though the consequences for Actions A and A are the same, as are the consequences for Actions B and B (Tversky & Kahneman, 1981).

Figure 10.2 How framing affects choices.

Image from ESB Professional\shutterstock.com.

Overcoming the Effects of Framing and Sunk Costs

Given that our fear of losses can taint our judgment, what might be done to attenuate the effects of framing and sunk costs? First, when confronted with a decision, ask yourself if it can be framed in another way. Let's say an insurance salesperson keeps pressuring you by pointing out everything you stand to lose if you do not purchase the most expensive package available. Before making a decision, consider the value of the money you would spend to purchase the package. Can you afford it? Would buying it prevent you from having or doing other things you enjoy? Second, keep in mind that once an investment has been made, sunk costs should not influence your future decisions. As the billionaire, Warren Buffet, once said, "The most important thing to do if you find yourself in a hole is to stop digging" (Harth, 2013). Rather than continuing to invest money in a losing stock or a car that's a lemon, cut your losses. Think about more enjoyable or profitable things you might do with your money or time. Likewise, if someone is making arguments such as "We can't pull out of this war now; too many lives have been lost," or "I've put every dime I had into this business," remind him or her about the sunk cost effect. Finally, if you are worried about looking bad because you've backed out of a failed endeavor, get over it. The longer you wait, the worse you'll look.

Availability: Whatever Comes to Mind

Which animals do you suppose are the most dangerous to humans—sharks, bears, alligators, or cows? If you guessed any of the carnivores, try again. It turns out that cows are 20 times more lethal than any of these other animals. Indeed, while each year in the U.S., sharks, bears, and gators kill about one person apiece, annual deaths by cows are estimated to be over 20 (Ingraham, 2015). Given such statistics, why do sharks, gators, and bears have such bad reputations? It could be because of something known as the *availability heuristic*.

According to Tversky and Kahneman (1974; Kahneman, 2011), when people use the availability heuristic they make judgments about things (e.g., the probability that something will happen) based on information that comes to mind easily. In other words, rather than search for more data, people tend to rely on the first thing that pops into their heads. This heuristic, of course, is fueled by how often people are exposed to certain information, how recently they were exposed to the information, and how vivid that information is. Take sharks, for example. Because they look frightening (15 rows of saw-like teeth) and are portrayed as man-eaters (*Jaws*) they are much scarier than cows, which include the likes of Elsie (from Borden Dairy Company), the laughing cow (from Laughing Cow Cheese), and that adorable spokesbovine from LACTAID®. As a result, shark attacks come to mind easily and lead us to misjudge how likely they are to occur.

Now that you are aware of the availability heuristic, suppose we asked you, "Which is more dangerous, a cow or a mosquito?" If you answered "a mosquito," you are correct, and you overcame the availability heuristic. Mosquitoes themselves aren't particularly fierce, but the diseases they transmit—malaria, Zika, yellow fever, West Nile, dengue, and more—can be deadly. Malaria alone kills nearly half a million people worldwide per year (Birkett, 2015).

Although the availability heuristic can result in reasonably accurate and efficient judgments, it might lead to biased thinking as well. Schick and Vaughn (2011), for example, suggested that when people rely on availability, they might reach conclusions about something on the

Figures 10.3 and 10.4 With whom would you rather selfie?

Figure 10.3 (shark): Kletr/shutterstock.com and Figure 10.4 (cow): Veronika 7833\shutterstock.com.

basis of very little evidence, thereby committing a fallacy known as a hasty generalization (see Chapter 7). Before dying of cancer, for instance, a relative of one of the authors insisted that her smoking habit couldn't be too bad considering she could think of several smokers she personally knew of who lived to ripe old ages.

Given the potential pitfalls of such thinking, what might you do to reduce your tendency to rely on available information? First, realize that whatever is "top of mind" may not be the most relevant information. As such, when faced with important decisions, do research and attempt to find additional data. Can you or someone you know think of contradictory examples? Are there statistics that might inform you? If so, make sure those statistics are based on a large enough sample size. For instance, if someone claims that three out of four dentists surveyed preferred one toothpaste to another leading brand, it's useful to know whether four dentists or 4,000 were surveyed.

Representativeness: It's Unlucky to Be Superstitious!

Before you read on, picture a person who owns a tractor, wears overalls, and feeds animals each morning. Got it? If so, what would you guess the chances are that this person is a farmer? Ninety percent? Fifty? Ten? If you estimated that the chances were unusually high, you may be relying on something known as the *representativeness heuristic*, which refers to people's tendency to use similarity to make judgments (Tversky & Kahneman, 1974; Kahneman, 2011). Specifically, if people think one thing is similar to another, they often conclude that the first thing is part of the second thing (e.g., a sample is part of a population), even when it is not. Research (Tversky & Kahneman, 1974) suggests that this heuristic leads to plenty of mistakes. Here, we'll examine just a few.

One mistake occurs when we misjudge which category something belongs to (*category membership*). In the case of farmers, for example, we might decide that a person who owns a tractor represents our stereotype of a farmer pretty well. In other words, the person and stereotype are similar. As a result, we overestimate the likelihood that the person is a farmer.

To see why this can be a mistake, picture yourself randomly Googling white pages for all the phone numbers in the United States and then randomly selecting one person's name from the list. How often do you think the person you pointed to would be a farmer? Hint: farmers comprise less than 1 percent of the US population. In other words, the *base rate* of farmers is low, so you won't find many in your phone book. Now, imagine you did the same thing, but this time you had to guess how likely it was that the person you selected owned a tractor. Hint: a lot of people use tractors for things other than farming, and there are different types of tractors, including utility tractors, industrial tractors, engineering tractors, and so on. One of your non-farming authors (who also owns overalls and feeds his pets in the morning) plows snow and mows weeds with his tractor. In short, your chances of randomly picking the name of someone who simply owns a tractor are far more likely than picking the name of a farmer. Even so, when estimating likelihoods, we tend to ignore such base rate information and go with our stereotypes instead, thus making mistakes when we categorize people and things.

Although this tendency can be harmless when it involves stereotypes about farmers, it can also, as Hastie and Dawes (2010) point out, be morally problematic. This is especially true when it involves not-so-innocent stereotypes about socially significant groups. As Hastie and Dawes (2010) note:

> Perhaps the most troublesome characteristics of . . . racial, gender and religious stereotypes is that they automatically evoke emotional reactions that affect our behavior toward members of the category. Once we've classified a person into a category with negative associations, we may not be able to help ourselves from reacting negatively to him or her. (p. 107)

A second mistake associated with representativeness occurs when we *misjudge random events*. For instance, have you ever suspected that your iPod's random play feature is broken? Do some artists seem to show up more than others? If you think so, you are not alone. According to Levy (2005), the apparent non-randomness of iPod's shuffle feature received so much attention in newspapers and blogs that Apple asked its engineers to verify that their algorithms were correct. Everything checked out, which leads to the natural question: If it's not the iPod, what is it?[1]

Once again, it may be because people are using similarity, or, in this case, dissimilarity, as a basis for their judgment. Indeed, it turns out that people's impressions of what randomness looks like are skewed. In a classic study (Bakan, 1960), for instance, students who were asked to generate sequences of heads and tails that would result from flipping a coin 300 times (e.g., HHTHTH . . .) did a lousy job, failing to include the occasional streak of heads or tails that tend to occur in real random processes.[2] Given this, it is not surprising that truly random events (e.g., coin flips, iPod tunes), when compared with our impressions of randomness, do not seem random at all. In fact, when such random streaks occur, we often make poor decisions and, in some cases, lose loads of loot to boot. For example, most people tend to think that once a flipped coin has landed on heads a bunch of times "it's due" to land on tails.

This notion—that randomly occurring events are influenced by events that occurred beforehand—is known as the *gambler's fallacy*. Its most famous example occurred in Monte Carlo, when a roulette wheel landed on black 26 times in a row (Lehrer, 2009)! Along the way, gamblers who mistakenly figured that red "was due," ended up hemorrhaging money, much to the casino owners' delight. Of course, the opposite notion (i.e., deciding that a streak might continue) is also irrational and can lead to some weird superstitions. In Texas Hold 'Em poker, for example, the odds of getting a royal flush (AKQJT of the same suit) are 30,940 to 1. When one of the authors got three royals within several hours, all the while wearing a new pair of pants, it was easy to start thinking how lucky those pants might be. Such thinking, of course, is silly; coins and roulette wheels have no memory of what happened in the past, and articles of clothing have absolutely no mystical abilities—unless you are Harry Potter.

Keeping this in mind, what might be done to attenuate the potentially negative effects of representative thinking? First, recognize that making assessments on the basis of general impressions and stereotypes can lead you astray, especially when your stereotypes are flawed. For instance, just because Ted Bundy, the serial killer, was intelligent and nice looking, did not mean he was trustworthy, as some folks falsely assumed.

Second, when making a judgment, don't ignore relevant information such as base rates, especially when such rates are extremely high or low. For example, considering that so few people get admitted to graduate school, it would be a mistake to assume that someone who was not admitted lacked academic talent (see Plous, 1993).

Third, don't assume that previous outcomes affect future events. In some cases, such assumptions might be well founded. In other cases, they are not. For example, all else being equal, it's reasonable to think that a sprinter who has won her last 100 races has a good chance of winning her next. On the other hand, investing in stocks with bad financial records because you believe their streaks of bad fortune are bound to end would be about as irrational as betting on a lottery number because it hadn't shown up for a long time.

Fourth, recognize that just because something seems bizarrely unlikely, does not mean that it is. What's more, resist the temptation to become superstitious, assuming, as some folks do, that you can control random events. Did you know, for instance, that gamblers tend to throw dice with greater force when trying to roll high numbers than when trying to roll low numbers (Hastie & Dawes, 2010), and that students can be convinced that they are better than the average person at predicting the outcome of coin tosses (Langer & Roth, 1975)?

Overconfidence: Am I Good or What?

When Garrison Keillor, former host of the radio show *A Prairie Home Companion*, told listeners that the fictional town of Lake Wobegon is "where all the women are strong, all the men are good looking, and all the children are above average," he did a nice job of summarizing how people in the real world tend to think about themselves. Indeed, research suggests that people are generally overconfident, a condition officially known as the *illusory superiority effect*, but playfully referred to as the Lake Wobegon Effect (Maxwell & Lopus, 1994). Such research indicates that both experts and nonexperts tend to believe that they are correct about things more often than they truly are (e.g., see Lichtenstein, Fischhoff & Phillips, 1982; Tetlock, 2005). Not only that, in one study, research participants who had actually performed the worst on a variety of tests (e.g., reasoning and logic) tended to be the most confident about their performances (Kruger & Dunning, 1999).

It's not difficult to imagine the possible problems that might result from overconfidence. For example, are you thinking about starting your own business? If so, be careful. While research shows that new business owners give themselves over an 80 percent chance of success (Cooper, Woo & Dunkelberg, 1988), the majority of businesses fail. Are you certain you'll finish your next project on time? If so, keep in mind that, in one study, the majority of students took weeks longer than they predicted to finish their theses (Buehler, Griffin & Ross, 1994). Are you thinking about getting in shape? If so, be warned that, when signing up for gym memberships, people tend to overestimate how often they'll work out, thereby wasting hundreds of dollars as a result (Della Vigna & Malmendier, 2006). Are you expecting to receive good health care? We hope you do, but also be aware that health-care specialists tend to overestimate their abilities and, as a result, often make decisions that are not based on the best evidence (Morris, Lee & Orme, 2017). What's more, if you ever get a life-threatening disease (we hope not!), be careful; doctors are likely to intimate that you are an above-average patient, thereby tainting the treatment advice you receive (Wolf & Wolf, 2013).

Considering this, perhaps some of the best advice we can give for dealing with overconfidence is to become well calibrated, using feedback to test your judgments. By way of example, one of the authors has a couple of police officers in his family who say that the most common claim they hear intoxicated drivers make is, "I had no idea I was legally drunk." To help drivers avoid such misperceptions, some bars and restaurants have installed retail breathalyzers, which provide feedback about blood alcohol content before a person gets behind the wheel. Likewise, you should consider feedback before making important decisions. For example, if you think you are a stock market wiz, you might keep and study records of how well you perform when investing play money before you spend your retirement savings on some hot new commodity. Similarly, you might ask yourself or others to play devil's advocate. For instance, if you are considering a tightrope feat across the Grand Canyon, can you think of anything that might defeat your feet? If so, pay attention to the feedback and act accordingly. To be sure, research shows that such feedback can help people become better calibrated (e.g., Arkes, Christensen, Lai & Blumer, 1987).

Confirmation Bias: Just as I Suspected

One thing that may contribute to overconfidence is the *confirmation bias*, which refers to our tendency to seek, favor, and remember evidence that supports our views while ignoring, scrutinizing, misinterpreting, and forgetting evidence that does not. For example, in a classic experiment, Lord, Ross, and Lepper (1979) presented students who either favored or opposed capital punishment with information about the results of two studies: one supporting capital punishment and the other opposing it. Results indicated that students believed the study that supported their views was conducted better and was more persuasive than the study that opposed their views.

Clearly, the confirmation bias is an impediment to critical thinking. First, selectively ignoring *any* information might promote ignorance. Second, it might bolster irrational beliefs and the misinterpretation of information. For instance, people who believe in astrology might interpret random events in their lives as confirmation of their superstitions. "You will encounter a musical stranger," for example, could mean listening to a new tune on the radio, seeing a songbird on your roof, or, since rumor has it that most American cars honk in the key of F,[3] having someone blast their horn at you.

There are several techniques you might use to attenuate the confirmation bias. First, before or after an argument, force yourself to *acknowledge or create opposing arguments* and evidence by *writing them down*. After developing a list, ask yourself, what are the opposition's *best* arguments? Then ask yourself, *what evidence was presented* for their arguments and which evidence is the *hardest to disprove*? Second, during an argument, acknowledge another's position by offering a *fair, unbiased summary* of his or her point of view. If the other person responds by saying "you're way off base," ask why. If the other person says you are on target, then go on to refute the argument, including the evidence supporting it. The advantage of this approach is that you'll be addressing both sides of the issue. Finally, be open to listening to opposing viewpoints. A liberal who listens solely to MSNBC and a conservative who listens solely to Fox News will only hear information that reinforces his or her point of view (for more on biases and heuristics, see Box 10.4).

Box 10.4   Additional Biases and Heuristics

Just in case you haven't gotten enough of biases and heuristics, here are some brief descriptions of a few more. If you are interested in details on these and a long list of other biases, check out Hastie and Dawes (2010), Gilovich, Griffin, and Kahneman (2002), Hardman (2009), Kahneman (2011), Kahneman, Slovic, and Tversky (1982), and Plous (1993).

- *Anchoring heuristic*—occurs when some starting value (anchor) influences estimates of an uncertain value. For example, after being asked to consider the last five digits of their social security numbers (anchor) and then estimate the length of the Nile, people with higher SSNs guess that the Nile is longer than do people with lower SSNs.
- *Hindsight bias*—occurs when people know what happened and suppose they could have predicted it beforehand. For example, once they know who won an election, people imagine they would have "known it all along."

- *Status quo bias*—occurs when people resist policies and behaviors that are new. The old saying "If it ain't broke, don't fix it," summarizes this bias, as do expressions suggesting that "you can't teach an old dog new tricks."
- *Illusory correlation*—occurs when people mistakenly believe there is an association between two things. For example, after seeing the word "salt" paired with the word "pepper" 20 times and with the word "telephone" 20 times, people estimate that "pepper" was paired most often with "salt" because the two words are linked in real life.
- *Hot hand fallacy*—occurs when people mistakenly think that basketball players who have made their last shot or two are more likely to make their next shot.
- *Optimism bias*—occurs when people overrate the likelihood that things will turn out well. For example, Timmy may buy expensive golf clubs because he is overly optimistic that he'll learn to play.
- *Conjunction fallacy*—occurs when people estimate that the probability of two events occurring is more likely than the probability of either of those two events occurring alone. For example, a person who learns that Babbs is introverted and analytical believes that Babbs is more likely to be a Republican and an accountant than either just a Republican or just an accountant.

A Procedural Approach to Problem Solving and Decision Making: Baby Steps

If you've ever tried untangling kite string, you know that starting in the wrong place can leave you with lots of knots. The same might be said about trying to solve complex problems. If you dive into a solution without much thought, you might make things messier than ever. With that in mind, for complex problems that involve multiple decisions, having a systematic thought-out plan can help you avoid some serious snarls. In fact, dozens of authors have described step-by-step guidelines for both individuals and groups that are faced with the task of finding solutions (e.g., see Beebe & Masterson, 2003; Bransford & Stein, 1984; Dewey, 1910; Hammond, Keeney & Raiffa, 1999; Hayes, 1981; Vaughn, 2007). Although such guidelines vary to some degree, practically all include some or most of the steps that we briefly outline in this section. Although abiding by such a "cookie cutter" approach does not guarantee success, we believe that, under most circumstances, considering these steps will help you avoid many common pitfalls that await unsuspecting problem solvers and decision makers.

Step 1: Define the Problem

The old saying, "A problem well stated is a problem half solved," suggests that taking time to articulate the problem and your assumptions about the problem is time well spent (Beebe & Masterson, 2003). As Hammond et al. (1999) noted, how you pose a problem has profound implications for the course of action you choose. For instance, if you've moved to a new city and ask "Which apartment should I pick?" you may prevent yourself from considering the possibility of renting a house, buying a condo, finding a roommate, and so forth (Hammond et al., 1999). With that in mind, Beebe and Masterson (2003) suggest that problem solvers start by asking themselves questions such as: What is the specific problem? Is the problem stated clearly? Who is harmed by the problem?

Figure 10.5 Cartoon: Mark Parisi, OffTheMark.com, 2009-11-02.

© Mark Parisi/OffTheMark.com.

Step 2: Analyze the Problem

In this step, problem solvers investigate causes and effects of the problem. Along the way, they gather facts that help them understand how serious the problem is, where it came from, and what obstacles might keep them from solving the problem. Skipping this step can lead to terrible results. For example, back when he was a student, one of the authors worked in a department store, selling men's suits on commission. One day, a new manager decided to hire more salespeople. Apparently, the manager noticed a lot of customers waiting around and concluded that there wasn't enough help on the sales floor. The *real* cause of the problem, however, was not enough tailors. The customers, it turns out, were not waiting to purchase suits. They were keeping themselves busy while waiting to be fitted! By not searching for facts, and misdiagnosing the cause of the problem, the manager made matters worse. Specifically, with less sales to go around, the star salespeople found jobs elsewhere, leaving mediocre staff behind. Not surprisingly, the department's profits plummeted.

Step 3: Establish Criteria

For this step, the problem solver determines what standards must be met in order for the problem to be considered resolved. By way of example, when shopping for a car, you might list several criteria—e.g., is it safe, comfortable, snazzy?—that need to be satisfied before deciding to make a purchase. In the same way, a manager in a suit department might decide that a problem is resolved if customers aren't waiting, salespeople are happy, profits are high, and so forth.

Step 4: Generate Possible Solutions

In this step, an approach known as *brainstorming*, which fosters the creative generation of ideas, can be useful. Although a number of techniques have been proposed (see Vaughn, 2007), the classic approach was created by Alex Osborn (1957). According to this approach, while working in groups, problem solvers should: 1) generate as many solutions, no matter how wild or outlandish, as possible; 2) avoid criticizing or judging any ideas for the time being; and 3) build on other people's ideas.

Step 5: Select the Best Solution

To accomplish this step, problem solvers might consider each possible solution alongside the criteria generated in Step 3, and then decide which solution seems to meet the criteria best. In addition, for each solution, problem solvers might generate a list of pros and cons. For example, although training salespeople to measure and mark suits for alteration (solution 1) might lessen the tailors' workload and provide continuity in customer service (pros), it could also lead to fewer sales and more alteration mistakes (cons). Once such a list is generated, the advantages and disadvantages of each solution can be compared and analyzed until the best solution is found.

Step 6: Implement the Solution

Just because a solution is found, does not necessarily mean it will be successful. Its chances are better, though, if some thought is put into how the solution will be put into effect. Thus, for this last step, problem solvers should consider questions such as: Who is in charge of applying the solution? What must be accomplished to implement the solution? How will the changes be explained to others? And how long will the implementation take?

Decision Making in Groups: Are Two (or More) Heads Better Than One?

Although old sayings such as "Too many cooks spoil the soup" or "A camel is a horse designed by a committee" suggest that groups are lousy problem solvers, if group members are able to pool resources while managing both social and task-related issues, the quality of their decisions will usually be higher than when working alone (Cathcart, Samovar & Henman, 1996). That "if" is a big one, though, and volumes have been written on how groups can be more effective. Although we don't have space to cover all the topics necessary to make you a group guru, we use the remainder of this chapter to warn you about two hurdles that can get in your way when you are working in groups.

Groupthink: Don't Rock the Boat!

In Chapter 2 we discussed a phenomenon known as *groupthink* (Janis, 1972), which, if you recall, occurs when members in a group are so concerned with getting along with each other that they make bad decisions. Among other things, such groups are characterized by overconfidence, closed-mindedness, and intolerance of disagreement within the group. With that in mind, if you ever find yourself in such a group, Janis (1972) suggested several tactics for reducing groupthink. Most of these focus on encouraging critical thinking and argumentation. For instance, disagreement should be encouraged from people inside the group and invited from people outside the group. Along the way, group members can be assigned the role of devil's advocate, or work individually or in smaller teams to consider alternative viewpoints.

Social Loafing: Couch Potatoes Need Not Apply

If you've ever caught yourself slacking off while riding a tandem bicycle, moving a heavy piece of furniture with others, or completing a group project, then you are already familiar with social loafing. According to Karau and Williams (1993), "social loafing is the reduction in motivation and effort when individuals work collectively compared with when they work individually or coactively" (p. 681). Previous research suggests that there are several potential causes for such loafing (for a review, see Gass & Seiter, 2018). Whatever the cause, however, it's clear that loafing can impede groups from reaching their full potential. With that in mind, what might be done to reduce social loafing? Previous research indicates that social loafing may be attenuated when people identify with the group and are held accountable for their work (Barreto & Ellemers, 2000). As such, building rapport in a group while monitoring performances might be a useful approach.

Summary

In this chapter we examined several topics related to judgment, decision making, and problem solving. First, we examined expected value and utility, normative models of decision making, rooted in economics and mathematics. Second, we saw that several heuristics and biases can function to hinder good judgment and decision making. These included sunk cost effects, message framing, the availability heuristic, the representativeness heuristic, overconfidence, and the confirmation bias. Third, we presented a procedural approach to problem solving and decision making that outlined the steps one might take individually or in groups when tackling a complex issue or decision. Finally, we talked about two phenomena, groupthink and social loafing, which can impede effective decision making in groups.

Notes

1 Technically speaking, whether or not a computer can generate a truly random number depends on what you mean by "random." For details, see Rubin (2011).
2 Likewise, people lack the capacity to generate other random responses such as pressing keys on a keyboard (see Baddeley, Emslie, Kolodny & Duncan, 1998).
3 Although we've not verified this rumor (to see it yourself, Google "car horn key f"), regardless of its accuracy, car horns honk in one key or another.

References

Aissia, D.B. (2016). Developments in non-expected utility theories: An empirical study of risk-aversion. *Journal of Economics and Finance, 30*(2), 299–318, doi: 10.1007/s12197-014-9305-3.

Arkes, H.R. & Blumer, C. (1985). The psychology of sunk costs. *Organizational Behavior and Human Decision Processes, 35*(1), 124–140, doi:10.1016/0749-5978(85)90049-4.

Arkes, H.R., Christensen, C., Lai, C. & Blumer, C. (1987). Two methods of reducing overconfidence. *Organizational Behavior and Human Decision Processes, 39*(1), 133–144, doi.org/10.1016/0749-5978(87)90049-5.

Baddeley, A., Emslie, H., Kolodny, J. & Duncan, J. (1998). Random generation and the executive control of working memory. *Quarterly Journal of Experimental Psychology, 51*(4), 819–852, doi: 10.1080/713755788.

Bakan, P. (1960). Response tendencies in attempts to generate random binary series. *American Journal of Psychology, 73*(1), 127–131, doi: 10.2307/1419124.

Barberis, N.C. (2013). Thirty years of prospect theory in economics: A review and assessment. *The Journal of Economic Perspectives, 27*(1), 173–195, doi: 10.1257/jep.27.1.173.

Barreto, M. & Ellemers, N. (2000). You can't always do what you want: Social identity and self-presentational determinants of the choice to work for a low-status group. *Personality and Social Psychology Bulletin, 26*(8), 891–906, doi: 10.1177/01461672002610001.

Barsalou, L.W. (1992). *Cognitive psychology: An overview for cognitive scientists.* Hillsdale, NJ: Erlbaum.

Beebe, S.A. & Masterson, J.T. (2003). *Communicating in small groups* (7th Ed.). Boston, MA: Allyn & Bacon.

Birkett, A.J. (2015). Status of vaccine research and development of vaccines for malaria. *Vaccine, 34*(26), 2915–2920, doi: 10.1016/j.vaccine.2015.12.074.

Bransford, J.D. & Stein, B.S. (1984). *The ideal problem solver: A guide for improving thinking, learning, and creativity.* New York: Freeman.

Buehler, R., Griffin, D. & Ross, M. (1994). Exploring the "planning fallacy": Why people underestimate their task completion times. *Journal of Personality and Social Psychology, 67*(3), 366–381, doi: rg/10.1037/0022-3514.67.3.366.

Cathcart, R.S., Samovar, L.A. & Henman, L.D. (1996). *Small group communication: Theory and practice* (7th Ed.). Madison, WI: Brown & Benchmark.

Chabris, C. & Simons, D. (2010). *The invisible gorilla and other ways our intuitions deceive us.* New York: Crown.

Cooper, A., Woo, C. & Dunkelberg, W. (1988). Entrepreneurs' perceived chances for success. *Journal of Business Venturing, 3*(2), 97–108, doi: org/10.1016/0883-9026(88)90020-1.

Della Vigna, S. & Malmendier, U. (2006). Paying not to go to the gym. *American Economic Review, 96*(3), 694–719, doi: 10.1257/aer.96.3.694.

de Roos, N. & Sarafidis, Y. (2010). Decision making under risk in *Deal or No Deal. Applied Economics, 25*(6), 987–1027, doi: 10.1002/jae.1110.

Dewey, J. (1910). *How we think.* New York: Heath.

Gass, R.H. & Seiter, J.S. (2018). *Persuasion, social influence, and compliance gaining* (6th Ed.). Boston, MA: Routledge.

Gilovich, T., Griffin, D. & Kahneman, D. (2002). *Heuristics and biases: The psychology of intuitive judgment.* Cambridge, MA: Cambridge University Press.

Gladwell, M. (2005). *Blink: The power of thinking without thinking.* New York: Little, Brown, and Company.

Hammond, J.S., Keeney, R.L. & Raiffa, H. (1999). *Smart choices: A practical guide to making better decisions.* New York: Broadway Books.

Hardman, D. (2009). *Judgment and decision making: Psychological perspectives.* Oxford: Blackwell.

Harth, M. (2013, April 16). 5 tips from Warren Buffet on mindfulness [Blog post]. *Huffington Post.* Retrieved on December 22, 2017 from: www.huffingtonpost.com/melanie-harth-phd-lmhc/5-tips-from-warren-buffet_b_3085586.html.

Hastie, R. & Dawes, R.M. (2010). *Rational choice in an uncertain world: The psychology of judgment and decision making* (2nd Ed.). Los Angeles, CA: Sage.

Hayes, J.R. (1981). *The complete problem solver.* Philadelphia, PA: Franklin Institute Press.

Hogarth, R.M., Karelaia, N. & Trujillo, C.A. (2012). When should I quit? Gender differences in exiting competitions. *Journal of Economic Behavior & Organization, 83*(1), 136–150, doi: 10.1016/j.jebo.2011.06.021.

Ingraham, C. (2015, June 16). Chart: The animals that are most likely to kill you this summer. *Washington Post.* Retrieved on December 22, 2017 from: www.washingtonpost.com/news/wonk/wp/2015/06/16/chart-the-animals-that-are-most-likely-to-kill-you-this-summer/?utm_term=.c19482e1519e.

Janis, I.L. (1972). *Victims of groupthink.* Boston, MA: Houghton Mifflin.

Kahneman, D. (2011). *Thinking, fast and slow.* New York: Farrar, Straus, and Giroux.

Kahneman, D., Knetsch, J.L. & Thaler, R.H. (1990). Experimental tests of the endowment effect and the Coase theorem. *Journal of Political Economy, 98*(6), 1325–1348, doi: 10.1086/261737.

Kahneman, D., Slovic, P. & Tversky, A. (1982). *Judgment under uncertainty: Heuristics and biases.* Cambridge, MA: Cambridge University Press.

Kahneman, D. & Tversky, A. (2013). Prospect theory: An analysis of decision under risk. In L.C. MacLean & W.T. Ziemba (Eds), *Handbook of the fundamentals of financial decision making* (Part 1, pp. 99–127). Toh Tuck Link, Singapore: World Scientific Publishing.

Kahyaoglu, M.B. & Ican, O. (2017). Risk aversion and emotions in DoND. *International Journal of Economics and Finance, 9*(1), 32–46, doi: 10.5539/ijef.v9n1p32.

Karau, S.J. & Williams, K.D. (1993). Social loafing: A meta-analytic review and theoretical integration. *Journal of Personality and Social Psychology, 65*(4), 681–706, doi: org/10.1037/0022-3514.65.4.681.

Kruger, J. & Dunning, D. (1999). Unskilled and unaware of it: How difficulties in recognizing one's own incompetence lead to inflated self-assessments. *Journal of Personality and Social Psychology, 77*(6), 1121–1134, doi: 10.1037//0022-3514.77.6.1121.

Langer, E.J. & Roth, J. (1975). Heads I win, tails it's chance: The illusion of control as a function of the sequence of outcomes in a purely chance task. *Journal of Personality and Social Psychology, 32*(6), 951–955, doi: 10.1037/0022-3514.32.6.951.

Lehrer, J. (2009). *How we decide.* Boston, MA: Houghton Mifflin Harcourt.

Levy, S. (2005, February 6). Does your iPod play favorites? *Newsweek online.* Retrieved on August 24, 2018 from: www.newsweek.com/does-your-ipod-play-favorites-116739.

Lichtenstein, S., Fischhoff, B. & Phillips, L.D. (1982). Calibration of probabilities: The state of the art to 1980. In D. Kahneman, P. Slovic, & A. Tversky (Eds), *Judgment under uncertainty: Heuristics and biases* (pp. 306–334). Cambridge, MA: Cambridge University Press.

Lord, C.G., Ross, L. & Lepper, M.R. (1979). Biased assimilation and attitude polarization: The effects of prior theories on subsequently considered evidence. *Journal of Personality and Social Psychology, 37*(11), 2098–2109, doi: org/10.1037/0022-3514.37.11.2098.

Maxwell, N.L. & Lopus, J.S. (1994). The Lake Wobegon Effect in student self-reported data. *The American Economic Review, 84*(2), 201–205.

McKenzie, C.R.M. (2005). Judgment and decision making. In K. Lamberts & R.L. Goldstone (Eds), *The handbook of cognition* (pp. 321–338). London: Sage.

Morris, A.H., Lee, K.H. & Orme, J. (2017). Illusory superiority: A barrier to reaching clinical practice goals [Abstract]. *American Journal of Respiratory and Critical Care Medicine, 195*, A1226.

Osborn, A.F. (1957). *Applied imagination.* New York: Scribner.

Payne, J.W., Bettman, J.R. & Johnson, E.J. (1988). Adaptive strategy selection in decision making. *Journal of Experimental Psychology: Learning, Memory, and Cognition, 14*(3), 534–552, doi: org/10.1037/0278-7393.14.3.534.

Plous, S. (1993). *The psychology of judgment and decision making.* New York: McGraw-Hill.

Post, T., van den Assem, M.J., Baltussen, G. & Thaler, R.H. (2008). Deal or no deal? Decision making under risk in a large-payoff game show. *American Economic Review, 98*(1), 38–71, doi: 10.1257/aer.98.1.38.

Rubin, J.M. (2011, November 1). Can a computer generate a truly random number? *Ask an Engineer.* Retrieved February 23, 2019 from: https://engineering.mit.edu/engage/ask-an-engineer/can-a-computer-generate-a-truly-random-number.

Savage, L.J. (1954). *The foundations of statistics.* New York: Wiley.

Schick, T.Jr. & Vaughn, L. (2011). *How to think about weird things: Critical thinking for a new age* (6th Ed.). New York: McGraw Hill.

Simon, H.A. (1956). Rational choice and the structure of the environment. *Psychological Review, 63*, 129–138.

Simons, D.J. & Chabris, C.F. (2010, May 30). The trouble with intuition. *The Chronicle of Higher Education.* Retrieved on June 6, 2010 from: http://chronicle.com/article/The-Trouble-With-Intuition/65674.

Tetlock, P.E. (2005). *Expert political judgment: How good is it? How can we know?* Princeton, NJ: Princeton University Press.

Tversky, A. & Kahneman, D. (1974). Judgment under uncertainty: Heuristics and biases. *Science, 185*(4157), 1124–1130, doi: 10.1126/science.185.4157.1124.

Tversky, A. & Kahneman, D. (1981). The framing of decisions and the psychology of choice. *Science, 211*(4481), 453–458, doi:10.1126/science.7455683.

Vaughn, R.H. (2007). *Decision making and problem solving in management* (3rd Ed.). Brunswick, OH: Crown Custom Publishing.

von Neumann, J. & Morgenstern, O. (1947). *Theory of games and economic behavior* (3rd Ed.). New York: Science editions.

Wilson, T.D. & Schooler, J.W. (1991). Thinking too much: Introspection can reduce the quality of preferences and decisions. *Journal of Personality and Social Psychology, 60*(2), 181–192, doi.org/10.1037/0022-3514.60.2.181.

Wolf, J.H. & Wolf, K.S. (2013). The Lake Wobegon Effect: Are all cancer patients above average? *Milbank Quarterly, 91*(4), 690–728, doi: 10.1111/1468-0009.12030.

Chapter 11

Deductive Reasoning

Sherlock Holmes and his ever-affable yet slow-witted sidekick Dr. Watson go camping. They pitch their tent and go to sleep, but Holmes awakens in the middle of the night. He nudges his companion and says, "Watson, look at the sky. What do you see?"

"Millions and millions of stars," replies Watson.

"And what's that tell you?"

"If only a few of those stars have planets, it's possible that some of those planets are like Earth. If some of those planets are like Earth, there must be life out there." Watson turns his head. "And what does it tell you?"

Holmes replies, "Watson, you idiot. Somebody stole our tent."

If you enjoyed this joke, you're not alone. In one survey it was voted the funniest out of 50,000 entries (see Radford, 2001). Many people think of Sherlock Holmes as the personification of deductive reasoning. But is deduction *really* Holmes' *modus operandi*? At times, the great detective did employ deduction. More often than not, however, Holmes relied on *inductive reasoning* (Kincaid, 2015). That is, he gathered facts to arrive at a probable inference rather than a certain conclusion. Others have suggested that he used *abductive reasoning*, which entails reasoning from the available data to the best hypothesis possible (Lyne, 2005; Walton 2005). With *deductive reasoning*, however, a person seeks to reach a certain, inescapable conclusion. The conclusion isn't merely probable, it is indisputable. When using deduction, the conclusion *necessarily follows* from the premises.

In this chapter we examine such reasoning. After exploring deduction's applicability to everyday life, you will learn about its role in a variety of fields and contexts. Next, we will look at rules for testing the validity of syllogisms, which are one of the most common types of deductive reasoning. But first, let's take a closer look at the difference between inductive and deductive reasoning.

Deductive Versus Inductive Reasoning: A Whole Different Animal

As we learned in previous chapters, *inductive reasoning* deals with probabilities. Returning to a Sherlock Holmes example, in *The Hound of the Baskervilles* (Doyle, 1902), Holmes inferred that whoever mailed a letter made of cut and pasted letters must be well educated because:

the utmost pains have been taken to remove all clues. The address, you observe, is printed in rough characters. But *The Times* is a paper which is seldom found in any hands but those of the highly educated. We may take it, therefore, that the letter was composed by an educated man who wished to pose as an uneducated one. (p. 32)

However, the conclusion doesn't *necessarily* follow from the assumptions as it would if deductive reasoning were being used. A less-educated person could have found a copy of the newspaper

*"Well, by that logic no one would ever shave
a clock onto a monkey."*

Figure 11.1 Caught up in a logical quandary. Paul Noth, cartoonbank.com, 2010-09-13, TCB-34912.
© Paul Noth/*The New Yorker* Collection/www.cartoonbank.com.

lying about on a bus, or a train, or in a pub. Deductive reasoning deals with certainties. To see why, let's examine a common type of deductive argument, known as a *categorical syllogism*, which looks like this:

Premise #1: All tortoises are vegetarians.

Premise #2: Bessie is a tortoise.

Conclusion: Therefore, Bessie is a vegetarian.

As you can see, a categorical syllogism has two premises followed by a conclusion. If both premises are true, the conclusion is a sure thing. In this case, Bessie is a vegetarian, no doubt about it.

What Is Formal Logic?

The word *logic* often conjures up images of cold calculation. For example, Mr. Spock from the *Star Trek* series is ultra-logical, perhaps because he's only half human. That said, formal logic and deduction are not as perplexing as they sometimes seem. Simply stated, *formal logic* is the science of correct reasoning, which leads to valid, rather than invalid, conclusions. *Deduction* is a method of logical reasoning.

Formal logic has rules, which, if followed correctly, lead to valid conclusions. These rules have to do with the *form* of arguments. In other words, it is the arrangement of the premises and conclusion that determine whether a deductive argument is valid or invalid. In addition, the specific wording of premises and conclusions matters too. Ordinary language is often vague or ambiguous. As such, when fashioning logical statements, you must be careful to make the wording clear and precise (see Box 11.1).

Box 11.1   Wording Counts: Casting Ordinary Language into Syllogistic Form

Because the form of a syllogism determines its validity, language must be precise. This may seem like nitpicking, but ambiguous language can render an otherwise valid syllogism invalid. The following are key considerations when wording syllogisms.

1   Unless otherwise stated, the subject term (first term) in a premise is *presumed to be universal*. Thus, the premise "Donuts have holes" is synonymous with saying "*All* donuts have holes." Proper nouns are also treated as universal. It sounds odd, but the premise "Socrates is a man" means *all* Socrates, implying that there is a class or category of persons named Socrates with only one member.

   "Lonnie has a short temper" means "[all of the person we refer to as] Lonnie has a short temper."

   "Toyota is the world's biggest car maker" means "[all of the company known as] Toyota is the world's biggest car maker."

2   Importantly, the predicate term (second term) is *not* presumed to be universal, unless the premise is negative. The statement "all bowtie wearers are dapper dressers" should be interpreted as "all bowtie wearers are [among those who are] dapper dressers," not "all bowtie wearers are the *only ones* who are dapper dressers." With a negative statement, however, both terms are universal. Saying "No French fries are healthy foods" is equivalent to saying "no healthy foods are French fries."

3   Quantifiers are limited to "all," "none," or "some." Quantifiers such as "many," "most," or "several" are not allowed.

   Allowed: Some CEOs of Fortune 500 companies are women.

   Not allowed: Few CEOs of Fortune 500 companies are women.

4   The quantifier "some" means "at least one." Thus, saying "Some people with disabilities are athletes" is synonymous with saying "At least one person with a disability is an athlete." Saying "Some hockey players are missing front teeth" really means "At least one hockey player is missing front teeth."

5   Technically speaking, the major term and minor term should be nouns or noun phrases. Rather than saying "Some cab drivers are smelly," one should say "Some cab drivers are smelly *people*." Rather than saying "Weevils are annoying," one could say "Weevils are annoying *varmints*." This requirement is often ignored with no serious consequences, as long as everyone understands what is meant. Most people can easily make sense of both premises below, even though one is technically incorrect.

   Technically correct: Some two year olds are [children who are] incorrigible.

   Technically incorrect: Some two year olds are incorrigible.

6   The *copula*, which is the verb connecting the major, minor, and middle terms, must be some form of the verb *to be*, such as "is," "are," or "are not." This may require some rewording. On the other hand, people often understand the copula just fine even though it is not technically correct.

   The premise "Some baboons have red butts," should be reworded to "Some baboons [are monkeys] with red butts."

   The premise "All stoners love Cheetos," should be rephrased as "All stoners are [people who love] Cheetos."

   Also, the copula cannot be qualified, as in "is probably is . . ." "are mostly . . ." "often are . . . ."

Are People Naturally Logical?

Early on, scholars subscribed to the doctrine that "logic provides the basis for rational human thought" (Evans, 2002, p. 979). According to this view, human beings are naturally logical and deductive thinking is hard-wired into our brains. There is some merit to this point of view. For example, some evidence suggests that people intuitively prefer valid over invalid arguments (Morsanyi & Handley, 2012). What's more, logical thinking is correlated with intelligence

(Newstead, Handley, Harley, Wright & Farrelly, 2004; Stanovich, 1999). Nonetheless, as we saw in previous chapters, people are often anything but logical in their thinking.[1] Among other things, they allow subjective biases to get in the way (Evans, Newstead & Byrne, 1993; Khemlani & Johnson-Laird, 2012). Studies reveal, for example, that ordinary people can accurately distinguish valid from invalid syllogisms only 37–55 percent of the time (Jacobs, Allen, Jackson & Petrel, 1985; Johnson-Laird & Bara, 1984; Johnson-Laird & Steedman, 1978). Worse yet, and somewhat surprisingly, did you know that being in a positive mood hinders your ability to assess syllogisms (Melton, 1995)? Our advice; try stubbing your toe before taking the LSAT, MCAT, or GRE.

Cognitive Fitness: Don Your Thinking Cap

The good news is that, with training and practice, you can improve your powers of deduction (Neilens, Handley & Newstead, 2009), especially on more difficult reasoning tasks (Leighton, 2006). Better yet, scholars have come to view deductive reasoning as a useful mental exercise, sort of like calisthenics for your brain. In fact, regularly engaging in mental exercise, or what has been dubbed *neurobics*, can help you stave off cognitive decline (Katz & Rubin, 1999). In the same way that playing Sudoku, crossword puzzles, and other "brain teasers" can sharpen your mind, analyzing syllogisms can hone your reasoning skills.

Deduction in Everyday Life: It's What the Cool Kids Are Doing

Does logic apply to everyday life, or is it an obscure pursuit of logicians, mathematicians, and computer programmers? We believe that ordinary people rely on deduction much more than they realize. Suppose some hot-shot music guru tells you, "None of the great rock guitarists read music." If you say, "I beg to differ. Jerry Garcia (from the Grateful Dead), Brian May (from Queen), and Frank Zappa (from the Mothers of Invention) can, or could, all read sheet music," you would invalidate the know-it-all's claim.[2] How? Because a *universal claim* ("all swans are white") is disproven by a *single negative instance* ("There is at least one black swan"). It doesn't matter how many famous lead guitarists could not read music. Logically speaking, a single negative example (in this case, three negative examples), disproves the universal claim that "*none of the great rock guitarists read music.*"

Another example of everyday logic involves ruling out possibilities. Let's say your car won't start. You assume that *either* the battery is dead *or* the car is out of gas. If you test the battery and find it is working, you can conclude the car is out of gas. Conversely, if you verify there is gas in the tank, then the battery must be at fault. Of course, there could be other reasons your car won't start; a faulty ignition switch, clogged fuel filter, etc. But, by using the same process of elimination, you or a mechanic could rule them out one by one.

Another practical illustration of deduction relies on *if–then* inferences. Let's say Mimi's history professor tells her, "*If* you get an A on the final exam, *then* you will get an A in the class." When Mimi learns she aced the final she jumps for joy, because she may logically conclude she earned an A in the class. Suppose, however, that Mimi got a B on the final exam. Should she assume that her chances for an A in the class were sunk? If so, she'd be making an error in logical thinking known as *denying the antecedent*, a problem we'll return to later in this chapter. Here is the quick explanation: Mimi's professor said that if she got an A on the test, then she would get an

A in the class, but her professor did not say that *only if* she got an A on the final would she earn an A in the class. It is logically possible that if Mimi had gotten a B on the test, she also would have received an A in the class.

These are just three examples of how deductive reasoning can be applied to everyday life. People may not recognize all the occasions on which they use logic, but every human being has the capacity for deductive reasoning. And whatever a person's skill level, there is room for improvement.

Deduction in Specific Fields and Contexts: Putting Logic to Work

As the above examples illustrate, deduction is not limited to the fields of mathematics, symbolic logic, or computer programming. Deductive reasoning is used in a variety of other fields and contexts, often alongside inductive reasoning. Let's consider a few of them next.

Gunshot Residue (GSR): Calling the Shots with Forensic Science

Much of what we see on television shows like CSI involves inductive reasoning. However, a good deal of forensic science uses deductive reasoning based on scientific tests. Such tests allow investigators to determine a specific cause of death, rule out a particular suspect, or reach a definitive conclusion about some aspect of a crime.

Imagine that police officers hear gunshots. They enter a residence and find a man holding a gun, standing over a body. The victim was shot and there are shell casings on the floor. Based on *circumstantial evidence* (e.g., sign reasoning), the cops might infer that the man holding the gun shot the victim. This would entail inductive reasoning. But what if the man swore that he entered the room *after* the shots were fired? What if he claims he picked up the gun to protect himself in case the murderer was lingering nearby?

By testing for gunshot residue (GSR), crime scene investigators could logically deduce whether the man was, or was not, in the room when the gun was fired. That's because when a gun is fired, gun powder vaporizes into fine particles that attach themselves to anything near the weapon, including the skin and clothing of the shooter. The GSR tests can determine, with near certainty, if a person was nearby when a gun was fired. As Trimpe notes, "the technology behind the analysis of gunshot residue is unquestionably scientifically sound" (2011, p. 31). The deductive process would go something like this:

- Premise: When the gun was fired, the man was either outside the room, as he claims, or inside the room, as he denies.
- Premise: Anyone who was outside the room will have no GSR on his or her skin or clothing.
- Premise: Anyone inside the room, in close proximity to the gun, will have GSR on his or her skin or clothing.
- Premise: The man has GSR on his skin and clothing.
- Conclusion: Therefore, the man was in the room and near the gun when it was fired.

If all the premises are true (the sample must have been gathered and analyzed correctly), then the only logical conclusion is that the man was in the room when the gun was fired. Of course, GSR cannot prove that he was the shooter, only that he was in the room.

Medical Diagnosis: I've Got Good News and Bad News

Medical diagnosis is another field in which both inductive and deductive reasoning join forces. Inductive reasoning, such as observing symptoms, is typically used to form a preliminary diagnosis. For example, if a woman complained to her doctor of nausea, dizziness, and frequent urination, the doctor might suspect she was pregnant. The doctor could then use deduction to rule other explanations in or out, such as flu or food poisoning. For instance, if the woman had a normal regular period after she last engaged in sexual activity, then she could not be pregnant.[3] The deductive reasoning would be as follows.

- Premise: A woman who has a regular period cannot be pregnant.
- Premise: This woman had a regular period.
- Premise: Therefore, this woman cannot be pregnant.

Alternatively, the doctor might order a blood pregnancy test to determine conclusively whether the woman was pregnant or not. The test identifies the presence and amount of the hormone hCG in the bloodstream. The deductive process would be:

- Premise: hCG levels in the range of 5–25 mlU/ml are proof of pregnancy.
- Premise: This woman's hCG levels fall within the 5–25 mlU/ml range.
- Conclusion: This woman is pregnant.

If the first two premises are correct, it logically follows that she is pregnant. However, because some medications can invalidate a blood pregnancy test, either by producing a false positive or false negative, the doctor would have to ensure the woman was not taking those medications.

Human Ancestry: Shagging 'neath the Family Tree

Neanderthals lived alongside Homo sapiens (that's us) until some 30,000 years ago. Occasionally, they "hooked up" with one another. How do we know? The field of biological anthropology offers an illustration of how deduction can be used to reach conclusions about human ancestry. Since the discovery of early hominid bones, there has been speculation about the relationship of Homo sapiens (modern humans) to Neanderthals. One theory is that, although the two coexisted, they are completely unrelated. Using a family tree analogy, Homo sapiens are on one tree, Neanderthals are on a different tree altogether. A second theory suggests that Neanderthals were our forebears and modern humans evolved from them. Returning to the family tree analogy, Neanderthals were the trunk of the tree and modern humans are a branch. A third, more recent view, called the "out of Africa" theory, maintains that although Neanderthals and Homo sapiens share a distant common ancestor, they separated early on and followed different evolutionary paths. Using the tree analogy, there was a fork in the tree, low on the trunk, and each branch went its own separate way. A fourth, even more recent theory, called the "assimilation model," suggests that after separating from a distant common ancestor, Neanderthals and Homo sapiens intermingled. That is, the two branches of the tree later became intertwined. According to this theory, Homo sapiens and Neanderthals were making "booty calls," at least occasionally.

Which theory is correct? Advances in genetic sequencing have ruled out two of these theories. The human genome was first sequenced in 2003. The Neanderthal genome was sequenced in 2010, using bone fragments (Green, Krause, Briggs et al., 2010). Comparing the two sets of DNA reveals that many modern humans inherited 1–4 percent of their DNA from Neanderthals. Logically, this eliminates the "two trees" theory. Homo sapiens and Neanderthals are not completely unrelated. The deductive process would be:

- Premise: If Neanderthal DNA is found in modern humans' DNA, then our ancestors interbred with Neanderthals.
- Premise: Neanderthal DNA is present in modern humans' DNA.
- Conclusion: Therefore, our ancestors interbred with Neanderthals.

Moreover, based on the small amount of shared DNA, the second theory also can be eliminated. Modern humans don't share enough DNA for Neanderthals to be our direct ancestors. That leaves the "out of Africa" and "assimilation model" in the running.

Genetic testing alone cannot determine which of the two remaining theories is correct, at least not yet. When inductive reasoning is added into the mix, however, the evidence seems to support the assimilation model. It is probable that modern humans and Neanderthals were "doing the humpity bumpity" as recently as 47,000 years ago (Choi, 2012; Sankararaman, Patterson, Li, Pääbo & Reich, 2012).[4]

Validity and Invalidity

Thus far, we've used the term "validity" several times. It's important to realize that the meaning of the term, as we've used it, is not the same as in ordinary usage. In everyday life, a person might say "You have a valid point there," meaning that the other person's argument is strong or compelling. In formal logic, however, the term *validity* has a precise meaning. It means that the conclusion is more than just convincing; it is indisputable. More specifically, in formal logic, *an argument is valid if the conclusion necessarily follows from the premises*, assuming the premises are true.

As you can see from this definition, validity is a property of the whole argument, premises and conclusion, not just the conclusion itself. Furthermore, as we noted earlier, the actual *form* or *structure* of a deductive argument determines its validity. Valid arguments are stated in such a way that if the premises are true, then the conclusion must follow. For this reason, logicians often say the conclusion is *entailed* in the premises, meaning the conclusion is contained in, or necessitated by, the premises. With this understanding in mind, let's take a closer look at the concept of validity and a related concept, soundness.

It Is or It Isn't

When it comes to the validity of deductive arguments, there are no gray areas. A deductive argument is *either* valid or invalid; it cannot be "pretty valid," "mostly valid," or "valid-ish." A deductive argument cannot be "kind of" valid any more than a woman can be "sort of" pregnant or a corpse can be "kinda" dead. It wouldn't do, for example, to argue that "all mammals are warm-blooded, and all dolphins are mammals, so dolphins are 'probably' warm-blooded." If the first two premises are true, then dolphins *must* be warm-blooded.

Soundness: Both True and Valid

Thus far, we've been relying on a big "if." We've said that in a valid argument, *if* the premises are true, then the conclusion necessarily follows. We've taken the truth of the premises for granted. But what if one or more of the premises is false? This is a matter of *soundness*. Specifically, if any of the premises are false and the reasoning is valid, the argument is said to be *unsound*. If, on the other hand, the premises are true *and* the reasoning is valid, then an argument is said to be *sound* (see Table 11.1). Thus, the argument "All Mormons drink whiskey, and Elder Bingham is a Mormon, so Elder Bingham drinks whiskey" would be valid, but unsound, because the first premise ("All Mormons drink whiskey") is false.

Here's the rub, a deductive argument cannot prove the truth of its own premises. The truth of the premises must be established by some other means. Thus, the statement "Canada has more donut shops per capita than any other country" could be used as a premise, but its accuracy would have to be verified independently from the argument itself. In this case, the premise is based on Snapple fast fact #339. Snapple bottle caps can only tell you so much, however. What's considered "true" is often up for debate. In the syllogism below, some people (pro-life types) would accept the truth of the premises, while others (pro-choice sorts) would not.

- Premise: All fetuses are living persons.
- Premise: All living persons are entitled to the right to life, liberty, and the pursuit of happiness.
- Conclusion: Therefore, all fetuses are entitled to the right to life, liberty, and the pursuit of happiness.

This syllogism is valid, based on its form alone. That said, some people would consider it sound whereas others would regard it as unsound. By way of summary, then, truth or falsity is a characteristic of premises. Validity versus invalidity is a characteristic of deductive reasoning. Soundness or lack of soundness is a characteristic of both.

Syllogistic Reasoning: It's Only Logical

Earlier, we alluded to a common type of deductive argument called a *syllogism*. Because syllogisms are such a valuable tool for understanding arguments, let's take a closer look at them now. A syllogism consists of three statements; a *major premise*, a *minor premise*, and a *conclusion*, in that exact order. For example, consider the following syllogism:

- Major premise: All zombies can be killed by a bullet to the brain.
- Minor premise: Edna is a zombie.
- Conclusion: Therefore, Edna can be killed by a bullet to the brain.

Table 11.1 Valid versus sound arguments

	True premises	False premise(s)
Valid reasoning	Sound	Valid, but unsound
Invalid reasoning	Invalid	Invalid and unsound

Each premise contains two terms; a subject term and a predicate term. The *subject term* is first and the *predicate term* is second. In the major premise above, the subject term is "all zombies" and the predicate term is "bullet to the brain." In the minor premise, the subject term is "Edna" and the predicate term is "zombie."

Remember that in deductive reasoning, the truth of the premises is assumed. This applies to syllogisms as well. The premise "all dragons breathe fire" may not be true, but, as the premise of a syllogism, it is presumed to be true. Hence, even imaginary arguments can be valid or invalid (although not necessarily sound). For example, in the zombie syllogism, the form of the reasoning is valid even though zombies do not exist.

With these assumptions in mind, we now consider three types of syllogisms, the first of which is known as a categorical syllogism.

Categorical Syllogisms: No Koalas Are Bears

Did you know that koala bears are not really bears at all? They are marsupials (meaning they mature in their mother's pouch). The fact that they are marsupials, not bears, can help us understand a bit more about categorical syllogisms. Specifically, as their name suggests, *categorical syllogisms* categorize things into different classes or groups. If someone began an argument by saying "All koalas are bears" the person would essentially be saying that all koalas can be *categorized* as bears. The person would be wrong, though, as anyone who watches *Animal Planet* surely knows!

Universal and Particular Premises

There are different words you can use to categorize koalas. For example, some terms, such as "all" or "none," refer to *universal* categories, whereas others, like "some" or "a few," refer to *particular* categories. The premise "No koalas are bears" is universal because it includes every koala bear *in the universe* (get it?). Some premises, on the other hand, are particular. As their name implies, particular premises classify *some* things into a category, but not all of those things. For instance, the premise "Some koalas are female" is particular. Others are male. Technically speaking, the term "some" means "at least one." Thus, the premise "Some koalas have chlamydia" is true if at least one koala has the disease.[5] Now you try. Can you tell which premise below is universal and which is particular? How about the conclusion? Is it particular or universal?

- Major premise: *All* koalas have opposable digits.
- Minor premise: *Some* marsupials are koalas.
- Conclusion: Therefore, *some* marsupials have opposable digits.

Affirmative and Negative Premises

In addition to being universal or particular, premises are also *affirmative* or *negative*. They either affirm or negate that something belongs in a category. For example, the premise "All adult koalas eat eucalyptus leaves" is affirmative and universal. The premise "No koalas are carnivores" is negative and universal. The premise "Some koalas live in zoos" is affirmative and particular, whereas the premise "Some koalas are not cute and cuddly" is negative and particular. Can you tell which premise below is affirmative and universal and which is negative and universal? What about the conclusion?

- Major premise: All koalas are marsupials.
- Minor premise: No bears are marsupials.
- Conclusion: Therefore, no bears are koalas.

Major, Middle, and Minor Terms

As we've noted, all syllogisms contain three statements known as the major premise, the minor premise, and the conclusion.[6] Every syllogism also includes three terms (or concepts) known as the *major term*, the *minor term*, and the *middle term*. Knowing how to identify each of these terms is important because, as we'll see, it will help you evaluate syllogisms. In the syllogism below (see Figure 11.2) the middle term is "marsupials," the major term is "bears," and the minor term is "koalas." You'll notice that each term appears twice and only twice in the syllogism. Each statement describes the relationship between two of terms.

The major term, "bears," is always found in the major premise, but it may be the first (subject) or second (predicate) term of that premise. Likewise, the minor term, "koalas," is always found in the minor premise, but may appear first or second in that premise. In the conclusion, however, the minor term *always appears first* (as the subject), while the major term *always appears second* (as the predicate). The middle term, in this case "marsupials," is easy to identify because it is always found in *both* premises, but *not* in the conclusion. Thanks to koalas (Figure 11.3), you now understand the elements of a categorical syllogism.

Evaluating Syllogisms: Form Over Substance

Examining deductive arguments to assess their validity might seem like a daunting task. In fact, it is a fairly straightforward process. Since it is the *form* of a syllogism that determines its validity, the content or substance of a syllogism matters little. In terms of validity, saying "All

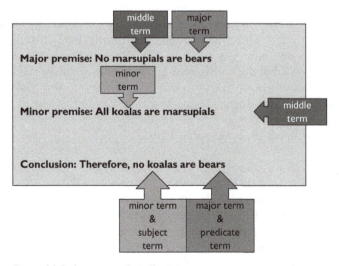

Figure 11.2 Anatomy of a syllogism.

Figure 11.3 "Who you callin' a bear?"
RuthCho\Shutterstock.com.

leprechauns are male" or "No unicorns are black" is the same as saying "All A are B," or "No A are B," respectively. As a form of shorthand, logicians are fond of substituting letters for terms. Specifically, since the minor term always appears as the *subject* of the conclusion, it is designated with the letter S. Since the major term always appears as the predicate of the conclusion, it is designated with the letter P. And M is used to designate the middle term. Regardless of their content, then, the following syllogisms are all valid based on their form alone.

All *M* are *P*	All jerks are inconsiderate people.
Some *S* are *M*	Some people who talk on cellphones are jerks.
Therefore, some *S* are *P*	Therefore, some people who talk on cell phones are inconsiderate people.

No *M* is *P*	No vampires are sunbathers.
All *S* is *M*	Count Dracula is a vampire.
Therefore, no *S* is *P*	Therefore, Count Dracula is not a sunbather.

No *M* are *P*	No two-eyed creatures are Cyclops.
Some *S* are *M*	Some ogres are two-eyed creatures.
Therefore, some *S* are not *P*	Therefore, some ogres are not Cyclops.

All *P* are *M*	All kraits are venomous snakes.
No *S* is *M*	No king snake is a venomous snake.
Therefore, no *S* is *P*	Therefore, no king snake is a krait.

All *P* are *M*	All sprinters are fleet of foot.
Some *S* are not *M*	Some joggers are not fleet of foot.
Therefore, some *S* are not *P*	Therefore, some joggers are not sprinters.

These are just five of the 256 possible combinations of valid categorical syllogisms. That said, *only 15 of those combinations are unconditionally valid*. How, then, do you separate the wheat from the chaff, syllogistically speaking? You could rely on intuition, but thinking through a syllogism to see if it *seems* logical may trip you up. You could also memorize all 15 valid forms, but that's a lot to remember.

Figure 11.4 Penguin logic.
© Randy Glasbergen/Glasbergen Cartoon Service.

Fortunately, there is an easier way using a simple mental checklist consisting of six rules. If no rules are violated, the syllogism is valid. If any rules are broken, the syllogism is invalid. It's that simple. With this in mind, let's consider six rules for determining the validity of a categorical syllogism.

The Big Six: Rules for Valid Syllogisms

RULE 1: THREE AND ONLY THREE TERMS ARE ALLOWED AND EACH TERM MUST HAVE THE SAME MEANING THROUGHOUT

A syllogism with more than three terms is automatically invalid. For example, the argument below, which has four terms, is invalid.

- Major premise: All Democrats are liberal.
- Minor premise: All Republicans are conservative.
- Conclusion: Therefore, no Democrats are conservative.

This type of argument, dubbed the *four-term fallacy*, may seem valid, but it is not. The fact that it contains four terms—Democrats, liberals, Republicans, and conservatives—renders it invalid.

This is easy to spot if you're on your toes. In addition, Rule 1 requires that *the meaning of a term remains consistent*. A term cannot be ambiguous, have multiple meanings, or morph into something else. Sometimes, however, arguers use *equivocation* to shift the meaning of a term. This shift, in turn, allows arguers to sneak in a fourth term, which can be seen in the argument below.

- Major premise: All super heroes have super powers.
- Minor premise: All super powers have nuclear weapons.
- Conclusion: Therefore, all super heroes have nuclear weapons.

Here the term "super power" has two different meanings, which essentially makes it two separate terms, for a total of four. The first term refers to super-human abilities, such as x-ray vision or spider senses. The second refers to nations with considerable economic and military might. Based on Rule 1, can you spot the flaw in the syllogism below?

- Major premise: All marching bands have horns.
- Minor premise: All devils have horns.
- Conclusion: Therefore, all marching bands have devils.

RULE 2: THE MIDDLE TERM MUST BE DISTRIBUTED IN AT LEAST ONE PREMISE

A term is *distributed* if it refers to an entire class or all members of a category. For example, if a middle term referred to "all magicians," or "no clowns," it would represent the whole class of magicians or clowns, thereby making the term distributed. If, on the other hand, a middle term referred to "some pickpockets" or "some witches," it would not include every member of those categories, making it undistributed. Two useful guidelines are that 1) only universal terms, e.g., those with "all," distribute the subject term, and 2) only negative terms, e.g., those with the word "no," distribute the predicate term. With that in mind, consider the following syllogism:

- Major premise: All snakes are legless creatures.
- Minor premise: All fish are legless creatures.
- Conclusion: Therefore, all snakes are fish.

Does it seem odd or a bit off? The reason has to do with the middle term, "legless creatures," which is undistributed. Remember, to be distributed, the term must include every member of the class to which it refers. Also remember that unless the premise is negative, the predicate term is particular. Obviously, since the subject terms "all snakes" and "all fish" include every snake and every fish, they are distributed. In contrast, because there are other types of legless creatures (e.g., earthworms, eels, snails), the term "legless creatures" is undistributed in this example.

With this understanding in mind, let's return to Rule #2, which says *the middle term must be distributed in at least one premise*. This rule applies specifically to the middle term, which appears in both premises but never in the conclusion. Thus, in the example above, since the middle term, "legless creatures," is undistributed, the conclusion is invalid.

Based on what you learned so far, see if you can tell which terms below are distributed and which are not. If you must peek, the answers are in parentheses.

- All monkeys are primates (the term "monkeys" is distributed, "primates" is not).
- Monkeys are bad pets (as the subject term, "monkeys" is presumed to be universal, and therefore distributed, but "pets" is not distributed).
- No apes have tails (both terms, "apes" and "tails," are distributed).
- Some apes fling their poo (neither term is distributed).

As you've probably noticed, categorical syllogisms can be worded differently. Regardless of wording, though, the subject term is only distributed if it includes "all" and the predicate term is only distributed if the premise is negative, e.g., includes "no."

RULE 3: ANY TERM THAT IS UNIVERSAL IN THE CONCLUSION MUST BE UNIVERSAL IN THE PREMISE IN WHICH IT APPEARS

The conclusion of a syllogism cannot encompass more than its premises. A syllogism is invalid if a term refers to all members of a category in the conclusion, but only some members of the category in either premise. One variation of this problem is dubbed the fallacy of the *illicit minor*. An example of this fallacy is:

- Major premise: All politicians are liars.
- Minor premise: All politicians are scoundrels.
- Conclusion: Therefore, all scoundrels are liars.

As you can see, the minor term "scoundrels" is universal in the conclusion, but not in the minor premise, hence the illicit minor. Another example is:

- Major premise: No gnomes are elves.
- Minor premise: All gnomes are short creatures.
- Conclusion: Therefore, no short creatures are elves.

In this example, the minor term, "short creatures," is universal in the conclusion, but not in the minor premise. That's because a lot of non-elfin creatures, besides gnomes, are also vertically challenged, including hobbits, pixies, and goblins. The real difference, of course, is that elves bake cookies in trees and gnomes advertise travel deals. A second variation of this problem, termed the *fallacy of the illicit major*, occurs when the major term is not universal. An example of this pitfall follows.

- Major premise: All professors are absent-minded.
- Minor premise: No students are professors.
- Conclusion: Therefore, no students are absent-minded.

As can be seen, the major term, "absent-minded," is not distributed in the major premise, but is distributed in the conclusion. The same is true in this example:

- Major premise: All heroin users are drug addicts.
- Minor premise: Rodney is not a heroin user.
- Conclusion: Therefore, Rodney is not a drug addict.

Since the major term, "drug addict," is non-universal in the major premise, this syllogism runs afoul of the illicit major fallacy. Rodney could be addicted to meth or OxyContin.

RULE 4: IF ANY PREMISE IS NEGATIVE, THE CONCLUSION MUST BE NEGATIVE

If either premise is negative, only a negative conclusion may be drawn. This may be the easiest of the rules to apply; a negative premise always requires a negative conclusion. For example,

- Major premise: No movie made before 1967 used the "f" word.
- Minor premise: *The Wizard of Oz* was made before 1967.
- Conclusion: Therefore, *The Wizard of Oz* does not use the "f" word.

That said, when the Wicked Witch was melting, she might have been thinking it!

RULE 5: A VALID SYLLOGISM MAY NOT HAVE TWO NEGATIVE PREMISES

The old axiom "two wrongs don't make a right" is used to renounce retaliation, but, if you ask us, it's also a handy mnemonic device for remembering our next rule: if both premises are negative, no valid conclusion may be drawn. This is often referred to as the *fallacy of exclusive premises*. Can you see how the syllogism below violates this rule?

- Major premise: No junk food is healthy.
- Minor premise: No organic food is junk food.
- Conclusion: All organic food is healthy.

Clearly, both of the premises are negative. That said, this syllogism would *still be invalid* even if it reached a negative conclusion, such as "No organic food is unhealthy," because both premises are negative. As another mnemonic device, remember that, "two negatives are a no no."

RULE 6: A PARTICULAR PREMISE REQUIRES A PARTICULAR CONCLUSION AND TWO PARTICULAR PREMISES ARE NOT ALLOWED

No valid conclusion may be derived from two particular premises, which is another way of saying that valid syllogisms require at least one universal premise. You might liken a particular premise to a particular fussy person. Two particular fussy people cannot get along with each other. One particular person, though, and one accommodating person, can get along. The syllogism below violates Rule 6, because both premises are particular.

- Major premise: Some 60 year olds are nudists.
- Minor premise: Some nudists are 20 years old.
- Conclusion: Therefore, some 60 year-olds are 20 years old.

It turns out that syllogisms also run into trouble when a particular conclusion is drawn from two universal premises, resulting in what is known as the *existential fallacy*. Admittedly, this can be a bit tricky. In fact, Aristotle considered this type of syllogism valid. However, some folks, known as Boolean logicians, assume that universal premises have no *existential import*. That is, universal premises may refer to an empty class or a category with no members. For example, the premise "All three-headed people are friendly" refers to a class of people without a single member. True, there are rare cases of dicephalic conjoined twins, where two separate heads share the same body. However, there are no three-headed triplets who share the same body (not living, anyway). Two heads may be better than one, but three is a crowd.

Just remember that in formal logic a universal premise may have no actual members, as in the premise "All centaurs are male." In formal logic, however, when the word "some" is used in a particular premise, it means that "at least one" member of the category exists. To illustrate, imagine that someone said "All the shoes in this closet are black." In formal logic, that doesn't guarantee that there are any shoes in the closet. But if someone said "Some of the shoes in this closet are white" it would guarantee the existence of at least one white shoe inside the closet. We know, it is a weird rule.

Now that you know how to assess the validity of a categorical syllogism using the six basic rules, we turn our attention to a second type of syllogism.

Conditional Syllogisms: If You Don't Stop Crying, I'll Give You Something to Cry About

Another common type of syllogism is the *conditional syllogism*. To say that something is conditional means that it depends on another thing. For example, a parent might tell a teenager, "If your GPA is 3.0 or higher this semester, then you may get your learner's permit to drive." As another example, a meteorologist might say "If it is 0 degrees Celsius, then water will freeze." An example of a conditional if–then syllogism appears below.

- Major premise: If a black cat crosses your path, then you'll have bad luck.
- Minor premise: A black cat did, indeed, cross your path.
- Conclusion: Therefore, you will have bad luck.

Like categorical syllogisms, conditional syllogisms also contain two premises followed by a conclusion. The premises are hypothetical in nature, that is, they consist of "if–then" statements.

Valid Conditional Syllogisms

As with all syllogisms, the *form* of a conditional syllogism determines its validity. If the form is valid, the conclusion necessarily follows from the premises. A common valid form, known as *modus ponens*[7] or *affirming the antecedent*, looks like this:

- Major premise: If *P*, then *Q*.
- Minor premise: *P*.
- Conclusion: Therefore, *Q*.

As you can see, the "If *P*" requirement in the first premise (the antecedent) is satisfied in the second premise "*P*," hence the antecedent is affirmed. Translating the symbols into words we get:

If *P*, then *Q*	If an antecedent event occurs, then a consequent event will occur.
P	The antecedent event does occur.
Therefore, *Q*	Therefore, the consequent event will occur.

Here's an example of this form, adapted from a speech by Dr. Martin Luther King Jr:

If *P*, then *Q*	If one person is oppressed, then no person is truly free.
P	One person is oppressed.
Therefore, *Q*	Therefore, no person is truly free.

Another valid form, known as *modus tollens*[8] or *denying the consequent*, looks like this:

If *P*, then *Q*	If an antecedent event occurs, then a consequent event will occur.
Not *Q*	The consequent event does not occur.
Therefore, not *P*	Therefore, the antecedent event did not occur.

An illustration of this form is as follows.

If *P*, then *Q*	If a person is bitten by a werewolf, then that person will become a werewolf.
Not *Q*	Gustavo did not become a werewolf.
Therefore, not *P*	Therefore, Gustavo was not bitten by a werewolf.

Interestingly, studies show that ordinary people are much better at evaluating the *modus ponens* form for validity (roughly 60–75 percent accuracy) than the *modus tollens* form (roughly 45 percent accuracy) (Evans, 2002; Evans, Newstead & Byrne, 1993). Why? Apparently, the inclusion of a negative premise tends to trip them up (Leighton, 2006). They exhibit what is called a *negative conclusion bias*, meaning that they err on the side of caution by rejecting syllogisms with negative premises (Evans, 1982).

Invalid Conditional Syllogisms

In addition to the two valid forms of conditional syllogisms, there are two invalid forms as well. Although they resemble the valid forms superficially, beware, because they are imposters. Not only that, research shows that, without training, people are not very good at spotting them. Their ability to do so correctly varies from 17–75 percent, depending on the fallacy (Perkins, 2002). With that in mind, let's get some practice.

AFFIRMING THE CONSEQUENT

The first invalid form of a conditional syllogism, known as *affirming the consequent*, looks like this:

- Major premise: If P, then Q
- Minor premise: Q
- Conclusion: Therefore, P

This form can appear deceptively logical, but, if you look closely, the conclusion does not necessarily follow from the premises, even if both premises are true. Why? Because the conclusion assumes the first premise is *bidirectional*. The faulty assumption is that "if P, then Q" is equivalent to "if Q, then P." Conditional premises, however, are *not reversible*. "If an animal is a tiger, then it is a feline" does not imply the reverse, that "if an animal is a feline, then it is a tiger." Indeed, lions, leopards, and house cats are felines too. Let's consider an example in plain, ordinary language.

If P, then Q	All evangelical Christians are opposed to abortion.
Q	Nadine is opposed to abortion.
Therefore, P	Therefore, Nadine is an evangelical Christian.

This syllogism is invalid because saying that "All evangelical Christians are opposed to abortion" is not the same as saying "all those opposed to abortion are evangelical Christians." Nadine could be a devout Catholic, for example, and still be opposed to abortion. Putting it another way, the first premise does not say "*Only* Christian evangelicals are opposed to abortion." Other religious groups may be opposed as well.

Here is another example of the fallacy of affirming the consequent.

- If a musician plays in a symphonic orchestra, then she or he can read sheet music.
- Betty can read sheet music.
- Therefore, Betty plays in a symphonic orchestra.

Once again, the first premise is non-reversible. While all orchestral musicians may be able to read sheet music, so can many non-orchestral musicians. A music teacher, for example, could read music without necessarily playing in an orchestra. Without training, people are generally not good at spotting this fallacy. Their ability to do so correctly varies from 23–75 percent of the time (Perkins, 2002).

DENYING THE ANTECEDENT

A second fallacy involving conditional syllogisms is known as *denying the antecedent*. Also called the *inverse fallacy* by some, this syllogism takes the following form:

- Major premise: If *P*, then *Q*
- Minor premise: Not *P*
- Conclusion: Therefore, not *Q*

Here is an example of denying the antecedent in action.

- Major premise: If Ralph is a safe cracker, then he will own a stethoscope.
- Minor premise: Ralph is not a safe cracker.
- Conclusion: Therefore, Ralph does not own a stethoscope.

Can you see the problem with this syllogism? If not, ask yourself whether Ralph could be in another line of work that requires a stethoscope. Is it possible that Ralph is a medical doctor or a bomb disposal expert? Let's consider one more example of denying the antecedent:

- If you have acute appendicitis, then you will require immediate surgery.
- You do not have acute appendicitis.
- Therefore, you will not require immediate surgery.

Can you see the problem here? If not, ask yourself whether other medical conditions might require immediate surgery too. For example, a blocked airway might require an emergency tracheotomy.

It is worth noting that a conditional "if–then" premise is *not* equivalent to an "if *and only* if" premise. The latter is known as a *biconditional* premise. In the above example, if the first premise were "*If and only if* you have acute appendicitis, then you will require immediate surgery," then the conclusion would logically follow.

Disjunctive Syllogisms: You Can't Have Your Cake and Eat It Too

In the New Testament (Matthew 12:30) Jesus says, "Whoever is not with me is against me." The verse includes an "either–or" statement. Similarly, the *disjunctive syllogism* relies on "either–or" premises. Each alternative is called a *disjunct*. According to scripture, a person either accepts Jesus or doesn't. There's no in-between. As with the other syllogisms, there are valid and invalid forms (Bobzien, 2002).

Valid Disjunctives

Suppose you are unsure what time a final exam will take place. You text a classmate, who replies, "Either 8 am or 2 pm. Can't remember which." You text another classmate, who responds,

"IDK, but not 2 pm." If their information is correct, then you may logically conclude the final exam is at 8:00 am. Most people, including children, are able to make such logical inferences by exclusion (Hill, Collier-Baker & Suddendorf, 2012). Let's say you put a ping pong ball under one of two cups and ask a person to guess which cup hides the ball. If the person's first guess is wrong, the person can logically deduce that the ball is under the remaining cup (unless you are cheating). There are only two valid types of disjunctive syllogisms.[9] If you fancy Latin, both are referred to as *modus tollendo ponens*.[10] The first takes the form:

- Major premise: Either *P* or *Q*
- Minor premise: Not *P*
- Conclusion: Therefore, *Q*

An example, adapted from the movie *The Hangover*, is:

Either *P* or *Q*	Either tigers love cinnamon, or they love pepper.
Not *P*	Tigers hate cinnamon.
Therefore, *Q*	Therefore, tigers love pepper.

The other valid form, based on a t-shirt slogan we saw, is:

Either *P* or *Q*	Either you love bacon, or you are wrong.
Not *Q*	You are not wrong.
Therefore, *P*	Therefore, you love bacon.

Invalid Disjunctives

Importantly, a disjunctive syllogism is valid only if the second premise *negates* one of the disjuncts. If the second premise *affirms* one of the disjuncts, the syllogism must be *invalid*. The issue here has to do with whether the alternatives are truly mutually exclusive, meaning that both alternatives cannot exist at the same time (e.g., a coin cannot land on heads *and* tails). If they are not mutually exclusive, the fallacy known as *modus ponendo tollens* is committed. For example,

Either *P* or *Q*	Either a defendant will stand trial in a criminal court or in a civil court.
P	The defendant is tried in a criminal court.
Therefore, *Q*	Therefore the defendant will not stand trial in a civil court.

Trial in a criminal court, however, does not preclude trial in a civil court. The two are not mutually exclusive. The first premise could be interpreted as saying a defendant won't be tried *simultaneously* in both criminal and civil court. But a defendant could be tried in one court first, then the other. For example, O.J. Simpson was tried in a criminal court and, once acquitted, was subsequently named in a wrongful death suit in civil court. Here is another invalid example.

Either *P* or *Q*	Either you check into rehab or your spouse will leave you.
P	You do check into rehab.
Therefore, *Q*	Therefore, your spouse won't leave you.

But what if your spouse leaves you anyway? Again, the problem has to do with whether the alternatives are truly mutually exclusive. This is not so much a problem with the form of the syllogism as it is a problem with the interpretation of the word "or," which we address next.

Confusion Over "Or"

When you are evaluating disjunctive syllogisms, keep in mind that some vagaries of ordinary language may come into play. If you're not careful, the word "or" can trip you up. That's because the word "or" can be used *exclusively* or *inclusively*. In the exclusive sense, "or" means "one or the other, but not both." Typically, when people say "A or B" they mean that the alternatives are mutually exclusive. That is, "A *and/or* B" is not an option. In baseball, for example, a pitch is either a strike or a ball. It can't be both. Similarly, the premise "Either Marge will be in London at noon or she'll be in Paris at noon" is also exclusive. Marge cannot be in two places at once.

However, the word "or" can also be used inclusively, meaning "at least one alternative is the case." If Pilar said "Either you can reach me on my cell phone or at my home phone" she might mean you could reach her at *either or both* numbers. Similarly, if you knew that Billy failed algebra three times, you might say, "Either Billy is horrible at algebra, or his teacher is inept." Both could be true, however. Billy might stink at math *and* his teacher might be incompetent.

Unfortunately, logic itself can't tell you the sense in which the term "or" is being used. You must rely on informal reasoning to determine whether "or" is exclusive or inclusive. Suppose, for example, that Mabel told you "Either I'm getting a tongue stud today, or I'm getting my navel pierced." If you knew Mabel to be impulsive, you might infer that she might well get both. You'd be opting for the inclusive meaning. If, on the other hand, a food server said "Your dinner comes with either soup or salad," and you said "I'll have soup," you would know you were not getting salad. You could reasonably infer the "or" in "soup or salad" was not inclusive, e.g., the dinner doesn't include both soup *and* salad.

In the case of an inclusive "or," the only way to ensure the validity of the syllogism is to negate all of the alternatives but one. If the alternatives are A, B, and A+B, then eliminating A and A+B as options leaves only B remaining. This is essentially a process of elimination. If someone were a Cubs fan, a Bears fan, or a Cubs and Bears fan, you would have to eliminate two possibilities to be certain of the third.

Summary

Deductive reasoning is used in science, law, medicine, and many other fields. It is also used in everyday life. Although deciphering syllogisms may seem daunting at first, with practice you can improve your ability to think and reason logically. As Leighton (2006) commented:

> Deductive reasoning is a cornerstone of scientific research in which claims to new knowledge are evaluated rigorously. Scientists, however, are not the only ones who should profit from systematic thinking. Students stand to become better decision makers, problem solvers, and thinkers when they learn to reason systematically. (pp. 109–110)

In this chapter we examined deductive reasoning. Unlike inductive reasoning, which deals with probabilities, deduction reasons from known premises, or premises taken to be true, to reach certain conclusions. Ordinary people are not particularly adept at distinguishing valid from invalid arguments. However, their ability to use deduction increases with training and practice. Deduction has practical applications to everyday life, though we may not always realize when we are using it. The syllogism is one of the most common ways of learning to assess validity and invalidity. Three types of syllogisms were examined; categorical, conditional, and disjunctive. Rules and strategies for evaluating each type were also provided. With practice, the rules become almost second nature.

Notes

1 One could just as easily argue that people are naturally given to mystical or magical thinking.
2 For the record, Frank Zappa is listed as #22 on *Rolling Stone*'s greatest guitarists of all-time list. Brian May is #26 and Jerry Garcia #46. Other guitarists such as Ry Cooder, Steve Vai (Whitesnake), Alice Cooper, and Joe Satriani (Deep Purple), also read music.
3 Some pregnancies might include vaginal bleeding, which could be mistaken for a period, but that is not the same as menstruation.
4 The reasoning is as follows: If Neanderthals and humans diverged onto separate evolutionary paths long ago (say, 400 thousand years) *and remained separated*, then humans in different parts of the world should have roughly the same amount of Neanderthal DNA. Such is not the case, however. Some human populations have more Neanderthal DNA than others. Northern Chinese people share more Neanderthal DNA than do southern Chinese people. Europeans and North Africans have more Neanderthal DNA than sub-Saharan Africans. This suggests that any "bonking" occurred more recently.
5 Sadly, chlamydia is one of the leading killers of koalas.
6 We are referring to syllogisms that follow the *standard form* here, e.g., major premise, minor premise, conclusion.
7 The Latin phrase *modus ponens* or, more properly, *modus ponendo ponens*, roughly translates into "a method that affirms by affirming."
8 The Latin phrase *modus tollens* or, more properly, *modus tollendo tollens*, roughly translates into "a method that denies by denying."
9 Parry & Hacker (1991) identify one valid and three invalid forms of the disjunctive syllogism; *modus tollendo ponens* is valid, but *ponendo tollens, tollendo tollens* and *ponendo ponens* are all invalid (p. 387).
10 *Modus tollendo ponens* translates as "a method that affirms by denying."

References

Bobzien, S. (2002). The development of *modus ponens* in antiquity: From Aristotle to the 2nd century AD. *Phronesis*, *47*(4), 359–394, doi: 10.1163/156852802321016541.

Choi, C.Q. (2012). Humans broke off Neanderthal sex after discovering Eurasia. *Livescience.com*. Retrieved on August 1, 2018 from: www.livescience.com/23730-neanderthals-modern-humans-interbreeding.html.

Doyle, A.C. (1902). *The hound of the Baskervilles*. London: George Nunes Ltd.

Evans, J.St.B.T. (1982). *The psychology of deductive reasoning*. London: Routledge.

Evans, J.St.B.T. (2002). Logic and human reasoning: An assessment of the deduction paradigm. *Psychological Bulletin*, *128*(6), 978–996, doi: 10.1037//0033-2909.128.6.978.

Evans, J.St.B.T., Newstead, S.E. & Byrne, R.M.J. (1993). *Human reasoning: The psychology of deduction*. Hove: Erlbaum.

Green, R.E., Krause, J., Briggs, A.W., Maricic, T., Stenzel, U., Kircher, M., Patterson, N. et al. (2010). A draft sequence of the Neanderthal genome. *Science*, *328*(5979), 710–722, doi: 10.1126/science.1188021.

Hill, A., Collier-Baker, E. & Suddendorf, T. (2012). Inferential reasoning by exclusion in children (Homo sapiens). *Journal of Comparative Psychology*, *126*(3), 243–254, doi:10.1037/a0024449.

Jacobs, S., Allen, M., Jackson, S. & Petrel, D. (1985). Can ordinary arguers recognize a valid conclusion if it walks up and bites them in the butt? In J.R. Cox, M.O. Sillars & G.B. Walker (Eds), *Argument and social practice: Proceedings of the Fourth SCA/AFA conference on argumentation* (pp. 665–674). Annandale, VA: Speech Communication Association.

Johnson-Laird, P.N. & Bara, B.G. (1984). Syllogistic inference. *Cognition*, *16*(1), 1–61, doi:10.1016/0010-0277(84)90035-0.

Johnson-Laird, P.N. & Steedman, M.J. (1978). The psychology of syllogisms. *Cognitive Psychology*, *10*(1), 64–99, doi:10.1016/00100285(78)90019-10285(78)90019-1.

Katz, L.C. & Rubin, M. (1999). *Keep your brain alive: 83 neurobic exercises to help prevent memory loss and increase mental fitness*. New York: Workman Publishing Company.

Khemlani, S. & Johnson-Laird, P.N. (2012). Theories of the syllogism: A meta-analysis. *Psychological Bulletin*, *138*(3), 427–457, doi: 10.1037/a0026841.

Kincaid, D.K. (2015, February 17). The Sherlock Holmes conundrum, or the difference between deductive and inductive reasoning. *Medium*. Retrieved February 26, 2019 from: https://medium.com/@daniellekkincaid/the-sherlock-holmes-conundrum-or-the-difference-between-deductive-and-inductive-reasoning-ec1eb2686112.

Leighton, J.P. (2006). Teaching and assessing deductive reasoning skills. *The Journal of Experimental Education*, *74*(2), 109–136.

Lyne, J. (2005). Abductive reasoning. *Argumentation & Advocacy*, *42*(2), 114–116.

Melton, R.J. (1995). The role of positive affect in syllogism performance. *Personality & Social Psychology Bulletin*, *21*(8), 788–794, doi: 10.1177/0146167295218001.

Morsanyi, K. & Handley, S.J. (2012). Logic feels so good—I like it! Evidence for intuitive detection of logicality in syllogistic reasoning. *Journal of Experimental Psychology: Learning, Memory, and Cognition*, *38*(3), 596–616, doi:10.1037/a0026099.

Neilens, H.L., Handley, S.J. & Newstead, S.E. (2009). Effects of training and instruction on analytic and belief-based reasoning. *Thinking & Reasoning*, *15*(1), 37–68, doi: org/10.1080/13546780802535865.

Newstead, S.E., Handley, S.J., Harley, C., Wright, H. & Farrelly, D. (2004). Individual differences in deductive reasoning. *Quarterly Journal of Experimental Psychology Section A: Human Experimental Psychology*, *57*(1), 33–60, doi: org/10.1080/02724980343000116.

Parry, W.T. & Hacker, E.A. (1991). *Aristotelian logic*. Albany, NY: State University of New York.

Perkins, D.N. (2002). Standard logic as a model of reasoning: The empirical critique. In D.M. Gabbay, R.H. Johnson, H.J. Ohlbach, & J. Woods (Eds), *Handbook of the logic of argument and inference* (pp. 187–223). Amsterdam: Elsevier.

Radford, T. (2001, December 20). Scientists close in on world's funniest joke. *The Guardian*. Retrieved February 26, 2019 from: www.theguardian.com/uk/2001/dec/20/humanities.research.

Sankararaman, S., Patterson, N., Li, H., Pääbo, S. & Reich, D. (2012) The date of interbreeding between Neanderthals and modern humans. *PLoS Genetics*, 8(10), e1002947, doi:10.1371/journal.pgen.1002947.

Stanovich, K.E. (1999). *Who is rational? Studies of individual differences in reasoning*. Mahwah, NJ: Erlbaum.

Trimpe, M. (2011). The current status of GSR examinations. *FBI Law Enforcement Bulletin*, 80(5), 24–32.

Walton, D. (2005). *Abductive reasoning*. Tuscaloosa, AL: University of Alabama Press.

Chapter 12

Effective Advocacy and Refutation

It's one thing to read about how to argue and quite another thing to do it. Just as you can't learn to tango without hitting the dance floor, you can't hone your argumentation skills without engaging in some verbal scrimmages. Although we cannot provide you with practice, we can offer guidance on how to advance an effective, well-reasoned case, and, in turn, on how to refute an opponent's case. Before we get to the details, it's important to understand your responsibilities in a dispute. In the same way that people dancing the tango mustn't step on each other's feet, effective arguers must understand and follow their obligations in an argument.

Sorry to Burden You: Argumentative Obligations and Responsibilities

Burden of Proof and Presumption: I Demand Proof

If a friend claimed "Bigfoot is real," you'd most likely expect your friend to provide proof for the claim. In argumentation parlance, this standard is known as the *burden of proof*, which centers on *who has an obligation to prove something and to what degree of certainty he or she must prove it*. In this example, what would constitute sufficient proof that Bigfoot exists? If your buddy provided some eyewitness accounts and a fuzzy photo, would that suffice? What about a highway sign warning of Bigfoot crossings? (Figure 12.1.) How about an article in the prestigious journal *Nature*, announcing the discovery of a new human-like species, based on DNA evidence from hair fibers?

On the flip side of the coin, the concept of *presumption* suggests that an existing position is assumed to have merit and deserves preference until a better one comes along. That is, presumption favors the *status quo* or the existing order. In the example above, because your friend is advancing the claim, you would typically enjoy presumption or what has also been called "the preoccupation of argumentative ground" (Whately, 1963; Godden & Walton, 2007). As we'll see in a moment, however, the matter of who shoulders the burden of proof and who enjoys presumption is not always cut and dried. In some contexts, argumentative burdens are officially assigned, while in others, people themselves must argue about who must prove or disprove something and what constitutes sufficient proof. It is important to clarify these issues at the very outset. Otherwise, you might find yourself shouldering someone else's burden in an argument.

Figure 12.1 Bigfoot crossing sign. Shutterstock image: ID: 613014212.
Rudy Riva\shutterstock.com.

Burdens in Everyday Arguments: I Want Proof Positive

In ordinary informal arguments, no one is officially assigned the burden of proof or presumption. Nevertheless, an audience may have a psychological expectation of what the arguer's burden should be (Sproule, 1976). What's more, argumentation scholars agree that a basic social norm in everyday arguments is that *the person advancing a claim is obliged to support that claim* (Godden & Walton, 2007; Walton, 1988; van Eemeren & Grootendorst, 2004). For instance, if your close friend Olga said "I hate to be the one to tell you, but Chris is cheating on you," it would be reasonable to expect her to offer some form of proof. If Olga went on to say, "I saw Chris making out with that food server who works at the vegan restaurant," her eyewitness testimony might establish that Chris was a two-timer.

Prima Facie Case: The Opening Salvo

An advocate satisfies his or her initial burden of proof by presenting a *prima facie* case. Prima facie is Latin for "on its face" or "at first glance" and simply refers to an argument that stands on its own, absent any refutation. Generally speaking, an arguer who supports a claim with "good and sufficient reasons" has satisfied the initial burden of proof. Offering a prima facie case, however, doesn't end a discussion. It begins one. A prima facie case is one that is strong enough to merit a reply.

Legal Burdens: Reasonable Doubt

If you're familiar with the phrases "beyond a reasonable doubt" or "presumption of innocence," you already know something about the burden of proof and presumption in legal contexts. In a criminal trial in the U.S., the prosecution has the burden of proof. Specifically, the prosecution must demonstrate a defendant's guilt *beyond a reasonable doubt*. The defendant, on the other hand, enjoys a *presumption of innocence*. The defendant is presumed to be innocent until proven guilty. In other legal contexts, the burden of proof varies (see Box 12.1). For example, in a civil suit, the default standard is the *preponderance of evidence*. If the weight of the evidence favors the plaintiff, the plaintiff wins. If the weight of the evidence tilts toward the defendant's side, the defendant wins.

Box 12.1   Legal Standards of Proof

Beyond a reasonable doubt: The prosecution must prove its case so convincingly that a reasonable person would not question a defendant's guilt.	Criminal trials
Clear and convincing case: A plaintiff in a civil suit must provide evidence that is highly and substantially more likely to be true than false.	Fraud, wills, patent infringement, terminating life support, insanity pleas
Probable cause: Law enforcement must show there are facts and circumstances that would lead a reasonable person to believe a crime has been committed.	Arrest warrants, search and seizure cases, grand jury proceedings
Preponderance of evidence: A plaintiff must demonstrate that the balance of probabilities favors his/her side. If the plaintiff's case is more likely than not, the plaintiff prevails.	Civil suits, small claims court, child support cases
Reasonable suspicion: Law enforcement has the burden of proof, which requires a specific, identifiable rationale. A hunch or gut instinct does not suffice.	Traffic stops or brief detentions, frisking and pat downs, school searches such as lockers and backpacks

Burdens in Non-Legal Contexts: Stands to Reason

Outside the courtroom, other burdens of proof are in effect. In a case that is tried in the "court of public opinion," for example, there are no due process guarantees. Of course, journalists are supposed to fact-check claims, corroborate evidence, and rely on multiple independent sources, but bloggers, tweeters, and other media outlets are free to say or write whatever they choose, short of committing libel and slander.

In another context, NFL football, fans can scream their heads off over a referee's call, but the National Football League requires "incontrovertible visual evidence" for instant replay footage to overturn the call on the field. In other words, presumption lies with the initial ruling made on the field.

In social science research, results are said to be significant if they meet the $p < .05$ level of statistical significance. This entails a statistical burden of proof requiring researchers to be 95 percent confident that their findings are not due to chance before claiming to have found a significant result. A 5 percent margin of error is allowed. The presumption is that no claim of a relationship between variables can be made unless it can be demonstrated with 95 percent or greater confidence.

Shifting Burdens: I've Got Nothing to Prove

Although people advancing a claim are often expected to assume the burden of proof, there are cases where the burden might be shifted the other way round. A boss, for instance, may tell a subordinate, "Boswell, we're downsizing! Give me one good reason why I shouldn't fire you." The boss has shifted the burden of proof to Boswell, but the employee would be well-advised to come up with two or three reasons why he is essential to the company's operation.

As another example, not all nations adhere to the doctrine of presumed innocence. In many places across the globe, a prisoner is presumed guilty and subject to incarceration until proven innocent at trial. Of course, it is tough to prove one's innocence while behind bars. At present, roughly 3.3 million people are being held in detention worldwide (Open Societies Foundation, 2014, p. 1). Many are innocent and are eventually acquitted at trial (Open Societies Foundation, 2014, p. 11). Many others languish in jail for years before getting their day in court.

The burden of proof may also depend on the urgency of the situation. In an emergency room, for example, there might not be time to argue. Instead, quick, decisive action might be needed to save a patient's life. The same might apply in a disaster, where quick thinking rather than slow deliberation is required.

Misplaced Burdens: Prove Me Wrong

Sometimes arguers try to shirk their burden of proof. Suppose your neighbor, Vlad, said "Your dog dug up my roses." When you ask "How do you know?" Vlad replies, "Gut instinct." In this case, you might reasonably question whether a mere hunch was sufficient to support the allegation. But what if, instead, Vlad replies, "How do you know your mutt didn't dig up my roses?" Notice that he is attempting to reverse the burden of proof by asserting that *you* must prove his argument *false*. This particular fallacy, which was discussed in Chapter 9, is known as an *appeal to ignorance* (or, in Latin, *argumentum ad ignorantium*). Specifically, by asserting that something is true because it hasn't been proven false, Vlad is evading his burden of proof. If you're like most people, you have a fairly good sense of when someone has shifted the burden of proof illicitly (Ricco, 2011). In this case, you'd have every right to tell Vlad, "You're the one making the accusation. I'm willing to make amends, but I'm going to need to see some proof first."

Burden of Rebuttal: Get Ready to Rumble

Once one arguer satisfies the burden of proof, the other party is obliged to respond. This is known as the *burden of rebuttal* (sometimes referred to as the *burden of clash* or *burden of rejoinder*). Suppose a high school principal summons Jeter, a freshman, to her office. The principal declares "Drugs were found in your backpack. What have you got to say for yourself?" As you might imagine, the manner of rebuttal can take many forms. Jeter might say "That isn't my backpack," "Someone else planted the drugs there," or "Those medications are prescribed by my doctor." If Jeter could supply proof for any of these defenses, the burden of proof would revert back to the principal, then to Jeter, and so on.

In this way, an argument is like a tennis match, but with less grunting. One side serves the argumentative ball by meeting his or her burden of proof. The other side returns serve by rebutting the argument in play. The server is then obligated to clash with the rebuttal or lose the argumentative volley. As in tennis, arguers sometimes "whiff" the argumentative ball by completely missing the other side's argument.

Arguing about Arguing

A final point regarding argumentative burdens is worth noting. Arguing is an activity in which the rules themselves are subject to dispute, including who has the burden of proof and who has presumption. In an argument over the topic of abortion, for example, one party may claim presumption that human life begins at the moment of conception and a fetus is therefore a person. According to this view, the burden of proof would fall on a pro-choice advocate who favored "killing" an unborn "child." The other party, however, might claim that presumption favors a woman's reproductive freedom and that a fetus is not a person until it is viable, e.g., capable of surviving outside the womb. According to this view, the burden of proof would rest with the pro-life proponent who sought to deny a woman her reproductive rights. In Box 12.2, who do you think should be assigned the burden of proof in each controversy?

Box 12.2 In Each Scenario Below, Which Party Should Shoulder the Burden of Proof?

- A theist claims that God exists, while an atheist says there is no God. *Who should have the burden of proof? What if one is an agnostic?*
- As Trudy is about to leave a party, Mona warns her "You shouldn't be driving. You've had a lot to drink." Trudy says, "I'm fine." *Does Mona have to prove Trudy is drunk, or does Trudy have to prove she is sober?*
- A traveler has just returned from a country experiencing a disease outbreak. The traveler is asymptomatic, but government officials want to quarantine him or her out

of "an abundance of caution." *Does the government have to prove there is a risk of infection, or does the traveler have to prove she or he poses no risk?*

- A female employee complains to the human resources director that a male colleague is constantly ogling her, leering at her, and mentally undressing her with his eyes. When asked about this, the male employee says that he never looks at her in a sexualized way and that simply looking at someone doesn't constitute sexual harassment. *Which employee should have the burden of proof?*

Case Building: On Solid Ground

Once argumentative burdens have been established, it's time to make your case. But how do you know which arguments to make? Building and advancing a cogent well-reasoned case requires that you discover the best arguments and evidence available and that you match them to the type of claim, a topic we turn to next.

Invention: Discovering the Issues

The process of discovering arguments, known as *invention*, requires investigating a topic thoroughly. The term invention, however, is somewhat misleading. Ethical advocates don't "invent" their arguments out of thin air. Instead, *invention refers to the careful systematic discovery of key issues, arguments, and evidence surrounding a controversy*. In other words, invention requires more than simply using Google or Wikipedia. Discovering what arguments and evidence to present requires research using scholarly, scientific, or professional publications that are dependable, timely, and reliable. Invention also involves identifying credible sources with expertise on the subject. What's more, key arguments are always specific to a topic or issue and must take the audience into account. Arguments for or against a moratorium on capital punishment, for example, would probably resonate differently with members of Amnesty International than with supporters of Justice For All.

The key arguments that help build a case are always specific to a particular topic or issue. For example, the central issues involved in a debate over whether capital punishment should be abolished (e.g., deterrent effect, racial bias, cruel and unusual punishment) are not the same as the issues in deciding which car to buy (e.g., safety, reliability, mileage). The concerns surrounding a decision to send an aging parent to an assisted living facility are not the same as the concerns surrounding a new phone plan.

Stock Issues: Touching All the Bases

Considering that there are more controversial topics than pages in this book, we obviously cannot tell you all the relevant arguments on every controversial topic or issue. We can, however, suggest some common templates or *stock issues* that you can use for building a case. These stock issues are recurring and are based on the type of claim being made. In other words, they are featured explicitly or implicitly any time a claim of that type is advanced. In Chapter 5, we identified four types of claims: fact, value/judgment, policy, and definition. How you build your case depends on which type of claim you are making. With that in mind, let's examine each of these claims and their accompanying stock issues.

Policy Claims: Should I or Shouldn't I?

Policy disputes center on what course of action should be taken to solve a problem. Such disputes focus on three key stock issues known as significance, or the significance of a harm, inherency, or the underlying cause of a problem, and solvency, or the solution to the problem and any accompanying advantages. These three stock issues are sometimes referred to as *ill, blame,* and *cure.*

Significance: What's the Harm?

The stock issue of *significance*, or *harm* as it is sometimes called, focuses on negative consequences or an "ill" that needs to be cured. The emphasis is on who or what is being harmed by an existing policy or the *status quo*. To establish significance, a person advocating a change must prove that a problem is serious or pervasive. This could be done by demonstrating the quantity or severity of the harm. For example, an estimated 400,000 Americans die per year from preventable hospital errors (James, 2013). That is a staggering figure. As another example, the International Labor Organization (2012) estimates that "there are 20.9 million victims of human trafficking globally (para. 1)." Sheer numbers aren't all that matters, however. If only one person were being denied his or her constitutional rights or human rights that would be significant as well. The Supreme Court often upholds or overturns laws based on a single plaintiff's rights. What's more, the harm need not entail a human toll. Economic costs, environmental harms, and animal welfare are ills as well.

Inherency: What's the Cause or Who Is to Blame?

The stock issue of *inherency* focuses on the cause(s) of a problem or the barrier(s) to its solution. Because there are various kinds of obstacles to change, there are also different ways to demonstrate the inherent nature of a problem. Let's examine a few of these.

First, as its name implies, *structural inherency* refers to structural barriers that are "on the books." Examples include collective bargaining agreements, contracts, corporate policies, legal precedents, prenuptial agreements, religious doctrines, and other codified rules. By way of illustration, multiple states have legalized recreational marijuana use. However, inmates already serving prison time for nonviolent marijuana offenses under the old laws remain incarcerated. Why? The inherent barrier to releasing them is mandatory minimum sentences. Under the old laws, judges had no discretion when sentencing a person for selling pot. Some prisoners serving time for marijuana offenses received stiffer sentences than airplane hijackers and child pornographers (Mak, 2015). A number of states have begun reforming mandatory minimum sentencing laws so they are less draconian.

Second, *attitudinal inherency* focuses on attitudes or mindsets that pose barriers to change. Indeed, some attitudes are more entrenched than laws. For example, women are decidedly underrepresented in senior management positions in the corporate world, an obstacle known as the "glass ceiling." In 2018, only 24 women were CEOs of Fortune 500 companies. Laws don't necessarily prohibit females from ascending the corporate ladder, but pernicious stereotypes do. In fact, Joan Williams and Rachel Dempsey (2014) argue that negative stereotypes about women in management positions are so ingrained that they prevent women from upward mobility in the business world.

A third means of demonstrating the source of harm is existential in nature. Specifically, *existential inherency* posits that the existence and persistence of a harm speaks to its inherent nature. That is, if there is a problem and it doesn't go away, there must be a reason why. For instance, one might argue that the ongoing rash of African-American shootings by police officers demonstrates that something is wrong with police departments across the country. In Ferguson, Missouri, for example, violent protests took place after a white officer shot an unarmed black man. A Department of Justice report (2015) found that in Ferguson, "Nearly 90% of documented force used by FPD officers was used against African Americans. In every canine bite incident for which racial information is available, the person bitten was African American" (p. 5).

Solvency: The Best Laid Plans

A final stock issue for policy propositions is *solvency*, which focuses on whether there is a workable solution to the problem. To illustrate, imagine that sewage has been leaking into your city's drinking water supply for months. When you shower, wash dishes, or brush your teeth, the smell is repulsive. "Not to worry," your mayor declares, "free cans of air freshener will be distributed to every household." Problem solved? Of course not! The mayor's solution treats the symptom, e.g., the smell, not the problem, which is the seepage.

As this example illustrates, an advocate for a policy change—in this case, the mayor—must propose an efficacious plan of action. You, on the other hand, could show that the plan is not workable or effective in solving the problem. Not only that, you could argue that the plan might be circumvented or thwarted by those who oppose the policy change.

COMPARATIVE ADVANTAGE: MORE PROS THAN CONS

Related to the stock issue of solvency is the concept of *comparative advantages*. A plan of action needn't be perfect. It may have some flaws or drawbacks. Overall, though, the advantages of enacting the policy change must outweigh the disadvantages. A balancing test may be used to weigh the pros and cons of a proposed policy change. An opponent of change would, of course, argue that the negative effects of the plan would outweigh any good it might achieve. Using an illness metaphor, for example, an opponent might argue that the cure was worse than the disease.

Value Claims: The Good, the Bad, and the Ugly

Given a choice, would you rather work outdoors with your hands or indoors on a computer? Are there some causes you would die for and others for which you wouldn't lift a finger? Issues about which people feel strongly are often rooted in their value systems. When one person's values, principles, or standards are at odds with another's, a value argument may ensue.

Value disputes may center on *moral or ethical issues* such as what is right or wrong, good or bad, fair or unfair, and kind or cruel. They also may focus on *aesthetic* issues. Aesthetic values involve matters of taste; whether something evokes pleasure or displeasure, is beautiful or ugly, in good or bad taste, or is classy or vulgar. Some tastes are purely subjective. If Bubba prefers chocolate and Babbs prefers vanilla, there isn't much point in arguing. That said, in our view, when value disputes arise, people are too quick to trot out the old chestnut, "I guess we'll just have to agree to disagree." The conversation below illustrates this tendency.

Lola: "Paparazzi are slimeballs. They make their living stalking celebrities and invading privacy."
Norm: "But celebrities are public figures. Fame has its price."
Lola: "I guess we will just have to agree to disagree then."

In our view, Lola and Norm are being intellectually lazy. Agreeing to disagree may shorten the argument, but it doesn't resolve the issue. By continuing to wrestle with ideas, people may clarify what is really at issue and find a way to resolve, or at least manage, their differences. What if Lola and Norm had pursued the argument further?

Lola: "Celebrities are public figures, but not government officials or public servants. What public interest is being served by hounding a celebrity leaving a restaurant or stalking a celebrity on vacation?"
Norm: "The sidewalk outside a restaurant is still a public place. So are public beaches if that's where celebs are vacationing."
Lola: "But paparazzi use long-distance lenses and drones to take photos on private property."
Norm: "In that case, there are laws against trespassing. Paparazzi can be prosecuted for trespassing."
Lola: "So we agree that celebrities are entitled to privacy on their own property. You just believe existing laws are sufficient to regulate such violations."
Norm: "Pretty much. Drones are new, so the government needs to clarify where they're permitted to fly."

By continuing to argue, Lola and Norm manage to reach an accord of sorts. They agree that privacy is more important in some places than others, and that new technology may require laws to be revised. In fact, laws in some states, like California, already ban the use of long-distance lenses and drones to photograph celebrities on private property (Megerian, 2015).

Values and Policies Are Close Cousins

Value and policy disputes are not separate and distinct. They are intertwined. Holding a particular value, such as the belief that capital punishment is immoral, also carries with it a policy implication, e.g., that capital punishment should be abolished. Similarly, favoring a policy, such as wealth redistribution, entails certain values, such as the importance of social justice.

Types of Value Disputes

Contradictory Values: You Can't Have It Both Ways

A vegan and a steak lover walk into a restaurant. Can they agree on anything to eat? The vegan may believe that "eating meat is murder," while the steak lover may believe "beef is delicious."

Sometimes people are at loggerheads, or at least appear to be. Still, it may be possible to find common ground. If the vegan's objection is primarily moral—e.g., eating meat makes animals suffer—would eating oysters or mussels be acceptable (some vegans eat them)? How about roadkill? Or synthetic meat grown in a laboratory, which may one day be commercially viable (Ferdman, 2015; Zaraska, 2016)? Admittedly, these examples are on the fringe, but they demonstrate that people's values may not be as far apart as they believe.

On the other hand, sometimes values are truly at odds, requiring us to roll up our sleeves and argue for the merits of our viewpoints. For example, consider Edward Snowden, the former CIA employee who leaked classified government information over the internet. While one person might view Snowden as a hero who sacrificed his career to expose the U.S. government's surveillance of its citizens, another might view him as a traitor who harmed U.S. national security. When people hold such seemingly irreconcilable views, should they avoid arguing? We suggest that they can still have constructive arguments that clarify the basis of their disagreement. The two sides might not be any closer together, but each would have a better understanding of the other's reasons.

Value Hierarchy: Whose Value Is More Valuable?

If you had to give up one of your senses, vision, hearing, taste, smell, or touch, which would it be? All of our senses are precious, but which do you prize most? Sometimes value disputes involve ranking what is valued more and less. Indeed, even when people share values, they may disagree over the importance of one value over another. In such cases, they tend to argue for the primacy of one value compared with another. For example, the courts have consistently held that political free speech, e.g., that which deals with public policy issues, enjoys more protection than commercial speech, which involves advertising goods and services.

What's more, a person can argue for the primacy of one value by arguing that it is necessary or essential to realize other values. With respect to the Bill of Rights, a person might argue that the 1st amendment is preeminent because, without free speech, you couldn't voice objections to infringements on your other rights. A strong case also could be made for the 13th amendment, which abolished slavery. After all, if people are regarded as property, they have no rights. Many would argue that the right to bear arms, provided by the 2nd amendment, is the most important because firearms offer physical protection against the violation of other rights.

Value Balancing: More of One, Less of the Other

Another type of value dispute tries to strike a balance between values by focusing on how much weight or importance to assign one value over another. Think of this as a discussion about how to divvy up a pie. Which value deserves a larger slice of the pie and which deserves a smaller one? By way of example, some people value pristine wilderness areas and argue in favor of preserving lands for future generations. Others value recreation and argue for limited access to wilderness areas for hiking, camping, fishing, biking, and so forth. Still others see commercial value in wilderness areas and argue in favor of logging and mining to create jobs and promote economic growth. Of course, advocates for each position argue that their value deserves a bigger slice of the "wilderness pie." Ultimately, a government agency, the congress, or the courts might decide how best to strike a balance between these competing values.

Instrumental and Terminal Values: Ends vs Means

Another approach to value disputes focuses on what's more important, *ends or means*. To clarify, Milton Rokeach (1973) differentiated between *terminal* values, which are desirable end states in and of themselves, and *instrumental* values, which help achieve a goal or objective. Having good health, for example, is a terminal value for most people. To maintain or achieve good health, a person might exercise regularly, adopt good nutrition habits, avoid smoking and drinking, and diet periodically. These are instrumental values that contribute to the terminal value of enjoying good health. Other terminal values include happiness, freedom, friendship, wisdom, salvation, or less lofty goals such as learning to play guitar or taking up ballroom dancing. Other instrumental values include having basic food and shelter, having access to medical care, saving for retirement, or just having reliable transportation.

If you guessed that terminal values are generally considered superior to instrumental ones, you are on the right track. Indeed, making an instrumental value more important than a terminal value, one could argue, is akin to "letting the tail wag the dog." For instance, when trying to balance work life and family life, a couple might discuss whether it is better for one partner to turn down a promotion and pay raise to spend more quality time with the family. As a means to an end, work may be valued less highly than family time, which is an end in and of itself.

Simple enough. But what if people clash over two terminal values? Supreme Court judges, for example, often grapple with competing values such as the public's right to know versus an individual's right to privacy. Likewise, value disputes might focus on competing instrumental values. As an illustration, wildlife conservationists differ over the best strategy for protecting endangered African rhinoceroses (rhinoprotect.org). Poachers kill rhinos for their horns, which fetch hefty sums on the black market. Some conservationists have proposed legalizing the sale of rhino horns. Rhinos could be raised on ranches. Their horns could be removed safely without harming the animals. The horns could then be sold for a profit. Another approach is to dehorn rhinos in the wild. Game wardens could remove their horns, thereby removing the incentive for killing the animals. Still others have recommended injecting rhino horns with colored dye, a procedure that is harmless to the animal, but makes their horns less valuable and more visible to x-ray scanners. Some have even called for injecting poison into rhino horns, which would make them unfit for human consumption. All wildlife conservationists agree on the end goal of saving rhinos from extinction. They disagree on the means for accomplishing the goal.

Finally, whether a value should be considered instrumental or terminal is, itself, arguable. One could argue that getting a college degree is a means to an end; landing a good job. One could also argue that a college education has intrinsic value; knowledge is its own reward. In addition, what one person perceives as an instrumental value, another person may see as a terminal value. For example, one person might value hard work, determination, and perseverance as a means to an end. All that hard work should pay off. Another person may view a strong work ethic as an end in itself; a character strength or measure of a person's moral fiber.

Value Consistency: Waver Not

The last type of value dispute centers on the consistency of values. A person may argue that holding a particular value is consistent with a personal or societal value system or that values are being applied inconsistently. Imagine, for instance, that Jane and Doyle are discussing Doyle's penchant for downloading movies for free on the internet.

Jane: "I know you've seen the anti-piracy ads. You wouldn't steal a car. You wouldn't steal a purse. Downloading pirated movies is stealing too."

Doyle: "The situations aren't the same. If I steal a stranger's car, I deprive the stranger of his or her car. If I download a movie, I don't deprive another person of the movie."

Jane: "No, but you deprive the filmmakers of their royalties and maybe even the cast and crew of their jobs."

Doyle: "I think the movie industry is doing pretty well. They don't need my money to survive."

Jane: "By that reasoning, it would be okay to steal a rich person's car, because she or he owned other cars or could afford to buy a new one."

In this dispute, Jane suggests that if stealing personal property is wrong, then stealing intellectual property is equally wrong. Jane is pointing out an inconsistency in Doyle's values because both forms of theft negatively impact others.

One might ask why holding consistent values even matters. Consistency in one's value system makes one's actions more predictable to oneself and to others. In Western culture, consistency also tends to be equated with rationality. A person whose values are inconsistent may be viewed as erratic, two-faced, fickle, or unreliable.

How to Build a Value Case

Now that you understand the different types of value disputes and that people can argue rationally about values, let's examine three basic stock issues for building a value case.

Clearly Defining the Value

First, it's important to *clearly define the value*. Indeed, values can be vague or nebulous. People may agree on a value at a high level of abstraction, but not see eye to eye when it comes to specifics. For example, most people embrace the importance of "family values." Yet people may not share the same concept of "family" (Edwards, McCarthy & Gillies, 2012; Weigel, 2008). Television shows, such as *The Brady Bunch, The Simpsons, Modern Family,* and *The Sopranos,* feature different constructs of family.

Clearly defining a value at the outset avoids confusion. Consider the debate over assisted suicide and end-of-life issues. One person may believe that assisted suicide is morally justified, while another may believe it is not. But what exactly is meant by the term "assisted suicide"? Does the advocate favor an active approach, such as administering a prescription drug to hasten a person's death, or a passive approach such as not resuscitating a person or withholding extraordinary live-saving measures? Does the advocate favor assisted suicide only for those who are terminally ill or for those with non-life-threatening conditions as well? Defining the specific circumstances under which an advocate favors assisted suicide is crucial to a meaningful discussion. No matter what the topic or issue is, then, clearly defining the nature and scope of the value is important.

Identifying Value Criteria

The second stock issue in building a value case is to *identify value criteria* or standards for evaluating the value in question. Returning to the above example, why is assisted suicide justified under the circumstances described? One criterion that favors assisted suicide is to limit pain and suffering. An advocate might argue that there is no justification for prolonging the agony of a person who is in excruciating pain. A second criterion that supports assisted suicide might center on the concept of death with dignity. An advocate might argue that a terminally ill person should have the right to die while in a sound state of mind rather than deteriorate into a comatose or vegetative state. A third criterion might involve personal autonomy or the "right to die." An advocate might maintain that a premium should be placed on the right of a terminally ill person to control his or her own body by choosing the time and place of his or her own death. In this case, then, the value of assisted suicide would be justified on the basis of the three criteria. Of course, the importance of establishing criteria to weigh or judge the value applies to other topics and issues as well.

Applying the Criteria

The final stock issue in building a value case is to apply the criteria to the value in question. With respect to the first criterion, relieving pain and suffering, an advocate could argue that assisted suicide is a compassionate response, not a malevolent one. The purpose is not to kill the patient, but to end suffering. In some cases, the only way to end pain is to hasten death. There is little value in prolonging someone's life if it is a life spent in agony.

Turning to the second criteria, death with dignity, an advocate might argue that terminally ill patients are entitled to end their lives before they become helpless, feeble, and pathetic. Drugs may alleviate pain, but leave the patient in a stupor, unable to think, communicate, or make decisions for him or herself. As Gentzler (2003) put it "death with dignity is more properly described as a life with dignity until its very end" (p. 462).

In applying the third criterion, the right-to-die advocate could argue that personal autonomy includes the right to make decisions about end-of-life issues. The right of self-determination should apply equally to a person's choices about life as well as death.

Factual Claims: Just the Facts, Ma'am

Comedian Stephen Colbert once coined the term "truthiness" to refer to knowledge claims that people believe, not because they are true, but because they want them to be true. But, as we saw in Chapter 5, factual claims are empirically verifiable. Thus, if several people are arguing over a fact, at least one of them is wrong. Some arguers view facts as nuisances to be ignored or swatted away. In many cases, however, the facts are clearly on one side of an issue. Denying those facts doesn't change them or make them go away. For example, the claim that "15 of the 16 warmest years on record have occurred since 2001" is empirically verifiable (Galimberti, 2016, para. 1; NASA, 2016). That doesn't necessarily prove that climate change is occurring, but it does prove that it's been hot lately.

Box 12.3   Fact-Checking: Don't Bother Me with Facts, I've Already Made Up My Mind

Thanks to the internet, answers to many factual questions are just a few mouse clicks away. How many Oscars has Meryl Streep won? Consult IMDB. Has sharia law been adopted in any U.S. cities? Check Snopes.com. Is Angelina Jolie feuding with Amal Clooney? See what GossipCop.com has to say. There are now more than 100 fact-checking outlets (Adair, 2016). Some of the most useful ones in the U.S. and abroad are listed in Chapter 5 and Chapter 6 (Box 6.2).

Even the fact-checkers, however, can get it wrong from time to time (Mantzarlis, 2015). There have also been accusations that the fact-checkers themselves harbor biases (Hemingway, 2011; Marietta, Barker & Bowser, 2015).

The Backfire Effect: Facts Are Stubborn Things

Suppose your roommate, Wilma, believes that camels store water in their humps. You cite a zoologist who states that is patently false. A camel's humps are mostly fat. Having presented Wilma with factual evidence refuting her belief, will she change her mind? Not necessarily. That's because presenting a person with corrective information can result in what is called the *backfire effect* (Nyhan & Reifler, 2010). Rather than changing her mistaken belief, Wilma's belief may become even more entrenched. Worse yet, people are more likely to remember false statements as true, than true statements as false (Peter & Koch, 2016).

Why do people dig in? First, it is easier to remember a false fact than to remember how the fact was learned in the first place. This is one reason urban myths spread so easily. Second, repeated exposure to a falsehood makes it seem truer. If Wilma repeatedly heard that camels' humps were water reservoirs, she might be more likely to accept it as fact. Third, in the case of closely held beliefs, the prospect of changing one's mind evokes cognitive dissonance. It is psychologically more comfortable to double-down on one's beliefs than to change them.

How can you counteract the backfire effect? The most effective strategy is to expose a false fact immediately. If people are asked to make an immediate determination about whether a fact is true or false, they are less likely to misremember it later (Lewandowsky, Ecker, Seifert, Schwarz & Cook, 2012). Once stored in memory, false beliefs are harder to eradicate. Inadmissible testimony, for example, is more likely to be discounted by jurors if a judge immediately admonishes them to ignore the evidence. This lends support to the view that news outlets should employ real-time fact-checking for evolving stories as they unfold and during political debates as claims are made (Reider, 2016). Some networks are already inserting fact-checking into chyrons (the scrolling text at the bottom of a screen).

For false facts that are stored in memory, your best approach is to ask people how they actually know something is a fact. You might say, "I'm curious, how do you know that?" or "How can I find that information?" If people cannot remember how they know something, you can follow up by mentioning, "If your memory is faulty, is there a chance the fact is wrong too?"

How to Build a Factual Case

Suppose that a factual dispute cannot be resolved with a quick online search. How should you go about advancing a factual claim? Here are four stock issues for demonstrating that a factual claim is true or false.

Source Qualifications: Consider the Source

The first method is to rely on a highly qualified authority, preferably one respected by all the parties involved in a dispute. If your aunt Clara says that toilets flush clockwise in the northern hemisphere and counter-clockwise in the southern hemisphere, ask who is the source of her information. If she says "I heard it on an episode of *The Simpsons*, titled 'Bart vs Australia'," you might reply "I like the Simpsons too, but not as a source of scientific information. No less an expert than Neil DeGrasse Tyson says that toilets flush in whatever direction they are designed to, no matter the hemisphere (Figure 12.2).

An expert's opinion trumps that of someone who says "I heard somewhere that . . .," which is more common than you might think. In presidential elections, for example, candidates are fond of saying "I'm hearing that . . ." or "People are saying . . ." without questioning the reliability of the source. You can counter such arguments by responding "You seem to be dressing a rumor up as a fact. I've heard the Loch Ness Monster is real, but I know better than to accept it as fact."

For many factual disputes, Wikipedia may be an acceptable source, especially if the stakes are low. As we noted in Chapter 6, however, Wikipedia relies on the "wisdom of the commons." In other words, anyone can add or edit material there. If the stakes are high and accuracy matters, expert sources, speaking within their field of expertise, are preferred. In a dispute over voter ID laws, for instance, if your pal, Grady, is citing Richard L. Hansen, a renowned expert on election laws, and Joyce is citing a chain email that her uncle forwarded, Grady should prevail.

Neil deGrasse Tyson ✔
@neiltyson

(Follow) ⌄

Toilet Bowls drain however they're designed to circulate water. It's irrelevant whether you live above or below the equator.

8:16 AM - 19 Sep 2014

1,730 Retweets **2,101** Likes

Figure 12.2 Tweet from Neil DeGrasse Tyson, September 19, 2014.
Twitter.com.

Scientific Studies: She Blinded Me with Science

A second stock method for advancing a factual claim is to cite a scientific study, clinical trial, or other empirical finding. Scientific studies carry considerable argumentative weight. As Funk and Rainie (2015) noted:

> science holds an esteemed place among citizens and professionals. Americans recognize the accomplishments of scientists in key fields and, despite considerable dispute about the role of government in other realms, there is broad public support for government investment in scientific research. (para. 2)

That said, not all arguers possess scientific literacy, e.g., the ability to understand basic scientific concepts as they apply to everyday life. What's more, some people are less enamored with science than others, especially on politically charged issues such as climate change, childhood vaccinations, and genetically modified foods. Nevertheless, "scientists continue to hold enormous clout with the public" even on controversial topics such as climate change (Cooper, 2011, p. 231).

How the public perceives scientific studies depends, in part, on how those studies are reported. Few laypersons read original research first-hand. Even then, they may rely on little more than an abstract (*PLOS Medicine* Editors, 2013). Most people's knowledge of scientific studies is filtered through the media, which often gets it wrong (Gonon, Konsman, Cohen & Boraud, 2012). When citing a study, then, it's important to provide information not only about the researcher's qualifications, but also about how the study was conducted. Even a modicum of information about a study's methodology can assuage doubts about its conclusions.

Bear in mind that not all scientific studies are equally good. Not all studies use random assignment of participants to treatment and control groups. Not all studies use a "double-blind" procedure, in which the participants and the experimenter are unaware of the conditions to which they've been assigned. Other factors such as sample size, validity of the measures, and control over confounding variables matter too. Unfortunately, news media aren't particularly good at reporting scientific findings to the public (Pew Research Center, 2015). Worse yet, the results of scientific studies can be manipulated, distorted, or politicized. Thus, when evaluating a study's merits, it's important that you verify the researcher's conclusions and not someone else's spin. Generally speaking, the best way to contest a scientific study is by providing a better scientific study.

Surveys and Polls: So Glad You Asked

Using public surveys and opinion polls is a third stock method of building a factual case, but you need to be careful. Indeed, people's *perceptions* can bias the way they process information. For example, if you ask Americans what percentage of the U.S. population is Muslim, they tend to guess around 15 percent when the real answer is one percent (Ipsos MORI, 2014). Liberals harbor misconceptions too, on topics such as nuclear power and fracking (Nisbet, Cooper & Garrett, 2015).

When assessing a public opinion poll, some key questions to ask include:

- Who conducted the poll and is there potential source bias?
- How was the poll conducted? A phone survey may yield different results than an online survey, a mail survey, or an in-person survey. The greater the anonymity of respondents, the less risk of *social desirability bias*, or the tendency to give a politically correct answer.

- What specific questions were asked? The wording of questions plays an important role as does the order of the questions.
- What was the sample size? A sample of as few as 1,200–1,500 people is sufficient for national polling if the sample is truly random.
- Were respondents selected at random? If, on the other hand, a pollster selected only senior citizens to survey, it might bias the representativeness of the sample.
- Is the *margin of error* reported in the results? Be suspicious of any poll that doesn't state the margin of error or what is called *sampling error* by statisticians. For most national polls, a margin of error of 3–5 percent is considered acceptable.

Finally, when relying on polling data, keep in mind that a single poll only provides a snapshot of opinion at a single point in time. To find out what people really think, look for multiple polls taken over an extended period.

Demonstration: This I Gotta See

A fourth stock method for supporting a factual claim is via an actual demonstration. If your friend, Wally, says "I can hold my breath under water for three minutes," you can offer to accompany him to a pool, bathtub, or fish aquarium so he can demonstrate the feat. Likewise, it is not unusual for job applicants to be asked to demonstrate specific skills, such as speaking a foreign language or working with Excel files, to verify claims made on their resumes.

Proving a fact by demonstrating it has appeal. It is harder to remain skeptical when you've witnessed something first-hand. Seeing, however, does not always warrant believing. One of the authors, for example, saw the magicians Penn and Teller turn pennies into goldfish. And who hasn't watched infomercial spokespersons hawking their wares by providing product demonstrations? As convincing as they seem, do you really believe you will develop rock-hard abs in only a few minutes a day or that an herbal supplement will melt pounds away?

In 2016, the rapper B.o.B sent a flurry of tweets claiming the Earth was flat. His proof? He'd seen it with his own eyes (Figure 12.3).

↻ You Retweeted

B.o.B ✓
@bobatl

No matter how high in elevation you are...
the horizon is always eye level ... sorry
cadets... I didn't wanna believe it either.

25/01/2016, 00:48

275 RETWEETS **245** LIKES

Figure 12.3 Tweet by the rapper B.o.B, January 24, 2016.
Twitter.com.

His claim is demonstrably false, however. As Schottlender noted in *Popular Science* magazine (2016), there are a number of simple ways to prove the Earth is round. For example, during a lunar eclipse, when the Earth shades the Moon from the Sun, the shadow cast by the Earth on the Moon is curved, not straight. You can see this for yourself if you shine a flashlight (serving as the Sun) at a basketball (standing in as the Earth) with a tennis ball (playing the Moon) behind it. You can also watch demonstrations of this on YouTube.

Definitional Claims: War of Words

Suppose that Rachel, who loves playing videogames, and her friend Joey, who enjoys playing Texas hold 'em, engage in the following argument.

Rachel: "E-sports, like *League of Legends*, should be considered legitimate sports."

Joey: "I say nay. A virtual sport is not a real sport."

Rachel: "In e-sports, there's competition between teams. Physical skill, such as eye–hand coordination, is required. Competitions draw huge crowds. There's even a world championship."

Joey: "Since when do competition and large crowds define a sport? The World Series of Poker draws large crowds. It's even broadcast on ESPN!"

Rachel: "There's a difference though. Poker requires mental skill, not physical skill."

Joey: "Au contraire. Poker requires stamina. Furthermore, controlling one's nonverbal cues to prevent 'tells' is a physical skill."

Rachel: "The stamina required for poker is more mental than physical. As for remaining stone-faced, it may be a skill, but it is hardly an athletic skill."

Rachel and Joey are arguing about what constitutes a "sport." Theirs is a definitional dispute. Although not as common as policy and value disputes, people also disagree on definitions of terms and concepts. Definitional disputes are often part of a larger debate over value or policy. Such controversies center on how to define a concept (e.g., "Is a hot dog a sandwich?"), how best to categorize something ("waterboarding is a form of torture"), or how to classify an action or behavior ("I didn't steal the car, officer, I borrowed it"). Some examples of definitional issues appear below.

- What distinguishes an electric bicycle, or e-bike, from a motor scooter or a motorcycle?
- What is the difference between a companion animal and a pet?
- Is Beyoncé a pop singer, rap/hip-hop artist, or R&B performer? Does it matter that nearly all of her Grammy wins are in the R&B category?
- What is the difference between an assault weapon and a hunting rifle? Are gun-control advocates conflating "semi-assault weapons" with automatic weapons, such as machine guns?
- What qualifies a film as a "documentary"? Movies that are "based on a true story" or "inspired by real events" aren't necessarily documentaries.

Building a Definitional Case: More Than Semantic Quibbling

The Dictionary Dilemma

There are a variety of ways to construct a definitional argument. A standard dictionary definition is a good place to begin. Dictionary definitions are not without their limitations, however. Dictionary definitions are based on common usage (i.e., the definitions are gleaned from recurring real-world use of terms). Language evolves. It takes time for dictionaries to adapt. Consider the meaning of the word "gay." In the traditional Christmas tune *Deck the Halls*, the phrase "Don we now our gay apparel," or the lyrics to the *Flintstones'* theme song, "We'll have a gay old time," the word "gay" had a different meaning than in modern-day parlance.

In addition to changes in meaning, it takes time for new words to find their way into a dictionary. The term "cisgender," or sometimes just "cis," to refer to straight people is an example. So are the terms "woke," "gig economy," and "microaggression." Culture bias may be lurking in the definitions of terms such as "marriage" or "racism" (Caplan-Bricker, 2016; Hoyt, 2012). As McKean (2009) cautions, "despite all the thought and work that go into them, definitions, surprisingly, turn out to be ill-suited for many of the tasks they have been set to—including their ostensible purpose of telling you the meaning of a word" (p. 16).

Advancing a Definition: Bright Lines or Blurry Boundaries?

Sometimes it is possible to draw a clear line between the meaning of two terms or concepts. Sometimes the dividing line is blurry. For example, imagine that two people are arguing about whether "human trafficking" is synonymous with "modern slavery" or distinct from "human smuggling"? What similarities do these terms share? What differences? Even experts disagree on the meaning of these terms (Crosset, 1997; Jansson, 2014; Siller, 2016; Weitzer, 2015). The way terms are defined shapes our perceptions of, and reactions to, them. With this in mind, we look at two stock issues for advancing a definition.

Identifying Definitional Criteria

The first stock issue for defining a term is to *identify definitional criteria*. Definitional criteria are the key questions or issues surrounding the term in question. For example, in formulating a definition of "human trafficking," as distinct from "modern slavery" or "human smuggling," one might employ the following criteria, which we highlight below.

- Human trafficking involves recruiting and exploiting people illegally. That is, *exploitation* is the essence of the crime. According to Siller (2016) "trafficking criminalizes the process of acquiring a person for their exploitation" (p. 407).
- Human smuggling, on the other hand, involves *moving people across borders* illegally. In this regard, Pierce (2014) emphasized that "smugglers always move migrants across national borders . . . In fact, the UNODC estimates that approximately one quarter of human trafficking victims are exploited within their country of origin" (para. 5).
- In contrast, slavery refers to a person as being *owned by*, or the *property of*, another, whether the person is relocated or not. As Paz-Fuchs (2016) observes, "the core concept of slavery and the contemporary revulsion from it, is strongly associated with the idea than one individual can *own* another" (p. 764).
- Human trafficking, in contrast to human smuggling, is *involuntary*, taking place without the victim's consent. As Richmond (2015) notes, "often, individuals pay significant amounts to smugglers to help them cross a border because they desire to be transported into the

country. In contrast, human trafficking by definition is always involuntary because it occurs by prohibited coercive means" (p. 21).

- Finally, human trafficking involves some form of *coercion, force, deception,* or *fraud.* According to Hume and Sidun (2017), "both the UN and the U.S. definitions emphasize that traffickers use some means (e.g., force, fraud, coercion, abuse of a position of authority) to exploit individuals for commercial gain" (pp. 8–9).

These criteria—illegally exploiting people, against their will, but not necessarily transporting them, or owning them, while using force or coercion—form the basis of a reasonable definition of human trafficking.

Applying Definitional Criteria

The second stock issue for advocating a definition is to *apply the definitional criteria.* This involves incorporating the criteria you've identified into a workable definition. To illustrate, the United Nations' definition of human trafficking, known as the Palermo Protocol (2000), happens to incorporate many of the same criteria we just identified. Specifically, it argues that trafficking in persons involves:

> the threat or use of force or other forms of coercion, of abduction, of fraud, of deception, of the abuse of power or of a position of vulnerability or of the giving or receiving of payments or benefits to achieve the consent of a person having control over another person, for the purpose of exploitation. (article 3-a)

Some would take issue with this definition, arguing that human trafficking is a form of modern slavery (Leary, 2015). Nevertheless, the criteria provided above would establish a *prima facie* case for a definition of human trafficking.

Refuting a Definitional Argument

Suppose that you are not advancing a definition, but rather refuting an opponent's definition. To do so, you have three basic options available. First, you can dispute your opponent's definitional criteria. You might, for example, revise the criteria offered. Second, you can contend that the definition offered does not satisfy its own criteria. That is, the definition is inconsistent with one or more of the criteria presented. Third, you can offer an alternative definition altogether. To illustrate how this might work, let's return to our earlier example involving Rachel and Joey: Does *League of Legends*, a popular multi-player fantasy game, meet the requirements for a "real" sport? Lagaert and Roose (2014) offer the following definition of a sport.

> the normal English meaning of 'sport' requires: (1) the application of some significant element of physical activity; (2) that such physical activity is itself an aim, or that it will have a direct effect on the outcome of the activity; and (3) that physical skill – of which mental skill may be a part, and which includes physical endurance – is important to the outcome. To our minds sport normally connotes a game with an athletic element rather than simply a game. (p. 485)

To counter Rachel's position that *League of Legends* qualifies as a sport, Joey could show that it fails to meet at least one of these definitional criteria. For example, he could acknowledge that videogames require limited physical skills, but that pressing buttons with one's thumbs does not constitute "a significant element of physical activity" as the definition requires.

Second, Joey could argue that unlike high jumping or gymnastics, in which the "physical activity is itself an aim," operating the controller in an e-sport is *only a means to an end*. The end is manipulating a virtual character or object.

Third, Joey could also introduce an alternative definition. For example, ESPN shows some e-sports on their network, but ESPN's president John Skipper said "It's not a sport—it's a competition. Chess is a competition. Checkers is a competition" (cited by Tassi, 2014, para. 2).

Summary and Conclusion

In this chapter we examined arguer's burdens, including the concepts of burden of proof, presumption, prima facie case, and burden of rebuttal. Argumentative burdens vary from field to field. In everyday arguments, the person making a claim has the burden of proof to support that claim. Arguers may attempt to shift the burden of proof unfairly, a fallacy known as appeal to ignorance. Invention is the process of discovering the available arguments and evidence to advance or refute a claim. There are stock issues for advancing different kinds of claims; policy, value or judgment, definition, and fact.

References

Adair, B. (2016, August 15). It's time to fact-check all the news. *Poynter.com*. Retrieved on August 27, 2016 from: www.poynter.org/2016/its-time-to-fact-check-all-the-news/426261.

Caplan-Bricker, N. (2016, February 23). Should dictionaries do more to confront sexism? *The New Yorker*. Retrieved August 21, 2018 from: www.newyorker.com/books/page-turner/should-dictionaries-do-more-to-confront-sexism.

Cooper, C.B. (2011). Media literacy is a key strategy toward improving public acceptance of climate change. *BioScience*, *61*(3), 231–237, doi: 10.1525/bio.2011.61.3.8.

Crosset, N. (1997, July 27). What modern slavery is, and isn't. *New York Times*, pp. 400–401. Accessed via Proquest, retrieved from: http://search.proquest.com/docview/430815996?accountid=9840.

Department of Justice, Civil Rights Division (2015, March 4). *Investigation of the Ferguson Police Department*. Retrieved August 21, 2018 from: www.justice.gov/sites/default/files/opa/press-releases/attachments/2015/03/04/ferguson_police_department_report.pdf.

Edwards, R., McCarthy, J. & Gillies, V. (2012). The politics of concepts: Family and its (putative) replacements. *British Journal of Sociology*, *63*(4), 730–746, doi.org/10.1111/j.1468-4446.2012.01434.x.

Ferdman, R. (2015, May 20). This is the future of meat. *Washington Post*. Retrieved on August 10, 2018 from: www.washingtonpost.com/news/wonk/wp/2015/05/20/meet-the-future-of-meat-a-10-lab-grown-hamburger-that-tastes-as-good-as-the-real-thing/?utm_term=.585ff32c3fdc.

Funk, C. & Rainie, L. (2015, January 29). *Public and scientists' views on science and society*. Washington, DC: Pew Research Center. Retrieved on September 2, 2016 from: www.pewinternet.org/2015/01/29/public-and-scientists-views-on-science-and-society.

Galimberti, K. (2016, January 25). *2015 shatters record for warmest year globally by largest margin yet*. State College, PA: Accuweather.com. Retrieved on September 21, 2016 from: www.accuweather.com/en/weather-news/2015-shatters-warmest-year-on-record-global-temperature-noaa-nasa/54892807.

Gentzler, J. (2003). What is a death with dignity? *Journal of Medicine and Philosophy*, *28*(4), 461–487, doi: 10.1076/jmep.28.4.461.15968.

Godden, D.M. & Walton, D. (2007). A theory of presumption for everyday argumentation. *Pragmatics and Cognition*, *15*(2), 313–346, doi: 10.1075/pc.15.2.06god.

Gonon, F., Konsman, J.-P., Cohen, D. & Boraud, T. (2012). Why most biomedical findings echoed by newspapers turn out to be false: The case of attention deficit hyperactivity disorder. *PLOS One*, *7*(9), 1–11, doi: 10.1371/journal.pone.0044275.

Harvard Business Review (2013). Women in the workplace: A research roundup. *Harvard Business Review*, *91*(9), 86–89.

Hemingway, M. (2011, December 19). Lies, damned lies, and 'fact-checking'. *The Weekly Standard*. Retrieved on August 18, 2016 from: www.weeklystandard.com/lies-damned-lies-and-fact-checking/article/611854.

Hoyt, Jr., C. (2012). The pedagogy of the meaning of racism: Reconciling a discordant discourse. *Social Work*, *57*(3), 225–234, doi: org/10.1093/sw/sws009.

Hume, D.L. & Sidun, N.M. (2017). Human trafficking of women and girls: Characteristics, commonalities, and complexities. *Women & Therapy*, *40*(1–2), 7–11, doi: 10.1080/02703149.2016.1205904.

International Labor Organization (ILO) (2012). *ILO global estimate of forced labour: 20.9 million victims*. Geneva: International Labor Organization. Retrieved January 3, 2015 from: www.ilo.org/global/about-the-ilo/newsroom/news/WCMS_182109/lang--en/index.htm.

Ipsos MORI (2014, September 19). *Perceptions are not reality: Things the world gets wrong*. London: Ipsos MORI. Retrieved on September 19, 2016 from: www.ipsos-mori.com/researchpublications/researcharchive/3466/Perceptions-are-not-reality-10-things-the-world-gets-wrong.aspx.

James, J.T. (2013). A new, evidence-based estimate of patient harms associated with hospital care. *Journal of Patient Safety*, *9*(3), 122–128, doi: 10.1097/PTS.0b013e3182948a69.

Jansson, D.B. (2014). *Modern slavery: A comparative study of the definition of trafficking in persons*. Boston, MA: Brill-Nijhoff.

Judicial Watch (2014, August 5). *DOJ report: Nearly half of Fed crimes near border*. Washington, DC: Judicial Watch. Retrieved on July 5, 2015 from: www.judicialwatch.org/blog/2014/08/doj-report-nearly-half-fed-crimes-near-mexican-border/?utm_source=facebook&utm_medium=post&utm_campaign=080514.

Lagaert, S. & Roose, H. (2014). Exploring the adequacy and validity of "sport": Reflections on a contested and open concept. *International Review for the Sociology of Sport*, *51*(4), 485–498, doi.org/10.1177%2F1012690214529295.

Leary, M.G. (2015). 'Modern day slavery'—Implications of a label. *St. Louis University Law Journal*, 60, online. Retrieved on August 1, 2018 from: https://ssrn.com/abstract=2705550.

Lewandowsky, S., Ecker, U.K.H., Seifert, C.M., Schwarz, N. & Cook, J. (2012). Misinformation and its correction: Continued influence and successful debiasing. *Psychological Science in the Public Interest*, *13*(3), 106–131, doi:10.1177/1529100612451018.

Mak, T. (2015, February 3). He'll rot for pot: 55 years for weed. *Daily Beast*. Retrieved on August 9, 2018 from: www.thedailybeast.com/hell-rot-for-pot-55-years-for-weed?ref=scroll.

Mantzarlis, A. (2015, October 28). Fact-checking the fact-checkers. *Poynter.com*. Retrieved on August 27, 2016 from: www.poynter.org/2015/fact-checking-the-fact-checkers/381458.

Marietta, M., Barker, D.C. & Bowser, T. (2015). Fact-checking politics: Does the fact-check industry provide consistent guidance on disputed realities? *Forum*, *13*(4), 577–596, doi: 10.1515/for-2015-0040.

McKean, E. (2009, December 20). Redefining definition. *New York Times Magazine*, p. 16.

Megerian, C. (2015, October 6). Governor Jerry Brown approves new limits on paparazzi drones. *Los Angeles Times*. Retrieved August 21, 2018 from: www.latimes.com/local/political/la-pol-sac-brown-drones-paparazzi-20151006-story.html.

National Aeronautics and Space Administration (NASA) (2016). *NASA, NOAA analyses reveal record-shattering global warm temperatures in 2015*. Washington, DC: National Aeronautics and Space Administration. Retrieved on September 23, 2016 from: www.nasa.gov/press-release/nasa-noaa-analyses-reveal-record-shattering-global-warm-temperatures-in-2015.

Nisbet, E.C., Cooper, K.E. & Garrett, R.K. (2015). The partisan brain: How dissonant messages lead conservatives and liberals to (dis)trust science. *The Annals of the American Academy of Political and Social Science, 658*(1), 36–66, doi.org/10.1177/0002716214555474.

Nyhan, B. & Reifler, J. (2010). When corrections fail: The persistence of political misperceptions. *Political Behavior, 32*(2), 303–330, doi: 10.1007/s11109-010-9112-2.

Open Societies Foundation (2014). *Presumption of guilt: The global overuse of pretrial detention.* New York: Open Societies Foundation. Retrieved on January 13, 2015 from: www.opensocietyfoundations.org/sites/default/files/presumption-guilt-09032014.pdf.

Palermo Protocol (2000, November 15). *A protocol to prevent, suppress and punish trafficking in persons, especially women and children, supplementing the United Nations Convention against transnational organized crime.* New York: United Nations. Retrieved on August 1, 2018 from: https://treaties.un.org/pages/viewdetails.aspx?src=ind&mtdsg_no=xviii-12-a&chapter=18&lang=en.

Paz-Fuchs, A. (2016). Badges of modern slavery. *The Modern Law Review, 79*(5), 757–785, doi: org/10.1111/1468-2230.12214.

Peter, C. & Koch, T. (2016). When debunking myths fails: The backfire effect in the context of journalistic coverage and immediate judgments as prevention strategy. *Science Communication, 38*(1), 3–25, doi: 10.1177/1075547015613523.

Pew Research Center (2015, February 15). *How scientist engage the public.* Washington, DC: Pew Research Center. Retrieved on September 21, 2016 from: www.pewinternet.org/2015/02/15/how-scientists-engage-public.

Pierce, S. (2014, November 12). The vital difference between human trafficking and migrant smuggling. *OpenDemocracy.net.* Retrieved on August 1, 2018 from: www.opendemocracy.net/beyondslavery/sarah-pierce/vital-difference-between-human-trafficking-and-migrant-smuggling.

PLOS Medicine Editors (2013). Better reporting of scientific studies: Why it matters. *PLOS Medicine, 10*(8), 1–3, doi.org/10.1371/journal.pmed.1001504.

Reider, R. (2016, June 6). Fact-checking pols in real-time. *USA Today.* Retrieved on August 27, 2016 from: www.usatoday.com/story/money/columnist/rieder/2016/06/06/rieder-fact-checking-pols-real-time/85487498.

Rhinosave.org. (2013, March 8). Retrieved August 21, 2018 from: www.expressoshow.com/articles/10-Realistic-Ways-To-Save-The-Rhino?articleID=4090.

Ricco, R.B. (2011). Individual differences in distinguishing licit from illicit ways of discharging the burden of proof. *Journal of Pragmatics, 43*(2), 616–631, doi:10.1016/j.pragma.2010.09.011.

Richmond, J.C. (2015). Human trafficking: Understanding the law and deconstructing myths. *Saint Louis University Law Journal, 60*(1), 1–42.

Rokeach, M. (1973). *The nature of human values.* New York: Free Press.

Schottlender, M. (2016, January 26). 10 easy ways you can tell for yourself that Earth is not flat. *Popular Science.* Retrieved on October 3, 2016 from: http://www.popsci.com/10-ways-you-can-prove-earth-is-round.

Siller, N. (2016). "Modern slavery": Does international law distinguish between slavery, enslavement, and trafficking? *Journal of International Criminal Justice, 14*(2), 405–427, doi:10.1093/jicj/mqv075.

Sproule, J.M. (1976). The psychological burden of proof: On the evolutionary development of Richard Whatley's theory of presumption. *Communication Monographs, 43*(2), 115–129, doi: 10.1080/03637757609375922.

Tassi, P. (2014, September 7). ESPN boss declares eSports 'not a sport.' *Forbes.* Retrieved August 21, 2018 from: www.forbes.com/sites/insertcoin/2014/09/07/espn-boss-declares-esports-not-a-sport/#5026f19055a8.

van Eemeren, F.H. & Grootendorst, R. (2004). *A systematic theory of argumentation: The pragma-dialectical approach.* Cambridge: Cambridge University Press.

Walton, D. (1988). Burden of proof. *Argumentation, 2*(2), 233–254, doi: 10.1007/BF00178024.

Weigel, D.J. (2008). The concept of family: An analysis of laypeople's views of family. *Journal of Family Issues, 29*(11), 1426–1447, doi.org/10.1177%2F0192513X08318488.

Weitzer, R. (2015). Human trafficking and contemporary slavery. *Annual Review of Sociology, 41*(1), 223–242, doi:10.1146/annurev-soc-073014-112506.

Whately, R. (1963). *Elements of rhetoric* (Rev. Ed.). Carbondale, IL: Southern Illinois Press.

Williams, J.C. & Dempsey, R.W. (2014). *What works for women at work: Four patterns working women need to know.* New York: New York University Press.

Zaraska, M. (2016, May 2). Lab-grown meat is in your future, and it may be healthier than the real stuff. *Washington Post.* Retrieved on August 21, 2018 from: www.washingtonpost.com/national/health-science/lab-grown-meat-is-in-your-future-and-it-may-be-healthier-than-the-real-stuff/2016/05/02/aa893f34-e630-11e5-a6f3-21ccdbc5f74e_story.html?utm_term=.9647d5e0ebdc.

Sample Debate Formats for In-Class Debates

Simple Pro–Con Format (For Many Speakers)

Pro speech   3 minutes maximum

1 minute cross-examination by opposing side

Con speech   3 minutes maximum

1 minute cross-examination by opposing side

Pro speech   3 minutes maximum

1 minute-cross examination by opposing side

Con speech   3 minutes maximum

1 minute-cross examination by opposing side

Repeat the cycle until every student has presented one speech and has been cross-examined on his or her speech. A speaker may argue on one side of the issue only. A speaker may not speak again until everyone else on that side of the issue has had an opportunity to speak.

The whole class debates the same topic. Be sure to choose a debate topic on which the class is roughly evenly divided. Otherwise, there will be a shortage of speakers on one side of the topic.

Oxford Style (Four-Person) Debate

Constructive Speeches

1st Affirmative speaker   6 minutes

2-minute cross-examination (usually by 2nd Negative speaker)

1st Negative speaker   6 minutes

2-minute cross-examination (usually by 1st Affirmative speaker)

2nd Affirmative speaker   6 minutes

2-minute cross-examination (usually by 1st Negative speaker)

2nd Negative speaker   6 minutes

2-minute cross-examination (usually by 2nd Affirmative speaker)

Rebuttal Speeches

1st Negative rebuttal   4 minutes

1st Affirmative rebuttal   4 minutes

2nd Negative rebuttal   4 minutes

2nd Affirmative rebuttal   4 minutes

Note: Typically, each team receives five minutes of preparation time, to be allocated between speeches. The Affirmative side speaks first and last. The Negative side speaks back to back, from the 2nd Negative constructive to the 1st Negative rebuttal (known as the "Negative block").

In a class of 20–30 students, groups of four students can select a topic for debate from a list of options provided by the instructor. Alternatively, the entire class could be assigned the same debate topic. The class can discuss possible topics, then vote on the one they prefer. Make sure there are roughly the same number of debaters on each side of the issue or there won't be enough teams to debate each other.

Lincoln–Douglas (One-on-One) Debate

Affirmative constructive   6 minutes

3-minute cross-examination by Negative speaker

Negative constructive   7 minutes

3-minute cross-examination by Affirmative speaker

1st Affirmative rebuttal   4 minutes

1st Negative rebuttal   6 minutes

2nd Affirmative rebuttal   3 minutes

Note: Typically, each debater receives three minutes of preparation time to be used between speeches. The Affirmative side speaks first and last and has two shorter rebuttal speeches. The Negative side has one longer rebuttal speech.

In a class of 20–30 students, pairs of students can select a topic for debate from a list of options provided by the instructor. Alternatively, the entire class could be assigned the same debate topic by the instructor. Make sure to select a topic on which the class is evenly, or nearly evenly, divided. Otherwise, you may have too many Lincolns and not enough Douglases or vice versa.

Author Index

Subject Index

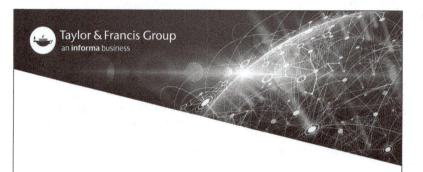